Second Edition

LITERATURE FOR CHILDREN
A Short Introduction

Second Edition

LITERATURE FOR CHILDREN
A Short Introduction

DAVID L. RUSSELL
Ferris State University

Longman
New York & London

Literature for Children, Second Edition

Longman, 10 Bank Street, White Plains, N.Y. 10606

Associated companies:
Longman Group Ltd., London
Longman Cheshire Pty., Melbourne
Longman Paul Pty., Auckland
Copp Clark Pitman, Toronto

Senior acquisitions editor: Laura McKenna
Development editor: Virginia L. Blanford
Production editor: Linda Moser
Cover design: Susan J. Moore
Cover illustration/photo: "Picture Books in Winter," *A Child's Garden of Verses,*
    by Robert Louis Stevenson, New York: Scribner's (Scribner's Illustrated
    Classics), 1905.
Production supervisor: Anne Armeny

Library of Congress Cataloging-in-Publication Data

Russell, David L.
    Literature for children / David L. Russell.—2nd ed.
        p.   cm.
    Includes bibliographical references and index.
    1. Children's literature—History and criticism   2. Children—
Books and reading.   I. Title.
PN1009.A1R7   1994
028.5—dc20   93–31351
ISBN 0-8013-1265-5   CIP

1 2 3 4 5 6 7 8 9 10 MA-96959493

Contents

Preface to the Second Edition   *xi*

PART I   THE CONTEXTS OF CHILDREN'S LITERATURE   **1**

CHAPTER 1   THE HISTORY OF CHILDREN'S LITERATURE   **3**

The Ancient World   *3*
The Middle Ages   *4*
   Reading in the Middle Ages 4, Medieval Epics 4, Medieval
   Romances 5, Fables and Other Tales 5
The European Renaissance   *6*
   The Printing Press 6, Social Changes 6, Instructional Books 6
The Seventeenth Century   *7*
   The Puritans 7, John Locke 9, Bunyan, Defoe, and Swift 9
The Eighteenth and Early Nineteenth Centuries   *11*
   John Newbery 11, Rousseau and the Moral Tale 11, The Rise of the
   Folktales 12
The Victorians: The Golden Age   *12*
   Fantasies 12, Adventure Stories 13, School Stories 13, Domestic
   Stories 14, Children's Book Illustration 15
The Twentieth Century: Widening Worlds   *15*
Adults and Children's Literature   *16*
Recommended Readings   *16*

CHAPTER 2 CHILD DEVELOPMENT AND LITERATURE   19

The Impact of Child Development on Reading   *19*
Modern Theories of Child Development   *19*
  Piaget's Cognitive Theory of Development 20, Erikson's Psychosocial
  Development Theory 23, Kohlberg's Theory of the Development of
  Moral Judgment 24
The Uses of Developmental Psychology   *26*
Recommended Readings   26

PART II   THE KINDS OF CHILDREN'S LITERATURE   29

CHAPTER 3 THE PICTURE BOOK: THE ILLUSTRATIONS   31

Definition of the Picture Book   *31*
Artistic Elements   *32*
  Line 32, Space 32, Shape 34, Color 34, Texture 37, Composition and
  Perspective 37
Artistic Styles   *38*
  Representationalism 38, Expressionism 39, Impressionism 41,
  Surrealism 41, Cartoon 41, Folk Art 42, Photography 42, Other
  Artistic Styles 43
Artistic Media   *43*
  Painterly Techniques 43, Graphic Techniques 45, Montage and
  Collage 46
Picture-Book Layout   *46*
Recommended Readings   47

CHAPTER 4 THE PICTURE BOOK: THE STORY   49

Types of Stories   *49*
  Folktales, Legends, and Myths 49, Modern Fantasy Stories 50, Talking
  Animal Stories 50, Realistic Stories 50
Narrative Elements   *51*
  Plot and Conflict 51, Character 52, Setting 52, Subject and Theme 52,
  Literary Style 53
Social Concerns and the Picture Storybook   *54*
Selected Bibliography of Picture Storybooks   55

CHAPTER 5   **ALPHABET, COUNTING, AND CONCEPT BOOKS**   **61**

Definitions   *61*
Alphabet Books   *62*
  Organization of Alphabet Books 62, Content of Alphabet Books 62,
  Design of Alphabet Books 64
Counting Books   *65*
  Content of Counting Books 66, Design of Counting Books 66
Concept Books   *67*
  Cognitive Development and Concept Books 67, Psychosocial
  Development and Concept Books 67, Design of Concept Books 68
Recommended Readings   68
Selected Bibliography of Alphabet, Counting, and Concept Books   69

CHAPTER 6   **MOTHER GOOSE RHYMES**   **73**

The Origins of Mother Goose Rhymes   *73*
The Importance of Mother Goose Rhymes   *74*
  Cognitive Development 74, Aesthetic Development 75, Emotional
  Development 76, Social and Physical Development 76
Choosing Mother Goose Books   *77*
  Illustrators of Mother Goose 77
Recommended Readings   84
Selected Bibliography of Mother Goose Books   85

CHAPTER 7   **POETRY**   **87**

Definition of Poetry   *87*
Poetry for the Very Young   *88*
The Forms of Poetry   *88*
  Narrative Poetry 89, Lyric Poetry 90
The Language of Poetry   *92*
  Imagery 92, Sound Patterns 94
The Meaning of Poetry   *95*
Sharing Poetry with Children   *96*
  Children's Preferences 96, Reading Poems 96, Selecting Poems and
  Anthologies 97
Recommended Readings   98
Selected Bibliography of Poetry Books for Children   98

CHAPTER 8   **FOLK LITERATURE**   103

Definition of Folk Literature   *103*
The Origin and Purposes of Folk Literature   *104*
Folktales   *104*
  Animal Tales 104, Fables 105, Märchen or Wonder Tales 105,
  Pourquoi Tales 106, Noodlehead Tales 106, Cumulative Tales 106,
  Tall Tales 107, Ghost Stories 107
Myths   *107*
  Classical Greek and Roman Mythology 108, Norse Mythology 108,
  American, African, and Oriental Mythologies 109
Epics and Legends   *109*
Artistic Elements   *110*
  Setting 110, Character 110, Plot 111, Theme and Conflict 111,
  Style 112
Issues in Folk Literature   *113*
Collectors, Retellers, and Adapters   *113*
The Appeal of Folk Literature   *114*
Recommended Readings   115
Selected Bibliography of Folk Literature, Myths, and Legends   115

CHAPTER 9   **FANTASY**   119

Definition of Fantasy   *119*
Types of Fantasy   *120*
  The Literary Fairy Tale 120, Animal Fantasy 120, Toy Fantasy 121,
  Eccentric and Extraordinary Characters 122, Enchanted Journeys and
  Imaginary Lands 122, Heroic or Quest Fantasy 124, Supernatural and
  Time Fantasy 125, Science Fiction and Space Fantasy 125
Special Characteristics of Fantasy   *126*
  Originality 127, Believability 127
The Rewards of Fantasy   *128*
Recommended Readings   128
Selected Bibliography of Fantasy Fiction   129

CHAPTER 10   **REALISTIC FICTION**   133

Definition of Realistic Fiction   *133*
Types of Realism   *133*
  Adventure and Survival Stories 134, Domestic Realism or Family
  Stories 135, Social Realism 137, Psychological Novels and Problem
  Novels 137, Realistic Animal Stories 139
Special Characteristics of Realistic Fiction   *140*
  Coming of Age 140, The Need for Others 140
The Value of Realistic Fiction   *140*
Recommended Readings   141
Selected Bibliography of Realistic Fiction for Children   141

CHAPTER 11   **HISTORICAL FICTION AND BIOGRAPHY**   **145**

Definition of Historical Fiction   *145*
The Development of Historical Fiction   *146*
Special Characteristics of Historical Fiction   *147*
  Unobtrusive History 147, Authenticity 147, Sensitivity 148
The Rewards of Historical Fiction   *149*
Definition and Development of Biography   *150*
Approaches to Biography   *150*
  Authentic Biography 150, Fictionalized Biography 151
The Forms of Biography   *151*
  Complete Biographies 152, Partial Biographies 152, Collective
  Biographies 152
The Elements of Biographical Writing   *153*
  Subject 153, Accuracy 153, Balance 154, Style 155, Theme 155
Special Characteristics of Autobiography   *156*
Recommended Readings   *157*
Selected Bibliography of Historical Fiction   *158*
Selected Bibliography of Biographies and Autobiographies   *160*

CHAPTER 12   **INFORMATIONAL BOOKS**   **165**

Definition of Informational Books   *165*
Types of Informational Books   *166*
  Lands and Peoples 166, Science and Nature 167, Fine and Applied
  Arts 169, Human Development and Behavior 170
Evaluating Informational Books   *171*
  Purpose 171, Accuracy and Objectivity 171, Format and
  Organization 172, Style 173
Informational Books as Literature   *173*
Selected Bibliography of Critical Studies   *174*
Selected Bibliography of Informational Books   *174*

PART III   **THE CONCERNS OF CHILDREN'S LITERATURE**   **179**

CHAPTER 13   **CULTURAL AND SOCIAL DIVERSITY**   **181**

Cross-Cultural Diversity   *181*
  African Americans 182, Native Americans 184, Hispanic
  Americans 185, Asian Americans 186, World-Wide Cultures 187
Gender Awareness   *187*
  Gender-Biased Language 188, Gender Roles 188, Gender Behavior 188
Alternative Families and Lifestyles   *190*
The Physically, Emotionally, and Intellectually Challenged   *190*
Other Issues   *191*

Recommended Readings   *192*

Selected Bibliography of Books Emphasizing Cultural and Social
    Diversity   *193*

CHAPTER 14   THE STUDY OF LITERATURE   197

The Purpose of Criticism   *197*
The Reader-Response Approach   *198*
The Historical Approach   *198*
The Psychoanalytical Approach   *199*
The Feminist Approach   *201*
The Formalist Approach   *202*
The Elements of Literature   *202*
    Point of View 202, Setting 203, Characters 204, Plot and
    Conflict 206, Theme 208, Style 208, Tone 211
Literature as Art   *212*
Bibliography of Works Cited   *212*
Recommended Readings   *213*

CHAPTER 15   LITERATURE IN THE CLASSROOM   215

Sharing Literature with Children   *215*
The Reader-Centered Approach to Literature   *216*
    Reading Aloud 216, Storytelling 217, Book Discussions 218, Writing
    Experiences 220, Dramatic Responses to Literature 222, Art and
    Literature 225
Children's Books and the Censor   *226*
The Influence of Literature   *227*
Recommended Readings   *227*

APPENDIX   CHILDREN'S BOOK AWARDS   229

American Book Awards   *229*
International Awards   *251*

Index   *261*

Preface to the Second Edition

As with the first edition, I have aimed this work at undergraduate college students of children's literature, many of whom are heading toward careers in education, and many of whom are not especially well versed in the field. I have found that what these students need most of all is to read, read, and read some more—the classic authors, the contemporary favorites, the lesser-known gems. What they do not need is an exhaustive pedagogical study or endless plot summaries of books they should have read. Consequently, my method has been to require students to read as many of the primary works of literature as is feasible during the academic term, and to supplement those readings with this text, which gives them a handle on the study of children's literature in general.

Having used the first edition in more than a dozen different classes over the past three years, I have become aware of some of the shortcomings and have tried to address them in this revision. The most significant change is the division of the book into three major parts, rather than two: "The Contexts of Children's Literature," "The Kinds of Children's Literature," and "The Concerns of Children's Literature." The last of these is entirely new and incorporates the issues of social and cultural diversity (Chapter 13), literary criticism (Chapter 14), and classroom methods (Chapter 15). The logic behind placing these three chapters in a separate Part III at the end of this book is simply that they focus on all kinds of literature, not just a single genre. Placing them last in the book is not to suggest their relative importance; indeed, these are some of the most crucial concerns of literature. But how they are treated in a given course will vary dramatically from instructor to instructor. It is quite likely that some instructors may want to begin with one or more of these chapters, others may want to combine them with the reading of some of the chapters in Part II, and still others may want to focus on them last when the students have a fair amount of reading under their belts.

All these issues were treated in a rather cursory fashion in the first edition, and all deserved more thorough coverage. Chapter 13, "Cultural and Social Diversity," covers a multitude of subjects, and each one is worthy of book-length studies. In an introductory study, it simply is not feasible to cover all the possibilities of human diversity; rather, my purpose was to heighten the awareness of students as readers, to make them more sensitive to social and cultural differences as they are portrayed in literature. Chapter 14, "The Study of Literature," describes approaches to literary criticism and expands on a chapter in the first edition. That earlier chapter focused entirely on the form of literature and virtually ignored the current developments in literary criticism. I do not pretend to have done complete justice to the field of literary criticism, but I do believe that students today can benefit greatly from even brief exposure to feminist criticism or psychoanalytical criticism or historical criticism, if only to raise questions in their minds about their reading. And reader-response theory is extremely valuable for anyone attempting to use literature in the classroom. I have retained the rather thorough explanation of the literary elements, which some readers have found useful, if only to provide a common vocabulary for literary discussion. The final chapter, "Literature in the Classroom," is simply a much-needed expansion of part of a chapter in the original edition, although I have taken pains not to turn this text into a study of pedagogy. It is still primarily a text for the study of children's literature as literature.

Users of the first edition will also discover a minor reorganization in the second part with the division of the study of picture storybooks into two chapters, one on the illustrations and one on the stories. This separation is not intended to divorce the text and illustrations, for that is contrary to the very nature of the picture book, but the choice was made to avoid an unduly long chapter. One other change some readers will note is the move of historical fiction into the chapter on biography. The philosophical justification is explained within the chapter, but from a practical point of view this move also helps to balance the chapter lengths and allows for more thorough discussion of historical fiction, which was slighted in the first edition.

Every chapter has been revised to clarify points, expand on important ideas, and to incorporate more recent thinking. The bibliographies have been enlarged and updated (although of necessity they remain selective). The appendices have also been updated, and two additional awards have been added: the Coretta Scott King Award and the Scott O'Dell Award. My objectives in this revision were to retain the brevity, sharpen the clarity, fill in the gaps, and still have a reasonably priced and attractive book. I trust the readers will find that all of these objectives were achieved in some measure.

I would like to reiterate my sentiments from the first edition that it is my hope that readers will come away from this work with a keen interest in and healthy respect for children's literature, with an understanding of its complexities, and an appreciation of the importance of literature in the lives of young people. Reading is unquestionably the most fundamental of all academic skills, and the love of reading is among the richest gifts we can bestow upon our children. Our justification has been eloquently pronounced by the writer of Ecclesiasticus:

> If thou has gathered nothing in thy youth,
> how canst thou find anything in thine age?

ACKNOWLEDGEMENTS

I would like to thank the following reviewers, whose comments and suggestions enabled me to make this a better book:

Stan Bochtler, Buena Vista College

Catherine Coggins, Stetson University

Patricia DeMay, Livingston University

Delores Dickerson, Howard University

Constantine Georgiou, New York University

Betty Greenway, Youngstown State University

Marjorie Jones, Saint Martin's College

Sandra Imdieke, Northern Michigan University

Jean McWilliams, Rosemont College

Jeff Oliver, University of Colorado

Jennifer Smith, Northern Kentucky University

Monroe Whiting, Canisius College

PART I
The Contexts
of Children's Literature

CHAPTER 1

The History of Children's Literature

We begin our exploration of the rich field of children's literature with a brief history, for knowing where we have been gives us a fuller understanding of where we are—and perhaps a hint as to where we are going.

THE ANCIENT WORLD

There is little in humankind's first several thousand years on earth that can be labeled "children's literature." The earliest literature in the West (and very likely in the rest of the world as well) was the oral tale, passed on by word of mouth—a practice reaching beyond antiquity. We may imagine flickering hearth fires, guarding against the chill of night, around which storytellers shared their tales, perhaps to pass the time or to explain some natural phenomenon. Eventually these tales became more elaborate as society grew more complex; in time, fantastic tales of gods and heroes, princes and dragons, foolish peasants and clever animals were being disseminated all over the world. Naturally, no one thought of these as "children's literature," nor were they specifically intended for children; children just happened to have been in the audience or overheard their elders telling the tales.

So it is that most early literature was originally oral—that is, it was composed not to be read but to be heard. Children borrowed the stories they enjoyed from the ones adults told. There were very few works composed with only children in mind; consequently, we hear that the young of classical Greece (around 400 BC) enjoyed the famous poems attributed to Homer, the *Iliad,* the story of the Trojan War, and the *Odyssey,* the story of the adventures of the Greek hero Odysseus. Adults might be allured by the passionate love stories and the depth of human emotion in Homer's *Odyssey,* whereas younger listeners might relish the fanciful monsters and exciting adventures.

Aesop's *Fables,* those familiar animal tales with pointed morals attached, were almost certainly staple reading for young Greek students during this time. Children of ancient Rome (from about 50 BC to 500 AD) read Virgil's *Aeneid,* the story of the legendary progenitor of the Roman race, and Ovid's *Metamorphoses,* poetic versions of the classical myths. Virgil and Ovid drew on the oral tradition, although their works are definitely literary, for the ancient Romans tended to be highly educated. Virgil has not held the same appeal for modern children as Homer has, but it is possible to find many modern retellings of the myths in *Metamorphoses.* Their brevity and their imaginative qualities have kept them popular with children for centuries.

THE MIDDLE AGES

Reading in the Middle Ages

By the time of the European Middle Ages (from roughly 500 to 1500 AD), the state of literature for children was scarcely changed—except that almost certainly fewer children could read during this period than during the preceding classical ages in Greece and Rome. Education was largely carried on by the church and almost exclusively for the purpose of spreading Christianity. As in the earlier periods, childhood itself was largely ignored, and kept as brief as possible. Although medieval parents surely loved their children as much as modern parents do theirs, medieval people had little understanding of child development, and education (which was reserved primarily for the clergy and nobility) was extremely unenlightened.

There was also the very practical problem of the scarcity of books. It is difficult for us to imagine an era when every single book had to be laboriously hand-copied, as was the case prior to the introduction of the movable type printing press. It took up to three years for a single copy of the Bible to be produced. Books were extraordinarily costly in the Middle Ages, and libraries often chained them to the tables (forget about checking a book out for the weekend). The library of the Sorbonne, the principal library of the University of Paris, had an inventory of some 1,700 books in the early fourteenth century—and that must have been one of the finest libraries of the day. Given these circumstances, it is little wonder that the general populace did not bother to learn to read—there would have been very little for them to read anyway. It is not unusual to find medieval kings who could not read or write—the great ninth-century conqueror and emperor Charlemagne was frustrated his entire life because he never learned to read or write, and the practice of affixing a seal to an official document was necessitated by the fact that many rulers could not sign their own names.

Medieval Epics

It is, therefore, not surprising that medieval writers were as reluctant as classical writers to devote their talents and energies to writing for children. So, as during the classical period, medieval children had to be largely content with those adult stories that held some interest for them. Nevertheless, this left much for them to enjoy, for, as with classical literature, medieval literature preserved that capacious quality that made it appealing to a broadly based audience—the same story could be enjoyed by young and old alike. It is not unlikely that the Anglo-Saxon epic *Beowulf,* the exciting story of a hero's defeat of a terrible monster, was a favorite among young listeners. Although the poem was originally composed in about the eighth century AD, it can still be read with pleasure today in modern retellings for children, such as Rosemary Sutcliff's *Dragon Slayer.* Most likely, medieval children knew other epics, such as the French *Song of Roland,* a story of Charlemagne, and the Spanish *El Cid.*

Medieval Romances

The tales of King Arthur and his knights of the Round Table surely delighted many medieval children. Arthur is a half-legendary, half-historical figure who was made popular during the High Middle Ages (around the twelfth and thirteenth centuries), at least partly to generate patriotic spirit in the English. But the stories of Arthur and his knights were well known on the Continent as well. These *romances,* as they are called, are stories of high adventure, love, mystery, treachery, and magic. Adults might have been attracted to the love stories (some happy, some tragic) of the knights and the fair damsels; children might have been enthralled by the wondrous monsters—ogres and dragons—and the magic spells; and both might have been thrilled by the contests and battles. The great reteller of the tales of King Arthur is the fifteenth-century writer Thomas Malory, whose *Morte d'Artur* ("The Death of Arthur") is one of the great pieces of medieval English literature. Four and a half centuries later, Howard Pyle, an American writer, retold some of the tales of Arthur for younger audiences in *The Stories of King Arthur and His Knights* (1903).

Another literary hero of the Middle Ages who has survived into the modern era is Robin Hood. Some believe Robin Hood to be based upon a historical figure, a twelfth-century outlaw stealing from the rich and giving his booty to the poor. The nineteenth-century American writer, Howard Pyle, wrote one of the most popular adaptations for children, *The Merry Adventures of Robin Hood* (1883), recounting the stories of this medieval anti-hero.

Fables and Other Tales

In the late thirteenth century, a collection of tales and fables, all with morals prominently attached, appeared in England. This was called the *Gesta Romanorum* ("The Deeds of the Romans"). It proved to be a rich source of plots for many famous writers later on, including the great medieval Italian storyteller, Boccaccio, and the equally great medieval English writer, Geoffrey Chaucer. Children of the Middle Ages must have been very familiar with the tales of the *Gesta Romanorum.*

Animal stories have always been favorites of children, and it is not surprising that the beast epic *Reynard the Fox,* the story of a trickster, was also extremely popular during the Middle Ages and apparently loved by children. Barbara Cooney's *Chanticleer and the Fox* is a twentieth-century picture-book version of this tale, which has remained a favorite since the days of Chaucer.

In addition to these secular entertainments were the biblical stories, the lives of saints (typically embellished and improved), local legends (celebrating the great deeds of some half-real, half-mythical hero of the neighborhood), all of which sought to improve the moral and spiritual character of the audience. The lively medieval imagination drew no close distinction between fantasy and reality, and medieval storytellers were free to mingle magic, enchantment, and the downright ludicrous alongside the serious. For many medieval people, miracles were as real as taxes. If the children were content to share the literature of their parents it may be at least partly because that literature was rich with a childlike imagination, full of wonder, mystery, and excitement.

THE EUROPEAN RENAISSANCE

The Printing Press

By the mid-fifteenth century, dramatic changes began to take place in Europe. At that time the movable type printing press was introduced into the West (the Chinese apparently developed it first), which made it possible to print books in quantities, reducing the time and labor involved and making them cheaper—and thus more accessible. It is almost impossible to exaggerate the impact of this single invention, certainly the most important technical innovation since the introduction of the wheel. In a short time, a remarkable revolution would be taking place that resulted in increasing literacy, the growth of education, and the rapid dissemination and advancement of knowledge generally.

Social Changes

At the same time, several other factors were converging that were to change the face of Europe. (1) The Crusades, which had taken place chiefly in the eleventh and twelfth centuries, had opened up trade routes to the East as far as India and helped to bring wealth in the form of trade to Europe. (2) Strong central monarchies harnessed warring feudal lords—who had dominated much of the Middle Ages with their petty wars—and encouraged the growth of peaceful commerce and industry. (3) The European arrival in the Western Hemisphere (also known rather inaccurately as the "Discovery of the New World") brought untold wealth to some and opportunity to many Europeans (albeit disaster to the Native American peoples). The growing wealth during this time saw the rise of a substantial merchant middle class—a class that was almost nonexistent during the Middle Ages, when people were either aristocrats, peasants, or clergy. Whereas peasants could not afford to educate their children (and had no reason to anyway), the new middle class valued education. Merchants and traders needed to read and write to keep their accounts.

Instructional Books

Nevertheless, the children of Renaissance Europe, even though they were more literate than their medieval counterparts, still had to be content largely with reading instructional books or works written primarily for adults. Children still enjoyed the old legends and romances, Aesop's *Fables* and *Reynard the Fox*. Such instructional works as the so-called Books of Courtesy, showing children how to behave in society (a sort of Emily Post or Miss Manners for children), sprang up during the fifteenth and sixteenth centuries. Sir Thomas Elyot's *The Boke Named the Governor* (1531) and Roger Ascham's *The Scholemaster* (1570) are the best known. They illustrate society's growing interest in the education of children. John Foxe's *Book of Martyrs* (1563), an anti-Catholic work filled with horrific scenes of violent deaths for the sake of religion, was among the most popular reading material for children. Because of its religious theme, it was considered acceptable reading for children, and even early in the twentieth century we hear of children enjoying this work. A gentler work is John Comenius's *Orbis Sensualium Pictus* (1658), which is generally regarded as the earliest children's illustrated book (see Figure 1.1). It was, in fact, a Latin vocabulary book—a sort of "Latin through pictures"—that provides us today with an interesting look at seventeenth-century European society. By the end of the seventeenth century, social changes were well under way that could clear the path for a genuine literature for children.

THE SEVENTEENTH CENTURY

It was not until the seventeenth century that childhood began to take on a new importance, and adults began to recognize the special needs of childhood (among them, a need for childhood reading). We should be aware of at least two specific influences that brought to society a heightened sense of the special needs of the child. First is the rise of Puritanism, an influential branch of Protestantism that placed special emphasis on the individual's need to tend to his or her own salvation. And second is the work of John Locke, the English philosopher.

The Puritans

The Puritans were a very strict religious sect who believed in living simply and working hard. They abhorred fancy church ritual and tended to frown on the pleasures of the flesh. The Puritans suffered persecution in England because they refused to support the established Church of England, and this brought them to North America. They believed that one could achieve salvation through individual faith alone, and that a thorough knowledge of the Bible was necessary for every human being. Consequently, the ability to read and to understand the Bible was a principal requirement for Puritan children. The Puritans were not long in America before they found the need to establish a college, Harvard (1636), as if to emphasize their commitment to the primacy of education.

As might be expected, the Bible stories were staples for Puritan children, and virtually all the first books for these children were *didactic* books—that is, they were intended to instruct. Early schoolbooks included the so-called horn books. Commonly found in New England, these consisted of simple wooden slabs, usually with a handle, on which were attached parchment containing rudimentary language lessons (the alphabet, numerals, and so on). The slabs were then covered with transparent

CXXXVI.

Ludi Pueriles:

Boyes-Sport

Boys used to play either with *Bowling-stones* 1. or throwing a *Bowl*, 2. at *Nine-pins*, 3. or striking a *Ball*, through a *Ring*, 5. with a *Bandy*, 4. or scourging a *Top*, 6. with a *Whip*, 7. or shooting with a *Trunk*, 8. and a *Bow*, 9. or going upon *Stilts*, 10. or tossing and swinging themselves upon a *Merry-totter*, 11.

Pueri solent ludere vel *Globis fictilibus*, 1. vel jactantes *Globum*, 2. ad *Conas*, 3. vel *mittentes* Sphærulam per *Annulum*, 5. *Clava*, 4. versantes *Turbinem*, 6. *Flagello*, 7. vel jaculantes *Sclopo*, 8. & *Arcu*, 9. vel incidentes *Grallis*, 10. vel super *Petaurum* 11. se agitantes & oscillantes.

FIGURE 1.1 John Comenius's *Orbis Sensualium Pictus* is often considered the first children's picture book. It first appeared in 1658 as a German/Latin textbook and was an immediate success. It revolutionized Latin instruction, a necessity in a society in which Latin was still the language of scholarship. The English/Latin versions appeared in 1659. Although the woodblock illustrations appear crude, they provide a wealth of information about seventeenth-century European life.

horn (from cattle, sheep, goats), which served as a primitive form of lamination. These books—seventeenth-century versions of modern-day cardboard and cloth books— proved to be very durable. Surely the most famous of early schoolbooks was *The New England Primer,* first appearing sometime around 1685 to 1690 and continuing in print in some form or another until 1886. It was initially a Puritan publication introducing young children to the alphabet through rhymes ("In Adam's fall/We Sinned all" for A) and then to increasingly sophisticated reading material—all with a religious intent (see Figure 1.2).

John Locke

The second great influence on children's literature during this period was the work of English philosopher John Locke (1632–1704) who, in 1693, wrote a famous essay, *Thoughts Concerning Education.* In this work, he formulated his notion that the minds of young children were similar to blank slates (he called them *tabula rasa*) just waiting to be written upon and thus instructed. Locke effectively discounted the influence of heredity by suggesting that every child possessed the capacity for learning. Moreover, Locke believed it was the responsibility of adults to see to the proper education of children. The Puritans were interested in childhood for religious reasons—whereas Locke stressed the importance of childhood for intellectual reasons. So it was that the idea of books for children received the considerable support of both religion and philosophy.

Bunyan, Defoe, and Swift

English children also continued to adopt certain adult works of literature. They were especially drawn to the fanciful allegory of John Bunyan's *A Pilgrim's Progress* (1678), the story of a man's journey to Heaven—although children undoubtedly preferred the horrific monsters that plagued him on the trip to the religious ecstacy of his safe arrival in Heaven. Two other works were exceedingly popular in the early eighteenth century: Daniel Defoe's *Robinson Crusoe* (1719), the ancestor of numerous survival stories that remain appealing to children to this day, and Jonathan Swift's *Gulliver's Travels* (1726), a story that is still told to children and has been the subject of several movies for young people. For young readers, the favorite part of Swift's book is Gulliver's visit to Lilliput, a miniature land, another recurrent subject of modern children's fantasies (Mary Norton's *The Borrowers* and Carol Kendall's *The Gammage Cup,* for example). The moral and ethical messages of these works did not concern young readers, who were simply after a good tale. All of these works are built around the idea of a dangerous journey, which is one of the oldest motifs in literature and dates back as far as Homer's *Odyssey.* It is also one of the most successful literary patterns, and the excitement and adventure it provides undoubtedly accounts for its continued popularity, especially among young people.

A — In *Adam's* Fall We Sinned all.

B — Thy Life to Mend This *Book* Attend.

C — The *Cat* doth play And after flay.

D — A *Dog* will bite A Thief at night.

E — An *Eagles* flight Is out of fight.

F — The Idle *Fool* Is whipt at School.

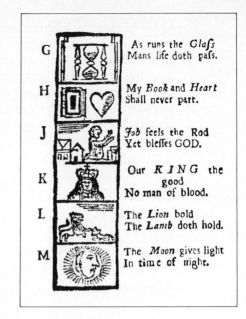

G — As runs the *Glass* Mans life doth pass.

H — My *Book* and *Heart* Shall never part.

J — *Job* feels the Rod Yet blesses GOD.

K — Our *KING* the good No man of blood.

L — The *Lion* bold The *Lamb* doth hold.

M — The *Moon* gives light In time of night.

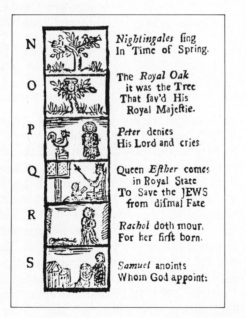

N — *Nightingales* sing In Time of Spring.

O — The *Royal Oak* it was the Tree That fav'd His Royal Majeſtie.

P — *Peter* denies His Lord and cries.

Q — Queen *Esther* comes in Royal State To Save the JEWS from dismal Fate

R — *Rachel* doth mour. For her first born.

S — *Samuel* anoints Whom God appoint.

T — *Time* cuts down all Both great and small.

U — *Uriah's* beauteous Wife Made *David* feek his Life.

W — *Whales* in the Sea God's Voice obey.

X — *Xerxes* the great did die, And so muſt you & I.

Y — *Youth* forward flips Death foonest nips.

Z — *Zacheus* he Did climb the Tree His Lord to fee.

FIGURE 1.2 *The New England Primer* was one of the longest-lived school texts in American history, flourishing from approximately 1680 to 1830. The earliest surviving copy is from 1727, from which these illustrations are taken. Intended to teach the children of the early Puritans how to live a godly life, the book is unabashedly didactic, which is evident even in its rhyming alphabet, recalling a time when church and state were not so completely separate as they are now.

THE EIGHTEENTH AND EARLY NINETEENTH CENTURIES

John Newbery

As a consequence of these influences, the way was paved for the serious publishing of children's books. Although he may not have been the first, John Newbery (1713–1767), an English entrepreneur, was certainly the most successful of the early publishers of books for children. His *Little Pretty Pocket Book* (1744) is now considered a landmark in children's literature as the first significant publication for children that sought not only their edification but their enjoyment as well. This collection of songs, moral tales, and crude woodblock illustrations marked the successful beginning of a publishing phenomenon that is still ballooning.

Rousseau and the Moral Tale

The French philosopher Jean Jacques Rousseau (1712–1778) added yet another angle to the concept of children's literature. His ideas about education were expressed in a book called *Emile* (1762), where he emphasized the importance of *moral* development (the Puritans' concern had been spiritual; Locke's had been intellectual). For Rousseau, proper moral development could be best accomplished through simplicity of living (even 200 years ago people were becoming distressed over the increasing complexity of life). It was a short jump from Rousseau's ideas to extremely didactic and moralistic books for children, books that supposedly taught them how to be good and proper human beings. (Newbery had, in fact, contributed his fair share of moralistic tales, *Little Goody Two Shoes* being the most famous.) A great many writers, most of them women (men still looked upon writing for children as an inferior occupation), churned out a great number of moralistic tales through the remainder of the eighteenth and well into the nineteenth centuries.

Among the best-known of these writers is Maria Edgeworth (1744–1817), whose most famous stories for children are "The Purple Jar" and her book *Simple Susan,* about a country girl whose goodness helps her to triumph over an ill-intentioned city lawyer. Sarah Trimmer (1741-1810) wrote the *History of the Robins,* an animal story unusual in a time when the device of talking animals was looked upon with suspicion (the eighteenth-century rationalists thought it was illogical). As one of the first reviewers of children's books, Mrs. Trimmer believed that literature must preach Christian morality above all, and she condemned fairy stories for children because they were sacrilegious and lacked moral purpose. Mrs. Anna Laetitia Barbauld (1743–1825) wrote in a similar vein; her most famous works, *Lessons for Children* and *Hymns in Prose for Children,* clearly suggest their purpose in their titles. Hannah More (1745–1833) and Mrs. Sherwood (1775–1851) were also part of this moralizing company, and Mrs. Sherwood's *History of the Fairchild Family* includes frighteningly vivid stories about the souls of impious children moldering in the cold grave or being consigned to the fires of hell. The reputations of most of these women have declined over the years, but their influence was tremendous. They deserve to be remembered as pioneers in a field that, until their time, received virtually no attention at all.

The Rise of the Folktales

The didactic element in children's books remained persistent through the early nineteenth century, and there was still little to distinguish children's literature. But concurrent with the heavily moralistic tales was another strain, although it was not initially considered to be children's literature. This was the resurrection of the old folktales from the oral tradition. Actually, folktales had been published in England much earlier—in 1729, *Tales of Mother Goose* by the Frenchman Charles Perrault, was first translated and published in English. These tales (originally published in France in the 1690s apparently for the diversion of the ladies of the Royal Court) were retellings of old folktales, including "Cinderella," "Little Red Riding Hood," "Sleeping Beauty," and so on. Of course, children adored them—as they always have—and throughout the eighteenth century, more and more retellings appeared, despite the admonitions of Mrs. Trimmer.

At the beginning of the nineteenth century, two German brothers, Jacob (1785–1863) and Wilhelm (1786–1859) Grimm, collected a great number of folktales and published them (once again, not expressly for children). Many adults considered the folktales, with their adult themes, their alarming frankness and violence, and their lack of moral messages, unsuitable for children. But the exciting, fast-paced, and imaginative stories captivated young readers, as they still do today. In 1846, Hans Christian Andersen's *Fairy Tales* were first published in English and have remained popular ever since. By the end of the nineteenth century, the collectors Joseph Jacobs *(English Fairy Tales)* and Andrew Lang (*The Blue Fairy Book, The Red Fairy Book,* and so on) were making available a wealth of folktales from the world over. Disputes still arise over the appropriateness of folktales for children's reading— although the disputes are always among adults, never among the children themselves who continue to read and love the old tales.

THE VICTORIANS: THE GOLDEN AGE

It was during the long reign of Britain's Queen Victoria (1837–1901) that children's literature first blossomed. The Victorians were influenced by the Romantic Movement of the early nineteenth century, a movement that idealized childhood and led to a greater interest in children in general. On both sides of the Atlantic, first-rate authors and illustrators began to turn their talents to children and their books.

Fantasies

In 1865, Lewis Carroll (the pseudonym for Charles Dodgson, a mathematics professor at Oxford University) published *Alice's Adventures in Wonderland* and thus began a new era in children's literature. *Alice in Wonderland* is the first significant publication for children that abandoned all pretense of instruction and was offered purely for enjoyment. It was this book that broke the bonds of didacticism that had so long gripped children's literature and thus opened the gates for a wealth of imaginative writing in both England and America. In the field of fantasy, we find Charles Kingsley's *The Water Babies* (1863) and George MacDonald's *The Princess and the Goblin* (1872) and *The Princess and the Curdie* (1877). L. Frank Baum's *The Wizard of Oz* (1900) grew out of this tradition of children's fantasy, as did Kenneth Grahame's classic *The Wind in the Willows* (1908).

Adventure Stories

Also especially popular in the nineteenth century were adventure stories for boys, of which Robert Louis Stevenson's *Treasure Island* (1883) and Mark Twain's *The Adventures of Tom Sawyer* (1876) and *The Adventures of Huckleberry Finn* (1884) are the most enduring. But hundreds of (mostly mediocre) adventure stories were published during the period. British children seemed to prefer stories set in faraway and unfamiliar places, and G. A. Henty (1832–1902) is among the most notable writers in this vein. A war correspondent, Henty traveled widely in the far-flung British Empire, and his books, such as *With Clive in India* (1884), reflect those experiences. American boys were more attracted to adventure stories set in their native land, sometimes in the romantic past of their still young nation, as with Mark Twain. Other writers focused on the present. One of the most successful was Horatio Alger, Jr. (1834–1899), whose immensely popular rags-to-riches stories (*Ragged Dick; or, Street Life in New York,* 1867, and many others) have made his name virtually a household word yet today, long after people have ceased to read his books. Alger's heroes were always downtrodden boys who struggled for fortune and respectability, both of which they ultimately gained, largely because of their moral uprightness. Exceedingly popular was William Taylor Adams (1822–1897), who wrote sensationalized formula fiction under the pen name of Oliver Optic. His works were only a notch above the so-called Dime Novels of the day—the forerunners of the modern-day paperbacks. Written by hack writers, Dime Novels were sensational, lacking in style and depth, cheap, and, therefore, immensely popular.

School Stories

Also primarily for boys was the so-called school story, about the antics of boys at boarding schools. *Tom Brown's School Days* (1857), by the British writer Thomas Hughes, is a prototype of this sort of fiction. In America, Edward Eggleston wrote *The Hoosier School-Boy* (1883), among the first American school stories. *The Hoosier Schoolmaster* (1871) is his most famous work, and it tells the school story from the teacher's point of view. The school story still occasionally appears in the twentieth century in works such as John Knowles's *A Separate Peace* and Robert Cormier's *The Chocolate War.* School stories are virtually always coming-of-age tales.

FIGURE 1.3   Randolph Caldecott, the great nineteenth-century English illustrator, was one of the pioneers of children's book illustration. His art is characterized by an economy of line and a playfulness of manner that make his work appealing today, more than a century after his death. The American Library Association annually awards the Caldecott Medal, named in his honor, to what it judges the most distinguished picture book published in the United States. This illustration from *The Frog He Would A-Wooing Go* (1883) depicts Caldecott's lively sense of humor.

Domestic Stories

For girls of this time, there were the popular domestic stories, tales of home and family life focusing on the activities of a virtuous heroine, usually coming from dire straits and achieving good fortune and ultimate happiness in the person of a handsome young man. (If both the Alger stories and the theme of the domestic stories sounds vaguely familiar, they should—they are essentially modern versions of the old folktales, in which persons of humble origins rise to wealth, fame, and happiness, primarily because they are moral and upright individuals.) Many of the domestic novels sank into maudlin sentimentality (Martha Finlay's *Elsie Dinsmore* series was the most popular and the most sentimental, with Elsie shedding tears on nearly every page). But

Louisa May Alcott's *Little Women* (1868) and L. N. Montgomery's *Anne of Green Gables* (1908), both domestic novels, rank among the minor classics of children's literature.

Children's Book Illustration

Children's books of the eighteenth century and earlier either lacked illustrations altogether or contained crude woodblock illustrations such as those in *Orbis Sensualium Pictus.* Serious artists could not be enticed to draw for children's books. But the growth of children's book publishing and the development of printing technology that allowed for full-colored printing attracted many talented artists to the field by the end of the century. The earliest great illustrator of English children's books was George Cruikshank (1792—1878), who in 1823 illustrated the first English translation of Grimms' fairy tales. He was also the first illustrator for Charles Dickens's works, most notably for *Oliver Twist* (1838). Randolph Caldecott (1846–1886), whose name would be immortalized by an annual American award for distinguished children's book illustration, illustrated *John Gilpin's Ride* (1878) and numerous other poems and nursery rhymes in a stunning series for children (see Figure 1.3). Kate Greenaway (1846–1901), whose name was given the British counterpart of the American award for book illustration, illustrated Browning's *The Pied Piper of Hamelin* (1888) and other works, including some of her own poetry (see Figure 6.5 for an example). Walter Crane (1845–1915) produced lavish illustrations for many children's books, including *The Baby's Opera* (1877), a collection of nursery rhymes complete with music.

By the end of the nineteenth century, stunningly illustrated children's books were available at reasonable prices, and by the first quarter of the twentieth century, libraries were designating children's rooms (or at least children's shelves). Children's literature had at last come of age.

THE TWENTIETH CENTURY: WIDENING WORLDS

Children's books of extraordinary quality have continued to appear throughout the twentieth century, and these will be the primary focus of Part II. Suffice it to say that this century has been characterized by even greater diversity in all kinds of children's literature, from picture books to poetry to fantasy to realistic fiction to informational books. A greater appreciation for quality books has surfaced, as evidenced by the numerous book awards now being offered in children's literature, among the earliest being the Newbery Medal, named for John Newbery and honoring the most distinguished American book written for children during a given year, and the Caldecott Medal, named for Randolph Caldecott and honoring the most distinguished American contribution to children's book illustration.

We have come a considerable distance over the past two centuries—from the time when children's literature was relegated to the back room of intellectual life, and when children were regarded as embodiments of sin about to happen and therefore in need of constant instruction, admonition, and supervision. We have seen writers and illustrators acquire a greater respect for their children and a deeper awareness of children's needs. The result has been a body of extremely fine literature, rich in diversity and polished in form.

ADULTS AND CHILDREN'S LITERATURE

C. S. Lewis wrote: "When I was ten, I read fairy tales in secret and would have been ashamed if I had been found doing so. Now that I am fifty I read openly. When I became a man I put away childish things, including the fear of childishness and the desire to be very grownup" (210). He further reminds us that growth or maturation actually consists not of putting away old pleasures, but of adding new ones:

> I now enjoy Tolstoy and Jane Austen and Trollope as well as fairy tales and I call that growth; if I had had to lose the fairy tales in order to acquire the novelists, I would not say that I had grown but only that I had changed. A tree grows because it adds rings; a train doesn't grow by leaving one station behind and puffing on to the next. (211)

The general public is surprisingly uneducated about children's literature. Contrary to popular belief, having once been a child and having read some of the childhood classics does not qualify one as an authority on children's books. It has only been in the latter decades of this century that a serious study of children's literature has emerged. We should take heart that at last the field is being acknowledged as worthy of consideration. The study of children's literature is the study of childhood, of human aesthetic development, of human intellectual development, of social development. Without reading, civilization as we know it would disappear in one generation; the ideas of the past would be lost forever; we would be forced naked into the world. Perhaps the greatest end of the study of children's literature is to make readers of all children. The more that we, as adults, know about children's literature, the better equipped we will be to help children discover both the rewards and pleasures of reading.

RECOMMENDED READINGS

Aries, Philippe. *Centuries of Childhood: A Social History of Family Life.* New York: Knopf, 1962.

Bator, Robert, comp. *Signposts to Criticism of Children's Literature.* Chicago: American Library Association, 1983.

Carpenter, Humphrey, and Mari Prichard. *The Oxford Companion to Children's Literature.* Oxford: Oxford University Press, 1984.

Coody, Betty. *Using Literature with Young Children.* 2nd ed. Dubuque, IA: Wm. C. Brown, 1979.

Cott, Jonathan. *Pipers at the Gates of Dawn: The Wisdom of Children's Literature.* New York: Random House, 1981.

Darton, F. J. Harvey. *Children's Books in England, Five Centuries of Social Life.* 3rd ed. Rev. by Brian Alderson. Cambridge, U. K.: Cambridge University Press, 1982.

Egoff, Sheila A. *Only Connect: Readings on Children's Literature.* 2nd ed. Toronto: Oxford University, 1980.

———. *Thursday's Child: Trends and Patterns in Contemporary Children's Literature.* Chicago: American Library Association, 1981.

Fraser, James H., ed. *Society and Children's Literature.* Boston: Godine, 1978.

Harrison, Barbara, and Gregory Maguire, comps. and eds. *Innocence & Experience: Essays & Conversations on Children's Literature.* New York: Lothrop, Lee & Shepard, 1987.

Haviland, Virginia, ed. *Children and Literature: Views and Reviews.* Glenview, IL: Scott, Foresman, 1973.

Hazard, Paul. *Books, Children, and Men.* Boston: The Horn Book, 1983.

Hunter, Mollie. *Talent Is Not Enough.* New York: Harper & Row, 1976.

Inglis, Fred. *The Promise of Happiness: Meaning and Value in Children's Fiction.* Cambridge, U.K.: Cambridge University Press, 1981.

Jackson, Mary V. *Engines of Instruction, Mischief, and Magic: Children's Literature in England from Its Beginnings to 1839.* Omaha: University of Nebraska, 1990.

Lewis, C. S. "On Three Ways of Writing for Children." In *Only Connect.* Ed. Sheila Egoff. 2nd ed. New York: Oxford, 1980. 207–220.

Meek, Margaret, Aidan Warlow, and Griselda Barton. *The Cool Web: The Patterns of Children's Reading.* New York: Atheneum, 1978.

Meigs, Cornelia, Elizabeth Nesbitt, Anne Thaxter Eaton, and Ruth Hill. *A Critical History of Children's Literature: A Survey of Children's Books in English.* New York: Macmillan, 1969.

Pickering, Samuel F., Jr. *John Locke and Children's Books in Eighteenth-Century England.* Knoxville: University of Tennessee Press, 1981.

Sadker, Myra Pollack, and David Miller Sadker. *Now Upon a Time: A Contemporary View of Children's Literature.* New York: Harper & Row, 1977.

Thwaite, Mary F. *From Primer to Pleasure in Reading: An Introduction to the History of Children's Books in England.* Boston: The Horn Book, 1972.

Townsend, John Rowe. *Written for Children.* Boston: The Horn Book, 1974.

Trelease, Jim. *The Read-Aloud Handbook.* New York: Penguin, 1982.

CHAPTER 2

Child Development
and Literature

THE IMPACT OF CHILD DEVELOPMENT ON READING

Children were once regarded as miniature adults with simple minds and shallow feelings. But the twentieth century has taken virtually the opposite view as our understanding of childhood behavior and intellectual development grows. Modern theories of child development have revealed that children are indeed psychologically complex individuals, possessing a host of special needs as they mature. An awareness of these theories can give us a better understanding of both children and their books, or, more specifically, their relationships and interactions with books.

MODERN THEORIES OF CHILD DEVELOPMENT

We will look at three of the more prominent theories of child development, all of which complement each other (see Table 2.1). Jean Piaget was concerned with intellectual or cognitive development, Erik Erikson with social development, and Lawrence Kohlberg with the development of moral judgment. All three see an individual's development as occurring in a series of stages through which most people pass on their progress toward maturity.

Before these theories are described, a word of caution is in order. Both Piaget and Kohlberg have been criticized for ignoring female development, which, some argue, is not the same as male development. Males generally value competition, self-assertiveness, individual rights, and social rules. Females, on the other hand, value human relationships, responsibilities to others, cooperation, community values, and tolerance for opposing viewpoints. For example, females, some researchers argue, reach some of these developmental stages more quickly than males. Only recently has a

TABLE 2.1 Comparative chart of developmental stages identified by Piaget, Erikson, and Kohlberg

Piaget	Erikson	Kohlberg
Sensorimotor Period (0–2 years)	Trust vs. Mistrust (0–18 months)	Preconventional Level (0–7 years)
Preoperational Period (2–7 years)	Autonomy vs. Doubt	*Stage 1—Punishment/Obedience*
Preconceptual Stage (2–4 years)	(18 months–3 years)	*Orientation*
Intuitive Stage (4–7 years)	Initiative vs. Guilt (3–7 years)	*Stage 2—Instrumental/Relativist*
		Orientation
Period of Concrete Operations	Industry vs. Inferiority	Conventional Level (7–11 years)
(7–11 years)	(7–11 years)	*Stage 1—Interpersonal Concordance*
		Orientation
		Stage 2—"Law and Order" Orientation
Period of Formal Operations	Identity vs. Role Confusion	Postconventional Level
(11–15 years)	(11–15 years)	(Adolescence/Adulthood)
		Stage 1—Contractual/Legalistic
		Orientation
		Stage 2—Universal/Ethical/Principle
		Orientation

significant amount of work been done in the field of women's psychological development. We can note a similar neglect of the psychological development of members of minority groups. This is not to say that the work of the three psychologists below is invalid, but that these theories, as all theories, are not infallible, and they are offered here only as a general guide—until something better comes along.

Piaget's Cognitive Theory of Development

The *Cognitive Theory of Development,* devised by the Swiss psychologist Jean Piaget, is the earliest and perhaps the most famous of the theories of child development. Piaget saw a person's intellectual or mental development as occurring in steps, each building on the previous one. He outlined four major periods of intellectual development, some of which he subdivided into stages. It is important to note that once an individual has moved on to a higher stage some backsliding may occur, some temporary reverting to a previous stage. (It is rather like mountain climbing; if we don't have a sure footing or a firm grasp, we will slip back down the mountain.)Also, the movement between stages is gradual and almost imperceptible, with all individuals developing at different rates. Consequently, the age spans mentioned here can be only approximations and averages.

Sensorimotor Period (From Birth to Two Years). The first period Piaget identifies is the *Sensorimotor Period,* which he sees as lasting from birth to about two years of age, during which the child is incapable of establishing *object permanence*—in other words, infants in this period do not realize that objects continue to exist even if they cannot be seen. So far as an infant is concerned, when she can no longer see her mother, her mother simply does not exist; she may as well have fallen off the face of the earth. Out of sight is out of mind. Consequently, the infant's world is entirely egocentric, and what matters most is sensory experience, what the child sees, feels, hears, and smells. It is also during this period that the infant is concerned with the development of coordination, figuring out how to use the hands and arms and legs.

What impact does this early period of cognitive development have on reading? It is most important in these early years that we plant the seed of reading, encourage the physical handling of books, and establish habitual story times. Durable cardboard and cloth books are helpful in providing infants and toddlers with a sense of books' physical characteristics. Tactile books, such as Dorothy Kunhardt's *Pat the Bunny* in which the young child can touch the cottony fur of the bunny or feel the sandpaper roughness of daddy's facial stubble, can provide considerable entertainment. From the very beginning of life, the nursery rhymes can have appeal with their lilting rhythms and curious sounds (for example, "Higglety, pigglety, my black hen," or "Hickory, dickory dock"). The infant does not care so much for the sense as for the sound of the language, which is all new and endlessly fascinating.

Preoperational Period (From Two to Seven Years)

Preconceptual Stage.   Once children have acquired fundamental language skills, they begin to move into the second of Piaget's periods—the *Preoperational Period*—lasting between the ages of two and seven. During the first two or three years of this period, children are in what Piaget termed the *Preconceptual Stage,* characterized by a very subjective logic. By preconceptual, Piaget simply refers to the inability to grasp generalizations or abstract concepts. This is a time of great discovery for children, and they still rely heavily on sensory experiences. However, children at this stage tend to classify objects according to variable criteria; for example, inanimate objects that move (such as machines) may seem alive to them because they associate them with people and pets. There are numerous books about animated machines—Hardy Gramatky's *Little Toot* is the story of a tugboat, and Virginia Burton's *Mike Mulligan's Steamshovel* depicts the adventures of a steamshovel named Maryanne.

Also at this stage, children are still unable to grasp the concept of *conservation of quantity* (in Piaget's famous experiment, children believed that a tall thin jar contained more water than a short fat one, even though they observed the same quantity of water being transferred from one to the other), or of the *reversibility of operations* (the notion that certain things can be "undone"). Additionally, these children cannot readily grasp the concept of adaptation, which includes *assimilation* (using current knowledge to explain or otherwise deal with new information) and *accommodation* (revising current knowledge to respond to new information).

When we consider these characteristics, it is easy to understand how children between the ages of two and four can readily believe in Santa Claus and have no trouble with the fact that they might see half a dozen different Santas in the course of a single shopping trip. Only when they begin to understand such a concept as conservation of quantity do they begin to wonder how Santa can be in so many places at once. Also, it is easy to understand why these children might have great difficulty with a story containing flashbacks, for that concept requires a grasp of the notion of reversibility. We can also see why stories with repeated patterns are appealing, and why anthropomorphic tales and tales of magic are popular with these children. Essentially, it has not yet occurred to children of this age to question the logic of such literature.

Intuitive Stage.   The second stage of this *Preoperational Period* is what Piaget terms the *Intuitive Stage,* which occurs typically between the ages of four and seven. Rather than formal logic, children at this stage use, for lack of a better term, "intuition" or their feelings to help them make judgments about the world around them. They are developing language skills; they are becoming increasingly aware of the world around them; and, consequently, they are becoming less egocentric. Now stories about human relationships carry new meaning as do stories that explore inner emotions. Although fantasies remain popular with these children, realism often becomes more meaningful as they grow curious about other people and their own relationships with others. Robert McCloskey's *One Morning in Maine,* a picture book describing the simple pleasures of family life, and Edward Ardizzone's *Little Tim and the Brave Sea Captain,* a somewhat more adventurous tale, are two examples of realistic fiction for children in this age group. This is an extremely important time for children so far as reading is concerned, since this is a stage of exploration and it is at this time that children often discover hidden interests—reading a wide variety of books on many different topics can help them in this discovery process.

Period of Concrete Operations.   The third period—the *Period of Concrete Operations*—lasts roughly between the ages of seven and eleven. This is when children begin to use rudimentary logic and problem solving. They begin to understand time and spatial relationships. At this stage, young readers begin to read longer books that are divided into chapters, and they can comfortably pause between chapters and pick up the story at a later time. Younger children would have a difficult time picking up a story in midstream like this. Time sequencing is no longer a difficult problem, and episodic books (such as Beverly Cleary's *Dear Mr. Henshaw*) and mystery stories (such as Sobol's *Encyclopedia Brown* series) present logical challenges for these readers. Because children at this stage are more aware of people around them and of their own role in society, novels by such writers as Judy Blume (*Blubber* and *Tales of a Fourth Grade Nothing*) and Patricia MacLachlan (*Cassie Binegar* and *Unclaimed Treasures*) are popular. Such books focus on the personal and social problems of this age group and frequently depict the young protagonists in the process of problem solving.

Additionally, historical fiction becomes more meaningful at this period, since the children now have a grasp of the passage of time. Laura Ingalls Wilder's *Little House* series has been a long-time staple for readers in these years, and MacLachlan's *Sarah, Plain and Tall* is a recent popular historical novel. Stories about other lands, such as Lois Lowry's *Number the Stars,* an exciting story of Denmark during the the Second World War, become appealing as young readers begin to expand their horizons and explore the wider world.

Period of Formal Operations.   Finally, the *Period of Formal Operations* begins around the age of eleven and is completed at about fifteen (when full cognitive maturity, according to Piaget, is established). During this period, young people become capable of using formal logic, engaging in a true exchange of ideas, comprehending the viewpoints of others, and essentially understanding the world as a social phenomenon requiring human interaction. Most readers at this stage of development have already entered adolescence, or what many prefer to call young adulthood. Their reading tastes extend beyond the boundaries established for this book. But it is helpful to see where the typical reading development is headed. Examples of topics found in books for this age group include inner-city gang wars (S. E. Hinton's *The Outsiders*), homosexuality (John Donovan's *I'll Get There, It Better Be Worth the Trip* and Sandra Scoppettone's *Trying Hard to Hear You*), racial prejudice (Mildred Taylor's *Roll of Thunder, Hear My Cry*), and premarital sex (Judy Blume's *Then Again, Maybe I Won't*), just to name a few. The controversial works of Robert Cormier (*I Am the Cheese, The Bumblebee Flies Anyway,* and others) treat such subjects as social and government corruption and have overall negative tones. They remain popular because they address head-on some of the doubts, fears, and anxieties that active young minds naturally experience. Once we understand something about Piaget's discoveries concerning cognitive development, we, as adults, may not be so surprised by the appeal some of these works have for teenagers.

Erikson's Psychosocial Development Theory

In addition to developing intellectually, individuals develop in their social interaction. Erik Erikson's psychosocial development theory classifies the maturing process into a series of psychosocial conflicts, each of which must be resolved before one can move on to the next, in much the same way that Piaget sees successive levels in cognitive development. Erikson's theory includes five principal stages of development throughout childhood. As with Piaget's periods, this development can only be approximated and is different for each individual. Also, regression (or backsliding) does occur from time to time.

Trust vs. Mistrust. The first stage is focused on the conflict of *Trust versus Mistrust,* from birth to roughly eighteen months. This is when children have little option but to trust those who are their caregivers, and they must overcome fears of mistrust, such as the fear of abandonment when they are left to sleep in their own bed. Security provided by creature comforts and physical affection is extremely important at this stage when life is so full of new and potentially unsettling experiences. Margaret Wise Brown's classic *Goodnight Moon* has long been popular as a story for early childhood because it exudes warmth and coziness as we observe a little bunny saying good night to all his favorite possessions in the comfort of his womblike bedroom. For children, hearing familiar books read night after night provides a measure of comfort and security as well.

Autonomy vs. Doubt. Erikson's second stage, *Autonomy versus Doubt,* from eighteen months to about three years, is when children become aware of others around them, especially their caregivers and siblings. As they become mobile, they begin to exercise their first impulses toward autonomy or independence. But at the same time, they must overcome doubts about whether they can do what they attempt. Consequently, this is a period of exploration, which can be exasperating for parents who have labeled this time, "the terrible twos." Beatrix Potter's *The Tale of Peter*

Rabbit beautifully illustrates the moral dilemma that faces children at this stage, with the protagonist facing the conflict between acting on his own will and obeying the authority of his mother.

Initiative vs. Guilt.   The third stage, *Initiative versus Guilt,* occurring between the ages of three and seven, is when children begin to realize their own responsibilities and understand the interpersonal conflicts that arise between people. Children want to take the initiative, not only to do things on their own, but to decide what to do and when to do it. But they must also struggle with guilt when they make the wrong choices. In Ezra Jack Keats's *Peter's Chair* (1967), Peter exhibits hostility when his parents decide to paint all his baby furniture pink for his new sister. Peter decides to run away, but eventually comes to regret his selfish refusal to share his things (which he realizes he no longer needs), and he finally offers them to her of his own free will. Peter has arrived at a higher stage of social development than his rabbit counterpart in Beatrix Potter's tale, demonstrated by his resolve to alter his behavior.

Industry vs. Inferiority.   The fourth stage, *Industry versus Inferiority,* taking place between the ages of seven and eleven, is characterized by a determination to achieve success, often working in concert with others (that is, engaged in work or industry). At the same time, however, children have a tendency to measure themselves against their peers and find themselves wanting, hence feelings of inferiority may develop. Beverly Cleary's *Ramona* books wonderfully demonstrate these feelings; young readers view Ramona with a sympathetic eye as she strives for acceptance among her peers.

Identity vs. Role Confusion.   The fifth stage, achieved at adolescence, is *Identity versus Role Confusion.* Perhaps the great crisis of adolescence is the discovery of identity (not only personal identity, but cultural and social identity as well). Young adults are anxious to know what their roles in life are to be, what society expects of them, what they expect of themselves. All these are questions of identity. Naturally, because of the wealth of options available to young adults, role confusion is a constant threat. Individuals at this stage often appear to be fickle, and sometimes seem to be in a state of almost constant flux, as they explore the possibilities open to them. It is at this time as well that cultural and social differences are first fully realized, and young readers benefit from books that deal honestly and openly about these issues. Although many of the books that address these issues are young adult books and outside the realm of this text, readers in the intermediate grades—roughly fifth through seventh or eighth—have many good novels available to them that examine these issues. Virginia Hamilton's *M.C. Higgins, the Great,* Katherine Paterson's *The Great Gilly Hopkins,* and the fantasies of Ursula Le Guin's *Earthsea* cycle are all stories of the search for individual identity.

Kohlberg's Theory of the Development of Moral Judgment

Lawrence Kohlberg is interested in the development of moral reasoning and moral judgment—that is, how individuals determine what is right and wrong. He bases his work on that of John Dewey and Jean Piaget, and similarly sees development as occurring in a series of stages through which an individual must pass to reach moral maturity. Kohlberg's particular interest is in why moral judgments are made, and he identifies six stages, which he classifies into three different levels.

Preconventional Level.   The first level, the *Preconventional Level,* is characterized by children responding in terms of the immediate consequences of an action—chiefly to punishment or reward or to the superior strength of another. At this level, children move through two stages. The first, termed the *Punishment/Obedience Orientation,* is when a child judges an action to be good or bad, depending upon its physical consequences. What hurts is bad, and what gives pleasure is good. (A hot stove is bad; a chocolate chip cookie is good.)The second stage, the *Instrumental/Relativist Orientation,* is when a child judges an action in terms of its ability to satisfy his or her own needs, or perhaps the needs of others, but only when reciprocity is present (that is, "I'll do this for you if you do that for me"). For children to engage in this sort of activity, they must have reached Piaget's Preoperational Period and have some facility with language and some intuitive logic. Children readily see the actions of Potter's Peter Rabbit as bad because they are likely to cause him harm. Clearly, going into the garden has not satisfied Peter's needs, but only resulted in his illness.

Conventional Level.   The second level, the *Conventional Level,* roughly corresponding with Piaget's Period of Concrete Operations (ages seven to eleven), marks the point at which children begin to value the family, group, community, and nation. Conformity and loyalty to societial conventions or norms become important. The first stage in this level is the *Interpersonal Concordance (or "Good Boy/Nice Girl") Orientation.* To be good is to please others and to have the approval of others. "Normal" behavior is frequently the ideal, and what is "normal" is usually determined by a stereotyped image agreed upon by the majority. We can see a relationship between this stage and Erikson's fourth stage, *Industry versus Inferiority,* coming into play here, as this is the time when peer pressure begins to exert itself. Children now want to wear clothes like their friends wear, want to eat food like their friends eat, and, perhaps most importantly, they just want to have friends. What is good for the individual, therefore, is anything that makes him or her look good in the eyes of others. The second stage in this level, the *"Law and Order" Orientation,* occurs when children develop a respect for authority and for abiding by the "rules," and when they realize the necessity for carrying out their part in the social order. Eleanor Estes's classic family story, *The Moffats,* depicts Janey Moffat, although typically respectful of her elders, one day mimicking the peculiar walk of the superintendent. Then she is convinced that the chief of police is after her for this "crime," and she jumps into a large wooden breadbox at the grocer's to hide from him. It is a comical, but believable, reaction.

Postconventional Level.   The final level is the *Postconventional Level,* which occurs when the individual is capable of making rational, independent judgments apart from the authority of the group or society. This begins to take us outside the limits of this book, since it is a phenomenon not usually realized until adolescence. The first stage in this level is the *Contractual/Legalistic Orientation,* in which individuals define "right" according to terms of broadly based individual rights and the standards that a society establishes. There is no longer blind acceptance of the law, as in the Conventional Level, but rather a reasoned approach that might, in fact, determine that certain laws are wrong. The second stage is the *Universal/Ethical/ Principle Orientation,* in which an individual defines right by his or her own conscience and what he or she perceives to be logical, consistent, and universal principles of right and wrong. Acting according to the Golden Rule or some other abstract principle is an example of this type of moral reasoning. But it should be pointed out that psychologists disagree as to whether such a stage actually exists—or rather, whether human beings are actually capable of attaining this stage (perhaps prophets and saints come close, but few ordinary individuals). Books on social problems, such as S. E. Hinton's study of gang violence, *The Outsiders,* address readers at the *Postconventional Level.*

If we take a simple example (and this does admittedly oversimplify the matter, but it will serve our purposes nevertheless), we can illustrate the various stages of development in this way. When a parent requires a toddler to fasten her seatbelt in the car, the toddler responds because the parent is bigger and stronger and the toddler must do as she is told. This is the first level of moral development, the *Preconventional Level.* A child in early elementary school may fasten her seatbelt because she learns that all her friends fasten theirs, or she may do so because her parents have told her they might get arrested if she is caught out of her seatbelt. She is responding to the pressure of peers or to societal authority and is at the *Conventional Level* of moral development. A teenager fastens her seatbelt not only because she knows it is the law, but because she knows that it is an intelligent law designed to protect her. She is operating at the third level of moral development, the *Postconventional Level.*

THE USES OF DEVELOPMENTAL PSYCHOLOGY

There are probably as many developmental theories as there developmental psychologists to devise them, and to explore this issue further in an introductory work such as this would soon lead to the dilemma of diminishing returns. Suffice it to say that there is considerable agreement that human beings develop in stages, that these stages can only be roughly approximated in terms of years, that there is much overlapping in these stages, and that there may be occasional regression or a temporary going backwards as children develop. Healthy individuals progress successfully through these stages, generally moving from a period of complete egocentricism to maturation, when the needs and concerns of others begin to play a central role, perhaps even the pivotal role if the development is completely successful. Although they may not always be able to identify developmental stages by name or to recite psychological theory, the best writers have an instinctive understanding of human behavior, motives, and relationships. Their books speak to so many people because they speak to the human condition shared by us all.

RECOMMENDED READINGS

Cullinan, Bernice. *Literature and the Child.* 2nd ed. San Diego, CA: Harcourt, 1989.
Donelson, Kenneth L., and Alleen Pace Nilsen. *Literature for Today's Young Adults.* 2nd ed. Glenview, IL: Scott, Foresman, 1985.

Gilligan, Carol. *In a Different Voice: Psychological Theory and Women's Development.* Cambridge, MA: Harvard University Press, 1982.

Hendrick, Joanne. The Whole Child: Developmental Education for the Early Years. 5th ed. New York: Merrill, 1992.

Huck, Charlotte S., Susan Hepler, and Janet Hickman. *Children's Literature in the Elementary School.* 4th ed. New York: Holt, Rinehart & Winston, 1987.

Hyde, Janet Shibley. *Half the Human Experience: The Psychology of Women.* Lexington, MA: D. C. Heath, 1985.

Walsh, Mary Roth, ed. *The Psychology of Women: Ongoing Debates.* New Haven, CT: Yale University Press, 1987.

PART II
The Kinds
of Children's Literature

CHAPTER 3

The Picture Book:
The Illustrations

DEFINITION OF THE PICTURE BOOK

Few things in life are more rewarding than sharing a good picture book with a wide-eyed young child. The picture book—a collaboration of the talents of the writer and the artist—has the power to shape a child's lifelong tastes and attitudes toward reading. The *picture book* is best defined as a book in which the text and pictures are equally important, as opposed to an *illustrated book* in which the text is primary. Many books for adults—including this textbook—are "illustrated," that is, they include pictures. But in a true picture book, the pictures are as important as the text (and often more important), and the result can be described as a happy marriage between the text and pictures. In this chapter, we will examine the illustrations in picture books, and in the next we will consider the text.

There are very fine examples of *wordless picture books*—books containing only pictures—and there is much controversy over whether these works actually constitute "literature." They surely cannot be evaluated according to exactly the same criteria as a book with a written text. On the other hand, many wordless picture books (Mitsumasa Anno's *Anno's Journey* and Lynd Ward's *The Silver Pony,* for example) do tell stories and include points of view, themes, character studies, settings, tones—all literary elements we recognize in written texts. (See Cianciolo [1984] and Groff [1984], for two different viewpoints on the value of wordless picture books.)

There are also the so-called toy books—cardboard books, cloth books, pop-up books—which must be evaluated according to slightly different standards than normal picture storybooks. Usually these books are intended for the very youngest children, even babes in arms. Cardboard and cloth books are durable, can be easily washed, and will withstand insensitive treatment. They are excellent books with which to instruct children on the proper handling of books. And even very young children can be taught respect for books. Pop-up books provide great fun, and they can be extraordinarily complex. The Victorians developed the pop-up book and other books with movable parts (such as wheels, sliding panels, and so on) into an intricate art form. In this century, Mitsumasa Anno has produced *Anno's Sundial,* recalling the nineteenth-century sophistication in this medium.

ARTISTIC ELEMENTS

Picture-book illustrations are examples of *narrative art,* or art that tells a story. The best illustrations are those exhibiting the elements of good art. The finest picture-book artists are serious and talented artists—they have *not* chosen to draw for children because they lacked the talent to draw for adults. They respect their child audience. And they realize that condescension—usually in the form of "cuteness" and rounded, faceless, cuddly figures that all look alike—is insulting to children. The child audience deserves, instead, imaginative art that is both highly individualistic and skillfully executed.

The artist's work is actually the effective use of *illusion.* The artist makes us see things that are not really there—distance, depth, texture, and so on. And the magic extends even further, for the artist gives us an emotional experience as well. Illustrations can make us feel warm, happy, apprehensive, and so on. Indeed, perhaps the foremost prerequisite of children's book illustrations is that they project a mood that is appropriate to the text. It further stands to reason that the more we understand about the artist's craft, the better able we are to judge illustrations in children's picture books intelligently. Consequently, we will briefly consider the principal elements of the art of illustration, including line, space, shape, color, texture, composition, and perspective.

Line

Lines are used both to define objects and to suggest emotional responses. We all realize that lines outline figures and therefore give them definition or shape, but lines can also suggest movement, distance, and even feeling. Curves and circles suggest warmth, coziness, and security (perhaps recalling the safety of the womb and its circular shape). Sharp and zigzag lines suggest excitement and rapid movement. Horizontal lines suggest calm and stability (recalling firm, solid ground), whereas vertical lines suggest height and distance—figures at the top of a page appear to be farther away than those at the bottom or the sides. Imaginative use of line, such as the graceful, delicate lines in Marcia Brown's *Cinderella* or the lively raucous feeling created by Margot Zemach's lines in *Duffy and the Devil* (Figure 3.1), can capture the special spirit of a story.

Space

We often do not think of space—literally the blank parts of the page—as an artistic element, but it is, in fact, very powerful. There is an old story about a Japanese artist who, when asked what was the most important part of a painting, replied, "What is left

FIGURE 3.1 Margot Zemach's illustrations for *Duffy and the Devil* (retold by Harve Zemach) capture the lively, comical nature of this Cornish Rumpelstiltskin tale. Notice how movement and chaos are suggested by the ragged lines moving in every direction.

out." The use of space is actually what draws our attention to specific forms depicted on the page. If a page contains very little blank space, but is instead crowded with images, our eyes are forced to examine all the forms carefully. However, if a page contains a great deal of space, our eyes are immediately drawn to the objects that are left on the page, and all of our attention is focused on them. In this way the artist gives these objects special importance. Generous use of space in a picture can suggest emptiness, loneliness, isolation. Space may also create the illusion of distance. Conversely, the lack of open space on a page may contribute to a claustrophobic feeling (see *Jumanji*, Figure 3.2) or confusion or even chaos.

Shape

The predominant shapes in an illustration help to elicit emotional reactions. Massive grouped shapes may suggest stability, enclosure or confinement, or perhaps awkwardness (*Jumanji*, Figure 3.2). On the other hand, lighter, delicate shapes may suggest movement, grace, and freedom (*One Morning in Maine*, Figure 3.3). Sometimes illustrations consist chiefly of shapes to the exclusion of lines, as in collage. Rounded shapes may suggest emotional reactions similar to those of the curved and circular lines (*The Tale of Peter Rabbit*, Figure 3.5), and squarish, angular shapes may elicit more excitable responses (*Duffy and the Devil*, Figure 3.1).

Color

It is a misconception that children require brightly colored pictures. Some of the most enduringly popular picture books are illustrated in black and white or monochrome (with pictures done in a single hue, such as blue or sepia). Wanda Gag's *Millions of Cats*, Leaf and Lawson's *Ferdinand the Bull*, McCloskey's *One Morning in Maine* (Figure 3.3) and *Blueberries for Sal*, and, more recently, Chris Van Allsburg's *Jumanji* (Figure 3.2) are only a few of these classics. And most of these books would be far less effective if they were done in full color. When an artist does choose to illustrate in black and white or monochrome, he or she usually compensates for the absence of color by the effective use of line, space, and shape. Color, in fact, can often detract from a text, particularly if the color is overpowering or inappropriate. Remember, we said that a picture book is the happy marriage between text and illustrations—one must not outdo the other.

Surprisingly, color is one of the least imaginatively used of artistic elements in children's picture books. Color is chiefly used in a conventional fashion—skies are blue, grass is green, and so on. But children have been found to be acutely aware of subtle variations in hues and they certainly do not demand bold, bright colors. (Donnarae MacCann and Olga Richard tell us of a seven-year-old who used thirty-two shades of blue in a painting and asked for the names of each separate color. Of course, most of us are not quite that sensitive to color variations.) Colors do have the ability to evoke emotional responses—as opposed to driving children to distraction or boredom. Psychologists tell us that reds and yellows are warm or hot colors and suggest excitement, whereas blues and greens are cool or cold colors and suggest calm or quiet. There are also certain conventional responses to color—purple

FIGURE 3.2 We, the viewers, are at a chld's eye-level looking over the table and up at the menacing monkeys (made even more disturbing from this point of view) in this surrealistic pencil drawing from Chris VanAllsburg's *Jumanji.* The figures seem to crowd us, adding an almost claustrophobic feeling, and the whole scene appears to be a moment uncomfortably frozen in time—an appropriate mood for this story of a mysterious board game come to life.

SOURCE: Illustration from *Jumanji* by Chris Van Allsburg. Copyright © 1981 by Chris Van Allsburg. Reprinted by permission of Houghton Mifflin Company.

signifying royalty, green envy or illness, blue depression, yellow cowardice, and so on. (These conventions are cultural phenomena: In imperial China, the color yellow was reserved for the emperor, and white is a traditional color of mourning in the Orient.) Additionally, colors are used to suggest cultural distinctions. When illustrating a Navajo Indian story, *Arrow to the Sun,* Gerald McDermott used the colors of the Southwest—golds, yellows, desert browns, and oranges. In McDermott's *Anansi the Spider* (Figure 3.4), a traditional folktale of Africa, he turns to the bold, bright reds, greens, and sharply contrasting black reminiscent of the colorful regalia often associated with the folk culture of western Africa.

FIGURE 3.3 The stone lithography of Robert McCloskey's illustrations for *One Morning in Maine* help to provide the textured appearance—the fine grain we see in the pictures is actually created by the stone surface on which the drawing was made. McCloskey's style is a fine example of representational art; he has, in fact, used himself and his daughters as models in this true-to-life tale.

SOURCE: From *One Morning in Maine* by Robert McCloskey. Copyright © 1952, renewed © 1980 by Robert McCloskey. Reprinted by permission of the publisher. Viking Penguin, a division of Penguin Books USA Inc.

FIGURE 3.4   Gerald McDermott's illustrations for the African folktale *Anansi the Spider* were inspired by African folk art. The stylized figures are decorated with geometric shapes and colored boldly in primary colors. Despite the abstract quality of the pictures, children have no difficulty in identifying the scene as that of a fish swallowing a spider.

SOURCE: From *Anansi the Spider* adapted and illustrated by Gerald McDermott. Copyright © 1972 by Landmark Production, Inc. Reprinted by permission of Henry Holt and Company, Inc.

Texture

One of the illusions the artist creates is to give a flat surface (the paper) the characteristics of a three-dimensional surface—the suggestion of fur, wood grain, smooth silk. We refer to this quality of art as texture. An artist who wants to emphasize the realistic quality of a picture may pay great attention to texture (*Jumanji,* Figure 3.2. and *One Morning in Maine,* Figure 3.3). However, less realistic styles may make use of texture to enrich the visual experience and to stimulate the viewer's imagination (*Daddy Is a Monster . . . Sometimes,* Figure 3.7.).

Composition and Perspective

The composition of an illustration refers to the arrangement of the details in the picture. Composition is important to the narrative quality of the picture as well as to its emotional impact. The artist must consider where best to place the focal point, from what angle the picture is to be viewed, and what mood is to be conveyed. One important aspect of composition is the point of view or perspective—that is, from what vantage point are we, the viewers, looking at the objects or events depicted? The closer we appear to be to the action, the more engaged we are likely to be (*Jumanji,* Figure 3.2). The farther away we seem to be, the more detached we will feel. We may view events from a worm's eyes or small child's perspective or a bird's-eye view or from a fish-eye view. The artist may wish to change points of view from illustration to illustration—perhaps to avoid monotomy, but more probably to make us see and think about things in special ways. Good composition creates a sense of rhythm as we move from page to page—a rhythm that is suited to the nature of the narrative. Good composition also creates a sense of unity, with the illustrations and the text making a satisfying whole and evoking an effective mood.

ARTISTIC STYLES

Many children's illustrators are consummate artists at the top of their profession. Consequently, it should not be surprising that we find in picture books a rich variety of artistic styles, representing all the major schools of art. Of course, we need not spend inordinate amounts of time trying to determine the specific artistic style used by picture book artists. In fact, artists frequently combine features of more than one style, making it difficult to classify their efforts. Rather, our point here is that the art in good children's picture books is good art by any standards, and we are doing our children a disservice by not exposing them to the widest possible variety and the highest possible quality.

Children are very eclectic in their tastes; that is, they enjoy a wide variety of artistic styles and often seem to enjoy new and unusual techniques. Children have not yet learned artistic prejudice or narrow-mindedness, and are not nearly so set in their ways as are adults. There are wonderful stories of very young children going into museums and noting the similarities between the works of a great Flemish artist of the sixteenth century, Brueghel, and a popular twentieth-century children's illustrator, Richard Scarry. Children are wise enough to detect differences in artistic styles, and not yet jaded enough to reject the unfamiliar. Our task is simply to share with them a generous sampling of all that the world of picture books has to offer. Some of the principal styles found in children's picture books include the following.

Representationalism

Representational art seeks to present objects realistically, although not necessarily photographically. Nor need representational art depict realistic subjects. For example, Beatrix Potter (*The Tale of Peter Rabbit,* Figure 3.5) was almost fanatical in her desire to realistically depict the little animal characters in her books; nevertheless she felt compelled to clothe them in human clothes. We still regard her art as representational, and we see her goal as wishing us to believe that her characters are real. On the other hand, Robert McCloskey's *One Morning in Maine* (Figure 3.3) faithfully depicts an extremely realistic tale—the adventures of an average family on a typical

FIGURE 3.5 This watercolor from Beatrix Potter's *The Tale of Peter Rabbit* exudes warmth and security, appropriate after Peter's harrowing experience in Mr. MacGregor's garden. The soft, warm yellows and earthy browns are complemented by gently curved lines and rounded shapes, from the oval mass of Mrs. Rabbit bent before the embracing hearth to the little round tails of each of Peter's sisters. Peter himself, having caught cold from his mischief, is distanced to the right, but nonetheless secure under the rounded folds of his bed blankets.

SOURCE: Beatrix Potter, *The Tale of Peter Rabbit*. London: Warne, 1901.

day at their summer vacation home. McCloskey used his own family for his models, and his attention to detail heightens the sense of immediacy and realism. Representational art deals with recognizable shapes, realistic color (if color is used), and proper perspectives and proportions. Representational art allows us to enter into the experience and readily become a part of it—but at the same time we are shown a new, fresh way of looking at the world.

Expressionism

Expressionism as a school of painting was quite specific and flourished toward the end of the nineteenth century. It was a reaction to the photographic realism of earlier styles (styles made somewhat obsolete by the invention of photography). Since it was no longer necessary to portray objects or people with exacting accuracy, artists were forced to find new ways to express themselves. Painters like van Gogh found a new freedom of expression, for it allowed them to use color, line, space, and other elements in a highly individualistic and subjective manner—they could paint what they *felt* rather than simply what they *saw*.

Expressionistic art includes deliberate distortion and exaggeration, accompanying wide-ranging experiments with line, space, color, shape, texture, and composition. Expressionism represents an emotional response to things, and the art captures the artist's subjective feeling rather than a faithful portrayal of reality. Notice in Ludwig Bemelmans's *Madeline* (Figure 3.6) how the artist has distorted shapes, included exaggerated lines, and drawn everything with a childlike simplicity. This is the artist's *idea* of a convent of girls going on a walk with their teacher, not a faithfully detailed rendering.

Expressionism, taken to its logical end, results in *abstractionism,* in which the drawn figures only vaguely resemble the objects they portray. Complete abstraction-

FIGURE 3.6 Ludwig Bemelmans's popular picture storybook *Madeline* is a delightful comedy about a spunky little girl in a Parisian convent school. The illustrations are interesting examples of expressionistic art. Notice the angularity of the figures and the exaggerated height of the nun, Miss Clavel, accompanying the twelve little girls who walk, as we are told, in "two straight lines" (surely a commentary on convent school discipline). The trees are more like ideas of trees; there is no attempt at realistic depiction. There is a carefree jocularity in these pictures that aptly characterizes the mood of the story.

ism is seldom, if ever, found in children's picture books, since it effectively eliminates any narrative intent. (How can we retell the story from the pictures if we cannot identify what it is the picture is illustrating?) But one popular children's illustrator, Brian Wildsmith, has used a form of abstract art known as *cubism,* in which the figures are composed of varied geometric shapes (not always cubes as the name suggests). Wildsmith also loves color and uses it to great advantage to dramatize his unusual and provocative illustrations.

Impressionism

Impressionism derives from the late nineteenth-century French art movement of the same name, a movement characterized by experimentation with ways of looking at objects. Monet and Cezanne are among the most famous impressionists, but many modern artists have experimented with the style. Impressionistic art uses an interplay of color and light—usually created by using splashes, speckles, or dots of paint as opposed to longer brush strokes—to create a dreamlike effect. Many of Maurice Sendak's illustrations in Charlotte Zolotow's *Mr. Rabbit and the Lovely Present* capture this dreamlike quality of impressionism. John Burningham's illustrations for his *Mr. Gumpy's Outing,* Donald Carrick's delicate watercolors for Carol Carrick's *In the Moonlight, Waiting,* and John Schoenherr's Caldecott Medal–winning illustrations for Jane Yolen's *Owl Moon* all evoke the magical, almost dreamlike quality that is characteristic of impressionistic art. Through impressionistic art, we, the audience, are distanced from the action, and rarely allowed to fully participate in it. Instead, we view it from afar with detachment—and often with wonder. Impressionism is best suited to dreamlike fantasies and quiet, pensive moods or stories on the margin between fantasy and reality. It is the one artistic style that seems to demand color.

Surrealism

Surrealism, an artistic style explored most fully by the painter Salvador Dali, represents the artist's intellectual response to a subject (as opposed to the *emotional* response of expressionism). In Surrealistic art, objects may be depicted quite realistically, but they are subjected to unnatural juxtapositions and bizarre incongruities. Chris Van Allsburg's *Jumanji* (Figure 3.2) is a prime example of surrealistic art in a picture book. The illustrations in this and other books employing this artistic style include the disturbing qualities of surrealistic art—almost nightmarish when contrasted with the more pleasant dream qualities of impressionistic art—which may make it more appropriate for older readers. Nowhere is this more evident than in the two books by Eugene Ionesco called simply *Story Number 1* and *Story Number 2.* Wildly imaginative, the illustrations and the stories approach (some would say surpass) the grotesque, which was surely Ionesco's intent.

Cartoon

It is possible to see cartoon art as a form of expressionism, although cartoons actually predate that art movement. Cartoon art employs gross exaggerations and distortions always for a satiric or humorous effect. Political cartoons are still a regular feature in newspapers and magazines, lampooning public figures and representing abstractions with symbols (Uncle Sam, for example). Because of their broad and easily grasped humor, cartoons are particularly appealing to young children. Cartoon art avoids any subtlety, and instead relies on solid lines and absence of shading for its distinctive style. If color is used, it is almost always bold and never exhibits any subtlety of hue. Dr. Seuss's beloved books display his own special brand of cartoon art—and the cartoon style is particularly suited to his rollicking, comical tales. Whereas the animated Walt Disney cartoons can hardly be surpassed, the Disney-inspired books are often disappointing because the cartoon illustrations lack originality—all the characters in all the books resemble each other. The pictures of Steven Kellogg (for example, in *The Island of the Skog* or *The Day Jimmy's Boa Ate the Wash* written by Trinka Noble) are far more interesting, and the pictures of James Marshall (*Miss Nelson Is Missing* or *The Stupids Die,* both written by Harry Allard) are much funnier.

Folk Art

One of the most commonly used styles of art is *folk art.* Folk art is also the most widely varied of art forms and sometimes the most difficult to pinpoint. Folk art is based upon the designs and images peculiar to a specific culture (Native American, Eastern European, Middle Eastern, African, Japanese, and so on). Because there are as many different folk styles as there are folk cultures, it is difficult to make meaningful generalizations about folk art. Alice and Martin Provensen's *Peaceable Kingdom: The Shaker Abecedarius* (see Figure 5.2) and Margot Zemach's lively depiction of the Cornish folktale *Duffy and the Devil* (Figure 3.1) demonstrate two widely varied versions of folk art. Leo and Diane Dillon's illustrations for Margaret Musgrove's *Ashanti to Zulu: African Traditions* are exquisite art works capturing the flavor of native African culture. Gerald McDermott's illustrations for the West African folktale *Anansi the Spider* carry suggestions of African folk art in their use of color and geometric shapes (Figure 3.4.). In spite of the great differences in these illustrations, all attempt to recreate the atmosphere or pervasive mood of a specific culture. Almost by definition, folk art belongs to an earlier, simpler time and a predominantly agrarian society. Consequently, folk art is particularly suited to the illustration of folktales, in which the artist wishes to express the ingenuous flavor of the ethnic or regional culture that inspired the tales.

Photography

Photography may be considered a technique as much as an artistic style, but it is, nevertheless, an art. And the art of photography is the art of composition—of arranging objects within a frame so that the result is intellectually stimulating. In picture storybooks, we normally expect something more creative than Polaroid snapshots, and when photographs are used to tell stories, it is principally for realistic stories. But in informational books, photographs can be especially effective. Imaginatively used in black and white or in color, photography can be dramatic, beautiful, and highly effective. Tana Hoban's *Count and See* and *Look Again* demonstrate the uses of photography in children's informational books.

Other Artistic Styles

Many other styles of art can be found in children's picture books. Some of these are variations of expressionism. We have already mentioned Brian Wildsmith's use of cubism, an early offshoot of expressionistic art that relies principally on the juxtaposition of various geometric shapes. Another distinctive style is found in the bold, black lines, richly contrasting colors, and almost vibrating lines of John Steptoe's *Daddy Is a Monster . . . Sometimes* (Figure 3.7), which suggest stained-glass windows. These are all characteristic of another offshoot of expressionism termed *Les Fauves* (the "wild beasts" in French). The influence of the Art Deco movement of the 1930s can be seen in some of the illustrations in Rachel Isadora's *Ben's Trumpet,* with their bold, sleek designs and sharp contrast. *Pointillism* sprang from the impressionist movement and is distinguished by pictures composed of carefully positioned colored dots of equal size. Georges Seurat is the most famous practitioner in this style. Pointillism differs from impressionism in that it is less spontaneous in appearance, the placement of each dot and its choice of color requiring exact planning. Miroslav Sasek's *This Is New York* demonstrates a variation of style.

Of course, all good artists of talent create their own highly individualized styles, drawing their inspiration from many varied schools and sources, often, as pointed out above, combining features of more than one style or school to achieve their ends. Ideally, children will be exposed to a wide variety of artistic styles in their picture books.

ARTISTIC MEDIA

An artist, in addition to deciding the style of an illustration, must also decide upon the method of producing that illustration: Shall it be drawn with pencil or ink? Shall it be painted in oils or watercolors or tempera? Shall it be cut out on a block of wood or linoleum? Each illustration may represent an artistic style, but the illustration was accomplished through a specific medium. By *medium* we mean essentially the tool (or tools, hence the plural *media*) the artist chooses to work with. We can group media generally into the following three broad categories.

Painterly Techniques

Painterly techniques are those using paint as their primary medium. Paint itself consists of pigment (usually powdered) mixed with some liquid or paste to make it spreadable. Many variations are possible depending upon the medium used to mix with the pigment.

> *Watercolors,* as their name implies, use water as the medium, resulting in transparent, typically soft, delicate pictures as in Beatrix Potter's *The Tale of Peter Rabbit* (Figure 3.5).
>
> *Tempera* is made by mixing pigments with egg yolk—or some other albuminous substance. Tempera is not as transparent as watercolor and can

FIGURE 3.7 A child of expressionism, Les Fauves art includes distinctive strong, black lines separating parts of the picture—much like the lines made by the lead framing in stained-glass windows. Also characteristic of this artistic style is a certain vibrance of line that suggests motion—and emotion—as in this illustration from John Steptoe's *Daddy Is a Monster . . . Sometimes,* a story of parent/child relationships.

SOURCE: *Father/Daughter* illustration, p. 13, from *Daddy Is a Monster . . . Sometimes* by John Steptoe. (J. B. Lippincott). Copyright © 1980 by John Steptoe. Reprinted by permission of Harper & Row, Publishers, Inc.

produce some brilliant hues. It was used by Maurice Sendak in his classic *Where the Wild Things Are,* and Lynd Ward used tempera in shades of gray in *The Silver Pony.*

Gouache is a powdered paint similar to tempera, but mixed with a white base, resulting in a delicate hue. Gouache was the favorite medium of Margot Zemach (*Duffy and the Devil,* Figure 3.1).

Poster color is a coarser version of gouache and can be found in Jacob Lawrence's *Harriet and the Promised Land.* The colors tend to be bolder than in gouache.

Oil paint typically uses linseed oil as a base and is among the most opaque of media. One of the best examples is found in Paul O. Zelinsky's version of *Rumpelstiltskin.*

Acrylics use a plastic base, a product of twentieth-century technology, and they produce very brilliant colors. Barbara Cooney's illustrations for *The Ox-Cart Man* by Donald Hall are excellent examples.

Pastels differ from the rest in that they are typically applied in powdered form (often with the fingers). Chris Van Allsburg used pastels in his *The Wreck of the Zephyr.*

Chalk, Pencil, and Ink drawings, while technically not painting, follow the same general principles as painterly techniques. Chris Van Allsburg used pencil for *Jumanji* (Figure 3.2).

Crayons were used by John Burningham in his fanciful story *Come Away from the Water Shirley.*

Each of these media produces differing effects, and two or more may be used in combination as well. (See Figure 5.1 for an example of art combining watercolors, pastels, and acrylics.)

Graphic Techniques

Graphic techniques refer to those in which the artist prepares blocks or plates that are then inked and imprinted upon paper. As with painterly techniques, there are several varieties.

Woodblocks are the very earliest form of reproducible art. The very first printed book illustrations—dating from the late middle ages—were made from blocks of wood on which the artist carved away all the areas that were not to be printed. Today, woodblock illustrations can still be found is such books as Ed Emberley's *Drummer Hoff* (retold by Barbara Emberley), in which stylized woodblock illustrations give an old-fashioned flavor to a folk rhyme.

Linocuts are similar to woodblocks in principle, but the artist uses blocks of linoleum rather than wood. Barbara Cooney's *Dick Whittington and His Cat* is an example.

In *scratchboard* illustration, the artist paints deep, black ink over a smooth board (called, appropriately, a "scratchboard") and then, when the ink dries, scratches the design onto the surface with a sharp instrument. Leonard Everett Fisher is a master of this technique, using it in many of his informational books for children (*The Doctors, The Schoolmasters,* and many others).

Stone lithography is a complex process involving the drawing of a design with a grease mixture onto a flat stone, treating the stone with chemicals and oils so that the ungreased areas repel water. Then water and ink are successively applied, the greased areas absorb the ink but repel the water, and when paper is pressed onto the stone, an impression is made from the greased, inked areas. (Robert McCloskey's *One Morning in Maine,* Figure 3.3, is an example of stone lithography; if you look closely at the illustration you can detect the grainy surface of the stone imprinted on the paper.)

Montage and Collage

Montage (the collection and assembling of a variety of different pictures or designs to create a single picture) and *collage* (similar to montage, but employing materials in addition to pictures—string, cotton, weeds, anything that will work—to create a single picture) have been styles effectively used by Ezra Jack Keats in *The Snowy Day* and its sequels, and by Leo Lionni in such works as *Frederick* and *Fish Is Fish.*

PICTURE-BOOK LAYOUT

Before we consider the story elements of the picture book, we must look at one last feature, but one that is by no means the least important—and that is the layout of the book. If we examine a good picture book carefully, we will notice that the text has been carefully placed in relation to the pictures. That is, simply put, the pictures illustrate what the accompanying text describes. This is the concept of juxtaposition. It is quite annoying to have the text say one thing and the picture illustrate something else (and that does happen in poorly done books).

We also may want to consider where the pictures are placed on the page—are they all on the same side of the page and all the same size? Or do the placement and size vary from page to page? Is there a good reason for the placement and size—that is, do they reinforce some aspect of the whole story? Maurice Sendak's *Where the Wild Things Are* provides a good example of the way in which pictures and text can complement each other. As the story opens, Max, a rather naughty boy, is causing all manner of havoc about his house. The pictures are small with large white borders around them. Max is then sent to his room for his misbehavior, and soon the room seems to change into a forest. Now the pictures are gradually getting larger, eventually overlapping onto the facing page, and finally becoming full-page spreads. The text, in the meantime, is actually describing a dream that Max is having, and as he sinks deeper into his dream, the pictures come to overtake the page. At the end the story, as Max gradually emerges from his dream, and the pictures begin to recede in size.

Of course, we do not always find such powerful symbolism in a book's layout. Such a book can remind us that the size and placement of illustrations is not (or should not be) a random process, but rather a carefully conceived plan that helps to unite the pictures, the text, and the overall intent of the book.

RECOMMENDED READINGS

Alderson, Brian. *Looking at Picture Books 1973.* New York: Children's Book Council, 1974.

Bader, Barbara. *American Picturebooks from Noah's Ark to the Beast Within.* New York: Macmillan, 1976.

Barrett, Terry, and Kenneth Marantz. "Photographs as Illustrations." *The New Advocate* 17 (Fall 1989): 103–53.

Cianciolo, Patricia. *Illustrations in Children's Books.* 2nd ed. Dubuque, IA: Wm. C. Brown, 1976.

———. *Picture Books for Children.* 3rd ed. Chicago: American Library Association, 1990.

Dooley, Patricia. "The Window in the Book: Conventions in the Illustrations of Children's Books." *Wilson Library Bulletin* (October 1980): 108–12.

Freeman, La Verne, and Ruth Sunderlin Freeman. *The Child and His Picture Book.* New York: Century House, 1967.

Gainer, Ruth Straus. "Beyond Illustration: Information about Art in Children's Picture Books." *Art Education* (March 1982): 16–19.

Gottlieb, Gerald. *Early Children's Books and Their Illustrations.* Boston: Godine, 1975.

Groff, Patrick. "Children's Literature Versus Wordless Books?" In *Jump Over the Moon.* Eds. Pamela Petrick Barron and Jennifer Q. Burley. New York: Holt, 1984, 145–54.

Hopkins, Lee Bennett. "Pop Go the Books." *CLA Bulletin* 16 (Fall 1990): 10–12.

Hurlimann, Bettina. *Picture-Book World.* Cleveland: World, 1969.

Kingman, Lee, ed. *The Illustrator's Notebook.* Boston: The Horn Book, 1978.

Kingman, Lee, Joanna Foster, and Ruth Giles Lontoft, comps. *Illustrators of Children's Books, 1957–1966.* Boston: The Horn Book, 1968. (Also, *Illustrators of Children's Books, 1744–1945* and *Illustrators of Children's Books, 1946–1956.*)

Kingman, Lee, Grace Hogarth, and Harriet Quimby. *Illustrators of Children's Books, 1967–1976.* Boston: The Horn Book, 1978.

Lindauer, Shelley L. Knudsen. "Wordless Books: An Approach to Visual Literacy." *Children's Literature in Education* 19:3 (Fall 1988): 136–42.

MacCann, Donnarae, and Olga Richard. *The Child's First Books.* New York: Wilson, 1973.

Matthias, Margaret, and Graciela Italiano. "Louder Than a Thousand Words." In *Signposts of Criticism of Children's Literature.* Comp., Robert Bator. Chicago: American Library Association, 1983.

Nodelman, Perry. *Words About Pictures: The Narrative Art of Children's Picture Books.* Athens, GA: University of Georgia Press, 1988.

Pitz, Henry C. *Illustrating Children's Books: History, Technique, Production.* New York: Watson-Guptill, 1963.

Pritchard, David. " 'Daddy, Talk!' Thoughts on Reading Early Picture Books." *The Lion and the Unicorn* 7/8 (1983/84): 64–69.

Roxburgh, Stephen. "A Picture Equals How Many Words? Narrative Theory and Picture Books for Children." *The Lion and the Unicorn* 7/8 (1983/84): 20–33.

Shulevitz, Uri. *Writing with Pictures: How to Write and Illustrate Children's Books.* New York: Watson-Guptin, 1985.

CHAPTER 4

The Picture Book: The Story

TYPES OF STORIES

In the preceding chapter, we considered the illustrations of picture books; now we will turn our attention to the stories in these books. In the "old days," children had to be content with just hearing a story told to them, but modern technology has brought into the children's hands a myriad of beautifully illustrated books on an inexhaustible variety of subjects. In the picture storybook, very young children are introduced to the idea of storytelling, of making up tales for the purpose of entertainment. Indeed, one of the important results of reading to children is to help them make the distinction between fiction and reality. Over 2,000 picture books are published each year in the United States alone, and on a plethora of topics. Most of these picture books may be categorized roughly into four principal story types.

Folktales, Legends, and Myths

These remain age-old favorites and include the familiar stories that have been passed down, at least initially, by word of mouth through the generations. They adhere to the traditional storytelling patterns (often beginning with "Once upon a time" and ending with the hero or heroine living "happily ever after"); and they typically take place in some never-never land where magic is commonplace. Innumerable versions of "Cinderella," "Little Red Riding Hood," and "The Three Little Pigs" are available at any one time (and they make for interesting comparisons, incidentally). Folktales are also the basis for many modern fantasies (James Thurber's *Many Moons* comes to mind).

Modern Fantasy Stories

These include those tales, usually with modern settings, that employ magic as a principal feature. Unlike the folktales, the modern fantasies can be ascribed to specific authors and therefore do not appear in multiple versions. Maurice Sendak's classic, *Where the Wild Things Are*, fits into this category, as do Chris Van Allsburg's Christmas enchantment, *The Polar Express,* and Crocket Johnson's wonderfully imaginative tale, *Harold and the Purple Crayon.* As with folktales, modern fantasies build on the child's delight in worlds of make-believe, but whereas folktales generally distance the magic through time and place, many modern fantasies bring the magic into contemporary life. In this way, they appeal to the same drive that causes a child to want to believe in Santa Claus or the Tooth Fairy. (And, by the same token, most modern fantasies omit the potentially threatening forces of evil that characterize the folktales—Wicked Witches and Big Bad Wolves. This issue will be discussed at greater length in Chapter 6.)

Talking Animal Stories

Talking animals are popular in picture books, such as Beatrix Potter's *The Tale of Peter Rabbit* and *Benjamin Bunny* or Russell Hoban's many tales about Frances the Badger. Many talking animal stories avoid magic (outside the fact that the animal characters can talk and think like humans) and attempt to focus on everyday issues in quite realistic contemporary settings. In Arnold Lobel's *Frog and Toad Are Friends*, we witness the pleasant antics of the frog and toad, who wear clothes, go on outings together, and generally do everything that humans do and in the same manner. Other modern fantasies employ inanimate objects as their protagonists, such as boats (Hardy Gramatky's *Little Toot*), houses (Virginia Burton's *The Little House*), or machines (Virginia Burton's *Mike Mulligan and His Steam Shovel*). These books give young readers early exposure to symbolism, for they see the animal or inanimate characters as symbolizing facets of human nature. Also, children have little trouble imagining animals and even machines with human traits (in fact, they may have difficulty imagining animals, especially, without human traits), and most children have a fascination with animals (pets, for instance), making these fantasy stories great favorites.

Realistic Stories

Today, few subjects are taboo in children's picture books—modern books for children often deal with such social and psychological issues as death, divorce, sibling rivalry, and other social and psychological adjustments facing children. The emergence of these topics in picture books may suggest the faith that writers place in the ability of today's children to handle the complexities of our world. But picture books are not primarily tools for helping children cope with their problems. Instead, literature for children is foremost for enjoyment, and our first thought ought to be for a book's potential for entertaining the reader. Realistic stories depict reality as we understand it. They may be historical, such as Brinton Turkle's warm tale of colonial

New England, *Thy Friend, Obadiah,* or Donald Hall and Barbara Cooney's *The Ox-Cart Man,* set in New Hampshire in the early 1800s. Or they may take on a modern setting as does Lucille Clifton's *Some of the Days of Everett Anderson,* about a contemporary African-American boy growing up in a big city. Realistic stories provide an interesting way to expose children to other cultures, such as the traditional Chinese in Thomas Handforth's *Mei Lei,* and the French in Ludwig Bemelmans's *Madeline* and its successors. Marjorie Flack's *Story About Ping,* concerning the escapades of a duckling on the Yellow River in China, is a realistic story about an animal—although some may feel that Ping is given feelings that may be all too human. The appeal of realistic stories is often in their ability to depict sympathetic characters with whom young readers can identify or emphathize. In other words, children like to read stories about other children very much like themselves.

NARRATIVE ELEMENTS

Regardless of the nature of the story, all stories contain the principal narrative elements of storytelling—plot, character, setting, theme, and style. It may be useful to review some of these elements as they apply specifically to picture books.

Plot and Conflict

The plot—which is simply the sequence of events in a story leading to a specific goal—must be clear and fairly direct. The plot in a good picture book meets all the requirements of a well-told tale: It has a clearly defined beginning, middle, and end. Whether it be through such familiar phrases as "Once upon a time" or through simply establishing the setting ("In the great green room"), young children very early on learn to recognize the conventions of storytelling. Additionally, reading books teaches them very early on the distinction between fact and fiction. If young children could not make these distinctions, they would constantly face intellectual dilemmas. For example, every time they heard a story such as Beatrix Potter's *The Tale of Peter Rabbit,* they would be puzzled about the nature of animals (can they talk? do they really wear clothes? do they eat their berries with cream?). In fact, we might say that one of the most important results of childhood reading is the shaping of this distinction between fact and fiction. But experience with books helps them to see when something is "only a story," and this distinction allows them to enjoy a healthy fantasy world and, in fact, to lead normal lives.

The plot focuses on a *conflict,* which requires resolution. The conflict, whether it be internal (a struggle going on within a character) or external (a struggle between two or more characters) contributes to the tale's excitement and ultimately to its theme and purpose. A small rabbit disobeys his mother, goes into Mr. McGregor's garden and, after a series of adventures, barely escapes with his life. For the very young, the time frame must be simple chronology—no flashbacks, for example. With older children, more complex plot structures—such as the intriguing parallel plots of Robert McCloskey's *Blueberries for Sal*—are suitable. Young readers also enjoy action, suspense, and, of course, humor in their stories.

Character

Typically, the stories focus on a character—either a human (usually a child) or an animal who possesses childlike characteristics. The principal character provides someone with whom the child audience can identify. Peter Rabbit appeals to young children because most of them have encountered temptations similar to Peter's, and his desire to do the forbidden is quite familiar to them. Characterization in picture books is usually quite simple; the stories are just not long enough to depict complex character development.

But that does not mean that the characters cannot be genuine or real. Bernard Waber's *Ira Sleeps Over* shows us the very real anxieties of a young boy spending his first night away from home. Ira's biggest worry is how he is to get through the night without Tah Tah, his teddy bear, whom he leaves at home lest his "tough" friend, Reggie, think him silly. But he discovers that Reggie sleeps with a teddy bear named Foo Foo. Happily, Ira runs home to get Tah Tah. Both Ira and Reggie exhibit human emotions typical of children their age, and young readers readily identify and sympathize with them.

Setting

Since each page is accompanied by illustrations, most picture-book stories rely on the visual element to articulate the setting. Nevertheless, the setting remains a story element because when and where a story happens determine a great deal about how and why things happen. Consequently, when a folktale begins by announcing "Once upon a time in a kingdom far, far away" we are immediately prepared for a certain type of tale, a tale in which we might reasonably expect to encounter an ogre, a magical object, a talking animal. On the other hand, if the setting is modern suburbia, we might logically expect a very different kind of story with greater attention to realism (although magic is not necessarily ruled out). Settings in picture books tend to be simply described (but the illustrations may be lavishly detailed). Margaret Wise Brown's classic *Goodnight Moon,* about a young bunny bidding everything in his room goodnight before going to sleep himself, is a good example, with virtually every page depicting the "great green room" from the same point of view, but in various stages of darkness. Young children enjoy picking out the many details mentioned in the simple storyline. It is, of course, the great advantage of the picture book that the setting can be conveyed nonverbally, and consequently most picture books spend little time in scenic descriptions. Each page or double-page spread can be seen as a set piece, like the individual scenes of a motion picture, and the success of the picture book depends heavily upon the effective selection of scenes.

Subject and Theme

The *subject* of a good story holds meaning for a young child. A preschool picture book on the subject of toxic waste disposal would probably be a bit silly, but child disobedience is not an unreasonable subject (and is undoubtedly something with which many children will have had considerable firsthand experience).

The *theme* is the principal idea that governs the story. In *The Tale of Peter Rabbit,* the theme might be something like this: Disobedience of parental authority often results in dire consequences. But we might also identify some other themes such as "the most effective punishment is that which we inflict upon ourselves." The theme itself may be quite serious—even in books for the very young. But we should *not* confuse theme with moral or lesson. In Maurice Sendak's *Where the Wild Things Are,* Max is naughty and is sent to his room without supper. While in his room, he has a fanciful dream in which he sails off to the land of the Wild Things and becomes their king. Eventually, he longs for home and decides to sail back. He then awakens and smells his supper sitting on a table in his room. Is there a lesson to be learned from this story? Probably not, unless we believe that Max learned that his mother's love is unconditional—she loves him despite his mean streaks. Sendak is merely showing us childhood as it is—not necessarily as we would wish it to be nor as it should be.

The theme of a good picture book will be deftly woven into the story. Most child readers recognize the actions of Peter Rabbit as unwise and those of Max as downright bad, but we are fooling ourselves if we think that, after reading either of these books, children will become more dutifully obedient or better behaved. Learning from reading is a cumulative process. We learn the wisdom of obedience in the same way that Peter does—through personal experiences, some of them harrowing. A book may help to reinforce our convictions or cause us to think about things in a new way. But few books bring about dramatic changes in our lives and behavior. For children, the enduring stories are those that entertain well.

Works written primarily to teach lessons—moral or otherwise—are termed *didactic.* A prime example of didactic literature is the fable—those brief and simple animal tales that typically conclude with the formulaic phrase, "And the moral of the story is . . . ." Adults often read Aesop's *Fables* to young children with the mistaken belief that the moral lessons tagged onto the stories will be taken to heart. In fact, for preschoolers and even children in the primary grades, the lessons of the fables are too sophisticated and are therefore lost on the audience. If children enjoy Aesop, it is perhaps simply because they have an affinity for talking animals, and because the plots are straightforward and uncomplicated. But the morals to stories, like Sunday school lessons, always seem to be intended for somebody else.

Literary Style

Boredom results from one of two things: either something is too simple or it is too complicated. To keep a reader stimulated, readers demand books that are increasingly challenging, but not completely beyond their personal comprehension level. As children become more sophisticated in their reading, they demand more complex characters, intricate plots, serious and probing themes, broader vocabulary, and more refined sentences.

These issues bring us to the matter of style. Picture books are typically brief—most are designed to be read in a single sitting, with 2,000 words being an average length for a storybook. The vocabulary must not be condescending—writers must not talk down to their child readers, but rather must treat them respectfully. The vocabulary ought to broaden the child's language experience. It makes no sense to criticize a picture book because it contains some words that might be unfamiliar to the child audience. (Beatrix Potter's reference to "camomile tea" in *The Tale of Peter Rabbit* comes immediately to mind, as does the "porridge" in "The Three Bears.") After all, one of the results of our reading should be an expanded vocabulary. If the books we read contained only words we know, we would all still be talking in colorless monosyllables. Once again, the best book is one that challenges without overwhelming.

Since picture books are frequently written for nonreaders, one requisite is that the book read well aloud. In the best books, natural breaks come at the turning of the pages; otherwise the sharing of the book becomes awkward. The child's ears hear one thing as the eyes behold another. The books should be well-paced; for example, the adult reader should finish reading a page just as the child is ready to move on to the next one. Children—who love the sounds of language—respond enthusiastically to rhythm and rhyme. We should also look for fresh imagery and imaginative language. The rollicking refrain of "Hundreds of cat, thousands of cats, millions and billions and trillions of cats" in Wanda Gag's classic, *Millions of Cats,* has delighted young audiences for more than sixty years. In another vein are the soothing repetition of Margaret Wise Brown's *Goodnight Moon* and the subtle rhythms of Donald Hall's *The Ox-Cart Man,* echoing the rhythmic cycle of life throughout the four seasons. Picture books using dialogue of several characters (such as Jeffrey Allen and James Marshall's *Mary Alice, Operator Number Nine*) are delightful both to read and hear.

In short, we must expect from picture books the same high literary standards we expect from books written for older readers. Young children are perhaps in some ways even more sensitive to sound and meaning than we adults are. They and their reading should be approached with the proper healthy respect.

SOCIAL CONCERNS AND THE PICTURE STORYBOOK

Because the readers of picture books are young and impressionable, it is helpful to be aware of specific ways in which these books portray and interpret society. Children's picture books of the past have been guilty of stereotyping according to such features as race, gender, age, and physical handicap. For example, white male heroes have traditionally dominated children's books. Although there are notable adventurous heroines of strong character (Ludwig Bemelmans's *Madeline,* for instance), girls have been depicted too often as weak, submissive, and domestic, leaving rough and tumble adventures to the boys. A recent critical view suggests that the fault lies in our culture, which would seem to value rash and aggressive behavior (characterized by the male) over the sensible equanimity typified by fictional female characters (see Chapter 11 for a further discussion of this issue).

Too often minority groups such as African Americans have been ignored or unfairly stereotyped. In the 1930s and 1940s, African Americans were virtually absent from picture books; by the 1950s and 1960s, they were portrayed essentially as middle-class white people with brown skin (e.g., Ezra Jack Keats's *The Snowy Day,* 1962). Only in the 1970s were they at last portrayed faithfully both physically and socially. At last, picture books were depicting inner-city African-American children proud of their heritage (Lucille Clifton's *Everett Anderson* series provides notable examples). Native Americans are still being stereotyped by the majority of picture books in which they appear (and they appear in very few). The traditional European image of an American Indian in a feathered headdress and animal skins is still too often the norm in picture books. We lack good picture books that show modern Native Americans going about their daily lives.

By and large, writers of recent fiction have become more sensitive to minority groups, and it is possible to locate books about strong heroines, self-confident characters from many cultures, sympathetic elderly people (Tomi da Paola's *Nana Upstairs, Nana Downstairs,* 1973), children from broken homes (Patricia MacLachlan's *Mama One, Mama Two,* 1982), and children with physical or emotional handicaps (Taro Yashmia's *The Crow Boy,* 1955). There is still a need for more books of high quality that seek to dispel society's ignorance and prejudices. Although we do not, in fact, know the extent of the impact that reading has on an individual, it is safe to assume that extensive reading will *reinforce* beliefs. It is good for us to be aware of the underlying messages in children's books precisely because children are vulnerable and impressionable. This does *not* mean that we become censors and forbid certain books to our children (censorship always has a way of backfiring), but that we should make a concerted effort to see that our children's reading includes a diverse selection of social attitudes.

It bears repeating that a good picture book for children represents the marriage of two arts: writing and illustrating. A well-written book with illustrations suited to the mood and purpose, both accurately depicting and effectively extending the text, is a special delight for all children. Of course, the experts are the children themselves—the books are for them, and they often prove to be much wiser than adults in their responses to what they read. However, most children rely upon us, the adults, to bring them into contact with good books. This is a great responsibility. If children do not learn to love reading and books by the time they reach the ages of five or six (and some say that even then it is too late), they are in danger of growing up to be nonreaders. This is why a good picture book is so vitally important, for it gives young children positive and rewarding experiences with books from the very beginning. And the payoff will be with them for the rest of their lives.

SELECTED BIBLIOGRAPHY OF PICTURE STORYBOOKS

The following picture storybooks are organized according to type of story—folk literature, modern fantasy, talking animal stories, realistic stories—as described in this chapter. This is only the briefiest selection of the many wonderful picture books available to young readers. Be sure to find other works of the writers and artists represented in this list. Unless otherwise indicated, the author is also the illustrator.

Folk Literature

Aardema, Verna. *Bringing the Rain to Kapiti Plain.* Illus. Beatriz Vidal. New York: Dial, 1981.
——— . *Why Mosquitoes Buzz in People's Ears.* Illus. Leo and Diane Dillon. New York: Dial, 1975.
Andersen, Hans Christian. *The Nightingale.* Tr. Eva LeGallienne. Illus. Nancy Ekholm Burkert. New York: Harper, 1965.

Bishop, Claire Huchet. *The Five Chinese Brothers.* Illus. Kurt Wiese. New York: Coward, 1938.

Brown, Marcia. *Cinderella.* New York: Scribner's, 1954.

——— . *Dick Whittington and His Cat.* New York: Scribner's, 1950.

——— . *Once a Mouse.* New York: Scribner's, 1961.

Cendrars, Blaise. *Shadows.* Illus. Marcia Brown. New York: Scribner's, 1982.

Climo, Shirley. *The Egyptian Cinderella.* Illus. Ruth Heller. New York: Crowell, 1989.

Cooney, Barbara. *Chanticleer and the Fox.* New York: Crowell, 1958.

De Paola, Tomi. *Strega Nona.* New York: Prentice-Hall, 1975.

Domanska, Janina. *Little Red Hen.* New York: Macmillan, 1973.

Emberley, Barbara. *Drummer Hoff.* Illus. Ed Emberley. New York: Prentice-Hall, 1967.

Hodges, Margaret. *The Wave.* Illus. Blair Lent. Boston: Houghton Mifflin, 1964.

——— . *Saint George and the Dragon.* Illus. Trina Schart Hyman. Boston: Little, Brown, 1984.

Hogrogian, Nonny. *One Fine Day.* New York: Macmillan, 1971.

Jarrell, Randall, reteller. *Snow White and the Seven Dwarfs.* Illus. Nancy Ekholm Burkert. New York: Farrar, Straus & Giroux, 1972.

Louie, Ai-Ling. *Yeh-Shen: A Cinderella Story from China.* Illus. Ed Young. New York: Philomel, 1982.

McDermott, Gerald. *Anansi the Spider.* New York: Holt, 1972.

——— . *Arrow to the Sun.* New York: Viking, 1974.

——— . *Zomo the Rabbit.* New York: Harcourt, 1992.

Mosel, Arlene. *The Funny Little Woman.* Illus. Blair Lent. New York: Dutton, 1972.

——— . *Tikki Tikki Tembo.* Illus. Blair Lent. New York: Holt, 1968.

Ness, Evaline. *Tom Tit Tot.* New York: Scribner's, 1965.

Nic Leodhas, Sorche (pseud. of LeClaire G. Alger). *Always Room for One More.* Illus. Nonny Hogrogian. New York: Holt, 1965.

Ransome, Arthur. *The Fool of the World and the Flying Ship.* Illus. Uri Shulevitz. New York: Farrar, Straus & Giroux, 1968.

Robbins, Ruth. *Baboushka and the Three Kings.* Illus. Nicolas Sidjakov. Boston: Houghton Mifflin, 1960.

Sawyer, Ruth. *Journey Cake, Ho!* Illus. Robert McCloskey. New York: Viking, 1953.

Scieszka, Jon. *The Stinky Cheese Man and Other Fairly Stupid Tales.* Illus. Lane Smith. New York: Viking, 1992.

——— . *The True Story of the Three Little Pigs.* Illus. Lane Smith. New York: Viking, 1989.

Singer, Isaac Bashevis. *The Fearsome Inn.* Illus. Nonny Hogrogian. New York: Macmillan, 1984.

Slobodkina, Esphyr. *Caps for Sale.* Reading, MA: Addison-Wesley, 1940.

Zemach, Harve, reteller. *Duffy and the Devil.* Illus. Margot Zemach. New York: Farrar, Straus & Giroux, 1973.

Zemach, Margot, reteller. *The Little Red Hen.* New York: Farrar, Straus & Giroux, 1983.

——— . *The Three Little Pigs.* New York: Farrar, Straus & Giroux, 1988.

Modern Fantasy

Aiken, Joan. *The Moon's Revenge.* Illus. Alan Lee. New York: Knopf, 1987.

Blos, Joan. *Lottie's Circus.* Illus. Irene Trivas. New York: Morrow, 1989.

Brown, Margaret Wise. *The Little Island.* Illus. Leonard Weisgard. New York: Doubleday, 1946.

——— . *The Steamroller.* Illus. Evaline Ness. New York: Walker, 1974.

Burton, Virginia L. *The Little House.* Boston: Houghton Mifflin, 1942.

——— . *Mike Mulligan and His Steam Shovel.* Boston: Houghton Mifflin, 1939.

Burningham, John. *Mr. Gumpy's Motorcar.* New York: Crowell, 1976.

———— . *Mr. Gumpy's Outing.* New York: Holt, 1971.

Conrad, Pam. *The Tub People.* Illus. Richard Egielski. New York: Harper, 1989.

Daugherty, James. *Andy and the Lion.* New York: Viking, 1938.

De Regniers, Beatrice Schenk. *May I Bring a Friend?* Illus. Beni Montressor. New York: Atheneum, 1964.

Freeman, Don. *Corduroy.* New York: Viking, 1968.

———— . *Will's Quill.* New York: Penguin, 1977.

Gag, Wanda. *Millions of Cats.* New York: Coward, McCann, 1928.

Gramatky, Hardie. *Hercules.* New York: Putnam, 1960.

———— . *Little Toot.* Rpt. New York: Putnam, 1978.

Hale, Lucretia. *The Lady Who Put Salt in Her Coffee.* Illus. and Adapted by Amy Schwartz. New York: Harcourt, 1989.

Johnson, Crockett. *Harold and the Purple Crayon.* New York: Harper, 1981.

———— . *Harold's Circus.* New York: Scholastic, 1959.

Leaf, Munro. *The Story of Ferdinand.* Illus. Robert Lawson. New York: Viking, 1936.

Rey, A. H. *Curious George.* Boston: Houghton Mifflin, 1973.

Sendak, Maurice. *In the Night Kitchen.* New York: Harper, 1970.

———— . *Outside Over There.* New York: Harper, 1981.

———— . *Where the Wild Things Are.* New York: Harper, 1963.

Seuss, Dr. (pseud. of Theodore Geisel). *And to Think That I Saw It on Mulberry Street.* New York: Vanguard, 1973.

———— . *The Cat in the Hat.* New York: Random House, 1957.

Swift, Hildegarde. *The Little Red Lighthouse and the Great Gray Bridge.* Illus. Lynd Ward. New York: Harcourt, 1974.

Thurber, James. *Many Moons.* Illus. Marc Simont. New York: Harcourt, 1990.

Titus, Eve. *Anatole in Italy.* Illus. Paul Galdone. New York: McGraw Hill, 1973.

Ungerer, Tonie. *The Beast of Monsieur Racine.* New York: Farrar, Straus & Giroux, 1971.

Van Allsburg, Chris. *The Garden of Abdul Gasazi.* Boston: Houghton Mifflin, 1979.

———— . *Jumanji.* Boston: Houghton Mifflin, 1981.

———— . *The Wreck of the Zephyr.* Boston: Houghton Mifflin, 1983.

Willard, Nancy. *The Nightgown of the Sullen Moon.* Illus. David McPhail. New York: Harcourt, 1983.

———— . *A Visit to William Blake's Inn.* Illus. Alice and Martin Provensen. New York: Harcourt, 1981.

Willis, Val. *The Secret in the Matchbox.* Illus. John Shelley. New York: Farrar, Straus & Giroux, 1988.

Wood, Audrey. *King Bidgood's in the Bathtub.* Illus. Don Wood. New York: Harcourt, 1985.

Zemach, Margot. *Jake and Honeybunch Go to Heaven.* New York: Farrar, Straus & Giroux, 1982.

Zolotow, Charlotte. *Mr. Rabbit and the Lovely Present.* Illus. Maurice Sendak. New York: Harper, 1962.

Talking Animal Stories

Allen, Jeffrey. *Mary Alice, Operator Number 9.* Illus. James Marshall. Boston: Little, Brown, 1975.

Brooke, L. Leslie. *Johnny Crow's Garden.* 1903. London: Warne, 1978.

———— . *Johnny Crow's Party.* 1907. London: Warne, 1966.

Brown, Margaret Wise. *Goodnight Moon.* Illus. Clement Hurd. New York: Harper, 1947.

———— . *The Runaway Bunny.* Illus. Clement Hurd. New York: Harper, 1962.

Carle, Eric. *Do You Want to Be My Friend?* New York: Harper, 1987.

———— . *The Very Hungry Caterpillar.* Cleveland: World, 1970.

———— . *The Very Quiet Cricket.* New York: Philomel, 1990.

Dana, Doris. *The Elephant and His Secret.* Illus. Antonio Frasconi. New York: Knopf, 1989.

de Brunhoff, Jean. *The Story of Babar, the Little Elephant.* 1933. New York: Knopf, 1989.

Duvoisin, Roger. *Petunia.* New York: Knopf, 1950.

Fatio, Louise. *The Happy Lion.* Illus. Roger Duvoisin. 1954. New York: Scholastic, 1986.

Gerstein, Mordicai. *Arnold of the Ducks.* New York: Harper, 1983.

Henkes, Kevin. *Chrysanthemum.* New York: Greenwillow, 1991.

Hutchins Pat. *Good-Night Owl.* New York: Macmillan, 1972.

Kellogg, Steven. *The Island of the Skog.* New York: Dial, 1973.

Kraus, Robert. *Leo the Late Bloomer.* Illus. Jose and Ariane Aruego. New York: Simon & Schuster, 1987.

Kuskin, Karla. *The Bear Who Saw the Spring.* New York: Harper, 1961.

Langstaff, John M. *A Frog Went A-Courtin'.* Illus. Feodor Rojankovsky. Rpt. New York: Scholastic, 1985.

Lionni, Leo. *Alexander and the Wind-Up Mouse.* New York: Pantheon, 1969.

———— . *Fish Is Fish.* Rpt. New York: Knopf, 1987.

———— . *Frederick.* New York: Pantheon, 1967.

Lobel, Arnold. *Frog and Toad Are Friends.* New York: Harper, 1970.

———— . *Frog and Toad Together.* New York: Harper, 1972.

Meddaugh, Susan. *Martha Speaks.* Boston: Houghton Mifflin, 1992.

Minarik, Elsa Holmelund. *Little Bear.* Illus. Maurice Sendak. New York: Harper, 1957.

———— . *Little Bear's Visit.* Illus. Maurice Sendak. Rpt. New York: Harper, 1984.

Pearce, Philippa. *Emily's Own Elephant.* Illus. John Lawrence. New York: Greenwillow, 1988.

Peet, Bill. *Encore for Eleanor.* Boston: Houghton Mifflin, 1985.

Piatti, Celestino. *The Happy Owls.* New York: Atheneum, 1964.

Potter, Beatrix. *The Tale of Peter Rabbit.* London: Warne, 1901.

Steig, William. *Sylvester and the Magic Pebble.* New York: Windmill, 1969.

Waber, Bernard. *Lyle, Lyle, Crocodile.* Rpt. Boston: Houghton Mifflin, 1987.

———— . *The House on East 88th Street.* Boston: Houghton Mifflin, 1975.

Wells, Rosemary. *Noisy Nora.* New York: Dial, 1980.

———— . *Morris' Disappearing Bag.* New York: Dial, 1978.

Realistic Stories

Ackerman, Karen. *Song and Dance Man.* New York: Knopf, 1988.

Alexander, Lloyd. *The Fortune-Tellers.* Illus. Trina Schart Hyman. New York: Dutton, 1992.

Alexander, Martha. *Nobody Asked Me If I Wanted a Baby Sister.* New York: Dial, 1971.

Allard, Harry, and James Marshall. *Miss Nelson Is Missing.* Illus. James Marshall. Boston: Houghton Mifflin, 1977.

Anno, Mitsumasa. *Anno's Journey.* New York: Philomel, 1978.

Ardizzone, Edward. *Little Tim and the Brave Sea Captain.* 1936. New York: Penguin, 1983.

Asch, Frank. *Sand Cake.* New York: Crown, 1987.

Bang, Molly. *The Grey Lady and the Strawberry Snatcher.* New York: Four Winds, 1980.

———— . *The Paper Crane.* New York: Greenwillow, 1985.

Bedard, Michael. *Emily.* Illus. Barbara Cooney. New York: Doubleday, 1992.

Bemelmans, Ludwig. *Madeline.* New York: Viking, 1937.

——— . *Madeline's Rescue.* New York: Penguin, 1953.

Beskow, Elsa. *Pelle's New Suit.* New York: Harper, 1929.

Bunting, Eve. *Fly Away Home.* Illus. Ronald Himler. New York: Clarion, 1991.

Carrick, Carol. *In the Moonlight, Waiting.* Illus. Donald Carrick. New York: Clarion, 1990.

Clifton, Lucille. *Some of the Days of Everett Anderson.* Illus. Evaline Ness. New York: Holt, 1970.

Cooney, Barbara. *Island Boy.* New York: Viking, 1988.

——— . *Miss Rumphius.* New York: Viking, 1982.

de Angeli, Marguerite. *Thee Hannah!* New York: Doubleday, 1940.

de Paola, Tomie. *Nana Upstairs, Nana Downstairs.* New York: Penguin, 1978.

Dorros, Arthur. *Abuela.* New York: Dutton, 1991.

Ets, Marie Hall. *Play with Me.* New York: Penguin, 1955.

Flack, Marjorie. *Story About Ping.* Illus. Kurt Weise. New York: Penguin, 1933.

Fleischman, Sid. *The Scarebird.* Illus. Peter Sis. New York: Greenwillow, 1988.

Fox, Mem. *Night Noises.* Illus. Terry Denton. New York: Harcourt, 1989.

Goble, Paul. *The Girl Who Loved Wild Horses.* New York: Bradbury, 1978.

Greenfield, Eloise. *She Come Bringing Me That Little Baby Girl.* Illus. John Steptoe. Philadelphia: Lippincott, 1974.

Hall, Donald. *The Ox-Cart Man.* Illus. Barbara Cooney. New York: Penguin, 1983.

Handforth, Thomas. *Mei Lei.* New York: Doubleday, 1938.

Hader, Berta, and Elmer Hader. *The Big Snow.* New York: Macmillan, 1948.

Hellen, Nancy. *The Bus Stop.* New York: Watts, 1988.

Hoban, Julia. *Amy Loves the Rain.* Illus. Lillian Hoban. New York: Harper, 1989.

Hoffman, Mary. *Amazing Grace.* Illus. Caroline Binch. New York: Dial, 1991.

Hol, Colby. *A Visit to the Farm.* New York: North-South, 1989.

Keats, Ezra Jack. *Peter's Chair.* New York: Harper, 1967.

——— . *The Snowy Day.* New York: Viking, 1962.

Keeping, Charles. *Joseph's Yard.* New York: Watts, 1969.

Locker, Thomas. *Where the River Begins.* New York: Dial, 1984.

McCloskey, Robert. *Blueberries for Sal.* New York: Viking, 1948.

——— . *Make Way for Ducklings.* New York: Viking, 1941.

——— . *Time of Wonder.* New York: Viking, 1957.

McCully, Emily Arnold. *Mirette on the High Wire.* New York: Putnam, 1992.

MacDonald, Golden (pseud. of Margaret Wise Brown). *The Little Island.* Illus. Leonard Weisgard. New York: Doubleday, 1946.

Milhous, Katherine. *The Egg Tree.* New York: Macmillan, 1971.

Ness, Evaline. *Sam, Bangs & Moonshine.* New York: Holt, 1966.

Politi, Leo. *Song of the Swallows.* New York: Macmillan, 1986.

Provensen, Alice, and Martin Provensen. *The Glorious Flight: Across the Channel with Louis Bleriot.* New York: Viking, 1983.

Raskin, Ellen. *Nothing Ever Happens on My Block.* New York: Macmillan, 1966.

Rylant, Cynthia. *The Relatives Came.* Illus. Stephen Gammell. New York: Bradbury, 1985.

——— . *When I Was Young in the Mountains.* Illus. Diane Goode. New York: Dutton, 1982.

Shulevitz, Uri. *Rain, Rain, Rivers.* New York: Farrar, Straus & Giroux, 1969.

Spier, Peter. *Peter Spier's Rain.* New York: Doubleday, 1982.

Tejima, Keizaburo. *Fox's Dream.* New York: Philomel, 1987.

——— . *Owl Lake.* New York: Philomel, 1987.

Tresselt, Alvin. *Hide and Seek Fog.* Illus. Roger Duvoisin. New York: Lothrop, 1965.

——— . *White Snow, Bright Snow.* Illus. Roger Duvoisin. New York: Lothrop, 1947.

Turkle, Brinton. *Thy Friend, Obadiah.* New York: Viking, 1967.

Udry, Janice M. *The Moon Jumpers.* Illus. Maurice Sendak. New York: Harper, 1959.

————. *A Tree Is Nice.* Illus. Marc Simont. New York: Harper, 1956.

Viorst, Judith. *Alexander and the Terrible, Horrible, No Good, Very Bad Day.* Illus. by Ray Cruz. New York: Atheneum, 1972.

————. *The Tenth Good Thing About Barney.* Illus. Erik Blegvad. New York: Atheneum, 1971.

Waber, Bernard. *Ira Sleeps Over.* Boston: Houghton Mifflin, 1972.

Ward, Lynd K. *The Biggest Bear.* Boston: Houghton Mifflin, 1952.

Wild, Margaret. *The Queen's Holiday.* New York: Watts, 1992.

Williams, Vera B. *A Chair for My Mother.* New York: Greenwillow, 1982.

————. *"More More More," Said the Baby: Three Love Stories.* New York: Greenwillow, 1990.

Yashima, Taro (pseud. of Jun Iwamatsu). *The Crow Boy.* New York: Viking, 1955.

————. *Umbrella.* New York: Viking, 1958.

Yolen, Jane. *Owl Moon.* Illus. John Schoenherr. New York: Philomel, 1987.

Yorinks, Arthur. *Hey Al.* Illus. Richard Egielski. New York: Farrar, Straus & Giroux, 1988.

Zion, Gene. *Harry, the Dirty Dog.* Illus. Margaret Bloy Graham. New York: Harper, 1956.

————. *Harry and the Lady Next Door.* Illus. Margaret Bloy Graham. New York: Zion.

Zolotow, Charlotte. *William's Doll.* Illus. by William Pene du Bois. New York: Harper, 1972.

CHAPTER 5

Alphabet, Counting, and Concept Books

DEFINITIONS

A large and important body of picture books is expressly intended to instruct children—in numbers, letters, shapes, colors, sizes, elementary science, mathematics, and even human behavior. In this chapter, we will consider specifically *alphabet books,* which attempt to teach children the sounds and forms of the letters; *counting books,* which attempt to teach children forms and meanings of numbers; and those *concept books* that attempt to instruct the very young in cognitive or behavioral processes. Informational books for older children—many of which are extensions of the concept book—will be discussed in more detail in Chapter 12. The books with which we are presently concerned are all picture books and intended for younger audiences. Naturally, much of what we said of children's book illustration in Chapter 3 is applicable for these books as well.

Both alphabet and counting books are concept books; that is, they teach abstract concepts. They have been singled out in this discussion only because they represent a relatively larger share of the children's book market and have their own distinctive features. Alphabet, counting, and concept books are first and foremost instructional books; they are intended to teach children certain facts or ideas. These picture books demonstrate the same diverse qualities of art as do the picture storybooks, but since the texts are meant to teach as well as to entertain, they operate by a more specific set of guidelines and require that we view them from a somewhat different perspective.

ALPHABET BOOKS

Organization of Alphabet Books

Alphabet and counting books are similar in their purposes and approaches. There are three general organizational patterns that alphabet and counting books typically follow, and these are based on the objects chosen to illustrate the concept.

1. A *theme book* is one that provides a thematic or topical focus for the objects depicted, an animal alphabet book, or an animal counting book, for example. Jan Garten's *The Alphabet Tale,* using wild animals to represent the letters of the alphabet, or Ezra Jack Keats's *Over in the Meadow,* using various animals in a meadow as the countable objects, are examples of theme books, as is Margaret Musgrove's *Ashanti to Zulu: African Traditions* (Figure 5.1), illustrated by Leo and Diane Dillon, and using words from African culture to represent the letters of the alphabet.

2. A *potpourri book* disregards any unity in subject matter; virtually anything may go, but the book is usually given some sense of unity through the style of its illustrations or its overall tone. *Anno's Alphabet* by Mitsumasa Anno, uses sophisticated *trompe l'oeil* artwork, in which each picture plays tricks with us. *Dr. Seuss's ABC,* on the other hand, uses decidedly unsophisticated, but thoroughly enjoyable cartoons. The potpourri book allows the artist the greatest freedom—but that, at the same time, is its limitation if an artist is a bit short of imagination (consequently we end up with a multitude of "A is for Apple" books).

3. The rarest is the *sequential-story book,* which illustrates the alphabet or numbers through a continuous storyline. Wanda Gag's *ABC Bunny* or Miska Miles's *Apricot ABC* are examples, and they are also books that demonstrate the difficulties of teaching the alphabet through well-plotted stories. Usually, the challenge of learning to recognize letters and their sounds is difficult enough for small children without further complicating matters for them by incorporating a plotline to follow as well.

Modern alphabet, counting, and concept books have become more than vehicles of education and purveyors of fact; they have joined the ranks of the picture storybooks in becoming works of art and objects of pleasure.

Content of Alphabet Books

Perhaps the most fundamental feature of the content of an alphabet book is that it be clear, or the purpose of teaching children the sounds of letters is defeated. *Dr. Seuss's ABC* comically reinforces the phonetic associations with such rollicking lines as "Big A, little a, what begins with A? Aunt Annie's Alligator—A—A—A" or "Y—A yawning, yellow yak and young Yolanda Yorgenson is yelling on his back." Three- or four-year-olds may not initially know what an alligator or a yak is, but the illustrations will quickly teach them and, after all, how are they to learn new concepts and facts if their

I/The Ikoma (ik·oh'·muh) gather honey to eat and sell. There is a tiny bird in their land which loves honey but cannot get into the beehives. When this bird sees a person, it becomes excited and flies to him. Fluttering and chattering, it leads the way through the bush to a hive. The Ikoma always reward the bird with a gift of honeycomb—otherwise, they say, it may never help them find honey again.

FIGURE 5.1 This illustration by Leo and Diane Dillon is taken from Margaret Musgrove's *Ashanti to Zulu: African Traditions,* a sophisticated alphabet book for older readers that associates the letters of the English alphabet with various African cultural traditions. This is an example of an alphabet book that is not really intended to teach the alphabet, but its exquisite artwork and informative text will appeal to a wide range of readers.

SOURCE: From *Ashanti to Zulu: African Traditions* by Margaret Musgrove, illustrated by Leo and Diane Dillon. Copyright © 1976 by Penguin Books, Inc. Reprinted by permission of Penguin USA, Inc.

reading never introduces them? However, the other extreme can be found in Jane Walsh Anglund's *A Is for Always*, where we find "C [for] Courteous"; "D [for] Determined"; "E [for] Exuberant"; and so on. Such abstract concepts are lost on preschoolers, most of whom simply do not have the cognitive development to grasp the ideas.

Additionally, we are usually dealing with phonetic sounds when teaching the alphabet. In other words, the purpose of the alphabet is to help the child associate the shape of a letter with the sound it customarily makes. This is not as simple as it sounds. Vowels, for instance, make several sounds, from long to short to everything in between. So the letter "A" can be accurately represented by an "apple" or by an "ape" or by an "auto." Some alphabet books (such as Gyo Fujikawa's *A to Z Picture Book*) take care of this problem by offering several objects on the same page to represent the letter. *Dr. Seuss's ABC* demonstrates the various sounds in the text: "Oscar's only ostrich oiled an orange owl today" demonstrates the "O" sounds.

Consonants as well can present problems. Two consonants—"C" and "G"—can be hard or soft. So "G" may be represented by a giraffe or a gorilla, for example. And then there is the troublesome "X." Most books rely on "Xylophone" for "X"—but the phonetic sound is closer to "Z." Dr. Seuss perhaps has a sensible compromise, by using such words as "Ax" and "Extra Fox." A peculiar mistake in alphabet books for the very young—but one that can be found—is identifying a letter such as "K" with a word such as "Knife" or "G" with "Gnat." These books confuse phonics, the sounds of letters, with spelling, which can be another matter altogether. Children need challenges, but not unnecessary confusion.

It is unlikely, therefore, that a single alphabet book will accommodate all the quirks of the English language. On the bright side, this simply gives us an excuse to read several different alphabet books to our children, so their language experiences will become richer and more varied, and they will begin to understand the extraordinary flexibility of English.

Design of Alphabet Books

The design and the illustrations of a good alphabet book are appropriate for the intended age level. This means that the visual representation of the letter is understandable to the young reader. If the letters are drawn too fancifully (A, G, S, for example), children may have a difficult time recognizing them in other contexts. There are, of course, common distinctions between the way some letters are printed in texts and they way we normally write them in handwriting ("a" and "a" or "g" and "g", for instance). Eventually children will have to learn all forms of the letter. It is helpful if both upper and lower case letters are illustrated because children need to understand that letters appear in different forms.

Most alphabet books juxtapose the letters and the pictures that represent them—that is they are on the same page or facing pages, which, of course, makes the most sense. Van Allsburg departs from this tradition in *Z Was Zapped*—a book depicting all manner of violence befalling the letters of the alphabet. Many alphabet books, including Allsburg's, demonstrate picture-book art at its most creative. The works of Anno, Bert Kitchen, John Burningham, Helen Oxenbury, and Alice and Martin Provensen (Figure 5.2), to name only a few, clearly indicate that alphabet books have achieved a very high status among illustrators.

COUNTING BOOKS

Like alphabet books, counting books have an educational purpose and that purpose is best served when the book effectively combines design and content. Counting books are intended to present the concept of numbers and to help children with number recognition. Many of the statements made about alphabet books apply equally to counting books.

FIGURE 5.2   The spirit of the simple, industrious way of the Shakers, an early American religious sect, is depicted in this illustration by Alice and Martin Provensen for *A Peaceable Kingdom: The Shaker Abecedarius.* The lack of depth and the disproportionate scale (notice the woman's tiny feet and hands and the overly large katydid) are all characteristic of the folk art of rural New England, the home of the principal Shaker communities.

SOURCE: From *A Peaceable Kingdom: The Shaker Abecedarius* illustrated by Alice and Martin Provensen, afterword by Richard Meran Barsam. Illustrations copyright © 1978 by Alice and Martin Provensen. Reprinted by permission of the publisher, Viking Penguin, a division of Penguin Books USA Inc.

PERIWINKLE,

Ermine,   Katydid,   Hawk,

Content of Counting Books

Sometimes, as with simple alphabet books, counting books contain virtually no text, just the numbers and the objects to be counted. Although as adults we take counting for granted, we must remember that it is an extremely abstract concept. Counting requires that children know the names of the numbers and that they understand that those names can be transferred to any object. In other words, the numbers only identify the quantity. In counting books, of course, we expect to see the arabic numerals depicted (1, 2, 3), but even some very simple counting books include the spelling of the number words *(one, two, three)*.

Because of this complexity, perhaps the most important aspect of the content of a counting book is that the objects to be counted are things a young child can readily identify. It is also important that whatever is being counted is clearly obvious. Very young children require that the objects to be counted are nearly identical or closely related (in other words, small children will understand the counting of five apples before they will grasp the significance of counting five unrelated objects such as an apple, an orange, a book, a pencil, and a window). Naturally, animals are great favorites as are toys and other familiar items.

But counting books need not be totally simplistic. Only a writer's or an illustrator's imagination need restrict the possibilities. Molly Bang's award-winning *Ten, Nine, Eight* is an example of an effective counting book that counts backwards. Children can benefit from this kind of number play once they have mastered the fundamental elements of enumeration. Also for the somewhat more sophisticated reader is Russell Hoban's *Ten What? A Mystery Counting Book.* In the same vein is Arthur Geisert's *Pigs from 1 to 10,* which requires the reader to find the hidden numerals along with ten little pigs on the full-page spreads that are replete with inventive detail. Also, there are the familiar counting rhymes, such as "Over in the Meadow," which has inspired counting books by such noted illustrators as Feodor Rojankovsky and Ezra Jack Keats. The beautiful counting rhyme by S. T. Garne, *One White Sail,* takes the reader to the magic of the Caribbean with such evocative lines as "Five blue doors / in the baking hot sun / Six wooden windows / let the cool wind run."

Design of Counting Books

Once again, juxtaposition is an important feature. Since most counting books go only up to ten, they are often shorter than other books and make use of full-page spreads. Or, they may depict the number on one page with the illustrations on the facing page. It is important that the young child be able to point to the appropriate objects as they are being counted. When a large number of items appears on a single page, the artist can avoid a cluttered appearance and possible confusion by grouping the objects.

There are a number of very sophisticated counting (and alphabet) books that, even if they seem inappropriate for young children, we would not want to dismiss entirely, for they are books of extraordinary imagination and beauty, such as *Anno's Alphabet* and *Anno's Counting House,* both by Mitsumasa Anno, and Tom and Muriel Feelings's very beautiful counting book, *Moja Means One,* which is subtitled "A Swahili Counting Book." Such books go far beyond teaching numbers and letters, and suggest that we do not necessarily outgrow alphabet and counting books.

CONCEPT BOOKS

Although all the best storybooks have significant themes, it is the good plot and effective style, and not the lesson, that are paramount. But we can find an endless variety of picture books designed to teach very young children concepts and behaviors; their intention is didactic: the conveying of information. These are often called concept books because they attempt to convey a specific developmental concept—such as explaining the passage of time or the differences between geometric shapes or the feel of various textures. Other books are more akin to children's versions of adult books: picture-book biographies, cultural awareness books, histories, natural science, health and the human body, to mention only a few of the many subject areas addressed.

Cognitive Development and Concept Books

Concept books can be found dealing with almost any subject. Some concept books deal with sensory experiences such as textures, colors, or spatial relationships. Among the books for the very early years are those teaching basic colors. These are usually quite simple books, but that does not preclude them from being highly inventive, such as E. L. Konigsburg's *Samuel Todd's Book of Great Colors*. Bernice Kohn's *How High Is Up?* is a fine example of a book that teaches the concept of opposites, such as as "high"—"low," "rough"—"smooth" and "loud"—"quiet." Margaret Wise Brown's "Noisy" books *(The Indoor Noisy Book, The Outdoor Noisy Book, The Country Noisy Book)*, illustrated by Leonard Weisgard, are concept books illustrating various types of sounds. *All Shapes and Sizes* is just one of a series of books by Shirley Hughes stressing clarity and simplicity in conveying fundamental geometric concepts.

Other concept books focus on skills such as telling time, identifying the seasons, or naming the months of the year or the days of the week. Nancy Tafuri's stunningly illustrated *All Year Long* cleverly combines the recognition of seasonal changes, the months of the year, and the days of the week. *John Burningham's Opposites* effectively illustrates semantic meanings of common words—it serves, in fact, as a sort of pre-dictionary. Still other books may seek to define and illustrate specific objects or classes of objects, such as boats, supermarkets, animals, and even professions. Donald Crews's *Trucks* is a widely acclaimed example, as is his *Freight Trains*.

Psychosocial Development and Concept Books

Another type of concept book that is becoming increasingly popular is that dealing not with factual material, but with the formation of attitudes and coping with emotions; they deal with the child's psychosocial development. Catherine and Laurence Anholt's *All about You* is an example of a type of book becoming increasingly popular, encouraging children to examine their world, ask questions, and think about their lives. *All Kinds of Families* was an early concept book that sought to break down narrow stereotypes. Arnold Adoff's *Black Is Brown Is Tan* is similarly a concept book about interracial families. Linda Walvoord Girard's *Jeremy's First*

Haircut is a book that attempts to put into focus a potentially traumatic experience for young children. Books can also be found on visits to the dentist, the first day of school, and other "firsts" in life. Also by Girard, *Alex, the Kid with AIDS* demonstrates the degree of openness that both writers and publishers have adopted in recent years. Many of the picture books dealing with psychosocial development are written in the form of fictional stories and can be found in the bibliography in Chapter 4. As we can see, few subjects are taboo in picture books for young children.

Design of Concept Books

The design of concept books can vary greatly according to the purpose. Those concept books intended to teach facts, such as Tana Hoban's *Shapes and Things,* require clear, readily recognizable illustrations (simple silhouettes in black and white in this instance). Clarity and simplicity are the virtues of illustrating this sort of concept book; highly imaginative illustrations that do not clearly illustrate the concepts they are supposed to teach will defeat the purpose of the book. Naturally, it is most useful if the illustrations relate clearly to the text on the same or adjacent page.

However, concept books focusing on attitudes or emotions may contain illustrations more like the picture storybooks. In these books, we may wish to consider whether the illustrations match the intended mood—a picture book about dying (and there are such things) will require a very different type of illustration than one about the joys of raising ducks or life in the big city. A good concept book invites the child into its world and makes learning a fulfilling experience.

Concept books remain important throughout an individual's education—something that should last a lifetime. When concept books contain more advanced information, we generally refer to them as nonfiction books or informational books. These will be discussed in somewhat more detail in Chapter 12.

RECOMMENDED READINGS

Bodmer, George R. "The Post-Modern Alphabet: Extending the Limits of the Contemporary Alphabet Book, from Seuss to Gorey." *Children's Literature Association Quarterly* (Fall 1989): 115–17.

Debes, John L., and Clarence M. Williams. "The Power of Visuals." *Instructor* (December 1974): 32–39.

Hall, Mary Anne, and Jane Mantango. "Children's Literature: A Source for Concept Enrichment." *Elementary English* (April 1975): 487–94.

Kiefer, Barbara. "Critically Speaking: Literature for Children." *The Reading Teacher* (January 1985): 458–63.

Schoenfield, Madalynne. "Alphabet and Counting Books." *Day Care and Early Education* 10 (Winter 1982): 44.

Stewig, John Warren. "Alphabet Books: A Neglected Genre." In *Jump Over the Moon.* Ed. Pamela Barron and Jennifer Q. Burley. New York: Holt, 1984, 115–20.

Thomas, Della. "Count Down on the 1-2-3's." *School Library Journal* (15 March 1971): 95–102.

SELECTED BIBLIOGRAPHY OF ALPHABET, COUNTING, AND CONCEPT BOOKS

Alphabet Books

Anno, Mitsumasa. *Anno's Alphabet.* New York: Harper, 1975.

Bourke, Linda. *Eye Spy: A Mysterious Alphabet.* New York: Chronicle, 1991.

Brown, Marcia. *Peter Piper's Alphabet.* New York: Scribner's, 1959.

Burningham, John. *John Burningham's ABC's.* New York: Crown, 1985.

Duvoisin, Roger. *A for the Ark.* New York: Lee & Shepard, 1952.

Feelings, Muriel. *Jambo Means Hello: A Swahili Alphabet Book.* Illus. Tom Feelings. New York: Dial, 1974.

Fujikawa, Gyo. *A to Z Picture Book.* New York: Grosset & Dunlap, 1974.

Gag, Wanda. *The ABC Bunny.* New York: Coward-McCann, 1933.

Garten, Jan. *The Alphabet Tale.* New York: Random House, 1964.

Hoban, Tana. *A, B, See.* New York: Greenwillow, 1982.

Isadora, Rachel. *City Seen from A to Z.* New York: Greenwillow, 1983.

Kitamura, Satoshi. *From Acorn to Zoo: And Everything in Between in Alphabetical Order.* New York: Farrar, Straus & Giroux, 1992.

Kitchen, Bert. *Animal Alphabet.* New York: Dial, 1984.

Lionni, Leo. *The Alphabet Tree.* New York: Pantheon, 1968.

MacDonald, Suse. *Alphabatics.* New York: Bradbury, 1986.

Martin, Bill, Jr., and John Archambault. *Chicka Chicka Boom Boom.* Illus. Lois Ehlert. New York: Simon and Schuster, 1989.

Merriam, Eve. *Where Is Everybody? An Animal Alphabet.* New York: Simon and Schuster, 1989.

Miles, Miska. *Apricot ABC.* Illus. Peter Parnall. Boston: Little, Brown, 1969.

Munari, Bruno. *Bruno Munari's ABC.* New York: Philomel, 1960.

Musgrove, Margaret. *Ashanti to Zulu: African Traditions.* Illus. Leo and Diane Dillon. New York: Dial, 1976.

Oxenbury, Helen. *Helen Oxenbury's ABC.* New York: Delacorte, 1983.

Provensen, Alice and Martin. *A Peaceable Kingdom: The Shaker Abecedarius.* New York: Viking, 1978.

Rankin, Laura. *The Handmade Alphabet.* New York: Dial, 1991.

Seuss, Dr. (pseud. of Theodore Geisel). *Dr. Seuss' ABC.* New York: Random, 1988.

Tudor, Tasha. *A Is for Annabelle.* New York: Walck, 1954.

Van Allsburg, Chris. *Z Was Zapped.* Boston: Houghton Mifflin, 1987.

Wildsmith, Brian. *ABC.* New York: Watts, 1962.

Counting Books

Anno, Mitsumasa. *Anno's Counting Book.* New York: Crowell, 1977.

Bang, Molly. *Ten, Nine, Eight.* New York: Greenwillow, 1983.

Burningham, John. *John Burningham's 1,2,3's.* New York: Crown, 1985.

Carle, Eric. *1, 2, 3 to the Zoo.* Cleveland: World, 1968.

Feelings, Muriel. *Moja Means One: A Swahili Counting Book.* Illus. Tom Feelings. New York: Dutton, 1971.

Garne, S. T. *One White Sail.* San Marcos, CA: Green Tiger, 1992.

Geisert, Arthur. *Pigs from 1 to 10.* Boston: Houghton Mifflin, 1992.

Hoban, Russell. *Ten What? A Mystery Counting Book.* New York: Scribner's, 1974.

Hoban, Tana. *Count and See.* New York: Macmillan, 1972.

Keats, Ezra Jack. *Over in the Meadow.* New York: Scholastic, 1971.

Kitchen, Bert. *Animal Numbers.* New York: Dial, 1987.

Langstaff, John. *Over in the Meadow.* Illus. Feodor Rojankovsky. New York: Harbrace, 1973.

McMillan, Bruce. *Eating Fractions.* New York: Scholastic, 1991.

——— . *Here a Chick, There a Chick.* New York: Lothrop, 1983.

O'Keefe, Susan Heyboer. *One Hungry Monster: A Counting Book in Rhyme.* Boston: Little, Brown, 1989.

Reiss, John. *Numbers.* New York: Bradbury, 1971.

Wildsmith, Brian. *Brian Wildsmith's 1,2,3's.* New York: Watts, 1965.

Concept Books—Cognitive Development

Anno, Mitsumasa. *Anno's Sundial.* New York: Philomel, 1987.

Brown, Marcia. *Listen to a Shape.* New York: Watts, 1979.

Cole, Joanna. *Evolution.* New York: Crowell, 1987.

Burningham, John. *John Burningham's Opposites.* New York: Crown, 1986.

Crews, Donald. *Freight Train.* New York: Greenwillow, 1978.

——— . *Truck.* New York: Greenwillow, 1980.

Ehlert, Lois. *Color Farm.* New York: Lippincott, 1990.

——— . *Color Zoo.* New York: Lippincott, 1989.

Emberley, Rebecca. *City Sounds.* Boston: Little, Brown, 1989.

——— . *Jungle Sounds.* Boston: Little, Brown, 1989.

Grifalconi, Ann. *The Village of Round and Square Houses.* Boston: Little, Brown, 1986.

Hoban, Tana. *Shapes and Things.* New York: Macmillan, 1970.

Kohn, Bernice. *How High Is Up?* Illus. Jan Pyk. New York: Putnam, 1971.

Konigsburg, E. L. *Samuel Todd's Book of Great Colors.* New York: Atheneum, 1990.

——— . *Samuel Todd's Book of Great Inventions.* New York: Atheneum, 1991.

MacKinnon, Debbie. *What Shape?* New York: Dial, 1992.

McPhail, David. *Farm Boy's Year.* New York: Atheneum, 1992.

Maestro, Betsy, and Guilio Maestro. *Traffic: A Book of Opposites.* New York: Crown, 1981.

Oakes, Bill, and Suse MacDonald. *Puzzlers.* New York: Dial, 1989.

Pienkowski, Jan. *Shapes.* New York: Simon & Schuster, 1981.

Reiss, John. *Colors.* New York: Macmillan, 1987.

——— . *Shapes.* New York: Macmillan, 1987.

Robbins, Ken. *Tools.* New York: Macmillan, 1983.

Rockwell, Anne, and Harlow Rockwell. *Machines.* New York: Macmillan, 1972.

——— . *The Supermarket.* New York: Macmillan, 1979.

Ruben, Patricia. *True or False?* New York: Harper, 1978.

Schwartz, David M. *If You Made a Million.* Illus. Steven Kellogg. Photos. George Ancona. New York: Lothrop, 1989.

Spier, Peter. *Fast-Slow, High-Low: A Book of Opposites.* New York: Doubleday, 1972.

Tafuri, Nancy. *All Year Long.* New York: Penguin, 1984.

Testa, Fulvia. *If You Look Around You.* New York: Dial, 1983.

Walsh, Ellen Stoll. *Mouse Paint.* New York: Harcourt, 1989.

Concept Books—Psychosocial Development

Aliki. *Feelings.* New York: Greenwillow, 1984.

——— . *We Are Best Friends.* New York: Greenwillow, 1982.

Anholt, Catherine, and Laurence, Anholt. *All about You.* New York: Viking, 1992.

Girard, Linda Walvoord. *Alex, the Kid with AIDS.* Morton Grove, IL: A. Whitman, 1990.

————. *Jeremy's First Haircut.* Morton Grove, IL: A. Whitman, 1986.

————. *We Adopted You, Benjamin Koo.* Morton Grove, IL: A. Whitman, 1989.

Rockwell, Harlow. *My Dentist.* New York: Greenwillow, 1975.

————. *My Doctor.* New York: Harper, 1985.

Rosen, Michael J. *Home: A Collaboration of Thirty Distinguished Authors and Illustrators of Children's Books to Aid the Homeless.* New York: Harper, 1992.

CHAPTER 6

Mother Goose Rhymes

THE ORIGINS OF MOTHER GOOSE RHYMES

A great deal of time has been devoted to speculations on the origin of the term "Mother Goose." Suffice it to say that the seventeenth-century French reteller of folktales, Charles Perrault, named his book *Tales from Mother Goose,* and that by the end of the eighteenth century, "Mother Goose" was clearly associated with a mythical teller of nursery rhymes for young children—at least in the United States. No one is really sure where Perrault found the name. Mother Goose rhymes (in England they are called "nursery rhymes") are typically a child's first introduction to literature, beginning with the parents' singing of lullabies, such as "Rock-a-bye, Baby," or counting out tiny toes with "This little pig went to market."

Most Mother Goose rhymes are folk literature, songs that were passed down by word of mouth long before they were written down. Whereas some nursery rhymes are exceedingly old (the counting-out rhyme "Eena, meena, mona, my" and its variations seem to harken back to the sounds of ancient names for the numbers), most date from the sixteenth, seventeenth, and eighteenth centuries. "The Three Blind Mice" was set to music as early as 1609; "Jack Sprat" may have ridiculed a certain Archdeacon Spratt in the mid-seventeenth century, and some identify "Jack Horner" with Thomas Horner of Mells whose "plum" was much valuable land he acquired through Henry VIII's dissolution of the monasteries in 1536. Nursery rhymes are derived from a number of sources: war songs, romantic lyrics, proverbs, riddles, political jingles and lampoons, and street cries (the early counterparts of today's television commercials). But one thing can be said for certain: Few of these rhymes were initially intended for children.

Nursery rhymes are often delightfully irreverent, and their heroes come typically from the lower walks of life: Simple Simon, Tom the Piper's Son, Mother Hubbard, the Old Woman in the Shoe, and so on. Those that do include kings and queens frequently have a satirical bite to them. Scarcely hidden beneath the surface of these rhymes and jingles are the jibe and the barb.

It has often been pointed out that the nursery rhymes contain their share of violence. Some of this realism could be shocking if we take it literally: babes dropping from treetops, cradle and all; a farmer's wife cutting off the tails (some say "heads") of three blind mice; a beleaguered old woman giving her children broth without bread and soundly whipping them; a man imprisoning his troublesome wife in a pumpkin shell; and so on. One assiduous critic, Geoffrey Handley-Taylor, noted that in a single collection of 200 familiar nursery rhymes, he discovered clearly 100 rhymes with "unsavoury elements," including eight allusions to murder, two cases of choking to death, one case of decapitation, seven cases of severing of limbs, one case of body snatching, four cases of breaking of limbs, and the list goes on (cited in Baring-Gould 1962, 20). The important thing to realize is that this "violence" is not sensationalized, and the context of the violence is not only fictional but absurd. (Who puts wives in pumpkin shells? Who really lives in a shoe?) The violence is never presented realistically or seriously, and it may effectively serve to help children vent those hostilities and pent-up anxieties to which all human beings are subject. Further, there is not a single recorded instance of a child being transformed into a vicious human being from the influence of nursery rhymes.

THE IMPORTANCE OF MOTHER GOOSE RHYMES

Perhaps the only defense that Mother Goose rhymes need is that they are purely fun; their delightful nonsense and wonderful characters remain with us long beyond childhood. We should never underestimate the value of the sheer pleasure that literature can offer, but these rhymes, in fact, provide much more than an enjoyable pastime. Mother Goose rhymes may actually contribute significantly to a child's development in a surprising variety of ways.

Cognitive Development

With such rhymes as "One, two, buckle your shoe / Three, four, shut the door," and "One, two, three, four, five / Once I caught a fish alive," young children are encouraged to learn numbers and counting. The letters of the alphabet are subjects of such rhymes as "A—apple pie." Nursery rhymes—perhaps because many of them were originally intended for adults—often include challenging words. "Mary, Mary, quite *contrary*," "Jack be *nimble*" and "Peter Piper picked a *peck of pickled peppers*" all provide opportunities for young children to expand their vocabularies painlessly. There is never any need to shy away from big words in children's books so long as they are words that can be easily explained and do not involve abstract thinking beyond the children's capacity. And it is also good to remember that because the nursery rhymes are easily memorized, young children frequently are able to "pretend" to read them and soon, almost without realizing it, actually begin to read the words. In this way, Mother Goose can be a tremendous stimulant to reading.

Finally, the appreciation of nonsense, such as that in most nursery rhymes, requires a firm grasp of reality. Nonsense is only amusing if we see its absurdity and its incongruity when we place it next to what we know to be real. Therefore, it might be argued that Mother Goose rhymes help children in developing a sense of humor and that the rhymes force intellectual comparisons between fantasy and reality.

Aesthetic Development

By aesthetic development, we mean the forming of an appreciation for beautiful things; in the case of literature, we are referring specifically to an appreciation of the beauty of language. Mother Goose rhymes with their rollicking meter appeal to a child's natural sense of rhythm—perhaps learned in the womb from the steady rhythm of the mother's heartbeat. The repeated refrains also provide children with the pleasures of anticipating something familiar. The playful sounds, including those wonderful nonsense words ("Hickory, dickory dock," "Diddle, diddle dumpling, my son John," "Higgledy, piggledy, my black hen"), appeal to the natural delight most children find in language. The rhymes encourage the very young children to experiment in creating sounds—a necessary developmental process toward learning to speak. Children learn to make meaningful sounds through constant experimentation, aided by the encouraging responses of adults. Nursery rhymes do their small, but important, part in introducing a rich variety of sounds to eager ears.

In addition to providing children with a wonderful introduction to linguistic sounds, the nature of rhyming, and the joy of rhythm, nursery rhymes also develop a child's sensitivity to pattern. The idea of pattern forms the basis of much art, for pattern imposes form, order, and logic on life. "A little girl was sitting on the ground eating and was scared away by a spider" describes an event in life. But notice how much more memorable the scene is when we impose a pattern on it:

> Little Miss Muffet sat on a tuffet
> Eating her curds and whey;
> Along came a spider
> And sat down beside her
> And frightened Miss Muffet away.

Naturally, we hope that, with maturity, readers come to appreciate more sophisticated poetry than this, but without this foundation—verse forms and the repetition of sound that we call rhyme—a deeper appreciation is not very likely to develop.

Mother Goose rhymes may also help children recognize the distinction between fact and fiction—that is, understanding when something is a "story" and when it is "real life." Being able to draw a line between the events of a story and the events of the real world is a distinction that is absolutely essential if children are to lead psychologically healthy lives. In addition to recognizing a fictional work, children may also begin to comprehend rudimentary plot structures. The above example, "Little Miss Muffet," contains the basic elements of a simple plot structure: a conflict between a protagonist and antagonist, a climax with the confrontation, and a denouement or conclusion. Nursery rhymes are children's first introduction to fictional characters and fictional events, and these experiences can prepare them for the somewhat more complex fictional experiences awaiting them in folktales and the picture storybooks as well as later reading. And not least, nursery rhymes deal in concrete images that are easily visualized. The rhymes, with their vivid imagery and precise mental pictures, provide an important stimulus to young imaginations.

Emotional Development

Children return again and again to favorite nursery rhymes, which become like old friends, providing comfort and security. This is important for very young children, to whom every day presents a host of new and unusual experiences. Additionally, as was suggested above, the frank realism of many of the rhymes helps children in coping with aggressive behavior. Virtually everyone experiences aggressive impulses from time to time. The important thing is to find some socially acceptable way of expressing those feelings. Some psychologists believe that children who are able to vent aggressive feelings through literature and art are less likely to vent those feelings by throwing tantrums or popping their siblings and friends in the noses. In other words, literature can help us along the road to emotional maturity. Some critics believe that Mother Goose rhymes can provide important assistance in this emotional growth (see Bremner, "The World According to Mother Goose," and, for a related discussion but one focusing on folktales, see Bettelheim, *The Uses of Enchantment,* cited in Chapter 8).

Social and Physical Development

Many nursery rhymes are based on cooperative play—"Pat-a-cake, pat-a-cake" requires physical coordination and interpersonal contact, for example. Other rhymes, such as "Ring-a-ring o' roses" or "London Bridge Is Falling Down," call for the interaction of several children and thus encourage games and social interaction. Jump-rope rhymes are simply nursery rhymes gone to the playground, and they appear to be an almost worldwide childhood pastime (see Butler, *Skipping Around the World*). They also exhibit a considerable amount of aggression, and even hostility. Take this popular jump-rope jingle, for instance:

> Fudge, fudge, tell the judge
> Mother has a newborn baby;
> It isn't a girl and it isn't a boy;
> It's just a fair young lady.
> Wrap it up in tissue paper
> And send it up the elevator:
> First floor, miss;
> Second floor, miss;
> Third floor, miss;
> Fourth floor,
> Kick it out the elevator door.

In one playful action, the skipping children are developing large motor coordination skills, engaging in a cooperative social activity, and rather harmlessly verbalizing some of the hostility that is an inevitable part of every sibling relationship. It is more socially acceptable than punching out one's kid brother—and almost as efficacious.

CHOOSING MOTHER GOOSE BOOKS

A Mother Goose book is typically a picture book and may be evaluated along standards similar to those applied to picture books in the preceding chapters. However, there are also some specific elements to look for.

1. Is there a balance between the familiar rhymes and those that are less often anthologized?
2. Are rhymes from other cultures included—African, Asian, Native American, for example? (Mother Goose may be American, but cultures the world over have their equivalent of the child's folk rhyme.)
3. Are the illustrations examples of good illustrative art, both imaginative and well-executed?
4. Are the pages uncluttered in appearance and are the rhymes juxtaposed with the proper pictures?
5. Are there enough rhymes to justify the cost of the book?
6. Is there an index so specific rhymes can be easily located?
7. Does the book present an overall attractive appearance?

Every household should possess at least one good collection of Mother Goose rhymes. Perhaps the most difficult part is selecting just one from the many fine collections available. Of course, there is nothing at all wrong with having many Mother Goose books; it is almost guaranteed that they will be well-worn and that the investment will be returned manifold.

Illustrators of Mother Goose

Mother Goose rhymes are widely illustrated and have attracted some of the best children's artists. On the following pages are comparative examples of illustrations of two favorite rhymes—"Jack Sprat" and "Little Miss Muffet."

"Jack Sprat" has been especially popular among illustrators of Mother Goose rhymes and has inspired a wide variety of individual interpretations. The appeal of this nursery rhyme for illustrators has undoubtedly been the opportunity afforded by its two distinctive characters—each with a clearly defined character trait.

"Little Miss Muffet" is a wonderfully constructed tale, complete with setting, characters, conflict, climax, and resolution. With its clearly defined beginning, middle, and end, and its distinct characterization, this rhyme has been among the most popular of all Mother Goose verses. Most illustrators understandably choose to depict the moment just prior to the verse's climax: it provides the most drama and the greatest possibilities for interpretation.

J ACK SPRAT could eat no fat,
His wife could eat no lean:

And so, betwixt them both, you see,
They lick'd the platter clean.

FIGURE 6.1   L. Leslie Brooke depicts a decidedly older couple and from an earlier time—the costumes are Renaissance. As always with Brooke, a close examination of his illustration reveals his wry humor: notice the bovine fattened for market prominently displayed on the Sprats's coat-of-arms. Like many Victorian children's artists, Brooke imbued his representational drawings with rich, subtle details.

SOURCE: From *The Nursery Rhyme Book* by Andrew Lang. Illustrated by L. Leslie Brooke. Copyright 1972 by Dover Publications, Inc. Reprinted by permission.

FIGURE 6.2 Blanche Fisher Wright depicts an eighteenth-century husband and his solicitous mate. Typical of her illustrations for the popular collection, *The Real Mother Goose,* the lines are clean and sharp and her characters well-defined.

FIGURE 6.3 Marguerite de Angeli's lush painting of the Sprats, from her *Book of Nursery and Mother Goose Rhymes,* is a feast for the eye. Her illustration contrasts interestingly with Wright's, for although both artists have chosen virtually the same pose (even to the dog before the table), de Angeli's use of line makes her vision much more animated. De Angeli's style comes closer to expressionism, although she is still seeking that pictorial quality of representational art.

SOURCE: Excerpt(s) from *Book of Nursery and Mother Goose Rhymes* by Marguerite de Angeli, copyright © 1954 by Marguerite de Angeli. Used by permission of Doubleday, a division of Bantam, Doubleday, Dell Publishing Group, Inc.

FIGURE 6.4 Raymond Briggs's little drawing is quite different from the rest in that it captures the Sprats in their most bizarre behavior—that of licking the platter clean. Appropriate to the subject, Briggs's style is cartoon, which heightens the effect of the absurd.

SOURCE: Illustration by Raymond Briggs. Reprinted by permission of Coward, McCann & Geoghegan from *The Mother Goose Treasury* by Raymond Briggs, © 1966 by Raymond Briggs.

LITTLE MISS MUFFET

Little Miss Muffet
Sat on a tuffet,
Eating her curds and whey;
There came a big spider,
Who sat down beside her
And frightened Miss Muffet away.

FIGURE 6.5 Raymond Briggs portrays a looming creature, but his Miss Muffet looks more like a nineteenth-century school marm. The fact that Briggs's spider does not have the anatomically correct number of legs need not bother us, since the illustration is in a cartoon style, and exaggerations and distortions are to be expected.

SOURCE: Illustration by Raymond Briggs. Reprinted by permission of Coward, McCann & Geoghegan from *The Mother Goose Treasury* by Raymond Briggs, © 1966 by Raymond Briggs.

Little Miss Muffet,
Sat on a tuffet,
Eating some curds and whey;
There came a great spider,
And sat down beside her,
And frightened Miss Muffet away.

FIGURE 6.6 Kate Greenaway could not bring herself to include unsavory elements in her illustrations; consequently she detracts from the drama by focusing all attention on the prim and proper Miss Muffet. The spider is barely noticeable off to the left. The colors are subdued and contribute to the air of quietness belying the circumstances.

SOURCE: Kate Greenaway, *Mother Goose Nursery Rhymes.* London: Frederick Warne & Co., Ltd.

FIGURE 6.7 Arthur Rackham, on the other hand, portrays a truly monstrous-looking, but not ungentlemanly, spider. The spider's appearance completely overwhelms the picture, and there is a wonderful contrast between the sedate Miss Muffet (somewhat more mature than Greenaway's), her lip daintily pursed, and the grotesque creature about to interrupt her. Rackham's surrealistic, frequently nightmarish, quality is tempered here by a bit of wry humor as the spider gallantly doffs his hat.

SOURCE: Arthur Rackham, *Mother Goose Nursery Rhymes*. London: Chancellor Press.

Little Miss Muffet
Sat on a tuffet,
Eating her curds and whey;
Along came a spider,
Who sat down beside her
And frightened Miss Muffet away.

FIGURE 6.8   Alice and Martin Provensen depict the real moment of drama in the rhyme—Miss Muffet actually encountering the spider and her spilling of the curds and whey. The old-fashioned flavor of the illustration, reminiscent of eighteenth-century New England folk art, helps to distance the viewer from the action, so Miss Muffet's horror is not necessarily shared by the audience.

source: From *The Mother Goose Book* by Alice and Martin Provensen. Copyright 1976 by Alice and Martin Provensen. Reprinted by permission of Random House, Inc.

RECOMMENDED READINGS

Baring-Gould, William S., and Ceil Baring-Gould. *The Annotated Mother Goose.* New York: Potter, 1962.

Bodger, Joan. "Mother Goose: Is the Old Girl Relevant?" *Wilson Library Bulletin* (December 1969): 402–408.

Bremner, Moyra. "The World According to Mother Goose." *Parents Magazine* (December 1983): 61–67.

Butler, Francelia. "Skip-Rope Rhymes as a Reflection of American Culture." In *Sharing Literature with Children.* Ed. by Francelia Butler. New York: Longman, 1977. 8–14.

——— . *Skipping Around the World: The Ritual Nature of Folk Rhymes.* New York: Ballantine, 1989.

Chisolm, Margaret. "Mother Goose—Elucidated." *Elementary School English* (December 1972): 1141–44.

Eckenstein, Lina. *Comparative Studies in Nursery Rhymes.* 1906. Detroit: Singing Tree, 1968.

Green, Percy B. *A History of Nursery Rhymes.* Detroit: Singing Tree, 1968.

Nadasan, Ardell. "Mother Goose Sexist?" *Elementary School English* (March 1974): 375–78.

Opie, Iona, and Peter Opie. *The Oxford Dictionary of Nursery Rhymes.* Oxford: Oxford University Press (Clarendon Press), 1951.

Thomas, Katherine Lewis. *The Real Personages of Mother Goose.* New York: Lothrop, 1930.

SELECTED BIBLIOGRAPHY OF MOTHER GOOSE BOOKS

Alderson, Brian, comp. *The Helen Oxenbury Nursery Rhyme Book.* Illus. Helen Oxenbury. New York: Morrow, 1986.

Baring-Gould, William S., and Ceil Baring-Gould, eds. *The Annotated Mother Goose.* New York: New American Library, 1967.

Briggs, Raymond, illus. *The Mother Goose Treasury.* New York: Coward, McCann & Geoghegan, 1966.

de Angeli, Marguerite, illus. *Book of Nursery and Mother Goose Rhymes.* Garden City: NY: Doubleday, 1953.

Hader, Berta, and Elmer Hader. *Picture Book of Mother Goose.* 1930. New York: Crown, 1987.

Lang, Andrew, ed. *The Nursery Rhyme Book.* Illus. L. Leslie Brooke. New York: Dover 1972.

Lines, Kathleen, ed. *Lavender's Blue.* Illus. Harold Jones. New York: Watts, 1973.

Lobel, Arnold, illus. *The Random House Book of Mother Goose.* New York: Random House, 1986.

Marcus, Leonard S., and Amy Schwartz, selectors. *Mother Goose's Little Misfortunes.* Illus. Amy Schwartz. New York: Bradbury, 1990.

Opie, Iona, and Peter Opie, eds. *The Oxford Nursery Rhyme Book.* New York: Oxford University Press (Clarendon Press), 1955.

Petersham, Maud, and Miska Petersham, illus. *The Rooster Crows: A Book of American Rhymes and Jingles.* New York: Macmillan, 1945.

Provensen, Alice, and Martin Provensen, illus. *The Mother Goose Book.* New York: Random House, 1976.

Rackham, Arthur, illus. *Mother Goose.* 1913. New York: Marathon, 1978.

Reed, Philip, illus. *Mother Goose and Nursery Rhymes.* New York: Atheneum, 1963.

Scarry, Richard, illus. *Richard Scarry's Mother Goose.* New York: Western, 1983.

Smith, Jessie Willcox, illus. *The Jessie Willcox Smith Mother Goose.* New York: Derrydale, 1986.

Tripp, Wallace, illus. *Granfa' Grig Had a Pig and Other Rhymes Without Reason from Mother Goose.* Boston: Little, Brown, 1976.

Tudor, Tasha, illus. *Mother Goose: Seventy-Seven Verses with Pictures by Tasha Tudor.* New York: Oxford University Press, 1944.

Wildsmith, Brian, illus. *Brian Wildsmith's Mother Goose.* New York: Watts, 1965.

Withers, Carl, collector. *A Rocket in My Pocket: The Rhymes and Chants of Young America.* Illus. Susane Suba. New York: Holt, 1946.

Wright, Blanche Fisher, illus. *The Real Mother Goose.* New York: Rand McNally, 1916.

CHAPTER 7

Poetry

DEFINITION OF POETRY

Perhaps one of the loveliest descriptions of poetry comes from the poet Paul Roche who remarked that poetry is like a stained-glass window: It lets the light shine through but exists for its own beauty. The "light" is a metaphor for knowledge, wisdom, or truth. The "beauty" refers to both the sounds and the poet's imaginative use of the language, creating fresh and stimulating imagery. Good poetry is the effective combination of sound and sense. As adults we typically have little use for beautiful sounding words if they make no sense. However, most nonsense verse—such as that of Edward Lear or Lewis Carroll—possesses its own internal logic (even if it is a logical contradiction of logic). Conversely, a profound thought expressed in a clumsy, inarticulate fashion would hardly be labeled poetic.

Poetry is the most personal of all literary forms, and as such is the most misunderstood. In their anthology of poetry for children, *Knock at a Star*, X. J. and Dorothy M. Kennedy answer the question, "What do poems do?" with the following five points: (1) *they make us laugh*—from the nonsense of Lear to the comedy of Shel Silverstein, good children's poets have recognized this as one of the best ways into the child's world; (2) *they tell us stories*—just as some of the Mother Goose rhymes do, poems can set scenes, establish characters, and convey plots; (3) *they send us messages*—poets usually have points to make, ideas to get across, and even comic verse often has some food for thought; (4) *they share feelings with us*—from joy to sorrow to anger to excitement to serenity, poets ask us to come into their world and, for a time, to share their deepest feelings and sensations, and the poet is often well aware of our feelings as well; and (5) *they start us wondering*—the poet forces us to see things in ways we may never have thought of before and encourages us to stretch our minds and exercise our imaginations. Poetry—good poetry at least—is not intended to be obscure or to "muddy" things up, but is supposed to enlighten us, to make us see something we have not seen before, feel something we have never felt. The best poetry is a union of beauty and truth, but we must not forget that the best poets speak to us with *beauty that we can appreciate* and in *truths that we can understand.*

POETRY FOR THE VERY YOUNG

Toddlers and preschoolers, as we might expect, respond first to the beauty of poetry and not its truth. Infants and preschoolers are captivated by the sounds of "Pat-a-cake, pat-a-cake," or "Hickory dickory dock"—the fact that these are largely nonsense sounds is decidedly secondary to the enjoyment. And Lewis Carroll's "Jabberwocky" remains a pleasure to listen to and to read, however obscure its meaning. All poetry is musical, and rhythm is a fundamental quality of poetry. Babies respond to rhythmical patterns almost from birth, whether it be swaying or rocking or a simple caressing of the back. So it should not be surprising that they demonstrate an early love of the rhythms of language. As mentioned in chapter 6, Mother Goose rhymes are among the earliest delights of young children. Beyond that, nursery rhymes offer benefits in the cognitive, emotional, and social realms as well. We should remember the joy these simple poems give children and the delight they find in memorizing and repeating them. This early exposure to the wonder of language is crucial. Poetry and music spring from the same impulse, and it may even be that the love of poetry and music is a natural impulse, for both echo the rhythmic patterns of nature. It seems quite likely that music, dancing, and poetry are all parts of our earliest artistic expression.

But poetry is as much an appeal to the mind's eye as it is to the ear. Once children begin to comprehend meaning through language, they begin to demand vivid mental images in their stories and poems. (Hence, we have one of the reasons that the folktales are so successful with the very young, for those tales rely heavily on sharp, concrete images to convey their messages.) Imagery in literature is simply the quality that allows language to paint pictures with words. The Mother Goose rhymes are filled with memorable mental pictures: Miss Muffet on her tuffet, Jack and Jill tumbling down the hill, another Jack suspended in midair over a candlestick, and the miserable Old Woman attempting to corral her unruly children into an oversized shoe. It is no accident that nursery rhymes are among the most-often illustrated of children's literature. The vivid pictures conveyed by the words so readily lend themselves to the artist's brush and pen.

THE FORMS OF POETRY

When we talk about poetry, it is easy to get bogged down with complex terminology and obscure references, and it is certainly not necessary for children to be able to recognize and label poetic techniques. But in order for us, as adults, to appreciate fully the craft of the poet, it is helpful to have at least a passing acquaintance with the poet's "tools." There are two sets of tools: the poem's *external form* (usually identified as a stanza) and the poem's *internal sound and imagery.* Let us start by considering the external forms of poetry.

Narrative Poetry

A *narrative poem* is a story in verse. (To narrate, of course, means simply to tell a story.) The most accessible narrative poems for children are ballads. Ballads are typically straightforward and easy to understand; like a story, they include a setting, character, and events with a climax. Many readers find ballads less intimidating than the shorter, more compact *lyric poems*. The typical ballad follows a four-line scheme with the second and fourth lines rhyming, such as in this famous opening stanza to the anonymous ballad, "Barbara Allen's Cruelty":

> In Scarlet town, where I was born,
> There was a fair maid dwellin',
> Made every youth cry *Well-a-way*!
> Her name was Barbara Allen.

As with most good story beginnings, we are given a definite setting and introduced to the main character, the devastating Barbara Allen. Ballads have been popular since the Middle Ages and have proven quite adaptable. They are frequently tragic and plaintive, such as this example of an anonymous ballad from the American West called "The Dying Cowboy" or "The Streets of Laredo":

> Let sixteen gamblers come handle my coffin,
> Let sixteen young cowboys come sing me a song,
> Take me to the green valley and lay the sod o'er me,
> For I'm a poor cowboy and I know I've done wrong.

Occasionally ballads are set to music, and the perennial favorite "Wreck of the Edmund Fitzgerald" by Gordon Lightfoot is an interesting example of a modern-day disaster supplying the inspiration for a modern-day ballad. And country and western music thrives on the ballad form.

Not all narrative poems are ballads. In fact, some of the world's oldest literature includes the 3,000-year-old Sumerian epic, *Gilgamesh,* and the great narrative poems of Homer, *The Iliad and The Odyssey.* These are lengthy stories in poetry form that were actually intended to be recited to audiences (rather than read by them). A hundred years ago, lengthy narrative poems still enjoyed some popularity, but today few readers have the patience required to read them. Nevertheless, Robert Browning's "The Pied Piper of Hamelin" and Henry Wadsworth Longfellow's "The Song of Hiawatha" are examples of nineteenth-century narrative verse still found in print. The early twentieth-century poet Alfred Noyes wrote narrative poems imbued with drama on subjects that appeal to readers in the upper elementary years—"The Highwayman" and "A Song of Sherwood" are examples.

In a narrative poem, we look for a storylike structure, with a beginning, a middle, and an end. We look for character motivation (if not development), and we look for an underlying theme (the monumental theme of the triumph and tragedy of war in the great epic poems or the tender theme of the forsaken lover that is common to the ballad are examples).

Lyric Poetry

By far the most popular poetry enjoyed by children is *lyric poetry*. Lyric poetry expresses a poet's emotional or intellectual response to a subject. Unlike a narrative poem, a lyric does not so much tell a story as it does describe the feeling of a moment. Lyrics tend to focus on a single experience and are brief, which undoubtedly accounts for much of their popularity. In the absence of exciting narrative action, the lyric must depend heavily on musical and rhythmical qualities. There seems to be an endless variety of stanza forms in lyric poetry, and new ones are still being created.

Haiku. The Japanese *haiku* consists typically of seventeen syllables divided into three lines and is usually on the subject of nature and our relationship to nature, such as this by Ruby Lytle*:

> The moon is a week old—
> A dandelion to blow
> Scattering star seed.

In this haiku, the notion of the stars as tiny seeds blown from the moon, a whispery soft dandelion puff gone to seed, brings us at once closer to the starry night sky and reminds us of that curious interrelationship of all nature. Haiku in English possesses a subtle rhythm, but typically no rhyme. Its strength lies in its suggestive quality. Successful haiku uses metaphor (which will be further explained below) to give us a fresh and imaginative look at something we may view as quite ordinary.

Cinquain. The *cinquain* is a five-line stanza apparently of medieval origin. The term once seems to have included any five-line poem (*cinq* is French for "five"), but Adelaide Crapsey, in her volume entitled *Verse,* created more precise rules stipulating that the five lines should contain two, four, six, eight, and two syllables respectively. Her inspiration may have been the Japanese haiku, although little real similarity between the two forms exists. Cinquains, because their rules are less rigid than those of haiku, can be fun for children to imitate. The poet Myra Cohn Livingston sees the cinquain as a sort of mathematical puzzle, in which the writer must find expressions of the correct number of syllables placed in an intelligible order. Notice the pattern of syllables (2, 4, 6, 8, 2) in Adelaide Crapsey's cinquain, entitled "November Night":

> Listen . . .
> With faint dry sound,
> Like steps of passing ghosts,
> The leaves, frost-crisp'd, break from the trees
> And fall.

Notice how the poet plays on the double meaning of the last word. Like all poetry, the good cinquain shows us a fresh pespective, a new way of observing and thinking.

---

*From *What Is the Moon* by Ruby Lytle. Copyright 1965 by Charles E. Tuttle Company.

Concrete Poetry.   When the words of a poem are so arranged that they form a pictorial representation of the subject of the poem, we have what is called a *concrete poem.* These are really not new, for the English metaphysical poets were practicing this sort of poetry in the seventeenth century. George Herbert, for example, wrote "The Altar" so that the lines formed the shape of an altar; also popular were poems in the shapes of crosses, pyramids, and Herbert's "Easter Wings" was designed to suggest angel wings. In the twentieth century, much more liberty has been taken with this sort of thing, such as in this example by Robert Froman, in which the poet defines what he calls "A Seeing Poem"*:

Limerick.   Among the most popular poetic forms among children is the *limerick,* a six-line humorous poem, the first, second, and fifth lines rhyming, and the third and fourth rhyming. Part of the fun of the limerick is its rollicking rhythm, and the rest of the fun is in its broad humor. The following limerick has been attributed to President Woodrow Wilson:

> I sat next to the Duchess at tea;
> It was just as I thought it would be;
>   Her rumblings abdominal
>   Were simply phenomenal,
> And everyone thought it was me.

The limerick's form is easily imitated, and young children can have a great deal of fun creating their own.

Taken from *Seeing Things: A Book of Poems* by Robert Froman. Copyright © by Robert Froman. Reprinted by permission of the author.

Free Verse.   The twentieth century has popularized *free verse,* which adheres to no set of predetermined rules, but nevertheless good free verse establishes its own criteria for rhyming and rhythmical patterns. Free verse is much more demanding on the poet than most readers suppose, and it requires the same thoughtful choice of words and sentence patterns as the more rigid stanza forms. The following example, "The Fog,"* by Carl Sandburg focuses on a single concrete image:

> The fog comes
> on little cat feet.
>
> It sits looking
> over harbor and city
> on silent haunches
> and then, moves on.

There are potentially as many stanza forms as there are poets. Perhaps the best we can do for children is to make them aware of the vast array of choices open to them as both readers and writers of poetry, and in this way try to prevent the misconceptions that arise about what a poem is.

THE LANGUAGE OF POETRY

Poetry—like all literature—depends upon the effective union of form and content, but poetry is at once more compact than most literature and more reliant upon certain literary devices for its effect. The most memorable poems paint mental pictures for us by the effective use of *imagery,* and they also sound pleasing to our ears by the effective use of *sound patterns.*

Imagery

Imagery refers simply to mental pictures created by words. Since words are the poem's medium, their selection is the most crucial aspect of the poem's creation.

Direct Images.   Imagery may be direct, using a word or words to describe how our senses respond to a subject. Direct images appeal to one of our five physical senses. Consequently, images may be *visual,* referring to things we can see, or images may be *tactile,* appealing to our sense of touch. When Walter de la Mare writes "Through the green twilight of a hedge / I peered with cheek on the cool leaves pressed," he is using first visual imagery—*green twilight*—and then tactile—*cool leaves.* *Auditory* images suggest the sounds of things, as when Eve Merriam writes of a wrecking ball in her poem, "Bam, Bam, Bam"†:

---

* "Fog" from *Chicago Poems* by Carl Sandburg, reprinted by permission of Harcourt Brace and Company.

† From *Catch a Little Rhyme* by Eve Merriam. Copyright © 1966 by Eve Merriam. Reprinted by permission of Marion Reiner.

Crash goes a chimney,
Pow goes a hall,
Zowie goes a doorway,
Zam goes a wall.

Olfactory images suggest the smells of things, as in these lines from Shakespeare that mingle sound imagery with that of scent: "[The music] came o'er my ear like the sweet sound / That breathes upon a bank of violets, / Stealing and giving odor!" Dante Gabriel Rosetti suggests another olfactory image: "I know the grass beyond the door / The sweet keen smell." *Kinesthetic* images refer to actions or motions, as do these lines from Alan Cunningham's "At Sea":

A wet sheet and a flowing sea,
    A wind that follows fast
And fills the white and rustling sail
    And bends the gallant mast

And *gustatory* images suggest the tastes of things. These images are less common than others, but it is perhaps taste, texture, and color that Mary O'Neill had in mind when she wrote that "Brown is cinnamon / and morning toast" or that gray is "The bubbling of oatmeal mush."

Indirect Images.   Images may also be *indirect,* describing something by comparing it to another thing with which we are more familiar. The three common methods of comparison are through *similes, metaphors,* and *personification.*

A *simile* is a stated comparison, employing a connective such as "like" or "as"; take Robert Burns's famous line: "My love is like a red, red rose." The unknown is "My love" (presumably the poet's sweetheart), and the known is the "red, red rose" (a flower that is familiar to his audience). It is true that we may, as readers/listeners, have somewhat different conceptions and attitudes about the "red, red rose" (those who have violent allergies to roses are apt to think of them quite differently from most readers). But we must admit that most people think of roses as examples of extraordinary delicacy and beauty, and we would certainly have a very different conception of the lover if the poet had written, "My love is like a mighty oak." The point is that the poet's object was not to confuse us, but, rather, to help us share in his deep and passionate feelings about his lover.

A *metaphor* is an implied comparison—one not directly stated with words such as "like" and "as," and is sometimes more subtle to grasp. In a brief poem, "City,"* by Langston Hughes, the poet implies a comparison of a city in the morning with a songbird:

In the morning the city
Spreads its wings
Making a song
In stone that sings.

---

* Langston Hughs, "City," in *The Langston Hughes Reader.* Reprinted by permission of Harold Ober Associates Incorporated. Copyright 1958 by Langston Hughes. Copyright renewed 1986 by George Houston Bass.

This simple poem gives us an exhilarating feeling about the city. The short, musical lines, with their repeating "s" and "ing" and short "i" sounds, their end rhyme, help to convey a sense of the animated and joyous life in the bustling city. The effective metaphor helps us to understand the poet's message and attitude.

Personification is by its nature metaphorical, although not all metaphors are personification. Personification occurs when a poet describes an inanimate object, an abstract idea, or a force of nature as if it were alive. James Stephens is using personification when he writes: "The Night was creeping on the ground! / She crept and did not make a sound. . . ." It is also personification when Eleanor Averitt writes of the November wind that she "has plucked the trees / like pheasants, held / between her knees."

Sound Patterns

Rhythm.   Most poems are written expressly for oral delivery, and, consequently, how they sound is extremely important. All poetry is musical, and, as in music, rhythm is a fundamental quality of poetry. Babies respond to rhythmical patterns almost from birth, whether it be swaying or rocking or a simple caressing of the back. Who is to say that our first sensory experience is not, in fact, prenatal—that steady, rhythmical pulsation of our mother's body and the gentle undulations of the embryonic fluids sweeping about us? And, of course, rhythm is everpresent in nature, the orbiting of the planets and the rhythmical birth, flourishing, death, and rebirth revealed to us through the changing seasons. Rhythm—be it in nursery rhymes or Shakespeare—is inseparable from poetry.

Simply defined, *rhythm* is the pattern of stressed and unstressed syllables in a poem. (This pattern is also called *meter.*) The smallest unit of rhythmical pattern is called a *foot.* There are many variations of metrical feet, each having from two to three syllables. The most common are the following:

> *Iamb* (two syllables with the emphasis on the second: "When **wál**-king **ín** a **tí**-ny **ráin**")
>
> *Trochee* (two syllables with the emphasis on the first: "**Síng** a **sóng** of **sub**-ways")
>
> *Anapest* (three syllables with the emphasis on the last: "In the **morn**-ing the **cí**-ty")
>
> *Dactyl* (three syllables with the emphasis on the first: "**Sky**-scra-per, **sky**-scra-per")

Nursery rhymes tend to have very regular rhythms: "**Má**-ry **hád** a **lít**-tle **lámb**" (regular trochees). Following their example, much of the verse for the very young repeats similar singsong patterns. But if children are ever to appreciate poetry more fully, they must be brought beyond the notion that perfect, unvaried meter is the only rhythmical option available to poetry. Much poetry combines more than one rhythmical pattern to achieve a particular effect. When we read poetry to children, it is important that we are ourselves aware of any subtleties of rhythm the poem may contain, so that we may gain the best effect from our reading.

Rhyme.   *Rhyme,* the second important element of sound patterns, is achieved through the similarity of sound that exists between two or more words. When it comes to poetry for children, we customarily place too much emphasis on *end rhymes*—that is, rhyming "June" with "moon" and "spoon" and "soon." In fact, rhyme can occur anywhere sounds are repeated.

Alliteration, for example, is the repetition of initial sounds in two or more words, such as the **b** and **l** sounds in these lines by A. E. Housman:

> **B**y **b**rooks too **b**road for **l**eaping,
> The **l**ightfoot **b**oys are **l**aid.

Assonance is the repetition of identical vowel sounds, such as the long **a**, long **u**, and long **i** sounds in these lines by Carl Sandburg:

> "Let me be the **gr**e**a**t n**ai**l holding a skyscraper thr**ough** bl**u**e n**i**ghts into wh**i**te stars."

Consonance is the repetition of consonant sounds within words, often with a variation in adjoining vowels, such as the **f** and **d** sounds in these lines by William Jay Smith*:

> Butter**fl**ies . . .
> Gli**d**ing over **f**iel**d** and stream—
> Like **f**ans unfol**d**ing in a **d**ream.

Obviously, too much of any repetitive sound pattern becomes noticeable and begins to detract from the content. The good poet knows just how much to include to make music, and just when to stop before the result is tongue-tieing racket.

THE MEANING OF POETRY

All of the poet's pyrotechnics with language will not substitute for a shallowness of meaning. Poems can be written about anything. We are all familiar with poems about nature and love, but poets have demonstrated that memorable poems can be written about apartment houses ("A filing cabinet of human lives" says poet Gerald Raftery), or about toasters ("A silver-scaled Dragon with jaws flaming red" according to William Jay Smith), or about junkyards ("That junkyard fell down the side of the hill / like a river" writes Jeannette Nichols).

Poetry is condensed thought, and for that reason it is often more difficult to comprehend than typical prose, which explains things in greater detail. Poetry is also evocative—like a good piece of music, it appeals to our emotions, calls for reflection, invites rumination. A good poem is one to linger over, to read and reread, not just to

---

*Reprinted from *The Golden Journey: Poems for Young People* by William Jay Smith and Louise Bogan, © 1990. Used with permission of Contemporary Books, Inc., Chicago.

grasp its meaning, but to luxuriate in its sounds and its images. And even occasionally we will find a poem that we love to read and hear, even though we cannot claim to understand it, and that is all right, too.

SHARING POETRY WITH CHILDREN

Children's Preferences

Studies of children's poetry preferences suggest, among other things, that children prefer poetry that they can understand, that they prefer humorous poetry, that they prefer new poems to older ones, and that they do not like serious and contemplative poems (see Terry). This is not to suggest that we provide children only with what they like or think they like. After all, an important part of education is broadening experiences. But it is useful to know what prejudices and preconceptions children may have about poetry, so that we have some idea of where we must go. Too often in the schools we labor under the misconception that poetry is obscure (a puzzle to be unravelled by English teachers), "pretty" (without any particular meaning), and not about anything especially important (mostly flowers, birds, or fireflies). These are the very misconceptions that are passed on to children—the very children who could not get enough of Mother Goose rhymes or the delightful verses of Jack Prelutsky, Shel Silverstein, and others. And many of these children may have dabbled in writing poetry themselves in early elementary school. Unfortunately, the approach to poetry in many classrooms may actually encourage a fear and even a dislike of poetry among children.

Reading Poems

The best way to dispel these misconceptions is to make poetry a regular part of a child's reading program (rather than an intensive two-week unit to be forgotten as quickly as it was begun). Most poetry is best read aloud and—in the classroom, at least—it is best read frequently and not saved up for a marathon weeklong poetry drill once a year. There are wonderful poems suitable for special occasions (or even ordinary occasions—poems for a partly cloudy day, for instance). Poetry offers endless possibilities—a well-presented poem can fill a relatively small time slot in a day and provide some welcome, joyous relief. If we begin to think of poetry in this fashion, we may begin to dispel some of the notions of drudgery and perplexity that currently surround poetry.

And it is important to eliminate those tedious academic exercises (memorizing irrelevant poems, counting meters, scanning lines, and so on) that typically form the academic study of poetry. There is nothing wrong with discussing these matters with children and showing them how they might make use of them in their own poems, but it can be disastrous to make meaningless exercises of them.

The writing of original poetry may be encouraged and even required, and some children will find it fun and rewarding. Encouraging children to form collections of their own favorite poems is also an enriching experience (and every adult presenting poetry to children should do the same). Requiring students to memorize poems can result in happy experiences for some children, but it quickly devolves into drudgery for others. We need to be aware of children's individual differences and personal preferences.

Helping children to effectively read their favorite poems is always a worthwhile exercise. Inexperienced readers tend to want to dramatize the rhythm or the rhyme of a poem, to always make a definite pause at the end of a line whether the poet has punctuated it or not, and to overemphasize the singsong quality. Children learn best by example. We can demonstrate the effective reading of poetry, paying close attention to the poet's punctuation, avoiding a lapse into inappropriate nursery-rhyme rhythm, carefully enunciating the words, and emphasizing the meaning of those words by using natural and not artificial inflections. Practice in reading poetry is the key to accomplishment. Ideally, the reading of poetry will become a much anticipated part of the daily schedule—both a delight and a refreshment.

Selecting Poems and Anthologies

Too often children are asked to read poems that were clearly intended for adults. And then we wonder why the children are confused or bored. The truth is that much of the poetry of our most revered poets speaks about adult emotions and adult perceptions of the world. How can we expect children to identify with these subjects? And we need not expect them to do so; there are plenty of very good poems for young readers. There is little need to raid adult literature for suitable examples.

Every classroom and home should include a generous supply of poetry books, both anthologies and books by individual poets. With the wealth of good poetry available, every child—no matter how resistant to poetry—is bound to find some favorites. The key is, of course, to supply a wide and varied sampling—poems on all subjects, poems representing a myriad of stanza forms and rhyme schemes and rhythms.

We should say a few words about selecting poetry anthologies. Look for the following characteristics in the best anthologies:

1. There are both familiar and new names among the poets included.
2. There are a significant number of new poems included and not simply old poems that can already be found in many anthologies.
3. There is a balance of light and serious poems.
4. The poems *show* the reader (through effective imagery, metaphor, personification) rather than *tell* the reader the poet's thoughts.
5. The poems reflect a variety of verse forms.
6. The illustrations (if the book is illustrated) complement the poems without overpowering them.

As with all children's literature, if we wish to instill a love of reading poetry in children, we must begin with ourselves. The poet is a visionary, one who sees the world in fresh and unusual ways, and one who is capable of sharing that vision with the rest of us. We have been notoriously unsuccessful in conveying this notion of poetry to young people. It is important that we overcome our own fears and apprehensions about poetry so that we may share in its bounty. But, as with everything else in creation, the more we understand about poetry, and the better we come to know it, the richer our experience with it will be. And few literary forms offer so much in wealth of pleasure and knowledge than poetry. Lovers of poetry are not born, but made through patient and careful nurturing.

RECOMMENDED READINGS

Baskin, Barbara Holland, Karen H. Harris, and Coleen C. Salley. "Making the Poetry Connection." *The Reading Teacher* 30 (December 1976): 259–65.

Ciardi, John, and Miller Williams. *How Does a Poem Mean?* 2nd ed. Boston: Houghton Mifflin, 1975.

Fisher, Carol J., and Margaret A. Natarella. "Of Cabbages and Kings: Or What Kinds of Poetry Children Like." Language Arts 56: 4 (April 1979): 380–85.

Greenway, Betty, and William Greenway. "Meeting the Muse: Teaching Contemporary Poetry by Teaching Poetry Writing." *Children's Literature Association Quarterly* 15 (1990): 138–42.

Higginson, William J., with Penny Harter. *The Haiku Handbook: How to Write, Share and Teach Haiku.* New York: McGraw-Hill, 1985.

Hopkins, Lee Bennet. *Pass the Poetry Please.* New York: Citation Press, 1972.

Hurst, Carol. "What to Do with a Poem." *Early Years* 11(February 1980): 28–29, 68.

Kennedy, X. J. " 'Go and Get Your Candle Lit!' An Approach to Poetry." *Horn Book Magazine* 57: 3 (June 1981): 273–79.

Krogness, Mary Mercer. "Imagery and Image Making." *Elementary English* 51: 4 (April 1974): 488–90.

Larrick, Nancy, ed. *Somebody Turned on a Tap in These Kids.* New York: Delacoret, 1971.

Lewis, Marjorie. "Why Is a Poem a Four-Letter Word?" *School Library Journal* 23: 9 (May 1977): 38–39.

Livingston, Myra. *Climb into the Bell Tower: Essays on Poetry.* New York: Harper-Collins, 1990.

———. *Poem-Making: Ways to Begin Writing Poetry.* New York: Harper-Collins, 1991.

Shapiro, Jon E. *Using Literature and Poetry Affectively.* Newark, DE: International Reading Association, 1979.

Steiner, Barbara. "Writing Poetry for Children." *Writer's Digest* (February 1986): 34–35.

Terry, Ann. *Children's Poetry Preferences: A National Survey of the Upper Elementary Grades.* Urbana, IL: National Council of Teachers of English, 1984.

SELECTED BIBLIOGRAPHY OF POETRY BOOKS FOR CHILDREN

Poetry Anthologies

Abdul, Raoul, ed. *The Magic of Black Poetry.* Illus. Dane Burr. New York: Dodd, 1972.

Adoff, Arnold, ed. *The Poetry of Black America: An Anthology of the 20th Century.* New York: Harper, 1973.

———. *Celebrations: A New Anthology of Black American Poetry.* Chicago: Follett, 1977.

Arbuthnot, May Hill, and Shelton L. Root, eds. *Time for Poetry.* Illus. Arthur Paul. Glenview, IL: Scott, Foresman, 1968.

Blishen, Edward, comp. *Oxford Book of Poetry for Children.* Illus. Brian Wildsmith. New York: Watts, 1963.

Bryan, Ashley, selector and illus. *All Night, All Day: A Child's First Book of African-American Spirituals.* New York: Atheneum, 1991.

Carter, Anne, selector. *Birds, Beasts, and Fishes: A Selection of Animal Poems.* New York: Macmillan, 1991.

Cole, William, comp. *Poems of Magic and Spells.* Illus. Peggy Bacon. Cleveland: World, 1960.

de Gasztold, Carmen Bernos, selector. *Prayers from the Ark.* Tr. Rumer Godden. Illus. Barry Moser. New York: Viking, 1992.

De La Mare, Walter, ed. *Come Hither.* 3rd ed. Illus. Warren Chappell. New York: Knopf, 1957.

———. *Tom Tiddler's Ground.* Illus. Margery Gill. New York: Knopf, 1962.

Dunning, Stephen, Edward Lueders, and Hugh Smith, comps. *Reflections on a Gift of Watermelon Pickle.* Glenview, IL: Scott, Foresman, 1967.

———. *Some Haystacks Don't Even Have Any Needle.* Glenview, IL: Scott, Foresman, 1969.

Elledge, Scott, ed. *Wider Than the Sky: Poems to Grow Up With.* New York: Harper, 1990.

Hall, Donald, ed. *The Oxford Book of Children's Verse in America.* New York: Oxford University Press, 1985.

Houston, James, ed. *Songs of the Dream People.* New York: Atheneum, 1972. (Eskimo and other Native America poems)

Janesczko, Paul B., selector. *The Place My Words Are Looking For: What Poets Say about and through Their Work.* New York: Bradbury, 1990.

———. *Preposterous: Poems of Youth.* New York: Watts, 1991.

Jones, Hettie, selector. *The Trees Stand Shining: Poetry of the North American Indians.* Illus. Robert Andrew Parker. New York: Dial, 1971.

Kennedy, X. J., and Dorothy M. Kennedy, eds. *Knock at a Star: A Child's Introduction to Poetry.* Illus. Karen Ann Weinhaus. Boston: Little, Brown, 1982.

Larrick, Nancy, ed. *Piping Down the Valleys Wild.* Illus. Ellen Raskin. 1968. New York: Dell, 1982.

Livingston, Myra Cohn, comp. *Dilly Dilly Piccalilli: Poems for the Very Young.* New York: McElderry, 1989. (Nonsense verse)

Moore, Lilian, ed. *Go with the Poem.* New York: McGraw-Hill, 1979.

Moore, Lilian, and Judith Thurman, comps. *To See the World Afresh.* New York: Atheneum, 1974.

Opie, Iona, and Peter Opie, eds. *The Oxford Book of Children's Verse.* New York: Oxford University Press, 1973.

Sullivan, Charles, ed. *Imaginary Gardens: American Poetry and Art for Young People.* New York: Abrams, 1989.

Townsend, John Rowe, comp. *Modern Poetry.* Philadelphia: Lippincott, 1974.

Whipple, Laura, comp. *Animals Animals.* Illus. Eric Carle. New York: Philomel, 1989.

Books by Individual Poets

Adoff, Arnold. *All the Colors of the Race.* Illus. John Steptoe. New York: Lothrop, 1982.

Armour, Richard. *A Dozen Dinosaurs.* Illus. Paul Galdone. New York: McGraw-Hill, 1970.

Blake, William. *Songs of Innocence and Experience.* Illus. Harold Jones. New York: Barnes, 1961.

Bodeker, N. M. *Water Pennies: And Other Poems.* Illus. Erik Blegvad. New York: McElderry, 1991.

Cawthorne, William Alexander. *Who Killed Cockatoo?* Illus. Rodney McRea. New York: Farrar, Straus & Giroux, 1989. (Australian adaptation of "Who Killed Cock Robin?")

Ciardi, John. *The Man Who Sang the Sillies.* Illus. Edward Gorey. Philadelphia: Lippincott, 1961.

———— . *The Reason for the Pelican.* Illus. Madeleine Gekiere. Philadelphia: Lippincott, 1959.

Coatsworth, Elizabeth. *Under the Green Willow.* Illus. Janina Domanska. New York: Macmillan, 1971.

Cole, William, selector. *A Zooful of Animals.* Illus. Lynn Munsinger. Boston: Houghton, 1992.

cummings, e. e. *Hist Whist.* Illus. Deborah Kogan Ray. New York: Crown, 1989.

De La Mare, Walter. *Peacock Pie.* Illus. Barbara Cooney. New York: Knopf, 1961.

Demi, selector and illus. *In the Eyes of the Cat: Japanese Poetry for All Seasons.* Tr. Tze-si Huang. New York: Holt, 1992.

Dickinson, Emily. *Letter to the World.* Ed. Rumer Godden. Illus. Prudence Seward. New York: Macmillan, 1969.

Eliot, T. S. *Old Possum's Book of Practical Cats.* Illus. Edward Gorey. New York: Harcourt, Brace, Jovanovich, 1982.

Farjeon, Eleanor. *Then There Were Three.* Illus. Isobel and John Morton-Sale. Philadelphia: Lippincott, 1965.

Field, Rachel. *Poems.* New York: Macmillan, 1957.

Fisher, Aileen. *Cricket in a Thicket.* Illus. Feodor Rojankovsky. New York: Scribner's, 1963.

———— . *Feathered Ones and Furry.* Illus. Eric Carle. New York: Crowell, 1971.

Fleischman, Paul. *I Am Phoenix: Poems for Two Voices.* Illus. Ken Nutt. New York: Harper, 1985.

———— . *A Joyful Noise: Poems for Two Voices.* New York: Harper, 1988.

Froman, Robert. *Seeing Things: A Book of Poems.* New York: Crowell, 1974.

Frost, Robert. *Birches.* Illus. Ed Young. New York: Holt, 1988.

Giovanni, Nikki. *Spin a Soft Black Song.* Illus. George Martins. New York: Hill and Wang, 1985.

Greenfield, Eloise. *Night on Neighborhood Street.* Illus. Jan Spivey Gilchrist. New York: Dial, 1991.

Hughes, Langston. *Selected Poems.* New York: Knopf, 1959.

Hughes, Ted. *Moon-Whales and Other Moon Poems.* Illus. Leonard Baskin. New York: Viking, 1976.

Issa. *A Few Flies and I: Haiku by Issa.* Tr. R. H. Blyth and Nobuyaki Yuasa. Eds. Jean Merrill and Ronni Solbert. New York: Pantheon, 1969.

Kennedy, X. J. *Chastlies, Goops & Pincushions: Nonsense Verse.* Illus. Ron Barrett. New York: McElderry, 1989.

Kuskin, Karla. *Near the Window Tree.* New York: Harper, 1975.

Lear, Edward. *The Complete Nonsense Book.* Ed. Lady Strachey. New York: Dodd, 1942.

———— . *The Quangle-Wangle's Hat.* Illus. Helen Oxenbury. New York: Watts, 1969.

Lewis, J. Patrick. *A Hippopotamusn't: And Other Animal Verses.* Illus. Victoria Chess. New York: Dial, 1990.

Livingston, Myra Cohn. *The Way Things Are and Other Poems.* Illus. Jenni Oliver. New York: Atheneum, 1974.

———— . *Whispers and Other Poems.* Illus. Jacueline Chwast. New York: Harcourt, 1958.

McCord, David. *One at a Time: His Collected Poems for the Young.* Illus. Henry Kane. Boston: Little, Brown, 1986.

Mahy, Margaret. *Nonstop Nonsense.* Illus. Quentin Blake. New York: McElderry, 1989.

Merriam, Eve. *The Singing Green: New and Selected Poems for All Seasons.* New York: Morrow, 1992.

———— . *There Is No Rhyme for Silver.* Illus. Joseph Schindelman. New York: Atheneum, 1962.

Milne, A. A. *The World of Christopher Robin.* Illus. Ernest Shephard. New York: Dutton, 1924.

Moore, Lilian. *Adam Mouse's Book of Poems.* Illus. Kathleen Garry McCord. NewYork: Atheneum, 1992.

Nash, Ogden. *The Adventures of Isabel.* Illus. James Marshall. Boston: Little, 1991.

———. *Custard and Company: Poems by Ogden Nash.* Comp. and illus. Quentin Blake. Boston: Little, Brown, 1980.

O'Neill, Mary. *Hailstones and Halibut Bones.* Illus. John Wallner. New York: Doubleday, 1989.

Prelutsky, Jack. *Ride a Purple Pelican.* New York: Greenwillow, 1986.

———. *The Sheriff of Rottenshot.* Illus. Victoria Chess. New York: Greenwillow, 1982.

———. *Something Big Has Been Here.* Illus. James Stevenson. New York: Greenwillow, 1990.

Richards, Laura. *Tirra Lirra: Rhymes Old and New.* Illus. Marguerite Davis. Boston: Little, Brown, 1955.

Roethke, Theodore. *Dirty Dinky and Other Creatures.* Sel. Beatrice Roethke and Stephen Lushington. New York: Doubleday, 1973.

Schwartz, Alvin, selector. *And the Green Grass Grew All Around: Folk Poetry from Everyone.* Illus. Sue Truesdell. New York: Harper, 1992.

Seabrooke, Brenda. *Judy Scuppernong.* Illus. Ted Lewin. New York: Dutton, 1990.

Service, Robert W. *The Shooting of Dan McGrew.* Illus. Ted Harrison. Boston: Godine, 1988.

Silverstein, Shel. *A Light in the Attic.* New York: Harper, 1981.

———. *Where the Sidewalk Ends.* New York: Harper, 1974.

Soto, Gary. *A Fire in My Hands: A Book of Poems.* Illus. James M. Cardillo. New York: Scholastic, 1991. (Poems about Hispanic culture)

Starbird, Kaye. *The Covered Bridge House.* Illus. Jim Arnosky. New York: Four Winds, 1979.

Stevenson, Robert Louis. *A Child's Garden of Verses.* Illus. Jessie Willcox Smith. 1905. New York: Scribner's, 1969.

Viorst, Judith. *If I Were in Charge of the World and Other Worries.* Illus. Lyn Cherry. New York: Atheneum, 1969.

Whitman, Walt. *Voyages: Poems by Walt Whitman.* Sel. Lee Bennett Hopkins. Illus. Charles Mikolaycak. New York: Harcourt, 1988.

Wilbur, Richard. *Opposites.* New York: Harcourt, 1973.

Willard, Nancy. *Household Tales of Moon and Water.* New York: Harcourt, 1982.

———. *A Visit to William Blake's Inn.* Illus. Alice and Martin Provensen. New York: Harcourt, 1981.

CHAPTER 8

Folk Literature

DEFINITION OF FOLK LITERATURE

People told stories even before civilization began to record its history. The impulse to tell tales may come in part from our desire to impose order on our lives. Tales, with their defined characters and settings and patterns, are organized human experiences. They put into words what many of us feel intuitively but are unable to express and therefore often unable to understand. Once some formalized expression—through story, drama, poetry, or art—has been created, we are better able to grasp the meaning of these feelings. We all need to hear stories, to read stories, to see them enacted; they satisfy a need deep within us to comprehend ourselves and the world around us. Folktales are among the earliest expressions of this need, and perhaps the most enduring.

Folk literature (also referred to as traditional literature) consists of all those stories handed down from generation to generation, from old to young, by word of mouth. By definition, folk literature is not written down (at least at its inception). The body of folk literature includes not only what we—somewhat inaccurately—refer to as "fairy tales," but also the myths, legends, fables, tall tales, and other inventions associated with preliterate societies. Although now most of these stories have been committed to paper, for centuries they lived only in the oral tradition of the people. Consequently, folktales were apt to change with each successive telling (much as complicated phrases get altered as they pass from person to person in that childhood game of "Telephone"). We may find hundreds of variations for a single tale, each variation containing elements peculiar to the society and culture that produced it. These tales form the roots of all literature, and their storylines still form the foundations for virtually every book we read or every movie we watch. They speak to our most basic human emotions, to our deepest hopes and fears, and it is little wonder that even the youngest children feel a great affinity with these stories that have been with us for as long as civilization.

THE ORIGIN AND PURPOSES OF FOLK LITERATURE

Two principal theories attempt to explain the origins of folktales. *Monogenesis* is the theory that all tales were ultimately derived from a single source (such as a Mesopotamian culture) and were disseminated throughout the world gradually. *Polygenesis,* on the other hand, is the theory that tales emerged independently of each other in many different places throughout the world. Polygenesis attributes these marked similarities in form and content to the fundamental similarities in the human psyche: people around the world having similar human hopes, fears, dreams, and psychological needs. Neither theory has yet been absolutely substantiated, and the truth may lie somewhere in between—some tales emerging independently and others having been adopted from neighboring cultures.

Undoubtedly, folktales, myths, legends, and fables originally served a variety of purposes. Some stories served as educational tools for preliterate societies, passing on knowledge essential for survival. Others surely helped to reinforce cultural practices and social mores—the importance of certain virtues, the significance of marriage or of the established social or political order, the superiority of one's clan or tribe over its neighbors, and so on. Vital to nearly all peoples were creation myths—how the world, *their* world, came to be. And we should not forget what must have been one of the driving forces behind the telling of these tales—entertainment. These tales served primitive societies in place of books, plays, movies, and television, and, as such, they embodied the popular attitudes, beliefs, and values of the culture. If many of the tales remain meaningful for us today, it is probably because, inside us all, we still share a great deal more with our ancestors than we realize.

FOLKTALES

We can identify several different types of folk literature, from the religious to the secular, from the sober to the whimsical. We will examine some of the more common types, including folktales, myths, epics, and legends. Folktales are among the most commonly known; they are the brief stories, secular in nature, intended largely for entertainment. They may be serious or comical, and they come in various familiar forms.

Animal Tales

Animals that talk appear in a great number of folktales—remember the magic fish in "The Fisherman and His Wife" or the wolf in "Little Red Riding Hood." A true animal tale (also called a talking beast tale) is one in which the principal characters are anthropomorphized animals—that is, animals that talk and act like humans. Animals in these tales may, and often do, interact with humans, although the human roles are negligible and usually not depicted in the best light. In "The Bremen-Town Musicians," we may recall that the humans are the heartless farmers, who are ready to dispose of the aging animals, and the thieves whom the animals cleverly rout from their hideout.

Animal tales are perhaps the oldest of all tales. Early people had a strong affinity with animals. Not only did animals pose the greatest threats for them, but they also provided them with food, clothing, companionship, and even served as guides and protectors, so it is not surprising that animals would play significant roles in early stories and legends. In most animal tales, the animals serve as symbols for humans, and in no way do they behave as we would expect real-life animals to behave. These tales tend to be very popular with young children who enjoy a great affinity with most animals. It is not a difficult leap for a young child to make believe that an animal can speak and feel just as we do.

Fables

Fables are a form of animal tale in which animals portray human virtues and vices for the purpose of conveying a moral message. Most fables conclude with a blatantly stated moral directed toward human behavior and are, therefore, openly didactic. Aesop, a famed teacher of the ancient Greeks, is credited with the most famous of fables, and it is usually assumed that he used them in his teaching. Ironically, even though their form would suggest a strong appeal among young children, most fables demand abstract thinking, and their points are often lost on children. Nevertheless, adults continue to provide children with fables, occasionally with lavish illustrations—but we must suspect that, for the most part, the adults are the ones who appreciate them.

Märchen or Wonder Tales

The best-known of the traditional folktales are the *märchen* or *wonder tales.* Focusing on magical wonders long ago in faraway lands, these tales typically depict the conflict between good and evil, usually enacted by characters of royal birth. They typically conclude with the triumph of virtue and a happy marriage. "Cinderella," "Snow White and the Seven Dwarfs," and "Sleeping Beauty" are the classic examples. It is largely from these tales that the term "fairy tale" emerged, although most do not actually contain fairies. In *märchen,* the supernatural is a dominant element, whether it be a magical person (a fairy godmother, a wicked witch), a magical object (a wondrous beanstalk and a goose that lays golden eggs) or an enchantment (a miraculous sleep that lasts until love's first kiss). Sometimes these stories are narratives of the hero's or heroine's life from childhood through the accomplishment of some great deed, which more often than not concludes with a marriage. Because of the ages of the protagonists (usually they are in late adolescence) and the fact that matrimony is the end of many of these tales, we may wonder what appeal they have for preschoolers. Their popularity undoubtedly springs from their imaginative characters, their supernatural elements, their focus on action, their simple sense of justice, and their happy endings.

Pourquoi Tales

A *pourquoi tale* (the name derives from the French word for "why") seeks to explain natural phenomena—many familiar Native American folktales fall into this category. One particularly moving tale is that explaining the creation of the Sleeping Bear Dunes on the northwest coast of Michigan's lower peninsula. The massive dunes, according to the tale, cover the body of a mother bear mourning the loss of her two cubs who drowned in Lake Michigan, and North and South Manitou islands, just off the coast, represent the two cubs themselves. Some pourquoi tales take on deep religious significance—such as creation tales—and are more properly considered myths.

Noodlehead Tales

Noodlehead tales (also termed *merry, droll or simpleton tales*) include as their principal characters fools, albeit lovable fools. "Hans in Luck," in which the title character successively trades one possession for another of lesser value until he is left with nothing (except happiness), is an excellent example of such a tale. "The Three Wishes" is the story of a poor couple who are granted three wishes by a grateful magical creature whom they helped out of a jam. The foolish couple proceed to waste all three wishes, however, and end up no better off than they were at the beginning—although they are usually depicted as contented anyway. Often noodlehead tales include no supernatural elements—or, if they do, as in "The Three Wishes," they are not the focus of the story. Noodlehead tales typically focus on a single episode in the hero's life. The appeal in these tales is usually in their pure nonsense and jocularity, and sometimes we enjoy the triumph of the good-hearted simpleton over the craftier evil characters of the story. Occasionally, the simpleton is indeed far wiser than anyone else, suggesting that it is the world at large that is foolish and unable to recognize true wisdom. The noodlehead tale is fundamentally that of the underdog, always a popular character.

Cumulative Tales

Most folktales include repetitious patterns—three wishes to be made, three deeds to be accomplished, and so on. But certain tales rely on repetition for their total effect. As each new detail is added to earlier ones, the entire list is repeated in order, so that the accumulation becomes a kind of chorus—and a challenge to the memory of the listener/reader. These *cumulative tales* are generally brief, else they become tiresome, but their appeal lies in their musical quality and, often, in their flippant humor. The old rhyme "This Is the House that Jack Built" is an example of repeated language patterns, and those familiar tales, "The Gingerbread Boy" and "The Turnip," wherein additional characters are called in to assist in the accomplishment of some feat, are examples of the accumulation of repetitive action. By its very nature, the cumulative tale is a nonsense tale designed entirely for fun. Young children especially love these repeated patterns, which typically allow them to join in the telling.

Tall Tales

The numerous tales about Paul Bunyan's extraordinary exploits mark the American *tall tale*. Tall tales—those comic stories of preposterous exaggeration—illustrate the American preference for broad humor and overstatement, and they are, in a sense, modern secular versions of the saint's legend. Tall tales defy logic and are almost positively without moral lessons. Their delight is in their absurdity and in the wildly imaginative yarns, each succeeding one seeming to outdo the other.

Ghost Stories

Most young people enjoy, in the right circumstances, being frightened. The immense popularity of horror movies among teenagers (and even younger children) attests to the appeal of spinetinglers. Telling *ghost stories* around a campfire or beneath the blankets at a pajama party has long been a childhood entertainment staple. Most cultures have their own versions of chilling tales, ghosts and evil spirits walking the night, or tales that Richard Chase calls "jump tales," because the teller jumps out towards the listeners at the climax to surprise them. Because most children prefer to hear these stories in groups where there is safety in their numbers, and because many of these stories are more effective when delivered orally, ghost stories are perfect examples of the living folktale, told *by* the folk *to* the folk—with each tale adapted to the occasion. They also invite others in the audience to make up their own ghost stories.

MYTHS

Myths are the stories of gods, goddesses, and heroes of a given culture, and these stories serve a variety of purposes, combining science, religion, and even sociology and psychology. Myths may explain the ultimate origin of the world and of human beings—virtually every culture from the most primitive to the most advanced has some creation myth, such as those wonderfully recounted in Virginia Hamilton's *In the Beginning: Creation Stories from Around the World*. Myths also help explain the origins of customs and societal beliefs—ancient Greeks and Romans placed coins in the mouths of their dead that they might have the fare for Charon who would ferry them over the River Styx to the Underworld. Myths also provide explanations for natural phenomena—the most familiar perhaps being the myth of Persephone, whose kidnapping by Hades (Pluto in Roman mythology), the god of the Underworld, caused her mother, Demeter, goddess of the grain and harvest, to be plunged into deep sorrow, thus bringing the desolation of winter to the world.

Myths also help to define human relationships with the god (or gods and goddesses). Myths may reinforce cultural values, drawing attention to what the culture sees as primary good and evil. Not least, myths help to resolve humanity's fear of the unknown—whether it be fear of thunder and lightning (explained as activities of the gods) or fear of death (typically explained as a passage from one world into another).

Classical Greek and Roman Mythology

To people of Western cultures, the most familiar mythology outside the Judaeo-Christian tradition is that of ancient Greece and Rome. Our daily lives are imbued with references to the extensive pantheon and the notable heroes of that civilization—note the names of the planets, stars, and galaxies, and, on a more mundane level, months of the year, body parts *(Achilles tendon),* cleaning agents *(Ajax),* synthetic fibers *(Herculon),* automobiles *(Mercury* and *Saturn),* tires and map-books *(Atlas),* athletic games *(Olympics),* and so on. A knowledge of these myths is important if only to make us more culturally aware. But, in addition to recognizing the multitude of references to Greek and Roman mythology in the modern world, our interest in these tales might be both entertaining and spiritually edifying, in that these exciting stories also tell us—as do the folktales—a great deal about human nature. In classical Greece, the gods and goddesses were powerful figures who often struggled against one another for human favor and typically were pragmatic in their dealings with humans ("I'll do that for you if you do this for me"). The questions of humanity's obedience to a higher power, the relationships of men and women to one another, the power of love, and the strength of parental devotion are all addressed in this body of mythology. Perhaps more than any other world mythology, classical Greek and Roman mythology focuses on the significance of humanity in the world. Numerous retellings of the Greek and Roman myths exist for children.

Norse Mythology

Second only to Greek and Roman mythology in its influence on the Western tradition, Norse mythology reflects the harsh way of life engendered by the severe, yet dramatically beautiful, Scandinavian lands. In Norse mythology, the gods and goddesses were defenders of humanity against the mighty forces of evil. Like the Greek and Roman gods and goddesses, the Norse deities were anthropomorphic—that is, the gods and goddesses had human forms (a practice not all that common throughout the world, when we consider the many monsters, demons, multi-armed deities, feathered serpents, and animal forms worshiped throughout the world). But compared to the Greek deities, the Norse gods and goddesses tend to be a much more serious lot, engaged in a perpetual struggle with the forces of evil, a struggle that they were destined to lose eventually. Individual codes of honor were highly esteemed in this war-conscious society, and the thunder god, Thor, with his mighty hammer is among the most familiar images from Norse mythology. Thor is remembered weekly in our own culture, for Thursday was named for him, just as Tuesday, Wednesday, and Friday were named for other Norse deities: Tiw (the god of war), Woden (father of the gods), and Fria (goddess of fruits). The tales of Norse mythology are both exciting and moving, and among the versions for children we may especially note Padraic Colum's *The Children of Odin.*

American, African, and Oriental Mythologies

The cultures of Native America (including North, Central, and South America), Mesopotamia, Africa, India, and the Far East all developed highly complex and sophisticated mythologies. Unlike Greek, Roman, and Norse mythologies with their anthropomorphic deities, the deities of these cultures are frequently polymorphic, combining the forms of animals and/or humans. Sometimes, the gods and goddesses took extraordinary forms—humans having many arms, heads, eyes, and so on. The great majority of world mythologies are polytheistic—that is, they contain many gods and goddesses. In fact, animistic cultures tend to have hundreds, even thousands, of minor deities, for they believe that supernatural beings and spirits inhabit every tree, animal, and stream. Nevertheless, these disparate mythologies all have in common a need to explain our relationship to the wondrous and mysterious forces that drive the universe.

EPICS AND LEGENDS

Epics and *heroic legends* initially grew out of mythology, but instead of focusing on gods and goddesses, these stories had human beings as their heroes. Among the most popular of the Greek and Roman heroes are Achilles, Odysseus, Hector, Jason, and Perseus. They were indeed the first superheroes, the prototypes for Superman, Batman, and Wonder Woman. Although Homer's *Iliad* and *Odyssey* were obviously aimed at an adult audience, there is much in them to attract young readers, for they are adventure-filled and wrought with unworldly wonders. Padraic Colum also wrote fine versions for children (*The Children's Homer* and *The Golden Fleece*).

Medieval Europe saw the rise of epic tales deriving from Christian sources—King Arthur and the Knights of the Round Table, the Quest for the Holy Grail, and the Life of Charlemagne provided the sources of the most popular tales. These epics and legends are often more secular than religious, Malory's *The Death of Arthur* and the French epic *The Song of Roland* being among the most famous, and some of these tales have been successfully retold for young readers— Rosemary Sutcliff's story of the Quest for the Holy Grail, *The Light Beyond the Forest,* for example. Sutcliff's *The Dragon Slayer,* a modern version of the Old English epic *Beowulf,* is reminiscent of the thrilling adventures of Homer's *Odyssey* and *Iliad.*

Also popular in the Middle Ages were the *saints' legends,* recounting often aprocryphal tales of the lives and miracles of saints. These enjoy no modern popularity, but as late as the early part of the twentieth century, John Foxe's *Book of Martyrs,* a sixteenth-century work about the deaths of persecuted Christians, was still considered fare for children. In a similar fashion, *local legends* emerged, focusing on local secular (as opposed to religious) heroes and usually departing rather dramatically from reality. The typical legend grows up around real people, although the facts are soon lost—George Washington's chopping down the cherry tree, Davy Crocket's frontier exploits, Johnny Appleseed's horticultural contributions to the land.

ARTISTIC ELEMENTS

It is possible to identify certain artistic elements that most tales have in common. Since folktales are derived from the oral and not the literary or written tradition, we hesitate to term these literary elements, although they amount to the same thing. As might be expected, these elements are all decidedly influenced by the oral nature of the tales.

Setting

The settings of most folktales are not sharply defined. Often brief conventional phrases ("Once upon a time in a kingdom far, far away") are the norm. The time and place are usually vague and often distant. The purpose of most folktale settings would seem to be to remove the tale from the real world, taking the events to a world where magic can easily and unabashedly occur. Only occasionally do we find actual place names in tales, and even then we have the feeling that we could substitute the name of any city or forest or country (which is undoubtedly what early storytellers did as they tailored their recitations to individual audiences). Even when place names are used—as they might be in myths, tall tales, or local legends—the setting is still distanced by time, and descriptions are very sparse indeed.

Character

The characters in folktales are usually flat (with only one side to the personalities) and stereotyped. Stereotypical characters—powerful, wicked stepmothers; weak-willed, ineffectual fathers, jealous siblings—populate most tales. A character is typically either all good or all evil, and it is usually not difficult for the audience to separate the good from the bad. Physical appearance often readily defines a character—wicked witches are ugly, good princesses are beautiful, noble princes are fair. Of course, magic occasionally intervenes. The Beast in "Beauty and the Beast" has been transformed from his handsome self into a monstrosity by a jealous witch. And another witch transforms a handsome prince into a frog in "The Frog Prince." But, once the character's true nature has been acknowledged by the appropriate person—usually some unsuspecting and strikingly beautiful maiden—the deceptive guise vanishes. Only rarely do we find a truly beautiful character to be wicked—Snow White's stepmother is an example, but even her beauty is outshone by that of her virtuous stepdaughter, and she performs her most powerful magic when she assumes the disguise of an ugly hag. Truth cannot remain hidden long.

The main character—the hero or heroine—is often isolated and forced to act alone. More often than not, the hero/heroine is the youngest child (and thus pitted unfairly against older siblings) or is an only child and/or orphaned. (Not surprisingly, this feature of folktales makes them especially appealing to young children who see themselves as equally helpless against the adult world or against their older siblings.) The heroes or heroines are usually cast out into the open world or are apparently without any human friends. And, if that were not enough, the forces of evil seem unfairly stacked against them. Often the evil is represented by groups of characters—two wicked stepsisters and a stepmother, for example.Consequently, to offset the apparent imbalance, the hero/heroine must be aided by supernatural forces (such as magic or enchanted, talking animals). The hero/heroine is clearly blessed and not infrequently discovered to be of royal blood (most folktales place a great deal of importance on one's appropriate station in life).

In short, the folktale hero/heroine is someone very much like we, as young children, pictured ourselves—the helpless but well-meaning victims of powerful evil forces (sometimes appearing in the form of our parents!). And the evil characters are incredibly evil—symbolizing all of our fears and frustrations. Naturally, imbued with the hope of youth, the evil characters will get what is coming to them, and the good characters will triumph in the end. Similar exaggeration is found in myths and legends, where the characters are larger than life.

Plot

The plots, or the sequence of events, are among the most identifiable features of folk literature. Suspense and action are far more important to these tales than character development. Conflicts are quickly established, and events move swiftly to their conclusion; although there may be subsidiary plots or the events may at times seem to get sidetracked, the action never slows down.

Because these tales were not originally written down, they are characterized by considerable repetition of both words and actions, the repetition serving as a memory aid. This repetition may also be suggestive of the ritual nature of many folktales. Rituals depend upon repetition—repetition of the same prayers and rites in church, of the same oaths of allegiance in government, of the same practices at weddings and funerals. Folktales frequently deal with rites of passage, especially that passage from childhood into adulthood, which is a familiar theme in folk literature. And finally, the great majority of folktales end happily, with poetic justice being served, the good being rewarded and the wicked punished. This pattern remains true for much of folk literature, although we are more likely to find unhappy conclusions in mythological stories.

Theme and Conflict

Folktale themes are usually quite simple, but always serious and powerful. Themes deal with such subjects as escaping mighty and evil enemies, earning a place in the world, accomplishing monumental tasks, and so on. Values are clearly defined; there is seldom a question about what is right or wrong—folktale heroes and heroines usually do not wrestle with perplexing moral dilemmas. The choices are typically very clear—but they are also typically very demanding.

If we had to make a general statement about themes in folktales, we might well turn to themes of Greek tragedy: *Wisdom comes through suffering.* The message rings loud and clear that for every benefit there is a condition, that nothing in life comes without strings attached, responsibilities to be met, and bargains to be kept. And folktale themes—especially in the Western tradition—espouse the virtues of *compassion, generosity,* and *humility* over the vices of *greed, selfishness,* and *excessive* or *overweening pride.* (Pride, which has customarily been regarded in the Judaeo-Christian ethic as the worst sin is not to be confused with self-respect. Self-respect means that we see ourselves as just as good as everybody else; pride means that we see ourselves as better than the rest.)

Style

The style in folktales is largely regulated by the oral nature of their origins. The language is typically economical, with a minimal amount of description and a heavy reliance on formulaic patterns—conventional openings and closings, for instance ("Once upon a time in a kingdom, far, far away" and "They lived happily ever after"). Repetitious phrases are common; they supply a rhythmical quality desirable in oral tales, and undoubtedly they once served as mnemonic devices to make the tales easy to memorize. Dialogue is frequently used; in the best-told tales, the dialogue captures the nature of the character speaking—hence, a lowly peasant will speak in a folksy manner whereas the speech of a king or princess will be more refined. (The English retellings of Joseph Jacobs wonderfully capture these differences in speech patterns.)

Most folktales include examples of simple, but concrete and very powerful, images that leave us with indelible mental pictures. Many tales can easily be identified by their images—a glass slipper, a bean stalk and talking harp, golden eggs, a bloody handkerchief, a red riding hood, and so on. Related to these images are the *motifs* on which most tales rely. In art, a motif is a repeated figure or element in a larger design (decorative fads are easily recognized by their motifs—ducks or geese or hearts and flowers, and so on). Similarly, in literature, a motif is a recognizable element that recurs in different tales. A motif has been defined by folklorist Stith Thompson as "the smallest element in a tale having power to persist in tradition." Certainly one reason motifs are so common in folktales is that they assist oral storytellers in their memorizing. Examples of popularly used motifs include magical transformations (a beast is transformed into a handsome prince, usually after some expression of true love), the use of magical objects, the appearance of deceitful animals (or helpful animals), the making of foolish bargains. The list continues.

Many folktale motifs are examples of magic—helpful animals, transformations from human to beast and beast to human, granted wishes, and so on. One important stylistic feature of the folktale is that the magic, when it inevitably appears, is always greeted by the characters with matter-of-factness. Characters in folktales acknowledge magic as an almost normal part of life. No one is ever amazed or disbelieving when a wolf speaks politely, or a fairy godmother materializes out of thin air, or an elf make exotic promises. This accepting attitude toward magic on the part of every folktale character further distances the folktale from reality, and it provides an important distinction between folk literature and much of literary fantasy. In many literary fantasies (heroic fantasy being one of the exceptions), magical occurrences are not necessarily taken for granted, but may even be regarded with surprise, awe, and disbelief. (Both Alice and Dorothy, those most famous of child travelers in literary fantasies, are in constant wonder at the characters and circumstances they encounter.)

ISSUES IN FOLK LITERATURE

Among the issues most often discussed regarding folk literature is the prevalence of violence. Foolish and irresponsible little pigs are devoured, wolves are cooked in boiling water, witches are pushed into hot ovens, characters are mutilated in any number of ways—folktales have their fair share of violent acts. Certainly much of this violence is the product of earlier, less squeamish eras (and the same can be said for the violence in Mother Goose rhymes, as discussed in Chapter 6). But before we express our indignation over these violent elements or seek to exorcise them from stories for the young, perhaps we should consider the excessively graphic and despicably gruesome violence that we can observe on television at almost any time of the day or that too frequently clutters up our theater screens. Modern violence—not the least of which is found in children's Saturday morning cartoons—is often gratuitous, without sense or purpose other than to arouse or titillate the audience. This is clearly different from folktale violence, which is always handled without graphic description and which is seldom included without motivation. Violence perpetrated by the wicked always results in their downfall and deaths; violence perpetrated by the good is always a response to evil. It is interesting that, when given the choice, children most often prefer versions of "Little Red Riding Hood" in which grandmother is devoured and the wolf is ultimately killed—as opposed to those versions in which the ravenous wolf, after inexplicably tying up grandmother and tossing her in the closet, is miraculously reformed and promises to be good henceforth.

Perhaps more potentially damaging than the violence is the depiction of negative female stereotypes (the frail young girl in need of a good man) or the unfortunate deprecation of stepmothers in general. Modern attitudes demand that we attempt to balance our selection of folktales—it is possible to find folktales that have positive female role models ("Mollie Whuppie" and "Kate Crackernuts" are just two examples). We should also consider the possibility of contemporary adaptations of old folktales—making them more "politically correct," perhaps? We should remember that the resilience of these folktales is partly due to the fact that they have been continually adapted over the centuries to meet the changing needs of society.

COLLECTORS, RETELLERS, AND ADAPTERS

Almost as soon as human beings invented the art of writing, they began to record their oral tales—on stone, on papyrus, and on paper. So far as Western culture is concerned, virtually the entire body of ancient Greek literature consists of renderings and retellings of their myths, legends, and fables. The ancient Romans followed this practice similarly. The ancient Jews recorded their history with a generous dose of legend. The Christian Middle Ages built up a body of literature on the legendary lives of the saints as well as on the glorified deeds of heroes. But by and large, the vast majority of folktales remained only in oral form, except for a few recorded by such medieval writers as Chaucer in *The Canterbury Tales* and Boccaccio in *The Decameron*. Consequently, these stories survived chiefly by word of mouth until the seventeenth and eighteenth centuries when writers began to collect them and put them down on paper.

Among the first and most famous of these writers was Charles Perrault, whose *Tales of Mother Goose* made such stories as "Cinderella," "Sleeping Beauty," and "Little Red Riding Hood" standard fare in children's literature. In the early nineteenth century, the famous Grimm brothers gathered German folktales, which included, not surprisingly, versions of "Cinderella" ("Aschenputtel") and "Little Red Riding Hood" ("Little Red Cap"), as well as such familiar favorites as "Snow White and the Seven Dwarfs."

In fact, none of these early collectors recorded the tales specifically for children. Many people even thought folktales too harsh for children and sought to protect children from these stories. But children, of course, devoured the tales anyway. It was not until the last half of the nineteenth century that folktales were widely collected and retold for children by such people as Joseph Jacobs and Andrew Lang. Since that time, folktales have been largely the exclusive property of children. The twentieth century has seen an explosion in the interest in folklore, and countless collections of tales from all over the world have appeared. With each retelling, the tales are changed to suit the teller's individual tastes and purposes. The old tales have been told and retold, updated and embellished, distorted and expurgated; yet still they survive—an indication of their tough endurance.

THE APPEAL OF FOLK LITERATURE

Folktales appeal to children in a variety of ways. The theories of Piaget and Erikson (see Chapter 2) help explain much of this appeal. Among the significant (and less controversial) explanations, we may include the simple fact that children believe, or perhaps want to believe, that objects, actions, thoughts, and words can exert a magical influence over events. Also, children believe that inanimate objects have consciousness, and they freely accept a human consciousness in animals. The simple story lines, the emphasis on action rather than thought, the clearly delineated characters, and the triumph of good over evil all contribute to children's enjoyment. Additionally, it is easy for children to identify with folktale heroes and heroines, who are often seen as victims, beset by woes that they overcome partly through their own tenacity and willpower, and partly with the aid of magical or divine intervention. Folktales, in this way, provide what some feel to be the most important element of all children's literature—hope. Some theorists, notably Bruno Bettelheim, suggest that folktales, through their rich symbolism and evocative story patterns, actually fulfill unconscious psychological needs in some children. Bettelheim argues that children are able to vent anxieties and hostilities through the vicarious experience of art and literature, with folktales providing an especially healthy and much-needed emotional outlet. Critics often find Bettelheim too Freudian for modern tastes, but his theories do add a deeper dimension to the study of folktales. (For a sampling of Bettelheim's theory, see the discussion on "The Psychoanalytical Approach" in Chapter 14.)

Folk literature is among the most important of all our literature. The various forms of folk literature can help children to learn about human problems and show them that they are not alone in their troubles. Folk literature can broaden children's cultural experiences, show them about new and fascinating cultures, and teach them that we share the world with many diverse peoples. Folk literature can instruct them the art of the story itself, helping them to grasp the concepts of character, plot and conflict, theme, and so on. And not least, folk literature, with its powerful messages, can give children, when they most need it, hope that good will triumph.

Regardless of what critics may say, folk literature in its various forms has long stood the test of time, and it is not likely that what we adults say or do will change that fact. The chances are that these stories will be entertaining readers, young and old, long after the complaints of the purists and theories of the scholars have sunk into dust.

RECOMMENDED READINGS

Bettelheim, Bruno. *The Uses of Enchantment: The Meaning and Importance of Fairy Tales.* New York: Knopf, 1976.

Bosma, Betty. *Fairy Tales, Fables, Legends, and Myths: Using Folk Literature in Your Classroom.* 2nd ed. New York: Teachers' College Press, 1993.

Campbell, Joseph. *The Hero with a Thousand Faces.* 2nd ed. Princeton, NJ: Princeton University Press, 1968.

Chase, Richard. *American Folk Tales and Songs.* New York: Dover, 1971.

Cook, Elizabeth. *The Ordinary and the Fabulous.* Cambridge, U.K.: Cambridge University Press, 1969.

Krappe, Alexander H. *The Science of Folklore.* 1929. New York: Norton, 1964.

Luthi, Max. *Once Upon a Time: On the Nature of Fairy Tales.* Bloomington, IN: Indiana University Press, 1976.

Storr, Catherine. "Folk and Fairy Tales." *Children's Literature in Education* 17 (Spring 1986): 63–70.

Thompson, Stith. *The Folktale.* New York: Holt, Rinehart, and Winston, 1951.

Walker, Virginia, and Mary E. Lunz. "Symbols, Fairy Tales and School-Age Children." *The Elementary School Journal* (November 1976): 94–100.

Yolen, Jane. *Touch Magic.* New York: Philomel, 1981.

Zipes, Jack. *Breaking the Magic Spell: Radical Theories of Folk and Fairy Tales.* Austin, TX: University of Texas Press, 1979.

———. *Fairy Tales and the Art of Subversion: The Classical Genre for Children and the Process of Civilization.* London: Heinemann, 1983.

SELECTED BIBLIOGRAPHY OF FOLK LITERATURE, MYTHS, AND LEGENDS

Below is a brief selection from the vast number of collected folktales, fables, riddles, myths, and legends that are available. They are classified as either (1) Folktales and Fables or (2) Myths, Epics, and Legends. Check the booklist following Chapter 4 for picture book versions of individual tales.

Folktales and Fables

Aesop's Fables. Illus. Fritz Kredel. New York: Grosset, 1947.

Asbjornsen, Peter, and Jorgen Moe. *East O' the Sun and West O' the Moon.* New York: Dover, 1970. (Scandinavian folktales)

Bierhorst, John, ed. *Lightning Inside You: And Other Native American Riddles.* New York: Morrow, 1992.

Bloch, Marie Halun. *Ukrainian Folk Tales.* New York: Coward, McCann, 1964.

Briggs, Katharine. *British Folk Tales.* New York: Pantheon, 1977.

Bushnaq, Inea, tr. *Arab Folktales.* New York: Pantheon, 1986.

Calvino, Italo, ed. *Italian Folktales.* New York: Pantheon, 1980.

Chandler, Robert, tr. *Russian Folk Tales.* New York: Shambhala/Random House, 1980.

Chase, Richard. *The Jack Tales.* Boston: Houghton Mifflin, 1971. (American tall tales)

Cole, Joanna, selector. *Best-Loved Folktales of the World.* Garden City, NY: Doubleday, 1982.

Demi, adapter. *A Chinese Zoo: Fables and Proverbs.* New York: Harcourt, 1987.

de Wit, Dorothy. *The Talking Stone: An Anthology of Native American Tales and Legends.* New York: Greenwillow, 1979.

Finger, Charles. *Tales from Silver Lands.* New York: Doubleday, 1924. (Native Central American folktales)

Gag, Wanda. *Tales from Grimm.* New York: Coward, McCann & Geoghegan, 1981.

Glassie, Henry. *Irish Folk Tales.* New York: Pantheon, 1985.

Grimm, Jakob, and Wilhelm Grimm. *Household Stories.* Tr. Lucy Crane. New York: Dover, 1963.

Haley, Gail E., reteller and illustrator. *Mountain Jack Tales.* New York: Penguin, 1992.

Hamilton, Virginia. *In the Beginning: Creation Stories from Around the World.* New York: Harcourt Brace Jovanovich, 1988.

———. *The People Could Fly.* New York: Knopf, 1985. (African-American folktales)

Haviland, Virginia. *Favorite Tales Told in India.* Boston: Little, Brown, 1973.

Hodges, Margaret, reteller. *Hauntings: Ghosts and Ghouls from Around the World.* Boston: Little, 1991.

Hoogasian-Villa, Susie. *One Hundred Armenian Tales.* Detroit: Wayne State University Press, 1966.

Jacobs, Joseph. *Celtic Fairy Tales.* New York: Dover, 1968.

———. *English Fairy Tales.* New York: Dover, 1967.

James, Grace, reteller. *Green Willow and Other Japanese Fairy Tales.* New York: Avenel, 1987.

Kherdian, David, reteller. *Feathers and Tails: Animal Fables from Around the World.* New York: Putnam, 1992.

Lang, Andrew. *The Blue Fairy Book.* New York: Dover, 1965.

Lester, Julius. *Black Folktales.* New York: Richard W. Baron, 1969.

Lyons, Mary E., selector. *Raw Head, Bloody Bones: African-American Tales of the Supernatural.* New York: Scribner, 1991.

Neil, Philip, reteller. *Fairy Tales of Eastern Europe.* Boston: Houghton Mifflin, 1991.

Nic Leodhas, Sorche. *Thistle and Thyme: Tales and Legends from Scotland.* New York: Holt, Rinehart, and Winston, 1962.

Opie, Iona, and Peter Opie. *The Classic Fairy Tales.* New York: Oxford University Press, 1974.

Phelps, Ethel Johnson. *The Maid of the North: Feminist Folk Tales from Around the World.* New York: Holt, Rinehart, and Winston, 1981.

Schwartz, Alvin, reteller. *Ghosts!: Ghostly Tales from Folklore.* New York: Harper-Collins, 1991.

Schwarz, Howard, and Barbara Rush, retellers. *The Diamond Tree: Jewish Tales from Around the World.* New York: Harper-Collins, 1991.

Singer, Isaac Bashevis. *Zlateh the Goat and Other Stories.* New York: Harper, 1966. (Yiddish folktales)

Tehranchian, Hassan, adapter. *Kalilah and Dimnah: Fables from the Middle East.* New York: Harmony, 1985.

Wolkstein, Diane. *The Magic Orange and Other Haitian Folktales.* New York: Knopf, 1978.

Yeats, W. B., and Lady Gregory. *A Treasury of Irish Myth, Legend, and Folklore.* New York: Avenel, 1986.

Yep, Laurence, reteller. *Tongues of Jade.* New York: Harper-Collins, 1991. (Chinese)

Yolen, Jane, ed. *Favorite Folktales from Around the World.* New York: Pantheon, 1986.

Zipes, Jack, tr. *Beauties, Beasts, and Enchantment: Classic French Fairy Tales.* New York: Penguin, 1991.

———. *Spells of Enchantment: The Wondrous Fairy Tales of Western Culture.* New York: Viking, 1991.

Myths, Epics, and Legends

Colum, Padraic. *The Children of Odin: The Book of Northern Myths.* 1920. New York: Macmillan, 1984.

———. *The Children's Homer: The Adventures of Odysseus and the Tale of Troy.* 1919. New York: Macmillan, 1982.

———. *The Golden Fleece and the Heroes Who Lived Before Achilles.* 1921. New York: Macmillan, 1983.

Coolidge, Olivia. *Greek Myths.* Boston: Houghton Mifflin, 1949.

D'Aulaire, Ingri, and Edgar Parin D'Aulaire. *D'Aulaire's Book of Greek Myths.* New York: Doubleday, 1962.

Erdoes, Richard, and Alfonso Ortiz, eds. *American Indian Myths and Legends.* New York: Pantheon, 1984.

Goldston, Robert, reteller. *The Legend of the Cid.* Indianapolis: Bobbs-Merrill, 1963.

Green, Roger Lancelyn. *Heroes of Greece and Troy: Retold from the Ancient Authors.* Illus. Heather Copley and Christopher Chamberlain. New York: Walck, 1961.

Hieatt, Constance, reteller. *Sir Gawain and the Green Knight.* Illus. Walter Lorraine. New York: Crowell, 1967.

Highwater, Jamake. *Anpao: An American Indian Odyssey.* New York: Harper, 1977.

Kingsley, Charles. *The Heroes.* New York: Dutton, 1963.

MacLeod, Mary. *The Book of King Arthur and His Noble Knights.* Philadelphia: Lippincott, 1949.

Malcolmson, Anne, ed. *The Song of Robin Hood.* Boston: Houghton Mifflin, 1947.

McKinley, Robin. *The Outlaws of Sherwood.* New York: Greenwillow, 1988.

Philip, Neil. *The Tale of Sir Gawain.* Illus. Charles Keeping. New York: Philomel, 1987.

Pyle, Howard. *Some Merry Adventures of Robin Hood.* New York: Scribner's, 1954.

Sherwood, Merriam, tr. *The Song of Roland.* New York: McKay, 1938.

Sutcliff, Rosemary. *Beowulf.* London: Bodley Head, 1961. (Later published in the United States as *Dragon Slayer*)

———. *The Light Beyond the Forest: The Quest for the Holy Grail.* New York: Dutton, 1980.

Thompson, Brian. *The Story of Prince Rama.* New York: Viking, 1985.

Thompson, Vivian L. *Hawaiian Tales of Heroes and Champions.* New York: Holiday House, 1971.

Westwood, Jennifer, reteller. *Gilgamesh and Other Babylonian Tales.* New York: Coward McCann, 1970.

CHAPTER 9
Fantasy

DEFINITION OF FANTASY

What child has not been entranced by the enduring figures of the great fantasies—Alice, Dorothy and her loyal and motley companions, the irrepressible Mr. Toad of Toad Hall, Peter Pan, Wilbur the pig and Charlotte? These and other fantasy characters are fixed indelibly on the cultural consciousness of our society and have helped to shape our imaginations. It is difficult to exaggerate the influence that fantasy reading has on a young mind.

Fantasy may be simply defined as any story of the impossible, a tale including events that contradict the laws of the natural world; but we must distinguish it from folk literature, which is certainly the root of all fantasy. Whereas a folktale may have developed over several centuries and exists in many varied forms, a fantasy is an original story written by a specific author or authors. Fantasy is a *literary,* not an *oral,* creation. And although we can frequently find "retellings" or "adaptations" of fantasy stories—Walt Disney has adapted Grahame's *Wind the the Willows,* A. A. Milne's *Winnie-the-Pooh,* and Carroll's *Alice in Wonderland,* for example—it is possible to point to the original text and see what the author actually wrote. Because it is literary and not oral, fantasy tends to be more complex in structure than the folktale, with more character development and more detailed settings, and is generally more polished in literary style.

The first important fantasies specifically for children appeared in the nineteenth century. Hans Christian Andersen, in addition to retelling traditional tales, wrote original fairy stories heavily influenced by folk tradition. But it is Lewis Carroll's *Alice in Wonderland* that is remembered as one of the pioneers in book-length fantasy for children. (It is also considered one of the first books written primarily for the pleasure of children without heavy underlying didacticism.) Since that time, modern fantasy has prospered, producing some of the most memorable works of children's literature. Other early classics in modern fantasy for children include Carlo Collodi's *The Adventures of Pinocchio* (1881), Jules Verne's popular works of science fiction (*Twenty Thousand Leagues under the Sea* [1869] and others), L. Frank Baum's *The Wonderful Wizard of Oz* (1900), Kenneth Grahame's *The Wind in the Willows* (1908), and A. A. Milne's *Winnie-the-Pooh* (1926).

TYPES OF FANTASY

Fantasy comes in a wide variety of types, all with differing degrees of fantastic elements. There are many ways of classifying fantasy, and each classification method has its drawbacks. But, since fantasies, virtually by definition, contain some form of enchantment, some unreality, it makes a great deal of sense to classify fantasies according to the predominant type of enchantment. We will briefly consider some of the more common of these.

The Literary Fairy Tale

The traditional folktales have inspired modern counterparts—original tales by modern writers that have all the flavor of an old tale. Sometimes, unless we know the origin, it is difficult to distinguish between the literary fairy tale (the product of a specific author) and the oral folktale—and perhaps the writers of the literary fairy tales would take that as a sign of their success. Hans Christian Andersen was one of the earliest creators of the literary fairy tale, and he has proved one of the most enduring. His popularity inspired others, and, by the last half of the nineteenth century, many writers were experimenting with this form. George MacDonald's *The Light Princess* and *The Princess and the Curdie* and *The Princess and the Goblin* are all book-length works that we can label literary fairy tales. The literary fairy tale exhibits many of the same features as its oral counterparts: conventional settings in a distant "generic" kingdom, predominantly flat and stereotyped characters, an accepted magical element, and, of course, an inevitable happy ending. A modern variation on the literary fairy tale is a spoof or satire on the form, such as James Thurber's delightful *Many Moons,* which takes a comic twist. Satire results when writers feel a literary form has been exhausted and that it offers no other serious possibilities, consequently they begin to poke fun at it, and, in doing so, give the form a new lease on life.

Animal Fantasy

Animal fantasies focus on animals imbued with human traits. Young children are particularly fascinated by animals and, in fact, see them as possessing human characteristics: having familial relationships similar to humans, enjoying pleasures similar to humans, and going to some animal heaven when they die. So it is only natural that among the favorite fantasies of children are those with animals as the main characters.

There are essentially two ways that an author may present animal characters in a fantasy. Kenneth Grahame, in his classic *The Wind in the Willows,* creates animals who talk and behave almost entirely as humans. The animals live in houses (Mr. Toad inhabits a sprawling English manor house), use furniture and human modes of transportation, wear clothes, and even eat human food. So realistically does Grahame portray his characters that readers usually do not question the incongruity of a water rat and a mole eating cold chicken for a picnic lunch. Part of the success for this type of animal fantasy results from the author's creating an almost entirely animal world. However, Grahame does include enough of the animals' natural traits to separate them from the humans, who play a small role in the story and are generally treated satirically.

E. B. White, in his classic *Charlotte's Web,* depicts animals living in a predominantly human world. Hence, Wilbur the pig lives like a pig in a barnyard, eats like a pig, and generally has all the habits of a pig. The only difference between Wilbur and any other pig we might expect to find on a farm is that Wilbur (along with the other barnyard animals) can talk and has rather deep humanlike emotions. But Wilbur's power of speech is even restricted: Wilbur may be understood by his child friend Fern, but the animals never speak to adult humans. Charlotte, likewise, lives the life of a spider; we see her entrap a fly and suck its blood, for example, an activity that at first horrifies even Wilbur the pig. But, as is customary in animal fantasy, Wilbur and his friends exhibit human personality traits: Charlotte is kind and wise, Templeton is greedy and selfish, Wilbur is lovable, and so on. Nevertheless, White is bound more closely to the laws of nature than is Grahame, and we would be disturbed if Wilbur should suddenly take to wearing a spiffy jacket and top hat.

In all cases of animal fantasy, the premise is that the animals have human feelings, that we can emphathize with them, and that from their behavior we can learn something about ourselves and humanity in general. It is possible for us to draw significant conclusions about human behavior from reading either *The Wind in the Willows* or *Charlotte's Web.* By the same token, we learn very little reliable information about animal behavior. In other words, animal fantasy constitutes a form of literary symbolism, the animal characters symbolizing human counterparts, and these fantasies are often vehicles for exploring human emotions, values, and relationships.

Toy Fantasy

Similar to the animal fantasy, but with some distinct differences, is the *toy fantasy,* in which talking toys—usually dolls or stuffed animals—are the major characters. A frequent theme in the toy fantasy is the desire of the toys to become human. Collodi's *Pinocchio* is the classic of this type, in which the wooden puppet comes to life and wants nothing more than to become a real, live boy—a dream accomplished after a series of harrowing experiences that presumably make him worthy of the gift of life. Margery Nicholson's *The Velveteen Rabbit* is another perennial favorite with a similar theme, as is Leo Lionni's popular picture-book fantasy *Alexander and the Wind-up Mouse.* The implication is, of course, that it is much better to be a living, breathing human being than an inanimate object—although, curiously enough, the toys generally exhibit human traits before their magical transformations.

Other toy fantasies depict toys who are apparently contented with their lot, happy to interact with each other or with a loving child caretaker. A. A. Milne's *Winnie-the-Pooh* is a delightful example of this type of fantasy. Each of the toys, all of which are stuffed animals, has his or her own peculiar personality, and the prospect of becoming human is not a possibility (nor does it seem desirable). In another example of this type, Rachel Field's *Hitty, Her First Hundred Years,* the first-person memoirs of a doll over an entire century, we see some of the peculiar advantages of a toy protagonist, who can enjoy virtual immortality (barring wear and tear or natural disintegration, of course) and thereby witness the parade of history.

Eccentric and Extraordinary Characters

Many fantasies contain humor, but some fantasies rely on wild exaggeration and eccentricity for their effect rather than on any specific type of magic. Typically, the focus of the fantasy is an eccentric character, sometimes possessing magical powers, although not necessarily. An early example of this type is Lucretia Hale's *The Peterkin Papers.* These stories, written in the nineteenth century, are about the extraordinarily inept Peterkin family who must be extricated from their nonsensical predicaments by the conventional wisdom of the lady from Philadelphia. Their modern-day counterparts are Harry Allard and James Marshall's popular picture-book family, the Stupids, who, when a fuse is blown and their lights all go out, believe that they are dead.

These stories are closely related to the tall tale, a peculiarly American form of folklore deriving its strength from wildly fantastical exaggerations. Sid Fleischman is a master of the modern tall tale, and he has successfully developed the form into full-length books. His *The Ghost in the Noonday Sun* and *By the Great Horn Spoon!* are just two of his comical farces that skirt the border between fantasy and reality.

Some fantasies have as their focus a character who may possess some extraordinary power, such as P. L. Travers's *Mary Poppins,* about a nanny with an enchanted umbrella among other powers, or Astrid Lindgren's *Pippi Longstocking,* about an irrepressible young girl with extraordinary powers, or Hugh Loftis's *Dr. Doolittle,* who can communicate with the animals. These fantasies all emphasize the charm of eccentricity and the advantages of having the courage to be different. Since many are written for children in the middle grades when peer pressure to conform is at a peak, these stories may help to encourage a sense of individuality.

Enchanted Journeys and Imaginary Lands

The journey motif is one of the oldest in literature, going back to Homer's *Odyssey* and beyond. The great advantage to sending fictional characters on a journey is that the possibilities for plot variation are virtually endless. Everyone is familiar with those fantasies that take a character—almost always a child—from the Real World into an Other World, a sort of never-never land where all manner of wondrous things can occur. These fantasies are especially popular with younger readers, and some of these tales include the most famous books of childhood. Lewis Carroll's *Alice in Wonder-*

land, Frank Baum's *The Wizard of Oz,* Charles Kingsley's *Water Babies,* and James Barrie's *Peter Pan* come immediately to mind. The fantasy of the Enchanted Journey typically opens in the real world (also called the primary world); then, by some means or device—such as a cyclone or falling into a rabbit hole—the principal character enters the enchanted realm (the secondary world).

The journey may have some purpose (Dorothy wants to find the Emerald City and ultimately a way back home; Alice wants to find the Queen's Garden), but that purpose is usually overshadowed by the thrill and delight offered by the extraordinary events that can happen in the secondary world. The credibility of these stories is normally aided by the fact that the fanciful events can only happen in the secondary world and not in the primary world—the wicked witch has no authority in Kansas. The plots of these tales are frequently quite loose—sometimes episodic, simply stringing together a series of adventures—and we rely on the central character (the child human) to be our touchstone with reality. Alice and Dorothy judge everything they see in Wonderland and Oz, respectively, by the standards they knew at home.

Books such as William Pene du Bois's *Twenty-One Balloons* adhere more closely to reality—in fact, the island of Krakatoa, which constitutes the secondary world, did actually exist and was the site of one of history's greatest volcanic eruptions. Joan Aiken has written several fantasies that are quasi-historical, in that they are set in an eighteenth-century England that never was. *The Wolves of Willoughby Chase* and *Black Hearts of Battersea* are both melodramatic novels that include eccentric characters and inventive schemes that could succeed only in a fantasy. The Moomintroll fantasies by the Finnish writer Tove Janssen (who writes in Swedish) describe an entire fantasy world with marvelous creatures—some more or less human—who live in a gentle, distant valley with friends as peculiar as they are. (The Moomintroll family is introduced in *Tales from Moominvalley,* and their adventures are followed through nine books.)

Another type of secondary world is the land of miniaturized characters. Jonathan Swift is usually singled out as the prototype for this form, with his description of the journey to Lilliput in the first book of *Gulliver's Travels;* however, the adventures of the diminutive folktale hero, Tom Swift, predate *Swift.* Modern examples include L. Frank Baum's depiction of the Munchkins in *The Wonderful Wizard of Oz* and Mary Norton's *The Borrowers,* a tale of a family of miniature people living in the walls of a house (they are the ones responsible for all those items that inexplicably disappear). Carol Kendall's *The Gammage Cup,* about the struggles of the Minnipin society against their ancient enemies, the Mushroom People, contains many of the features of the heroic fantasy, just on a smaller scale. Young readers are attracted to these miniature worlds because they can identify with the diminutive characters, and because these stories often depict the clever triumph of the small and weak characters over the larger, but duller, bullies of the world.

Many fantasies, of course, cannot be so readily pigeonholed. Roald Dahl's *Charlie and the Chocolate Factory* and *James and the Giant Peach* combine elements of the fantasy of extraordinary character with enchanted journey. These journeys—one through a remarkable chocolate factory and the other across the Atlantic in an overgrown and magical peach—do not take us to a true secondary world, but demonstrate the fantastic possibilities in the primary world. In that sense, Dahl's work evokes a surrealistic quality that is at once fascinating and disturbing. The inventive fantasist will inevitably create his or her own special kind of fantasy.

Heroic or Quest Fantasy

Alice and Dorothy, although they perform several acts that might be interpreted as heroic, remain clearly grounded in the primary world, the touchstone against which the wonders of the fantasy world are measured. However, in the *heroic fantasy* (sometimes referred to as *quest fantasy* or *high fantasy*), we share the heroic exploits of a hero or heroine engaged in a monumental struggle against a seemingly all-powerful evil, and the fate of an entire civilization depends on the outcome of the struggle. Whereas the enchanted journey may be quite episodic, the heroic fantasy is often more tightly woven, with all the action directed toward a single end—the triumph of good over evil.

The presentation of the fantasy world may occur in one of three ways. Occasionally, heroic fantasies, such as Susan Cooper's *The Dark Is Rising* series, are set in the real (the primary) world, which is threatened by dark forces. In Cooper's series, most of the fantasy, although it takes place technically in the primary world, occurs on a psychological level understood only by certain "chosen" humans in the stories. In other heroic fantasies, the story begins in the primary world and contains a passage to the secondary world. C. S. Lewis's *The Lion, the Witch and the Wardrobe* is one of the best known examples, the children getting to the secondary world of Narnia through the back of an old wardrobe in a country house. (Passages to secondary worlds are not restricted to heroic fantasies, however. Alice's rabbit hole and looking-glass, and Dorothy's cyclone are among the most famous in literature.) And finally, many heroic fantasies, such as Ursula Le Guin's *Earthsea* cycle or Tolkien's *Lord of the Rings* trilogy, take place entirely in imaginary worlds inhabited by imaginary creatures (sometimes humanlike, sometimes not), in no way connected to the world as we know it. These works contain no passage between our world and the fantasy world, but focus on self-contained fictional worlds.

Heroic fantasies are most often structured around the hero's or heroine's *quest*—this frequently turns out to be a quest for identity, although the hero or heroine usually does not realize that at first. The fate of a nation or a people is often dependent upon the success or failure of the quest, and the hero or heroine becomes a figure of adulation and may even be rewarded with a crown by the story's end. The central character acts decisively, is altruistic, and eventually becomes the savior of a people. The plot typically consists of a series of remarkable *adventures*—usually impediments that the central character must overcome in order to achieve the quest. Because of the seriousness of the themes—the necessity for good to overcome evil, the defense of an entire society, the search for the rightful ruler, and so on—humor is either absent or a decidedly secondary element in heroic fantasy. (Lloyd Alexander's *Prydain* cycle, based on Welsh legend, is a good example of heroic fantasy employing comic elements, usually in the form of comic characters. However, the hero, even if sympathetic, is always quite serious.) Most heroic fantasies do not shy away from tragedy, and the message is frequently that good is not accomplished without some significant sacrifice. Heroic fantasy owes a great deal to the traditional märchen or wonder tales of folk literature, from which are derived themes, plot structures, even characters and settings. If we understand the folktales, we are more likely to understand heroic fantasy.

Supernatural and Time Fantasy

Supernatural and *time fantasy* are among the most popular of fantasy types, including ghost and witch stories, stories of the mysterious and unexplained occurrence, and stories of time travel—explained or otherwise. All are set in the primary world, and the fantasy element is often seen as a disturbing aspect that must be corrected before the story ends.

Ghost stories are perennial favorites with many young people. Robert Bright's *Georgie and the Robbers* is a picture book about a shy ghost, and the cartoon figure of Casper the Friendly Ghost has a long history. But older children often prefer more threatening ghosts; indeed, the more horrifying and gruesome the story is, the better some seem to like it. Many people have deep within them something of the ambulance chaser. Nevertheless, the best tales of the supernatural are not those that dramatize and glamorize the blood and horror. Perhaps the most thrilling tales are those that leave something to our imaginations. The finest supernatural stories do not capitalize on the horror, but explore the possibilities offered by the presence of the supernatural. Penelope Lively's *The Ghost of Thomas Kempe* is a popular and well-told example of a modern ghost story. Devoid of any grisly horror, Lively's novel explores the potential problems that a ghost from an earlier time might have in adapting to the modern world.

Sometimes a fantasy story will introduce a supernatural object, such as the magic stone in Penelope Farmer's book of that name, in which two children are able to enter bodily into any picture (an oil painting, a photograph, and so on). Lynn Reid Banks's *The Indian in the Cupboard* introduces a magical cupboard that turns toys into living creatures.

Related to the supernatural tales are those stories that involve playing tricks with time—a ghost, after all, is simply a human presence operating in a time other than that in which it lived. Philippa Pearce's *Tom's Midnight Garden* explores movement in and out of time, and deals sensitively and seriously with human relationships. In a similar vein are Lucy Boston's *Green Knowe* books and Alan Garner's *Owl Service,* the latter of which is a somewhat sophisticated tale of the occult, drawing on mysterious ancient powers.

Science Fiction and Space Fantasy

Mary Shelley's *Frankenstein* (1818) is usually credited with being the first true work of *science fiction,* followed by the works of Jules Verne (*Twenty Thousand Leagues Under the Sea* and *From Earth to the Moon Direct*), which achieved great popularity in the mid-nineteenth century. Today science fiction has a following among young readers who make up in enthusiasm what they may lack in actual numbers. Science fiction is speculative writing—usually focusing on life in the future, either on earth or on some other planet. (When the setting is the present, the plot depends upon some presumably advanced, and often secret, science or technology.) Much of science fiction is devoted to dramatizing the wonders of technology (although science fiction is usually not especially scientific). Science fiction, in fact, closely resembles heroic fantasy, with magic being replaced by technology, and the plots often unfold mighty struggles between the forces of good and evil, with the fate of civilization hanging in the balance. As one critic notes, "How different, after all, is a wizard with a magic wand from a scientist with a microminiaturized matter-transformer? The reader does not know how either gadget works" (Roberts 90).

There is typically as little humor in science fiction as in heroic fantasy, because the science fiction writer often wants to create the illusion that the world depicted is a world of possibility. There is no room for flippancy or lightheartedness. (The exception may be science fiction written for the younger reader from six to eight years old; these works are largely space travel adventures—Ruthven Todd's *Space Cat*—or perhaps robot stories—Lester Del Rey's *The Runaway Robot.*)

Some works we categorize as science fiction may be better termed *space fantasy.* This is the term preferred by Sylvia Engdahl, whose *Enchantress from the Stars* and *The Far Side of Evil,* among other works, are set in the future on distant planets, but otherwise are little concerned with scientific or technological achievements. Engdahl's works, despite their futuristic setting, are usually preferred by readers who are not science fiction buffs. Engdahl treats her futuristic setting as simply the framework through which she conveys her sense of the development of human civilization, socially and psychologically rather then scientifically and technologically.

There is, in fact, a strong didactic strain in science fiction, and many works deal with ethical problems facing humanity as science and technology progress, but human ethical values do not. Consequently, the question as to whether technological discoveries will be used for humanity's benefit or for its destruction frequently becomes a theme of science fiction. Madeleine L'Engle, best known for *A Wrinkle in Time,* addresses such issues in her science fiction.

SPECIAL CHARACTERISTICS OF FANTASY

Regardless of the type, Zilpha Snyder suggests that there are two things children demand from fantasy —that it contain no nonsense and that it contain no treachery (230). These, at first, may appear to be curious requirements, but they are quite important. Even though fantasy presents situations that we know to be impossible, we do expect them to be presented as if they *were* possible. Consequently, children insist that writers of fantasy establish certain rules that operate within the fantasy world itself, and that the writers abide by those rules. Also, children insist that the fantasy not be unfairly taken away at the book's end (such as pretending that it never happened, that it was all a dream, and so on). Such a betrayal on the writer's behalf usually generates a groan from readers. After all, part of the readers' delight in fantasy is that of being completely absorbed into the fantasy, and, once having made that commitment, readers do not like to find out that it has all been a trick or an elaborate deception. For example, the implication at the end of the MGM movie of *The Wizard of Oz* is that the entire adventure was just a dream, but Baum played no such trick on his readers. In the original book, Dorothy *really* went to Oz and back. Baum wants us to believe in that magical land, and so do we want to believe.

Originality

In addition to the general characteristics that we expect of all fiction, we expect good fantasy to meet some special requirements. Perhaps above all, we expect fantasy to be *original.* From a stylistic point of view, neither *The Wizard of Oz* nor *Peter Pan* is particularly well written, but the ideas in these works are so imaginative and so original that the stories remain with us throughout our lives. The characters of good fantasy—Alice, Mr. Toad of Toad Hall, Winnie-the-Pooh, the Scarecrow and the Tin Woodsman—remain indelibly marked in our minds and we inevitably measure every new character against these mainstays.

Believability

Secondly, we expect good fantasy to be *believable.* This may sound contradictory, but, in fact, fantasy may have to seem more believable than a realistic work. Readers want to believe in the fantasy, and we often resent it when an incompetent writer includes something that we immediately recognize as silly. ("Silly" is, of course, a relative term. We tolerate certain behavior in a toy fantasy such as *Winnie-the-Pooh* that we would not tolerate in C. S. Lewis's heroic fantasy *The Lion, the Witch, and the Wardrobe.* It is the writer who, in the creation of the fantasy, sets the limits of silliness, and those limits must not be overstepped.) A good writer achieves believability in fantasy by several means.

1. *The massing of detail* provides us with vivid descriptions of things seen and heard, and when we can visualize the scenes we are more apt to believe that the fantasy world does indeed exist. Whereas folktales are virtually devoid of physical description, fantasies are often lush with details, and the writers make the fantasies believable by fleshing them out and giving them substance.
2. *Maintaining consistency* is essential in good fantasy. Rules are established in every secondary world—there is only one way to get into the fantasy world, drinking from a certain fountain bestows immortality, the villain can be killed only by a special sword, and so on. The writer must abide by whatever rules are established.
3. *Restraining the fantastic* may sound contrary to the whole notion of fantasy, but, in fact, the good fantasy knows its limits. A fantasy in which "anything goes" is really no fun. The wizards in Le Guin's Earthsea cycle possess magical powers, but those powers are made more believable because they have their limitations, and Le Guin, once creating those limitations, makes sure her characters do not exceed these bounds.
4. Finally, good fantasy is rooted in *reality* and in *human nature.* Even if the characters are not human or not of this world, the good fantasist realizes that readers are human and that if the readers are to identify with the characters and the situations, they must be, disguised or otherwise, human characters and situations. Mr. Toad of Toad Hall may look like a toad, but he acts like a human and has human weaknesses. Winnie-the-Pooh, toy though he is, is capable of human adventures and

even human responses to those adventures (despite his protest that he is only a bear of little brain). Most fantasy, despite its wondrous dress, is imbued with a strong sense of reality and a deep seriousness. The imaginary world captures us; the underlying reality of it all moves us.

THE REWARDS OF FANTASY

Fantasy holds many treasures for us, not the least of which is the stimulation of our imaginations. Fantasy writer Joan Aiken has summarized what she sees to be the practical value of a developed imagination (in "On Imagination"). In addition to amusing us, Aiken points out our imagination keeps us hopeful, enabling us to see the myriad possibilities that life offers. It helps us to solve problems by allowing us to see things from different and fresh perspectives. It helps us see the points of view of others, thus serving as a check to fanaticism. Aiken goes further to suggest that the imagination is a bit like a muscle—if we do not exercise it, it becomes weak and ineffectual. Reading is the best way of exercising our imaginations. Although Aiken does not suggest that reading fantasy is a better exercise of the imagination than reading realism or nonfiction, we can safely say that fantasy does require a bit *more* exercise. Fantasy demands more of the reader than does realistic fiction, for fantasy creates not only its own characters and plots, but also its own peculiar set of laws with which we as readers must become acquainted.

Through the medium of fantasy, writers are able to explore complex ideas on a symbolic level that would be difficult to convey to young readers otherwise. Natalie Babbitt's *Tuck Everlasting* can cause us to think of the implications of immortality on earth, its advantages and disadvantages, in a way that would be impossible for a realistic story, and tedious in a nonfictional treatise. Fantasy is perfectly suited to the thoughtful exploration of philosophical issues at a level that can be understood and appreciated by the child reader. Fantasy deliberately challenges our perceptions of reality and forces us to explore new, uncharted realms of thought. And for those who are ready to accept the challenges fantasy presents us, the rewards can be manifold.

RECOMMENDED READINGS

Aiken, Joan. "On Imagination." *The Horn Book* (November/December 1984): 735–41.

Alexander, Lloyd. "High Fantasy and Heroic Romance." *Horn Book Magazine* 47: 6 (December 1971): 577–84.

Attebery, Brian. *The Fantasy Tradition in American Literature: From Irving to Le Guin.* Bloomington, IN: Indiana University Press, 1980.

Babbitt, Natalie. "Fantasy and the Classic Hero." *School Library Journal* (October 1987): 25–29.

Cameron, Eleanor. *The Green and Burning Tree.* Boston: Little, Brown, 1969.

Dickinson, Peter. "Fantasy: The Need for Realism." Children's Literature in Education 17: 1 (1986): 39–51.

Egoff, Sheila. *Worlds Within: Children's Fantasy from the Middle Ages to Today.* Chicago: American Library Association, 1988.

Engdahl, Sylvia. "The Changing Role of Science Fiction in Children's Literature." *Horn Book Magazine* 47: 5 (October 1971): 449–55.

Hume, Kathryn. *Fantasy and Mimesis.* New York and London: Methuen, 1984.

Le Guin, Ursula. *The Language of the Night.* Ed. Susan Wood. New York: G. P. Putnam's Sons, 1979.

Lewis, C. S. "Three Ways of Writing for Children." *Horn Book Magazine* 39: 5 (October 1963): 459–69.

Marcus, Leonard S. "Picture Books Animals: How Natural a History?" *The Lion and the Unicorn* 7/8 (1983/84): 127–39.

Raynor, Mary. "Some Thoughts on Animals in Children's Books" *Signal* 29 (May 1979): 81–87.

Roberts, Thomas J. "Science Fiction and the Adolescent." *Children's Literature: The Great Excluded* 2 (1973): 87–91.

Sale, Roger. *Fairy Tales and After: From Snow White to E. B. White.* Cambridge, MA: Harvard University Press, 1978.

Singer, Jerome. "Fantasy: The Foundation of Serenity." *Psychology Today* (July 1976): 33–37.

Snyder, Zylpha Keatley. "Afterword." *Tom's Midnight Garden* by Philippa Pearce. New York: Dell, 1986: 230–32.

Tolkien, J. R. R. *Tree and Leaf.* Boston: Houghton Mifflin, 1965.

Waggoner, Diana. *The Hills of Faraway: A Guide to Fantasy.* New York: Atheneum, 1978.

Wood, Michael. "Coffee Break for Sisyphus: The Point of Science Fiction." *New York Review of Books* 2 (October 1975): 3–4, 6–7.

SELECTED BIBLIOGRAPHY OF FANTASY FICTION

Literary Fairy Tales

Andersen, Hans Christian. *The Emperor and the Nightingale.* Tr. Eva LeGallienne. Illus. Nancy Burckert. New York: Harper, 1965.

———. *The Steadfast Tin Soldier.* Illus. David Jorgensen. New York: Knopf, 1986.

Babbitt, Natalie. *The Search for Delicious.* New York: Farrar, Straus & Giroux, 1969.

Enright, Elizabeth. *Tatsinda.* Illus. Irene Haas. New York: Harcourt, 1963.

Gardner, John. *Dragon, Dragon and Other Tales.* New York: Knopf, 1975.

Grahame, Kenneth. *The Reluctant Dragon.* Illus. Ernest Shepard. New York: Holiday, 1923.

MacDonald, George. *The Light Princess.* Illus. Maurice Sendak. New York: Farrar, Straus & Giroux, 1969.

———. *The Princess and the Curdie.* New York: Penguin, 1973.

Thurber, James. *Many Moons.* Illus. Louis Slobodkin. New York: Harcourt, 1943.

Yolen, Jane. *The Emperor and the Kite.* Illus. Ed Young. Cleveland: World, 1967.

Animal Fantasies

Adams, Richard. *Watership Down.* New York: Macmillan, 1974.

Ets, Marie Hall. *Mister Penny.* New York: Viking, 1935.

Grahame, Kenneth. *The Wind in the Willows.* 1908. (Several modern editions.)

Jarrell, Randall. *The Animal Family.* Illus. Maurice Sendak. New York: Pantheon, 1965.

King-Smith, Dick. Ace: *The Very Important Pig.* New York: Crown, 1990.

Lawson, Robert. *Rabbit Hill.* New York: Viking, 1944.

————. *The Tough Winter.* New York: Viking, 1970.

Marshall, James. *Rats on the Roof and Other Stories.* New York: Dial, 1991.

O'Brien, Robert. *Mrs. Frisby and the Rats of NIMH.* New York: Atheneum, 1971.

Rey, Hans A. *Curious George.* Boston: Houghton Mifflin, 1941.

Selden, George. *The Cricket in Times Square.* Illus. Garth Williams. New York: Farrar, Straus & Giroux, 1960.

Sharp, Margery. *The Rescuers.* Boston: Little, Brown, 1959.

Steig, William. *Abel's Island.* New York: Farrar, Straus & Giroux, 1976.

Titus, Eve. *Basil in Mexico.* Illus. Paul Galdone. New York: McGraw-Hill, 1976.

White, E. B. *Charlotte's Web.* New York: Harper, 1952.

————. *Stuart Little.* New York: Harper, 1945.

————. *The Trumpet of the Swan.* New York: Harper, 1970.

Toy Fantasies

Bailey, Caroline Sherwin. *Miss Hickory.* New York: Viking, 1968.

Clarke, Pauline. *The Return of the Twelves.* New York: Coward-McCann, 1964. (British title: *The Twelve and the Genii*)

Collodi, Carlo (pseud. for Carlo Lorenzini). *The Adventures of Pinocchio.* 1883. (Several modern editions.)

Field, Rachel. *Hitty, Her First Hundred Years.* New York: Macmillan, 1929.

Godden, Rumer. *The Dolls' House.* New York: Viking, 1962.

————. *Impunity Jane.* New York: Viking, 1964.

Hoban, Russell. *The Mouse and His Child.* New York: Harper, 1967.

Lionni, Leo. *Alexander and the Wind-Up Mouse.* New York: Pantheon, 1969.

Milne, A. A. *The House at Pooh Corner.* 1928. Illus. Ernest Shepard. New York: Dutton, 1961.

————. *Winnie-the-Pooh.* 1926. Illus. Ernest Shepard. New York: Dutton, 1961.

Nicholson, Margery. *The Velveteen Rabbit.* Illus. Michael Hague. New York: Holt, Rinehart & Winston, 1983.

Eccentric Beings and Extraordinary Characters

Allard, Harry. *The Stupids Step Out.* Boston: Houghton Mifflin, 1974.

Atwater, Richard, and Florence Atwater. *Mr. Popper's Penguins.* Illus. Robert Lawson. Boston: Little, Brown, 1938.

Dahl, Roald. *Charlie and the Chocolate Factory.* New York: Knopf, 1964.

————. *James and the Giant Peach.* New York: Knopf, 1961.

Farmer, Penelope. *The Summer Birds.* New York: Harcourt, 1962.

Fleischman, Sid. *By the Great Horn Spoon!* Boston: Little, Brown, 1963.

————. *Humbug Mountain.* Boston: Little, Brown, 1978.

Hale, Lucretia. *The Peterkin Papers.* 1880. Boston: Houghton Mifflin, 1960.

Kastner, Erich. *The Little Man.* Tr. James Kirkup. Illus. Rick Schreiter. New York: Knopf, 1966.

Lindgren, Astrid. *Pippi Longstocking.* New York: Viking, 1950.

Lofting, Hugh. *The Adventures of Dr. Doolittle.* Philadelphia: Lippincott, 1920.

Merrill, Jean. *The Pushcart War.* Reading, MA: Scott/Addison, 1964.

Travers, P. L. *Mary Poppins.* New York: Harcourt, 1934.

Enchanted Journeys and Imaginary Lands

Aiken, Joan. *Black Hearts in Battersea.* New York: Doubleday, 1964.

———. *The Wolves of Willoughby Chase.* New York: Doubleday, 1963.

Barrie, Sir James. *Peter Pan.* New York: Scribner's , 1950.

Baum, L. Frank. *The Wonderful Wizard of Oz.* 1900. (Several modern editions.)

Carroll, Lewis. *Alice's Adventures in Wonderland.* Illus. John Tenniel. London: Macmillan, 1984.

Du Bois, William Pene. *Twenty-One Balloons.* New York: Viking, 1947.

Fleischman, Sid. *The Midnight Horse.* New York: Morrow, 1990.

———. *The Whipping Boy.* New York: Morrow, 1986.

Janssen, Tove. *Comet in Moominland.* Tr. Elizabeth Portch. 1961. New York: Farrar, Straus & Giroux, 1990.

———. *Moominsummer Madness.* Tr. Thomas Warburton. 1964. New York: Farrar, Straus & Giroux, 1991.

Juster, Norton. *The Phantom Tollbooth.* New York: Random, 1961.

Kendall, Carol. *The Gammage Cup.* New York: Harcourt, 1959.

Kingsley, Charles. *The Water Babies.* New York: Watts, 1961.

Lagerlof, Selma. *The Wonderful Adventures of Nils.* 1906. New York: Doubleday & Page, 1907.

Norton, Mary. *The Borrowers.* New York: Harcourt, 1953.

Pedley, Ethel C. *Dot and the Kangaroo.* Sidney, Australia: Cornstalk, 1925.

Steele, Mary Q. *Journey Outside.* New York: Viking, 1969.

Townsend, John Rowe. *The Fortunate Isles.* New York: Lippincott, 1989.

Heroic Fantasies

Alexander, Lloyd. "The Prydain Chronicles," (New York: Holt): *The Book of Three* (1964); *The Black Cauldron* (1965); *The Castle of Llyr* (1965); *Taran Wanderer* (1967); *The High King* (1968).

Cooper, Susan. *"The Dark Is Rising"* series (New York: Atheneum): *Over Sea, Under Stone* (1966); *The Dark Is Rising* (1973); *Greenwitch* (1974); *The Grey King* (1975).

Doyle, Debra, and James D. Macdonald. *Knight's Wyrd.* New York: Harcourt, 1992.

Le Guin, Ursula. "The Earthsea Cycle" (New York: Atheneum): *A Wizard of Earthsea* (1968); *The Tombs of Atuan* (1971); *The Farthest Shore* (1972); *Tehanu: The Last Book of Earthsea* (1990).

Lewis, C. S. "The Narnia Chronicles" (New York: Macmillan): *The Lion, the Witch, and the Wardrobe* (1950); *Prince Caspian, The Return to Narnia* (1951); *The Voyage of the "Dawn Treader"* (1952); *The Silver Chair* (1953); *The Horse and His Boy* (1954); *The Magician's Nephew* (1954); *The Last Battle* (1956).

McCaffrey, Anne. *Dragondrums.* New York: Atheneum, 1979.

———. *Dragonsinger.* New York: Atheneum, 1977.

———. *Dragonsong.* New York: Atheneum, 1976.

McKinley, Robin. *The Hero and the Crown.* New York: Greenwillow, 1985.

Mayne, William. *Antar and the Eagles.* New York: Delacorte, 1990.

Tolkien, J. R. R. *The Hobbit.* Boston: Houghton, Mifflin, 1938. (Followed by the *Lord of the Rings* trilogy)

Yolen, Jane. *Dragon's Blood.* New York: Delacorte, 1982.

Supernatural and Time Fantasies

Aiken, Joan. *A Foot in the Grave.* New York: Viking, 1992.

Banks, Lynn Reid. *The Indian in the Cupboard.* New York: Doubleday, 1981.

Babbitt, Natalie. *Tuck Everlasting.* New York: Farrar, Straus & Giroux, 1975.

Boston, Lucy. *The Children of Greene Knowe.* New York: Harcourt, 1964.

Cameron, Eleanor. *The Court of the Stone Children.* New York: Dutton, 1973.

Cobalt, Martin (pseud. for William Mayne). *Pool of Swallows.* New York: Nelson, 1974.

Dunlop, Eileen. *Elizabeth, Elizabeth.* New York: Holt, 1977.

———. *The Valley of Deer.* New York: Holiday, 1989.

Farmer, Penelope. *A Castle of Bone.* New York: Philomel, 1982.

———. *Charlotte Sometimes.* New York: Harcourt, 1969.

Garfield, Leon. *Mister Corbett's Ghost.* New York: Pantheon, 1968.

———. *The Restless Ghost: Three Stories.* New York: Pantheon, 1969.

Garner, Alan. *The Owl Service.* New York: Walck, 1968.

Hamilton, Virginia. *Sweet Whispers, Brother Rush.* New York: Philomel, 1982.

Lively, Penelope. *The Ghost of Thomas Kempe.* Illus. Antony Maitland. New York: Dutton, 1973.

Mayne, William. *Earthfasts.* New York: Dutton, 1967.

———. *A Game of Dark.* New York: Dutton, 1971.

Morgan, Helen. *The Witch Doll.* New York: Viking, 1992.

Nesbit, E. *The Enchanted Castle.* Harmondsworth, Middlesex: Penguin, 1979.

Norton, Mary. *Bed-Knob and Broomstick.* Illus. Erik Blegvad. New York: Harcourt, 1957.

Pearce, Philippa. *Tom's Midnight Garden.* New York: Dell, 1986.

Pearson, Kit. *A Handful of Time.* New York: Viking, 1988.

Price, Susan. *Ghost Song.* New York: Farrar, Straus & Giroux, 1992.

Westall, Robert. *The Devil on the Road.* New York: Greenwillow, 1979.

Yolen, Jane, and Martin H. Greenberg, eds. *Things That Go Bump in the Night: A Collection of Original Stories.* New York: Harper, 1989.

Science Fiction and Space Fantasy

Cameron, Eleanor. *Wonderful Flight to the Mushroom Planet.* Illus. Robert Henneberger. Boston: Little, Brown, 1954.

Clarke, Arthur C. *Dolphin Island.* New York: Holt, 1963.

Christopher, John. *The White Mountains.* New York: Macmillan, 1967.

Del Rey, Lester. *The Runaway Robot.* Philadelphia: Westminster, 1965.

Dickinson, Peter. *Eva.* New York: Delacorte, 1989.

Engdahl, Sylvia. *Enchantress from the Stars.* New York: Macmillan, 1970.

———. *The Far Side of Evil.* New York: Macmillan, 1971.

Hamilton, Virginia. *Justice and Her Brothers.* New York: Greenwillow, 1978.

Heinlein, Robert. *Have Space Suit—Will Travel.* New York: Scribner's, 1958.

Lawrence, Louise. *Moonwind.* New York: Harper, 1986.

L'Engle, Madeleine. *A Wrinkle in Time.* New York: Farrar, Straus & Giroux, 1962.

Norton, Andre. *Moon of Three Rings.* New York: Viking, 1966.

Rubenstein, Gillian. *Beyond the Labyrinth.* New York: Watts, 1990.

Sleator, William. *Strange Attractors.* New York: Dutton, 1989.

Todd, Ruthven. *Space Cat.* Illus. Paul Galdone. New York: Scribner's, 1952.

Verne, Jules. *Twenty Thousand Leagues Under the Sea.* 1864. New York: Penguin, 1987.

Wells, H. G. *The Time Machine.* New York: Bantam, 1982.

———. *War of the Worlds.* New York: Putnam, 1978.

CHAPTER 10

Realistic Fiction

DEFINITION OF REALISTIC FICTION

Stories of life in the real world can be as exciting as any fantasy, as the readers of *Treasure Island* or *The Adventures of Huckleberry Finn* well know. They can also be thought-provoking and emotionally moving, as the readers of *The Secret Garden* or *Roll of Thunder, Hear My Cry* well know. *Realistic fiction* consists of those stories set in the world as we know it, governed by the laws of the natural world as we understand them, and intended to provide a believable verisimilitude to life as we experience it. This is in contrast to fantasy, which ignores the natural laws and establishes its own set of rules. The appeal of realistic fiction resides in its ability to give us a vision of the human condition and to help us to either identify or empathize with the characters and their predicaments.

Although by definition realistic fiction is a story that is *possible*, it need not always be especially *probable*. Realistic fiction may contain very ordinary or quite exaggerated characters and mundane or preposterous plots, but it does not violate the essential rules of nature. Reality is its touchstone. Consequently, realistic fiction presents us with an artist's view of the world we live in.

TYPES OF REALISM

Equally as diverse as fantasy, realism comes in a wide variety of forms, and it is possible to find realistic books on virtually every imaginable subject. We can identify some broad classes of realism; however, the lines are not easily drawn, and we often find a work that, because of the writer's inventiveness and ingenuity, refuses to fit neatly into a single category. Just as we have classified fantasy according to the predominant fantasy element in the story, we will classify realistic fiction according to the principal focus of the realistic element. The following classification will suggest the wealth of realistic fiction available to young readers between the ages of about eight and sixteen.

Adventure and Survival Stories

The oldest type of fictional story is undoubtedly the adventure story, going back to the earliest novels, Cervantes's *Don Quixote,* Defoe's *Robinson Crusoe,* and Swift's *Gulliver's Travels* (all of which have proven popular in one form or another among children). The adventure story is characterized by exciting, fast-moving plots; unusual, often bizarre, characters; and frequently exotic settings. The characters are often sharply defined, with strong and daring heroes and dastardly villains. The nineteenth century was rife with hack writers who cranked out formulaic adventure books primarily for boys. But some very fine stories were written as well, with thoughtful themes and well-drawn characters. Stevenson's *Treasure Island,* and Mark Twain's *Huckleberry Finn* and *Tom Sawyer* are classic adventure stories.

The best of the modern adventure stories are probably the *survival stories,* adventures that focus on an individual or individuals pitted usually against the forces of nature, which the protagonist must either outwit or (more likely) unite with in order to survive. Daniel Defoe's *Robinson Crusoe* is often regarded as the granddaddy of the survival story. But whereas Defoe has his hero taming the wild tropical paradise in which he finds himself (and his story has much of the flavor of romance), twentieth-century survival stories depict their heroes or heroines humbled before the forces of nature. The native girls, Karana in Scott O'Dell's *Island of the Blue Dolphins* (set on an island off the California coast) and Julie in Jean Craighead George's *Julie of the Wolves* (set in the arctic wilds), even adopt the ways of the wild animals inhabiting their environment. Instead of controlling nature, these brave protagonists learn to live with it—and, of course, the implication is that civilized people can learn much from these experiences. Theodore Taylor's *The Cay* and Harry Mazer's *Snowbound* and *The Island Keeper* are other examples of this popular form of fiction, with Mazer's works representing a combination of the adventure story with the problem novel.

The *mystery,* perhaps first popularized in the early nineteenth century by Edgar Allan Poe and later by Arthur Conan Doyle, the creator of Sherlock Holmes, has long been a favorite kind of adventure story for young readers. Such serial detective stories as Nancy Drew, the Hardy Boys, the Bobbsey Twins, and Donald Sobol's *Encyclopedia Brown* series are enormously popular. The mystery always involves the solving of a puzzle—typically, but not necessarily, a crime—and, consequently, depends heavily upon plot intricacy and clever twists. The success of a mystery depends upon the clever planting of clues and the ingenuity of the crime and its solution. Although most of the characters in mysteries tend to be stereotypes—the principal interest is, after all, in the plot—some writers enrich their tales by creating memorable detectives, usually with exaggerated personalities (such as Agatha Christie's Miss Marple or Hercule Poirot). There are examples of exceptionally fine mysteries for young people. E. L. Konigsburg's *From the Mixed-Up Files of Mrs. Basil E. Frankweiler* recounts the exploits of a young brother and sister detective as they follow clues to the unravelling of a mystery, largely set in the Metropolitan Museum of Art. And Ellen Raskin's *The Westing Game* likewise depicts a young detective searching out the word clues of a cleverly devised mystery, containing numerous surprising twists. Both of these works won the coveted Newbery Medal for the best American literary work for young people in their respective years of publication. Virginia Hamilton's *The House of Dies Drear* may be regarded as a mystery of sorts, weaving suspense into a tale of the discovery of African-American heritage. Hamilton has the uncanny ability to take seemingly ordinary people and places, and weave an almost magical story. Her characters are so richly developed that we come to believe in even the most bizarre of them.

Domestic Realism or Family Stories

The next popular form of fiction to be developed was the family story or domestic realism, which shares some common ground with the eighteenth century domestic romance focusing on the everyday manners, customs, and mores of English society. It is probably only natural that young readers should be interested in reading stories about home and family, since those are the principal focuses of their childhood experiences. The British author Charlotte Yonge is usually credited with writing the first domestic novel for young people: *The Daisy Chain* (1862). But the American writers were the ones who ultimately became most comfortable with this type, beginning with Louisa May Alcott's *Little Women* (1867). Alcott, drawing on her own girlhood experiences, presents us with a realistic portrayal of mid-nineteenth-century American family life with all its ups and downs. For Alcott, the family is a constant source of strength and stability, the parents are idealized role models, and the troubles of the outside world are kept at bay by the family's industry and good humor.

Alcott's successors (and there were many) include Margaret Sidney, author of the once enormously popular *The Five Little Peppers and How They Grew.* Unlike Alcott, Sidney was not able to restrain the sentimental, and her story of the destitute, but virtuous, Pepper family is too saccharine for most modern readers. The children are all self-sacrificing and dutiful, always doing more than their fair share for the family's well-being. The mother seems to draw strength from her poverty, and no one ever complains. Their patience and goodness are rewarded in the end with the almost miraculous bestowal of good fortune. In response to the public demand of that time, Margaret Sidney wrote numerous sequels.

Similar books for young readers include Johanna Spyri's *Heidi,* Eleanor Porter's *Pollyanna,* and Kate Douglas Wiggin's *Rebecca of Sunnybrook Farm,* all of which are highly sentimentalized portraits of young girls (rarely boys) of incredible goodness who bring much needed happiness to the adult world. That these were all the subjects of romantic movies of the 1930s, when the world was in the throes of the Great Depression, suggests their escapist qualities. Frances Hodgson Burnett's *The Secret Garden* is a refreshing change from the overly sweet domestic romance, for her heroine, Mary, is initially a rather unpleasant child placed in an even more unpleasant home—that of her wealthy, but very mysterious, uncle. It is the story of Mary's "humanization"—something she learns, not surprisingly, from the example of a large, and ecstatically happy, rustic family who lives nearby. *The Secret Garden* contains mystery and suspense, as well as engaging characters, making it one of the most enduring of childhood stories, and it is also difficult to pigeonhole, for although it celebrates the virtues of family life, it certainly is not a domestic tale in any traditional sense.

The Canadian writer L(ucy) M(aud) Montgomery created an equally appealing character in *Anne of Green Gables* and its sequels, set on Prince Edward Island in the first decade of the twentieth century. Anne is an orphaned child who is placed in a foster home with an elderly brother and sister who originally wanted a boy. The book combines sensitively drawn characters and gentle humor, while avoiding sentimentality.

Two notable writers, Eleanor Estes (of the *Moffat* series) and Elizabeth Enright (of the *Melendy* series), produced successful domestic fiction in the 1930s and 1940s. Both take a romantic view of the family and present us with households that, even though on the brink of poverty, are filled with warmth and caring. Both writers adopt the episodic plot, with the individual chapters loosely connected by some overriding theme. Estes's works might almost be considered historical fiction, for she sets them in the 1910s; whereas Enright's stories are set in the period contemporary with their writing—the 1940s.

In the 1950s and 1960s, writers such as Beverly Cleary (*Ramona the Pest* and *Ramona the Brave,* among others) and Madeleine L'Engle (*Meet the Austins* and others) continued the tradition of Estes and Enright, depicting stable family units knit together with love. But with the dramatic change in the family structure in the latter half of the twentieth century, the romantic family scenes described by Estes, Enright, Cleary, and L'Engle are becoming rare in literature—particularly in books for older readers. Today we more commonly find, in place of the happy family unit once exemplified by such television programs as "Father Knows Best," "The Donna Reed Show," and "Leave It to Beaver," stories of emotionally charged situations, broken homes, and nontraditional domestic arrangements. Cleary herself recognized and adapted to this transformation with her Newbery Award–winning book, *Dear Mr. Henshaw,* about a young boy coping with his parents' divorce. Bill and Vera Cleaver's *Where the Lilies Bloom* describes the trials of an Appalachian family of poor, orphaned children, who survive and are held together chiefly through the valiant efforts of the thirteen-year-old middle sister. Virginia Hamilton's *M. C. Higgins, the Great,* also about a mountain family—this one African American— likewise addresses the issues of family survival and family pride in the face of an increasingly insensitive technological world. Robert Newton Peck's *A Day No Pigs Would Die,* an account of a Shaker boyhood in New England of the late 1920s, reveals the clash of cultures as the simple Shaker life is challenged by the rapidly advancing world around it. Katherine Paterson's *Jacob Have I Loved* is the story of the tenuous relationship between twin sisters, focusing primarily on the emotional growth of one of the twins, who must come to terms with herself as well as with the rest of her family.

The trend of the domestic novel in the twentieth century has been toward greater realism and less sentimentality. This change has been inevitably necessitated by the changing nature of the family—a perfect example of the response of art to life.

Social Realism

Charles Dickens was certainly one of the fathers of social realism in fiction, with his portrayal of the seedy side of nineteenth-century England. Social realism focuses on societal problems—poverty, crime, education, working conditions, corruption—and how those problems affect the characters in the novel. It could be argued that the nineteenth-century writer of boy's success stories, Horatio Alger, Jr., was a pioneer in writing social realism for young people, with his stories of children growing up in the poverty of America's big cities. His heroes generally succeeded in gaining respectability (which is what they always wanted) largely because they were morally upright individuals.

However, social realism for young people has really come into its own in the latter half of the twentieth century, which has produced many decidedly unromantic works openly examining the important social issues facing the world. Some of the domestic novels we noted above actually transcend the distinction between domestic fiction and social realism. *Where the Lilies Bloom* can be read as a treatise on the plight of the rural poor and Mildred Taylor's *Roll of Thunder, Hear My Cry,* a moving account of the struggles of an African-American family in rural Mississippi in the 1930s, explores bigotry in our society. Some novels dealing with social issues take on the appearance of survival fiction. In an age when technology threatens the individual's sense of identity and, at times, even the nature of society and civilization as we know it, we may feel that growing up in a city slum or an Appalachian hovel is as much a challenge as being abandoned on a desert island or in the frozen arctic reaches.

Typically, the novels of social realism offer hope amid the struggle, although the message is usually that, if hardship is to be overcome, it will be through perseverance and determination, and not through some fortuitous event that sheds rich blessings upon the protagonist. Published in 1967, S. E. Hinton's *The Outsiders,* about the plight of inner city youth plagued by poverty and lack of guidance, was one of the books heralding what has come to be called the new realism. The new realism is characterized by frankness, absence of sentimentality, and, in some cases, a diminishing of hope. Robert Cormier's novels (including *I Am the Cheese, The Chocolate War, Beyond the Chocolate War,* and *Bumblebees Fly Anyway*) take a much bleaker look at society than most books for young people. In his works, adults and children alike may be depicted in the worst possible light—self-serving, vicious, unscrupulous, even downright evil. Society as Cormier paints it takes on an Orwellian flavor—Big Brother is watching every move, spies lurk around every corner and even infiltrate the sanctity of the home. Adults criticize Cormier's unhappy—even grimly depressing—endings but he has remained a consistently popular novelist with adolescents, proving once again that adults have underestimated the capacity of the young to deal with serious issues.

Psychological Novels and Problem Novels

The psychological novel is a product of the twentieth century—we could not have had it without the development of the science of psychology. The psychological novel focuses on a single individual's emotional reaction and adjustment to life's experiences. To be sure, psychological issues are often intermingled with societal issues—the rising divorce rate (a social phenomenon) has resulted in the need for emotional adjustment on the part of children from broken homes (a psychological issue). Nevertheless, it is possible to identify books whose primary focus is on the individual's response to specific personal crises or other problems, whereas the novel of social realism is more universal in its treatment. Psychological novels tend to be for older readers and are written on a somewhat more sophisticated plane, containing neither much of a social message (as we come to expect from the novels of social realism) nor the implication that every problem has a solution (as we come to believe from many problems novels, to be discussed below). Instead, they reveal life in all its fascinating complexity. Writers such as Irene Hunt (in *Up a Road Slowly*) Katherine Paterson (in *The Great Gilly Hopkins* and *A Bridge to Terabithia*) and Zibby Oneal (in *The Language of Goldfish* and *In Summer's Light*) sensitively explore the personal difficulties facing young people in the process of maturing, but more importantly, there is the implicit faith in the resilience and ultimate good sense of young people. Most, if not all, fiction for young readers ultimately is about the rites of passage, the initiation into adulthood (or into advancing stages of adolescence). But this initiation is the special focus of the psychological novel, the goal of which is to present an honest account of that passage as the writer sees it.

Almost an invention of the 1960s, the problem novel typically focuses on a single issue of immediate concern to young people—parents' divorce, the first date, the onset of puberty, adjusting to a new home, teenage pregnancy, drugs, homosexuality, and so on. Unlike the family story or domestic novel, where the family is often a source of strength or a haven from the rigors of the outside world, the problem novel usually depicts the family as either helpless or, just as likely, part of the problem. Consequently, the problem novel is a reflection of the perceived breakdown of the modern family structure (although we should note that the breakdown of the American family has been predicted since at least the Civil War). The solutions, therefore, come from outside the home—perhaps from a sympathetic adult or even a peer.

But the problem novel also represents an acknowledgement of the abilities of young people to face up to and effectively cope with serious troubles. Even for the very young we may find books, such as Charlotte Zolotow's *William's Doll* (about a boy's very natural desire to have a doll and the worries of his rather conventional father), which explore the problems of personal development. (See Chapter 4 for a discussion of concept picture books on these issues.) For readers in the middle and upper grades, such books as Judy Blume's *Are You There, God? It's Me, Margaret* (focusing in part on a girl's coming to terms with menstruation and the psychological confusion surrounding it), Betsy Byars's *The Summer of the Swans* (about mental retardation), Robert Lipsyte's *One Fat Summer* (about obesity), and Norma Klein's *Mom, the Wolf Man and Me* (about an illegitimate child's adjusting to her mother's marriage) are just a few examples of some of the popular titles in this category and of the range of topics problem novels explore.

The problem novel is extremely popular with many adolescents. They easily identify with the characters, their feelings and predicaments. Problem novels have been used as part of bibliotherapy, a process by which young people are assisted in coping with personal problems through directed reading, and there is evidence that bibliotherapy can be effective as a means of coping. On the other hand, there is the notion that problem novels themselves often encourage a rather self-indulgent attitude (see, especially, Nodelman, 1981). Teenagers, according to this theory, read only about other teenagers just like themselves who suffer the same traumas as they do, and this results in an inflated view of their problems. In other words, rather than giving them a fresh outlook on the problems, the books allow them to wallow in self-pity that eventually narrows instead of widens their world. However, it should be pointed out here that teenagers often have an inflated view of their own tribulations—the books they read do not create that dilemma. Perhaps a truly effective bibliotherapy is one which expands the reader's experiences, broadens the reader's minds, and thus multiplies the reader's possible responses to problems.

At its worst, the problem novel becomes formulaic, predictable, sometimes sensationalized, and often implies that problems have simple solutions. At its best, the problem novel explores significant psychological and sociological issues with sensitivity, and it gives us vivid characters with depth of emotion.

Realistic Animal Stories

Realistic animal stories first appeared in the late nineteenth and early twentieth centuries (most earlier animal stories were fantasies, dating back to ancient Greece and the fables of Aesop), and they originated in North America. Canadians Ernest Thompson Seton (*Wild Animals I Have Known*) and Charles G. D. Roberts (*Red Fox*) wrote stories depicting animals realistically, but giving them personalities. Jack London's popular *White Fang* and *Call of the Wild* soon followed. The animals in these stories live as animals, behave as animals, and are not empowered with human speech (although some readers may argue they are given human emotions).

Of course, young readers have always had particularly soft spots for animals of all kinds. Animal stories have proved to be among the most enduring of modern children's literature and are the frequent inspirations for the cinema. Often these books focus on the relationship between an animal and a youthful human companion, such as in Marjorie Kinnan Rawlings's *The Yearling*, or Mary O'Hara's *My Friend Flicka* and Eric Knight's *Lassie Come-Home*, the popular story of a heroic collie.

Farley Mowat's comical true-life adventures in *Owls in the Family* would be found in the nonfiction section of the library, since it is autobiographical, and is an excellent example of the sometimes fine line that exists between fiction and reality. One of the most loved of all is Wilson Rawls's *Where the Red Fern Grows*, about two hunting dogs and their boy master. Marguerite Henry's books about horses, *Misty of Chincoteague, King of the Wind,* and others, remain among the best animal stories in the realistic tradition.

Some animal stories focus on the animal and not on the animal-human relationship. One early Newbery Award–winner, Dhan Gopal Mukerji's *Gayneck, the Story of a Pigeon,* keeps its focus on the central animal character. Among the best known of these is Sheila Burnford's *The Incredible Journey,* in which a cat and two dogs undertake a hazardous trip across the Canadian wilderness. Some readers feel that Burnford oversteps the limits of credulity, with the animals assuming too much of human nature to be totally believable animals. This criticism suggests one of the difficulties of writing realistic animal fiction. But for many readers, making the animal characters too human is a minor technical flaw that does not essentially detract from the appeal of the story.

SPECIAL CHARACTERISTICS OF REALISTIC FICTION

Coming of Age

It might be argued that every realistic novel for young people is a novel of coming of age. Since its underlying theme is the struggle we all face when growing up. In most realistic novels, we see the protagonist having grown— socially or psychologically or spiritually or intellectually—by the end of the story. Another step toward maturity has been taken. Huckleberry Finn knows a great deal more about people and love and hate at the end of his story than he did at the beginning. It is often that the protagonist is, as the cliché goes, sadder but wiser, and at the end of the story embarks on a new stage of life, more capable and more self-assured. In most books for young readers, the protagonist does not completely mature, but only takes another step in that continuing process. (Do we ever completely mature?) This step is usually in the form of greater independence, of making decisions, of accepting responsibilities.

The Need for Others

But just as maturing means achieving a degree of independence, it also means acknowledging our need for others. Human beings are essentially social animals. Most of us learn, sooner or later, that life is considerably easier if we learn to live, work, and play with others. Many child protagonists grow from isolation and distrust to a reaching out, an acknowledgement of this social need. The recognition of this need for others is the story of Leigh Botts in Beverly Cleary's *Dear Mr. Henshaw,* as Leigh struggles to adjust to his parents' divorce and learns to put his trust in others once again. Realistic stories often depict protagonists learning to embrace the world.

THE VALUE OF REALISTIC FICTION

It should be obvious by now that realistic fiction for children is a rich and complex field, burgeoning with ideas and ready to serve a variety of purposes. The purpose of this chapter has been to look at the nature of realistic fiction and how writers address the many issues that children face or will face in this increasingly diverse and rapidly changing world. Writers are both philosophers and artists, and they mean to stimulate our thinking as well as satisfy our need for aesthetic pleasure. The novelist tells us a good story—we insist on that first of all. The novelist also shares with us a vision of the world and asks us to respond. We do not have to agree with this vision, but we do have to think about it, examine it in relation to our own lives, and ultimately make some decision about it. Perhaps the most valuable thing about children reading is that it results in children thinking.

RECOMMENDED READINGS

Abrahamson, Jane. "Still Playing It Safe: Restricted Realism in Teen Novels." *School Library Journal* 22 (May 1976): 38–39.

Dickinson, Peter. "In Defense of Rubbish." *Children's Literature in Education* 3 (November 1970): 7–10.

Ellis, Anne W. *The Family Story in the 1960's.* New York: Archon, 1970.

Frye, Northrup. *The Educated Imagination.* Bloomington, IN: Indiana University Press, 1964.

Hinton, S. E. "Teenagers Are for Real." *New York Times Book Review* 27 (August 1967): 26–29.

Hipple, T., and B. Bartholomew. "The Novels College Freshmen Have Read." *ALAN Review* (Winter 1982): 8–10.

Kingston, Carolyn. *The Tragic Mode in Children's Literature.* New York: Teachers College Press, 1974.

McDowell, Miles. "Fiction for Children and Adults: Some Essential Differences." *Children's Literature in Education* 10 (March 1973): 50–63.

Mertz, Maia Pank, and David A. England. "The Legitimacy of American Adolescent Fiction." *School Library Journal* 29 (October 1983): 119–23.

Moran, Barbara B., and Susan Stienfirst. "Why Johnny (and Jane) Read Whodunits in Series." *School Library Journal* (March 1985): 113–17.

Nixon, Joan Lowry. "Clues to the Juvenile Mystery." *The Writer* 90 (February 1977): 23–26.

Nodelman, Perry. "How Typical Children Read Typical Books." *Children's Literature in Education* 12 (Winter 1981): 177–85.

Paterson, Katherine. *Gates of Excellence: On Reading and Writing Books for Children.* New York: Elsevier/Nelson, 1981.

———. *The Spine Heart: More Thoughts on Reading and Writing Books for Children.* Chicago: American Library Association, 1989.

Peck, Richard. "Some Thoughts on Adolescent Literature." *News from ALAN* (September/October 1975): 4–7.

Rees, David. *The Marble in the Water.* Boston: The Horn Book, 1980.

———. *Painted Desert, Green Shade: Essays on Contemporary Writers for Children and Young Adults.* Boston: The Horn Book, 1984.

Soderbergh, Peter A. "The Stratemeyer Strain: Educators and the Juvenile Series Book, 1900–1980." In *Only Connect.* Eds. Sheila Egoff, G. T. Stubbs, and L. F. Ashely. 2nd ed. New York: Oxford, 1980, 63–73.

Wilkin, Binnie Tate. *Survival Themes in Fiction for Children and Young People.* New York: Scarecrow, 1978.

SELECTED BIBLIOGRAPHY OF REALISTIC FICTION FOR CHILDREN

The following list is representative of realistic fiction classified according to the categories outlined in this chapter. It is necessary to remember that many books quite easily fit into more than one category. This is only a sampling; look for other books by these authors as well.

See also the bibliography following Chapter 13 for other works of realistic fiction that focus on various cultural groups. Many of the books on this list also deal with a variety of world cultures.

Adventure Fiction (Including Mysteries and Survival Stories)

Corcoran, Barbara. *A Star to the North.* Philadelphia: Lippincott, 1970.

Konigsburg, E. L. *From the Mixed-Up Files of Mrs. Basil E. Frankweiler.* New York: Atheneum, 1967.

George, Jean Craighead. *Julie of the Wolves.* New York: Harper, 1972.

————. *My Side of the Mountain.* New York: Dutton, 1959.

Holman, Felice. *Slake's Limbo.* New York: Scribner's, 1974.

Houston, James. *Frozen Fire.* New York: Atheneum, 1977.

————. *Long Claw: An Arctic Adventure.* New York: Atheneum, 1981.

Mazer, Harry. *The Island Keeper.* New York: Delacorte, 1981.

————. *Snowbound.* New York: Dell, 1973.

Raskin, Ellen. *The Westing Game.* New York: Dutton, 1978.

O'Dell, Scott. *Island of the Blue Dolphins.* Boston: Houghton Mifflin, 1960.

Shecter, Ben. *Inspector Rose.* New York: Harper, 1969.

Sobol, Donald. *Encyclopedia Brown Saves the Day.* Nashville, TN: Nelson, 1970.

Speare, Elizabeth George. *The Sign of the Beaver.* Boston: Houghton Mifflin, 1983.

Stevenson, Robert Louis. *Treasure Island.* 1883. (Various modern editions.)

Streiber, Whitley. *Wolf of Shadows.* New York: Knopf, 1985.

Taylor, Theodore. *The Cay.* New York: Doubleday, 1969.

Twain, Mark. *The Adventures of Huckleberry Finn.* 1884. (Various modern editions.)

————. *The Adventures of Tom Sawyer.* 1876. (Various modern editions.)

Watson, Harvey. *Bob War and Poke.* Boston: Houghton Mifflin, 1991.

Westall, Robert. *The Kingdom by the Sea.* New York: Farrar, 1991.

Domestic Realism or Family Stories

Alcott, Louisa May. *Little Women.* 1868–69. (Various modern editions.)

Burnett, Francis Hodgson. *The Secret Garden.* 1909. (Various modern editions.)

Cleary, Beverly. *Ramona the Pest.* New York: Morrow, 1968.

Enright, Elizabeth. *Thimble Summer.* New York: Holt, 1938.

Estes, Eleanor. *The Moffats.* New York: Harcourt, 1941.

Fitzhugh, Louise. *Harriet the Spy.* New York: Harper, 1964.

Gates, Doris. *Blue Willow.* New York: Viking, 1940.

Hermes, Patricia. *Mama, Let's Dance.* Boston: Little, 1991.

Hunt, Irene. *Up a Road Slowly.* New York: Follett, 1967.

L'Engle, Madeleine. *Meet the Austins.* New York: Vanguard, 1960.

Lowry, Lois. *Attaboy, Sam!* Boston: Houghton Mifflin, 1992.

MacLachlan, Patricia. *Cassie Binegar.* New York: HarperCollins, 1982.

————. *Journey.* New York: Delacorte, 1991.

————. *Sarah, Plain and Tall.* New York: Harper, 1985.

Montgomery, L. L. *Anne of Green Gables.* (Various modern editions.)

Namioka, Lensey. *Yang the Youngest and His Terrible Ear.* Boston: Little, Brown, 1992.

Paterson, Katherine. *Jacob Have I Loved.* New York: Crowell, 1980.

Peck, Robert. *A Day No Pigs Would Die.* New York: Knopf, 1972.

Porter, Eleanor. *Pollyanna.* 1913. (Various modern editions.)

Sawyer, Ruth. *Roller Skates.* New York: Viking, 1936.

Sidney, Margaret. *The Five Little Peppers and How They Grew.* 1880. (Various modern editions.)

Sorenson, Virginia. *Miracles on Maple Hill.* New York: Harcourt, 1956.

Spyri. Johanna. *Heidi.* 1884. (Various modern editions.)

Voight, Cynthia. *Dicey's Song.* New York: Atheneum, 1982.

Wiggin, Kate Douglas. *Rebecca of Sunnybrook Farm.* (Various modern editions.)

Social Realism

Armstrong, William. *Sounder* New York: Harper, 1969.

Bonham, Frank. *Durango Street.* New York: Dutton, 1965.

——— . *The Nitty Gritty.* New York: Dutton, 1968.

Childress, Alice. *A Hero Ain't Nothin' but a Sandwich.* New York: Coward, 1973.

Cleaver, Bill, and Vera Cleaver. *Where the Lilies Bloom.* Philadelphia: Lippincott, 1969.

Cormier, Robert. *Beyond the Chocolate War.* New York: Knopf, 1985.

——— . *The Bumblebee Flies Anyway.* New York: Pantheon, 1983.

——— . *The Chocolate War.* New York: Pantheon, 1974.

——— . *I Am the Cheese.* New York: Dell, 1977.

Fox, Paula. *How Many Miles to Babylon?* Port Washington, NY: White, 1967.

Graham, Lorenz. *North Town.* New York: Crowell, 1965.

Hamilton, Virginia. *The Planet of Junior Brown.* New York: Macmillan, 1971.

Hicyilmaz, Gaye. *Against the Storm.* Boston: Little, Brown, 1992. (Set in modern Turkey.)

Hinton, S. E. *The Outsiders.* New York: Viking, 1967.

Hunter, Kristen. *Soul Brothers and Sister Lou.* New York: Scribner's, 1958.

Lipsyte, Robert. *The Brave.* New York: HarperCollins, 1991.

Myers, Walter Dean. *Me, Mop, and the Moondance Kid.* New York: Dell, 1985.

Spinelli, Jerry. *Maniac Magee.* Boston: Little, Brown, 1990.

Taylor, Mildred. *Roll of Thunder, Hear My Cry.* New York: Dial, 1976.

Zindel, Paul. *The Pigman.* New York: Harper, 1968.

The Psychological Novel (Including the Problem Novel)

Avery, Gillian. *Maria Escapes.* New York: Simon, 1992. (Originally published in 1957 in England as *The Warden's Niece.*)

Avi. *Nothing but the Truth: A Documentary Novel.* New York: Watts, 1991.

Blume, Judy. *Are You There, God? It's Me, Margaret.* New York: Bradbury, 1970.

——— . *Tiger Eyes.* Scarsdale, NY: Bradbury, 1981.

Byars, Betsy. *Summer of the Swans.* New York: Viking, 1970.

Cleary, Beverly. *Dear Mr. Henshaw.* New York: Morrow, 1983.

Daly, Maureen. *Seventeenth Summer.* New York: Dodd, 1942.

Danziger, Paula. *The Cat Ate My Gymsuit.* New York: Delacorte, 1974.

Greene, Bette. *Summer of My German Soldier.* New York: Dial, 1973.

——— . *Philip Hall Likes Me. I Reckon Maybe.* New York: Dial, 1974.

Honeycutt, Natalie. *Ask Me Something Easy.* New York: Watts, 1991.

Klein, Norma. *Mom, the Wolfman and Me.* New York: Patheon, 1972.

Konigsburg, E. L. *Jennifer, Hecate, Macbeth, William McKinley, and Me, Elizabeth.* New York: Atheneum, 1967.

Lipsyte, Robert. *One Fat Summer.* New York: Harper, 1977.

Lowry, Lois. *A Summer to Die.* Boston: Houghton Mifflin, 1977.

Oneal, Zibby. *The Language of Goldfish.* New York: Random House, 1980.

———. *In Summer Light.* New York: Viking, 1985.

Peck, Richard. *Secrets of the Shopping Mall.* New York: Delacorte, 1979.

Paterson, Katherine. *The Great Gilly Hopkins.* New York: Crowell, 1978.

Smith, Doris Buchanan. *A Taste of Blackberries.* New York: Crowell, 1973.

Voigt, Cynthia. *A Solitary Blue.* New York: Atheneum, 1983.

Wilson, Budge. *The Leaving.* New York: Philomel, 1992.

Realistic Animal Stories

Burnford, Sheila. *The Incredible Journey.* Boston: Little, Brown, 1961.

Byars, Betsy. *The Midnight Fox.* New York: Viking, 1968.

Cleary, Beverly. *Socks.* New York: Morrow, 1973.

DeJong, Meindert. *Hurry Home, Candy.* New York: Harper, 1953.

Gates, Doris. *Little Vic.* New York: Viking, 1951.

George, Jean. *The Cry of the Crow.* New York: Harper, 1980.

Gipson, Fred. *Old Yeller.* New York: Harper, 1956.

Griffiths, Helen. *The Greyhound.* New York: Doubleday, 1964.

———. *The Wild Heart.* New York: Doubleday, 1963.

Henry, Marguerite. *King of the Wind.* New York: Rand, 1948.

———. *Misty of Chincoteague.* New York: Rand, 1947.

Kjelgaard, Jim. *Big Red.* New York: Holiday, 1956.

James, Will. *Smoky, the Cow Horse.* New York: Scribner's, 1926.

London, Jack. *The Call of the Wild.* 1903. (Various modern editions.)

Mowat, Farley. *Owls in the Family.* Boston: Little, Brown, 1962.

Mukerji, Dhan Gopal. *Gayneck, the Story of a Pigeon.* New York: Dutton, 1927.

Naylor, Phyllis Reynolds. *Shiloh.* New York: Atheneum, 1991.

Rawlings, Marjorie Kinnan. *The Yearling.* New York: Scribner's 1938.

Rawls, Wilson. *Where the Red Fern Grows.* New York: Doubleday, 1961.

CHAPTER 11

Historical Fiction and Biography

Combining historical fiction with biography may seem like the proverbial mixing of apples and oranges, and indeed, there is good justification for including historical fiction with realistic fiction. They are included together here because both biography and historical fiction depend heavily upon a good story, an evocative atmosphere, and a depiction of the social milieu of the period, and at times both rely on the effective commingling of fact with fiction. Both are important in encouraging young readers to examine their heritage and in demonstrating the fundamental similarity of human thoughts and feelings regardless of the time and place.

DEFINITION OF HISTORICAL FICTION

Historical fiction consists of stories set in the past, usually realistic, although in the past thirty years there has been a trend toward combining historical fiction with other types of fiction, so we can find historical fantasy (as in Joan Aiken's *The Black Hearts of Battersea*), historical tall tales (as in Sid Fleischman's *By the Great Horn Spoon!*), and historical mystery stories (as in Leon Garfield's *Footsteps*). The distinguishing feature of historical fiction is that it seeks to recreate the aura of a time past, reconstructing characters, events, movements, ways of life, and the spirit of a bygone day. It is important to note that not all works set in the past can be strictly considered historical novels. Stevenson's *Treasure Island*, for example, is set in the 1740s the text tells us, but indeed very little in the book distinguishes the time period—the story would scarcely change if it were moved a hundred years backward or forward. The time period seems clearly incidental, so long as it is during an era of sailing ships. In true historical fiction, the time period is at the core of the story, and the writer assumes an obligation to recreate the historical flavor of an era.

Historical fiction often fits into one of the other classes of fiction we have identified. It may be, for instance, a domestic novel, such as Patricia MacLachlan's beautiful tale, *Sarah, Plain and Tall,* a unified work—albeit a very brief one—that sensitively explores the perceptions and feelings of a pioneer girl as she adjusts to a new stepmother (an experience all too common in the old West). Or it may be a psychological novel, such as Elizabeth George Speare's *The Witch of Blackbird Pond* (about a young woman's integration into New England life in colonial New England). Or it may be an adventure story, such as Leon Garfield's *Smith* and *The Drummer Boy* or Rosemary Sutcliff's *Mark of the Horse Lord.* Or it may be suggestive of social realism, such as Irene Hunt's *Across Five Aprils* (about the hardships caused by the Civil War), or Yoshikko Uchida's *Journey to Topaz* (the story of the Japanese-American internment during World War II), or Paula Fox's *The Slave Dancer* (about American slave trade in the 1840s), or James and Christopher Collier's *My Brother Sam Is Dead,* and Esther Forbes's *Johnny Tremain* (both about the Revolutionary War). Historical fiction is a rich field and includes some of the finest writing for young people.

THE DEVELOPMENT OF HISTORICAL FICTION

Historical fiction and fantasy both sprang from the romantic movement of the early nineteenth century, and both appeal to the romantic desire to escape from the present. The late nineteenth century saw a flowering of historical fiction for children, beginning with Charlotte Yonge's *The Dove in the Eagle's Nest* (1866) and including such popular writers as G. A. Henty and R. L. Stevenson (in such novels as *Kidnapped,* which, unlike *Treasure Island,* is appropriately labeled historical fiction). Rudyard Kipling's *Puck of Pook's Hill* (1906) is rightly considered an historical time travel fantasy. In the United States, most nineteenth-century writers of historical fiction looked to American history for their inspiration, but the most famous of them all, Howard Pyle, drew on medieval settings in *The Merry Adventures of Robin Hood* and *Otto of the Silver Hand.*

With the First World War, historical fiction fell into decline, perhaps partly as a result of the disillusionment resulting from that conflict. A revival occurred in the 1930s, and for the next thirty or more years historical fiction flourished. Unlike much of pre–World War I historical fiction, which tended to be idealized and steeped in patriotic sentiment, the later works were less romantic. Historical fiction became more eclectic, drawing on the histories of various cultures from ancient Ethiopia (Elizabeth Coatsworth's *The Princess and the Lion*) to Roman Britain (Rosemary Sutcliff's *The Lantern Bearers*) to the Spanish explorations of sixteenth-century America (Scott O'Dell's *The King's Fifth*). Many historical novels won major book awards and enjoyed great popularity. But the 1970s saw the youth rebellion and the subsequent rejection of the past and an insistence on "relevance." All this cast shadows on history in general and on the historical novel in particular. The genre has not yet recovered its former popularity, although some of the finest children's books written today are historical novels.

The most successful of modern historical novels are those that attempt to reassess and understand the past, rather than to extol it. In contrast to celebrating the patriotic glory of the Revolutionary War, Christopher and James Lincoln Collier paint a far more cynical picture in *My Brother Sam Is Dead.* Mildred Taylor reveals the ugliness of racial injustice in the South of the 1930s in *Roll of Thunder, Hear My Cry.* And many powerful stories of the inhumanity and sacrilege of the Second World War have been published, some of them fictional (Lois Lowry's *Number the Stars*) and others based on firsthand accounts (Aranka Siegal's *Upon the Head of the Goat: A Childhood in Hungary, 1939–1944*).

SPECIAL CHARACTERISTICS OF HISTORICAL FICTION

Unobtrusive History

Historical fiction depends heavily on a believable and reasonably accurate setting and often includes actual historical personages, but it is *not* history. The events are creations of the author's imagination. Unlike fiction set in contemporary times, historical fiction must provide considerably more background for the novice reader. The more remote and unfamiliar the historical period, the more background the author must supply, including political and social history, customs, and even psychological attitudes (it is unlikely, for example, that an ancient Egyptian slave or medieval peasant would wholeheartedly embrace a democratic way of life). Additionally, the writer must be aware of the state of science and technology during the period covered in a historical novel. For instance, an author of contemporary fiction need not explain modern methods of preserving food for us, because most of us already know that we just throw it in the freezer. But when writing about the American frontier of the mid-nineteenth century, a writer might have to describe briefly an ice house or the methods of preserving meat, such as salting or smoking.

On the other hand, readers are not reading the book primarily to learn about such things; the writer's task is instead to include such information as unobtrusively as possible. Joan Blos, herself a writer of some fine historical fiction (*A Gathering of Days* and *Brothers of the Heart*), has noted some of the pitfalls writers of historical fiction should avoid: overloading the text with historical background information, having characters reveal information in an artificial and inappropriate fashion, or using language unsuited to the historical time ("The Overstuffed Sentence" 38–39). The apparatus of writing, in other words, should never get in the way of the story.

Of course, we must remember that historical fiction is more fiction than history. What most young readers look for first is simply a good story. If it happens to be staged in ancient Egypt, so be it. But then this is the advantage of historical fiction over historical fact: The writer can create a work of art that is both pleasurable and informative. So the good story is indeed the first requisite for good historical fiction.

Authenticity

If historical fiction is not going to give us the flavor of the historical period, then it might as well be set in contemporary times. We expect the atmosphere to be authentic, to evoke the period, be filled with the sights, sounds, smells, and textures of the historical period. So Marguerite de Angeli opens her novel of medieval England, *The Door in the Wall,* with "Robin drew the coverlet close about his head and turned his face to the wall. He covered his ears and shut his eyes, for the sound of the bells was deafening. All the bells of London were ringing the hour of Nones" (1949, 7).

Part of the flavor of a period is the language the people speak. We know that nineteenth-century Americans did not speak the same way that twentieth-century Americans do. The following brief passage from Irene Hunt's Civil War story, *Across Five Aprils,* clearly shows how certain language is acceptable and even appropriate in historical fiction that would be out of place in a contemporary story:

> The young man got to his feet grinning. "Sure, Red, glad to oblige. Hear you been blowin' off at the mouth at some of the cracker-barrel heroes agin."
> Milton shrugged. "Word gets around fast."
> "Ben Harris was in fer a minute." The young man shook his head. "You jest ain't goin' to be happy till you git dressed up in tar and feathers, are you, Red?" (1986, 78)

The passage refers, of course, to an actual nineteenth-century practice of covering undesirable people with tar and feathers—a not-too-subtle means of public chastisement.

This brings us to another aspect of authenticity, and that is faithfulness to the facts. Historical fiction is not bound by the same rules as historical writing, but to be effective and not dismissed as purely fanciful, historical fiction ought to give us a fair depiction of the society. Only satire or nonsense would tolerate a story about George Washington plotting out Revolutionary War strategy on a computer. But the conscientious writer of historical fiction is meticulous in the use of details faithful to the period, and a great deal of research goes into this kind of writing. The writer must read not only other historical works about the period, but, when possible, read material written during the period—letters, newspapers, documents, books. Only in this way can a writer acquire a sense of what it may have been like to live in the era.

Sensitivity

Finally, an issue of which we have been increasingly aware is the need for writers to view history with a new sensitivity. White supremacy and nineteenth-century imperialism are no longer the accepted norm. We can only hope that never again will insensitive American Westerns depict idealized cowboys and gunfighters and savage, dehumanized Indians. The capable writer of historical fiction recognizes the nature of the historical period and, rather than romanticizing it, provides a balanced and intelligent viewpoint. Ignorance and prejudice have no place in any writing for children, but they can be especially unfortunate in historical fiction. Regrettably, we find virtually no works of historical fiction for children about the lands outside of Europe and North America—few novels exist about historical Africa or South America or India, for example. We can hope that in the future, budding writers will see the unexplored possibilities in this field.

THE REWARDS OF HISTORICAL FICTION

Historical fiction can give us a greater sense of and appreciation for the past. We are compelled to believe that humanity can learn from the mistakes of the past. This is why it is important that our children know of the Holocaust, for example, and the merciless killing of six million innocent Jews by Hitler during the 1930s and 1940s—the subject of Lowry's moving Newbery Award–winning *Number the Stars.* This is why it is important that our children learn of the reprehensible treatment by the European Americans of the Native Americans (the subject of Scott O'Dell's *Sing Down the Moon* and others) and the African Americans (the subject of Paula Fox's *The Slave Dancer*). Are these historical episodes we want repeated? Historical fiction can introduce young readers to humanity's past and insist that they look at the present with a new, enlightened perspective.

Perhaps readers are never too young to enjoy historical fiction. There are many enjoyable picture books that are also historical fiction (children in preschool and early elementary school have not yet been persuaded that history is dull and dry—and let us hope they never are). Brinton Turkle's *Thy Friend, Obadiah,* Cynthia Rylant's *When I Was Young in the Mountains,* and Donald Hall's *The Ox-Cart Man* are all examples of historical fiction for the very young. Of course, very young children have little conception of chronology, and many children will be unaware that these stories take place in the past (or they may be unaware of what the past is altogether). But this should not deter us from giving children this introduction.

It is not until about the middle years (from about seven or eight years and older) that children acquire a sense of the passage of time. Laura Ingalls Wilder's *Little House* books, published in the 1930s and 1940s, drew on the author's own childhood experiences from the latter half of the nineteenth century. Technically classified as fictionalized autobiography, these books combine the features of survival fiction with the family story, using the theme of familial love and the interdependence of humanity, and the whole work is underpinned by a tremendous sense of time and place—the Middle West and the Great Plains in the days of the American Western Frontier. Wilder does not hesitate to expose the grim side of that hard life, but the pervasive mood is highly romantic, and there is always the hint of nostalgic feeling that life in those simpler pioneer days was somehow better than it is today.

We may summarize by saying that a good piece of historical fiction:

1. tells a good story,
2. conveys the flavor of the historical period,
3. authentically captures the people of the period, their values, and their habits,
4. uses dialogue to make the characters sound authentic but not artificial,
5. faithfully uses historical knowledge to avoid distorting history,
6. fairly and sensitively portrays different sides of the compelling issues of the period, and
7. gives us insight into contemporary problems as well as helps us understand the problems of the past.

Historical fiction forms one of the great treasure houses of literature for children.

DEFINITION AND DEVELOPMENT OF BIOGRAPHY

A *biography* is a nonfictional work describing the life—or part of the life—of an individual. When a person writes the story of his or her own life, we call the work an *autobiography*. Biographies are among the most popular of nonfiction books for young people. We separate our discussion of biographies from other nonfiction primarily because biographies (and autobiographies) have traditionally been regarded as a sort of subgenre of literature, unlike other informational books. The biographer Paul Murray Kendall notes that biography lies between history and literature—and has never been fully embraced by either (3). Nevertheless, biography is a very old genre—the Gospels, in fact, are among the earliest biographies, describing, as they do, the life of Christ. And today biography has a devoted following (perhaps smaller than we should wish). In biographies we are reminded of the common thread of humanity that runs through us all. Biography can inspire us with portraits of the indomitable human spirit, or it can arouse us from complacency with portraits of human malice and insensitivity. The good biography probably does a little of both.

This century has seen many fine writers—both for children and adults—earn their literary reputations as biographers (Esther Forbes, Jean Fritz, James Daugherty, Ingri and Edgar Parin d'Aulaire, and Russell Freedman are just a few of the most famous biographical writers for young people). The field of biography has grown to yield a rich and varied harvest.

APPROACHES TO BIOGRAPHY

There are two widely recognized approaches to biography for children: one is the authentic biography, valuing faithful adherence to facts; the other is the fictionalized biography, valuing dramatic narrative. Each has its peculiar strengths and appeal.

Authentic Biography

If a biography attempts to convey the factual information of a person's life and times faithfully, we call it an *authentic biography*. An authentic biography will not use any facts that cannot be supported by solid and reliable research. Consequently, if dialogue is used (which is not common in authentic biography) it must be dialogue that can be substantiated by historical documents (such as letters or diaries) or reliable personal recollections. Although authentic biography attempts to be accurate in its presentation of the facts, we must remember that not even the most thorough and honest biographer is free from bias or wholly objective. By ignoring some facts and highlighting others, it is possible to slant even the most solid evidence, and readers need to be aware of such slanting.

James Daugherty was a pioneer of fine authentic biography for young people; his *Poor Richard,* the life of Benjamin Franklin, *Daniel Boone,* and *Abraham Lincoln* are justly celebrated. More recently, the works of Jean Fritz and Russell Freedman have established still more exacting standards for young people's biography. In fact,

Freedman's *Lincoln: A Photobiography* won the coveted Newbery Medal. In its careful research, including its extraordinary illustration with photographs from the period; its refusal to condescend to children in either vocabulary or selection of hard facts; and its honest and unsentimental portrayal of one of the great figures of American history, and avoiding both debunking and deifying him, Freedman's book should be a model for all future biographers for young people.

Fictionalized Biography

In writing for young people, some biographers have found it inviting to dramatize certain events—to give characters dialogue or perhaps even to invent believable scenes—presumably to make the story more interesting. These *fictionalized biographies* are readily recognizable by their dialogue. That is, if we are reading a biography of Benjamin Franklin and find extended conversations between young Franklin and his brother or his parents, we can be fairly certain that the author has invented these discussions, for it is unlikely that they are recorded with such detail in any surviving record. A true fictionalized biography will not invent scenes or events that did not happen, but rather dramatizes specific scenes, speculating on the details. Naturally, since its boundaries between truth and fiction are not precisely defined, fictionalized biography cannot be regarded with the same reliability as authentic fiction. We are much safer to regard a fictionalized biography as reading for entertainment than as a reliable source of historical information. Jean Lee Latham's *Carry On, Mr. Bowditch* is a good example of fictionalized biography. Most of this book consists of dramatized scenes depicting events that occurred in the late eighteenth century—scenes with dialogue to which no biographer could have been privy. Although she does not distort the essence of the life of the celebrated New England mathematician and navigator, neither does she pretend that this is authentic historical writing. We go to this sort of book primarily for entertainment and not for accurate or complete information.

A third approach to biographical writing is *biographical fiction,* which is characterized by pure fanciful invention with only passing regard to the historical facts. Biographical fiction should be considered as fiction and is classified as such in most libraries. Robert Lawson's wonderfully entertaining *Ben and Me,* for example, ostensibly describes the life of Benjamin Franklin as told by Amos, an irascible mouse that inhabits the great man's fur hat. Amos is an incurable egotist and takes most of the credit for Franklin's great works, describing how the Declaration of Independence was actually the work of mice fighting for their own liberty, and how Amos was responsible for the "first" French Revolution—that of the French mice. It is all a great deal of fun, but it is not, by any stretch of the imagination, a biography of Franklin, and it is more appropriately evaluated by the standards of fantasy.

THE FORMS OF BIOGRAPHY

In addition to these differences in degree of authenticity, biographies also differ according to their content and, particularly, the extent of their coverage. Biographies may cover a subject's entire life or only a part of it. Biographies may also examine a subject's life with relationship to others who share some common ground. Of course, each of these types can be either authentic or fictionalized biographies.

Complete Biographies

For older readers, we can find a multitude of complete biographies, which, as the name suggests, examine the whole of the subject's life from the cradle to the grave. A complete biography may be simple—such as Aliki's charming picture-book biographies *(The Story of Johnny Appleseed)* or complex—such as Russell Freedman's *Lincoln: A Photobiography.* Jean Fritz has produced a number of very brief biographies, which are nonetheless complete in that they survey the entire life of the subject. Fritz has successfully distilled the essence of the lives of her subjects (all figures of the American Revolution) into works of under 50 pages, and she writes with a warm sense of humor that helps to bring her subjects closer to her readers. Since complete biographies necessitate bringing together a considerable amount of information that may be only loosely related, these are often the most difficult to unify. Still, the complete biography is what most readers think of when biography is mentioned.

Partial Biographies

Occasionally, biographies will appear that focus on only one part or one aspect of a subject's life. These partial biographies allow the author to focus more clearly on a specific theme. For example, Johanna Johnston's fictionalized biography of Harriet Beecher Stowe—*Harriet and the Runaway Book*—focuses chiefly on Mrs. Stowe's writing of *Uncle Tom's Cabin.* Esther Hautzig's autobiographical *The Endless Steppe: Growing Up in Siberia* recounts five years in the author's youth spent in forced labor. And, of course, one of the most famous of all partial autobiographical works is Anne Frank's *The Diary of a Young Girl.* Of necessity, biographies of living persons are technically partial biographies, since the life is not yet completed. However, the real point of the partial biography is to limit the writer's scope.

A whole series of books appeared in the 1940s and 1950s on the childhoods of famous Americans. Unfortunately, these were not generally well written, and they represented fictionalized biography at its worst—using made-up dialogue, for example, between young Thomas Jefferson and his friends, that made them sound as if they were typical American schoolchildren of the mid-twentieth century. However, these books may remind us that often in biography for young readers, what most interests them, and that with which they can best identify, are the events of childhood and adolescence. The activities of an accomplished adult—the usual subject of a biography—may not always be suitable or readily accessible material for young readers. Max Bolliger's *David,* which follows the life of King David up until he became King of Israel, is a good example of a partial biography for young readers that focuses on the subject's formative years. In some cases, however, partial biographies for children can successfully focus on adult activities. For instance, F. N. Monjo's *Poor Richard in France* concentrates on Benjamin Franklin's mature years as the American emissary to the French capital during the American Revolution.

Collective Biographies

Many biographical works briefly examine the lives of several people who are linked by a common thread—scientists, First Ladies, sports figures, and musicians, for example. Collective biographies may take two general forms. Most commonly, brief biographical sketches are provided for each individual included, forming a collection of biographies. Henrietta Buckmaster's *Women Who Shaped History* deals with such influential women as Dorothea Dix, Harriet Tubman, and Mary Baker Eddy. One of the most famous of all collective biographies is President John F. Kennedy's best-selling *Profiles in Courage,* which has been edited for younger audiences. Occasionally we find biographies that weave into a single narrative the lives of two or more people who worked in collaboration. Jane Goodsell's biography of the founders of the famed clinic that bears their name, *The Mayo Brothers,* is an example.

The collective biography emphasizes above all the theme of an individual's life and work, and it further allows us to place that theme in a larger perspective. An additional benefit of the collective biography is that it can serve as a catalyst for further reading, prompting young readers to explore the life of one or more of the subjects involved, or perhaps to seek out biographies of others whose lives played on the same themes.

THE ELEMENTS OF BIOGRAPHICAL WRITING

Evaluating biography naturally requires a somewhat different set of criteria from fiction, since the two forms have quite different aims. Five basic elements of biographical writing deserve our special attention.

Subject

A subject's fame and glory are no guarantee that the biography will be interesting. Throughout the Middle Ages and the Renaissance, biographical writing generally focused on either saints or royalty, and in both cases the purpose was to glorify the subject. Only in the twentieth century has biography become truly democratized—now it is possible to locate biographies of dancers, teachers, mathematicians, scroundrels, and slaves. There are really no limits when it comes to the choice of a biographical subject. The biographer's role is to present the subject in an interesting manner (by choosing the right facts and expressing them in the right way, not by inventing "facts"). We expect a biography to convey a sense of the historical period and the geographic place in which the subject lived. Obviously, the more remote the historical period or the more distant and unfamiliar the place, the more background is needed. And finally, the good biography not only reveals to us the life of the subject, but it contributes to our broader and deeper understanding of humankind. In other words, when we are finished reading the biography we should not only feel that we know more about the individual whose life was presented, but we should feel that we know something more about people in general. Otherwise, the biography becomes simply a vehicle for idle gossip.

Accuracy

The material of a good biography is both accurate and authentic. If it is a fictionalized biography, we expect the author to faithfully convey the *essence* of the character, if not always the specific details of the life. There should be evidence of careful research—Jean Fritz has shown us through her use of endnotes that this can be done even in biographies for younger readers. We expect there to be no glaring omissions that would distort the reader's view or understanding of the subject. However, as one critic remarks: "Children's biography does not always present the whole truth about a subject. If a life contains tragic or unsavory aspects, these are generally omitted" (Gottlieb 174). There is disagreement over this issue, with some feeling that children may not have the emotional and intellectual capacity to handle certain themes, and others believing that the implied dishonesty in omitting these elements is a worse offense. Most biographers of Benjamin Franklin, for example, do not make a point of mentioning that his son was illegitimate, but Jean Fritz, in her biography *What's the Big Idea, Ben Franklin?*, explains in an endnote that we do not know who the son's mother was, a bold admission in a book for elementary children.

The illustrations in a good biography pay careful attention to authenticity and are appropriately juxtaposed with the text. We can again turn to biographies of Benjamin Franklin for an example. Several biographies for young people include illustrations of the famous kite-flying episode and depict a young boy, representing Franklin's son, accompanying Franklin in the storm. In fact, Franklin's son was a grown man of over 20 when the incident occurred. Careless illustration may cast doubt—rightly or wrongly—on the validity of the text.

It has only been in the last few years that biographers have begun to include supplementary material in their books for young people. Naturally, very young children will benefit little from such materials, but children in the middle and upper elementary grades are not too young to learn about footnotes, endnotes, bibliographies, and indexes. The works of Milton Meltzer (not primarily a biographer but a social historian) and Russell Freedman (notably his *Lincoln: A Photobiography* and *Franklin Delano Roosevelt*) are not only given added authority by their inclusion of supplementary materials, they also suggest that these writers hold their readers in high regard, seeing them as discerning and inquisitive individuals. In general, the writer of a good biography avoids oversimplification, sentimentality, and overt didacticism.

Balance

Early biographical writing tended to focus on the glorious exploits of "captains and kings," and they were often idealized and treated as virtual superhumans. When a biographer presents an idealized portrait of a seemingly superhuman hero, there is the danger that young readers may come to believe that success is unattainable by ordinary people. Today we prefer biographies that reveal the human side of people, their errors in judgment, their personality flaws, their peculiar and eccentric habits, and so on. These inclusions generally do not cause us to think less of the individual, but rather they develop in us a greater capacity for sympathetic or empathetic understanding.

This does not mean that we want our heroes debunked—a fault often found in popular biographies for adults (the perversions, sexual escapades, and criminal activities of public officials, sports heroes, movie stars, and so on). Young people want heroes or heroines to believe in. But at the same time, young readers want to know that even heroes have their weaknesses, and that what sets them apart from others is that they are able to triumph in spite of these weaknesses. It is probably better for our egos if we learn that Patrick Henry achieved fame and respectability despite a streak of laziness, as Jean Fritz points out *(Where Was Patrick Henry on the 29th of May?)*. We may suspect that there is hope for us. We want to be able to believe in the characters, to see them as flesh and blood individuals, and to feel comfortable with our heroes.

Style

There are writers who have produced what might have been thought impossible—a dreadfully dull book about a wonderfully interesting subject. A dull biography may result from an unwise selection of material, but more likely it is the result of a dry literary style. The good biographer writes with a style that is interesting, accessible, and appropriate to the subject. Necessary background material is carefully woven into the narrative—young people generally prefer action and dialogue to lengthy description. Dialogue, when it is used, is believable and authentic to the period. There is no good reason for a biographer to depict young Tom Jefferson talking to his buddies as if he grew up Detroit in the 1950s.

Naturally, the vocabulary and sentence structure of a good biography are suited to the intended audience, but need not be without reasonable challenge—remember, boredom results either from the absence of any challenge or from an overwhelming and thus discouraging challenge. Another means of attracting and keeping the reader's interest is through humor. Jean Fritz effectively employs humor in her biographies without diminishing the stature of her subjects. Because humor is so important to healthy human existence, it is difficult to understand why it appears so seldom in biography.

Theme

Finally, the theme of a good biography is both significant and sound. This is not to suggest that biography should be didactic, but without a theme to hold it together a biography is simply a loose collection of facts (something like a *Guinness Book of Records*—interesting to read in bits and pieces, but hardly a gripping story). Sometimes the theme is evident from the title. Jean Fritz's *The Double Life of Pocahontas* suggests the theme of a tragic woman caught between the conflicting values of two very different ways of life—that of her native Indian culture and that of her adoptive English culture. Milton Meltzer's *Benjamin Franklin: The New American* advances a rather standard view of Franklin as a man of rich and varied character with boundless physical energy and intellectual curiosity. The theme of a biography clarifies the writer's point of view concerning the character, and that may be to shed new light on what the author sees as old misunderstandings. Russell Freedman's portrait of Abraham Lincoln shows the sixteenth president as an extraordinarily complex and often troubled man, not without his significant shortcomings, but whose greatest strength was his sincere and warm humanity.

It is undoubtedly futile to hope that we have seen the last of the didactic biographies, those well-intentioned books that presume to teach us virtue through the examples of our heroes. But this is not to suggest that good biographies should contain no message for us. On the contrary, the best biographies are built upon very profound themes—themes that speak to the strength and resilience of the human spirit, themes that remind us that the life well lived is its own reward.

Not all young readers will become enthralled with biography, but those who do become passionate about it. Just as there are "science fiction buffs," there are "biography buffs" who make up in enthusiasm what they lack in numbers. Publishers have attempted to satisfy the appetites of these aficionados by producing the biography series. Dell has published its "Famous Americans Series," consisting of very brief biographies, widely varying in quality, and lacking such apparatus as indexes or bibliographies. Puffin's "Women of Our Time Series" includes some very fine authors, including Milton Meltzer on Betty Friedan, and Patricia Reilly Giff on Mother Theresa. These are authentic biographies, but they still adopt the format of a fictional work, lacking indexes, source lists, notes, and so on. We may hope that some of the recent excellent contributions to the field will pave the way for more biographies of high standards—biographies with uncompromising integrity and a healthy respect for the intellectual and emotional capacities of young readers.

SPECIAL CHARACTERISTICS OF AUTOBIOGRAPHY

Autobiography has some of its own special characteristics that set it apart from biography. Autobiography is often much more informal than biography, sometimes appearing in the form of memoirs or reminiscences. Individuals often feel they have no need to research their own lives, and therefore rely on their memories and their recollections to supply them with information. For example, specific dates are frequently missing from autobiographies, perhaps because the writers feel no need to prove authenticity—after all, they probably think, who should know their lives better than they themselves? Likewise, autobiographies typically lack references, often even tables of contents and indexes.

By the same token, we must be wary of what someone says in an autobiography, for it is difficult to find a more potentially biased source about an individual's life than the individual him- or herself. This does not mean that the autobiographer always puts him- or herself in the best light. Henry Adams's famous autobiography for adult readers, *The Education of Henry Adams,* is remarkably self-effacing and modest. Readers would hardly guess that the writer was a highly respected teacher, scholar, and public servant. What this shows is that autobiographies are often not particularly reliable sources of facts about people. Naturally, they are not complete lives—written as they are in the midst of one's life. Often, an autobiographer will write only about one part of his or her life—childhood and adolescence, for example, or early adult years, or specific career experiences.

On the other hand, they can be indispensable sources for discovering an individual's character traits, likes and dislikes, hopes and fears—these things are not easily hidden. The unique personal perspective of the autobiography can tell us things about a person we will find no place else. Autobiographies also have the advantage of immediacy—if they are well written—of making us feel as if we are right there next to the subject, sharing his or her life experiences.

Regrettably, few autobiographies are written especially for children. This is perhaps not surprising, for individuals who feel their lives are worth recording usually prefer to write for adult readers. However, recent years have seen more and more autobiographical writing for young readers. The series of autobiographical picture books about famous children's illustrators, including *Self-Portrait: Margot Zemach* and *Self-Portrait: Erik Blegvad,* provides an interesting variation on the autobiography whereby artists not only tell their own life stories, they illustrate them as well. These are some of the finer examples of autobiographies for children. A market surely exists for good, brief autobiographies for children by some of their favorite authors. Betsy Byars's *The Moon and I,* Phyllis Reynolds Naylor's *How I Came to Be a Writer,* and Roald Dahl's *Boy: Tales of Childhood* are three examples of autobiographies of children's writers for young readers. Aside from providing positive role models and uplifting examples, autobiographies are excellent sources for encouraging children to think about their own life experiences and to record those experiences in a diary or journal. Both biography and autobiography can inspire us all to examine our own lives and bring us to a deeper understanding of ourselves.

RECOMMENDED READINGS

Aiken, Joan. "Interpreting the Past." *Children's Literature in Education* 16 (Summer 1985): 67–83.

Bowen, Catherine Drinker. *Biography: The Craft and the Calling.* Boston: Little, Brown, 1968.

Berry, Thomas Elliott, ed. *The Biographer's Craft.* New York: Odyssey, 1967.

Blos, Joan. "The Overstuffed Sentence and Other Means for Assessing Historical Fiction for Children." *School Library Journal* 31 (November 1985): 38–39.

Burton, Hester. "The Writing of Historical Novels." In *Children and Literature: Views and Reviews.* Ed. Virginia Haviland. Glenview, IL: Scott, Foresman, 1973, 299–304.

Carr, Jo. "What Do We Do About Bad Biographies?" In *Beyond Fact.* Ed. Jo Carr. Chicago: American Library Association, 1982, 119–28.

Coolidge, Olivia. "My Struggle with Facts." *Wilson Library Bulletin* (October 1974): 146–51.

Fisher, Margery. "Life Course or Screaming Force." *Children's Literature in Education* (Autumn 1976): 107–27.

Forman, Jack. "Biography for Children: More Facts, Less Fiction." *Library Journal* 97 (September 15, 1972): 2968–69.

Fritz, Jean. "George Washington, My Father, and Walt Disney." *Horn Book Magazine* 52 (April 1976): 191–98.

Garfield, Leon. "Historical Fiction for Our Global Times." *The Horn Book Magazine* (November/December 1988): 736–42.

Gottleib, Robin. "On Nonfiction Books for Children: Tradition & Dissent." *Wilson Library Journal* (October 1974): 174–77.

Groff, Patrick. "Biography: The Bad or the Bountiful." *Top of the News* (April 1973): 210–17.

Higgins, Judith. "Biographies They Can Read." *School Library Journal* 18 (April 1971): 33–34.

Jurich, Marilyn. "What's Left Out of Biography for Children?" *Children's Literature* 1 (1972): 143–51.

Kendall, Paul Murray. *The Art of Biography.* New York: Norton, 1985.

Lochhead, Marion. "Clio Junior: Historical Novels for Children." In *Only Connect,* 2nd ed. Eds. Sheila Egoff, G. T. Stubbs, and L. F. Ashely. New York: Oxford University Press, 1980, 17–27.

Marcus, Leonard. "Life Drawing: Some Notes on Children's Picture Book Biographies." *The Lion and the Unicorn* 4 (Summer 1980): 15–31.

Moore, Ann W. "A Question of Accuracy: Errors in Children's Biographies." *School Library Journal* 31 (February 1985): 34–35.

Morman, Charles. *Kings & Captains: Variations on a Heroic Theme.* Louisville: University of Kentucky Press, 1971.

Rahn, Suzanne. "An Evolving Past: The Story of Historical Fiction and Nonfiction for Children." *The Lion and the Unicorn* 15 (June 1991): 1–26.

Segel, Elizabeth. "In Biographies for Young Readers, Nothing Is Impossible." *The Lion and the Unicorn* 4 (Summer 1980): 4–14.

Wilms, Denise M. "An Evaluation of Biography." In *Jump Over the Moon.* Eds. Pamela Barron and Jennifer Burley. New York: Holt, Rinehart, and Winson, 1984, 220–25.

SELECTED BIBLIOGRAPHY OF HISTORICAL FICTION

The following bibliography list a few of the many books of historical realism available for young readers. These have been classified according to broad regional and chronological categories. Also check out the bibliography following Chapter 13 for some other titles relating to historical subjects.

Ancient, Medieval, and Renaissance European History

Behn, Harry. *The Faraway Lurs.* New York: Putnam, 1963.

Brennan, J. H. *Shiva: An Adventure of the Ice Age.* New York: Lippincott, 1989.

Chute, Marchette. *The Innocent Wayfaring.* New York: Dutton, 1955.

de Angeli, Marguerite. *The Door in the Wall.* New York: Doubleday, 1949.

Dyer, T. A. *A Way of His Own.* Boston: Houghton Mifflin, 1981.

Gray, Elizabeth Janet. *Adam of the Road.* New York: Viking, 1942.

Haugaard, Erik Christian. *Hakon of Rogen's Saga.* Boston: Houghton Mifflin, 1963.

———. *Leif the Unlucky.* Boston: Houghton Mifflin, 1982.

———. *Orphans of the Wind.* New York: Dell, 1966.

Hunter, Mollie. *The Spanish Letters.* New York: Funk, 1967.

———. *The Stronghold.* New York: Harper, 1974.

Ish-Kishor, Sulamith. *A Boy of Old Prague.* New York: Pantheon, 1963.

Kelly, Eric P. *The Trumpeter of Krakow.* New York: Macmillan, 1928.

Konigsburg, E. L. *A Proud Taste for Scarlet and Miniver.* New York: Atheneum, 1973.

———. *The Second Mrs. Giaconda.* New York: Atheneum, 1975.

McGraw, Eloise Jarvis. *Mara, Daughter of the Nile.* New York: Coward, 1961.

Pyle, Howard. *Men of Iron.* 1890. (Various modern editions.)

———. *Otto of the Silver Hand.* 1888. (Various modern editions.)

Speare, Elizabeth George. *The Bronze Bow.* Boston: Houghton Mifflin, 1961.

Stolz, Mary. *Zekmet the Stone Carver: A Tale of Ancient Egypt.* Illus. Deborah Nourse Lattimore. New York: Harcourt, 1988.

Sutcliff, Rosemary. *The Lantern Bearers.* New York: Walck, 1959.

———. *The Mark of the Horse Lord.* New York: Walck, 1965.

Treace, Geoffrey. *The Red Towers of Granada.* New York: Vanguard, 1967.

Treece, Henry. *The Centurion.* Illus. Mary Russon. New York: Meredith, 1967.

Modern European History Since the Renaissance

Burton, Hester. *Time of Trial*. Cleveland: World, 1963.

Garfield, John. *December Rose*. New York: Viking, 1986.

———. *Smith*. New York: Pantheon, 1967.

———. *The Sound of Coaches*. New York: Viking, 1974.

Hesse, Karen. *Letters from Rifka*. New York: Holt, 1992.

Hunter, Mollie. *The Ghosts of Glencoe*. New York: Funk, 1969.

Lowry, Lois. *Number the Stars*. Boston: Houghton Mifflin, 1989.

Monjo, F. N. *The Sea Beggar's Son*. New York: Coward, 1975.

Orlev, Uri. *The Island on Bird Street*. Tr. Hillel Halkin. Boston: Houghton Mifflin, 1984.

Pelgrom, Els. *The Winter When Time Was Frozen*. Tr. Maryka and Rafael Rudnik. New York: Morrow, 1980.

Peyton, K. M. *The Edge of the Cloud*. Cleveland: World, 1970.

———. *Flambards*. Cleveland: World, 1968.

Richter, Hans Peter. *Friedrich*. New York: Holt, 1970.

Serraillier, Ian. *The Silver Sword*. New York: Criterion, 1959.

Siegal, Aranka. *Grace in the Wilderness: After the Liberation, 1945–1948*. New York: Farrar, Straus & Giroux, 1985.

———. *Upon the Head of the Goat: A Childhood in Hungary, 1939–1944*. New York: Farrar, Straus & Giroux, 1981.

North American History, Including Native America

Armer, Laura Adams. *Waterless Mountain*. New York: McKay, 1931.

Avi. *Encounter at Easton*. New York: Pantheon, 1980.

Bawdin, Nina. *Carrie's War*. New York: Lippincott, 1973.

Beatty, Patricia. *Jayhawker*. New York: Morrow, 1991.

Blos, Joan. *A Gathering of Days*. New York: Scribner's, 1979.

Brenner, Barbara. *Wagon Wheels*. Illus. Don Bolognese. New York: Harper, 1978.

Brink, Carol Ryrie. *Caddie Woodlawn*. 1936. (Various modern editions.)

Bulla, Clyde. *A Lion to Guard Us*. New York: Crowell, 1978.

Collier, James Lincoln, and Christopher Collier. *My Brother Sam Is Dead*. New York: Four Winds Press, 1974.

Dorris, Michael. *Morning Girl*. Boston: Hyperion, 1992.

Fleischman, Paul. *The Borning Room*. New York: Harper, 1991.

———. *Coming-and-Going Man*. New York: Harper, 1985.

Fleischman, Sid. *Mr. Mysterious & Company*. Boston: Little, Brown, 1962.

Forbes, Esther. *Johnny Tremain*. Boston: Houghton Mifflin, 1946.

Fox, Paula. *The Slave Dancer*. New York: Bradbury, 1973.

Fritz, Jean. *The Cabin Faced West*. New York: Coward, 1958.

Garrigue, Sheila. *The Eternal Spring of Mr. Ito*. New York: Bradbury, 1985.

Hudson, Jan. *Sweetgrass*. New York: Philomel, 1989.

Hunt, Irene. *Across Five Aprils*. New York: Follett, 1964.

Lyons, Mary E. *Letters from a Slave Girl: The Story of Harriet Jacobs*. New York: Scribner's, 1992.

MacLachlan, Patricia. *Sarah, Plain and Tall*. New York: Harper, 1985.

O'Dell, Scott. *Island of the Blue Dolphins*. Boston: Houghton Mifflin, 1960.

———. *The King's Fifth*. Boston: Houghton Mifflin, 1966.

———— . *Sing Down the Moon.* Boston: Houghton Mifflin, 1970.

Pellowski, Anne. *Winding Valley Farm: Annie's Story.* New York: Philomel, 1982.

Petry, Ann. *Tituba of Salem Village.* New York: Crowell, 1964.

Reeder, Carolyn. *Shades of Gray.* New York: Macmillan, 1989.

Richter, Conrad. *The Light in the Forest.* New York: Knopf, 1953.

Rostokowski, Margaret I. *After the Dancing Days.* New York: Harper, 1986.

Sebestyen, Ouida. *Words by Heart.* Boston: Little, Brown, 1979.

Speare, Elizabeth George. *The Sign of the Beaver.* Boston: Houghton Mifflin, 1983.

———— . *The Witch of Blackbird Pond.* Boston: Houghton Mifflin, 1958.

Taylor, Mildred. *Let the Circle Be Unbroken.* New York: Dial, 1981.

———— . *Roll of Thunder, Hear My Cry.* New York: Dial, 1976.

Wilder, Laura Ingalls. *By the Shores of Silver Lake.* 1939. New York: Harper, 1953.

———— . *Farmer Boy.* 1933. New York: Harper, 1953.

———— . *Little House in the Big Woods.* 1932. New York: Harper, 1953.

———— . *Little House on the Prairie.* 1935. New York: Harper, 1953.

———— . *Little Town on the Prairie.* 1941. New York: Harper, 1953.

———— . *The Long Winter.* 1940. New York: Harper, 1953.

———— . *On the Banks of Plum Creek.* 1937. New York: Harper, 1953.

———— . *Those Happy Golden Years.* 1943. New York: Harper, 1953.

Other Times and Places

De Jenkins, Lyll Becerra. *The Honorable Prison.* New York: Lodestar, 1988. (South America)

De Young, Meindert. *The House of Sixty Fathers.* New York: Harper, 1956. (China)

Dickinson, Peter. *The Dancing Bear.* Boston: Little, Brown, 1972. (Byzantium)

Fyson, J. G. *The Three Brothers of Ur.* Illus. Victor G. Ambrus. New York: Coward, 1966.

Ho Minfong. *The Clay Marble.* New York: Farrar, Straus & Giroux, 1991. (Cambodia)

Holman, Felice. *Wild Children.* New York: Scribner's, 1983. (Russia)

Lewis, Elizabeth Foreman. *Young Fu of the Upper Yangtze.* New York: Holt, 1932. (China)

Namioka, Lensey. *Island of Ogres.* New York: Harper, 1989. (Japan)

Paterson, Katherine. *The Master Puppeteer.* New York: T. Crowell, 1976. (Japan)

———— . *Of Nightingales That Weep.* New York: T. Crowell, 1974. (Japan)

———— . *Rebels of the Heavenly Kingdom.* New York: T. Crowell, 1983. (China)

———— . *The Sign of the Chrysanthemum.* New York: T. Crowell, 1973. (Japan)

Ritchie, Rita. *The Golden Hawks of Genghis Kahn.* New York: Dutton, 1958.

———— . *Secret Beyond the Mountains.* New York: Dutton, 1960. (China)

———— . *The Year of the Horse.* New York: Dutton, 1957. (China)

Walsh, Jill Paton. *The Emperor's Winding Sheet.* New York: Farrar, 1978. (Constantinople)

Yep, Laurence. *The Serpent's Children.* New York: Harper, 1984. (China)

SELECTED BIBLIOGRAPHY OF BIOGRAPHIES AND AUTOBIOGRAPHIES

Since many writers specialize in biographical writing, look for other biographies by many of the writers represented on this list.

Adoff, Arnold. *Malcolm X.* Illus. John Wilson. New York: Crowell, 1970.

Aliki (pseud. of Aliki Brandenburg). *The Story of Johnny Appleseed.* Englewood Cliffs, NJ: Prentice-Hall, 1963.

————. *A Weed Is a Flower: The Life of George Washington Carver.* Englewood Cliffs, NJ: Prentice-Hall, 1965.

Asimov, Isaac. *Breakthroughs in Science.* Boston: Houghton Mifflin, 1960.

Blegvad, Erik. *Self-Portrait: Erick Blegvad.* Reading, MA: Addison-Wesley, 1979.

Bolliger, Max. *David.* Illus. Edith Schindler. New York: Delacorte, 1967.

Brooks, Polly Schoyer. *Queen Eleanor: Independent Spirit of the Medieval World.* Philadelphia: Lippincott, 1983.

Buckminster, Henrietta. *Women Who Shaped History.* New York: Macmillan, 1966.

Bulla, Clyde. *Songs of St. Francis.* Illus. Valenti Angelo. New York: Crowell, 1952. (St. Francis of Assisi)

————. *Squanto, Friend of the Pilgrims.* Illus. Peter Burchard. New York: Crowell, 1954.

————. *Washington's Birthday.* Illus. Don Bolognese. New York: Crowell, 1957.

Burleigh, Robert. *Flight: The Journey of Charles Lindbergh.* New York: Philomel, 1991.

Carter, Dorothy S. *Queen Hatshepsut.* Illus. Cecil Leslie. New York: Faber, 1978.

Clayton, Ed. *Martin Luther King: The Peaceful Warrior.* Englewood Cliffs, NJ: Prentice-Hall, 1968.

Cleary, Beverly. *A Girl from Yamhill: A Memoir.* New York: Morrow, 1988.

Coolidge, Olivia. *Tom Paine: Revolutionary.* New York: Scribner's, 1969.

————. *Winston Churchill and the Story of Two World Wars.* Boston: Houghton, 1960.

Dahl, Roald. *Boy: Tales of Childhood.* New York: Farrar, Straus & Giroux, 1984.

Daugherty, James. *Abraham Lincoln.* New York: Viking, 1943.

————. *Daniel Boone.* New York: Viking, 1939.

d'Aulaire, Ingri, and Edgar Parin d'Aulaire. *Abraham Lincoln.* New York: Doubleday, 1939.

Davidson, Margaret. *The Story of Eleanor Roosevelt.* New York: Four Winds, 1969.

De Trevino, Elizabeth Borton. *I, Juan de Pareja.* New York: Farrar, Straus & Giroux, 1965.

Duncan, Lois. *Chapters: My Growth as a Writer.* Boston: Little, Brown, 1982.

Eaton, Jeanette. *America's Own Mark Twain.* Illus. Leonard Everett Fisher. New York: Morrow, 1958.

Faber, Doris. *Eleanor Roosevelt: First Lady of the World.* New York: Viking, 1985.

Ferris, Jeri. *Native American Doctor: The Story of Susan LaFlesche Picotte.* Minneapolis: Carolrhoda, 1991.

Fisher, Leonard Everett. *Galileo.* New York: Macmillan, 1992.

Freedman, Russell. *Franklin Delano Roosevelt.* New York: Clarion, 1990.

————. *Lincoln: A Photobiography.* New York: Clarion, 1987.

————. *The Wright Brothers: How They Invented the Airplane.* New York: Holiday, 1991.

Fritz, Jean. *Bully for You, Teddy Roosevelt!* New York: Putnam, 1991.

————. *Can't You Make Them Behave, King George?* Illus. Tomie da Paola. New York: Coward-McCann, 1977. (King George III)

————. *The Double Life of Pocahontas.* New York: Putnam, 1983.

————. *Homesick: My Own Story.* New York: Putnam, 1982. (Autobiography)

————. *Make Way for Sam Houston.* New York: Putnam, 1986.

————. *Where Was Patrick Henry on the 29th of May?* Illus. Margot Tomes. New York: Coward-McCann, 1975.

Goodsell, Jane. *The Mayo Brothers.* New York: Crowell, 1972.

Greenfield, Eloise. *Mary McLeod Bethune.* New York: Crowell, 1977.

Hamilton, Virginia. *W. E. B. DuBois: A Biography.* New York: Crowell, 1972.

Hanff, Helene. *Queen of England: The Story of Elizabeth I.* New York: Doubleday, 1969.

Haskins, James. *The Story of Stevie Wonder.* New York: Lothrop, 1976.

Henry, Marguerite, and Wesley Dennis. *Benjamin West and His Cat Grimalkin.* Illus. Wesley Dennis. Indianapolis: Bobbs-Merrill, 1947. (Early American artist Benjamin West)

Hoyt-Goldsmith, Diane. *Hoang Anh: A Vietnamese-American Boy.* New York: Holiday, 1992.

Hyman, Trina Schart. *Self-Portrait: Trina Schart Hyman.* 1981. New York: HarperCollins, 1989.

Judson, Clara Ingram. *Abraham Lincoln, Friend of the People.* Chicago: Wilcox and Follett, 1950.

———. *Admiral Christopher Columbus.* Chicago: Follett, 1965.

Kennedy, John F. *Profiles in Courage.* New York: Harper, 1964. (Abridged for young readers; stories of courageous Americans)

Kherdian, David. *The Road from Home: The Story of an Armenian Girl.* New York: Greenwillow, 1979.

Komroff, Manuel. *Mozart.* Illus. Warren Chappell. New York: Knopf, 1956.

Lacy, Leslie Alexander. *Cheer the Lonesome Traveler: The Life of W. E. B. DuBois.* New York: Dial, 1970.

Latham, Jean Lee. *Carry On, Mr. Bowditch.* Boston: Houghton Mifflin, 1955.

Lawrence, Jacob. *Harriet and the Promised Land.* New York: Windmill, 1968. (One-time slave and heroine of the underground railroad Harriet Tubman)

McKissack, Patricia C. *Jesse Jackson: A Biography.* New York: Scholastic, 1989.

McNeer, May. *America's Mark Twain.* Illus. Lynd Ward. Boston: Houghton Mifflin, 1962.

Mathis, Sharon Bell. *Ray Charles.* New York: Crowell, 1973.

Meigs, Cornelia. *Invincible Louisa.* Boston: Little, Brown, 1968.

Meltzer, Milton. *Benjamin Franklin: The New American.* New York: Watts, 1984.

———. *Dorothea Lange: Life Through the Camera.* New York: Viking, 1985.

———. *Langston Hughes: A Biography.* New York: Crowell, 1968.

Mitchison, Naomi. *African Heroes.* New York: Farrar, Straus & Giroux, 1969.

Monjo, F. N. *The One Bad Thing About Father.* New York: Harper, 1970. (Theodore Roosevelt)

———. *Poor Richard in France.* New York: Holt, 1973. (Benjamin Franklin)

Naylor, Phyllis Reynolds. *How I Came to Be a Writer.* 1978. New York: Aladdin, 1987.

Oneal, Zibby. *Grandma Moses: Painter of Rural America.* New York: Viking, 1986.

Peet, Bill. *Bill Peet: An Autobiography.* Boston: Houghton Mifflin, 1989.

Provensen, Alice, and Martin Provensen. *The Glorious Flight: Across the Channel with Louis Bleriot.* New York: Viking, 1983.

Raboff, Ernest. *Marc Chagall.* New York: Doubleday, 1968.

———. *Pablo Picasso.* New York: Doubleday, 1968.

Rylant, Cynthia. *Best Wishes.* Photos Carlo Ontal. Katonah, NY: Richard C. Owen, 1992. (Autobiography)

Sandburg, Carl. *Abe Lincoln Grows Up.* Illus. James Daugherty. New York: Harcourt, 1928.

Shiels, Barbara. *Winners: Women and the Nobel Prize.* Minneapolis: Dillon, 1985.

Shippen, Katherine. *Leif Eriksson: First Voyager to America.* New York: Harper, 1951.

Singer, Isaac Bashevis. *A Day of Pleasures: Stories of a Boy Growing Up in Warsaw.* New York: Farrar, Straus & Giroux, 1969.

Sis, Peter. *Follow the Dream.* New York: Knopf, 1991. (Christopher Columbus)

Stanley, Fay. *The Last Princess: The Story of Princess Ka'iulani of Hawai'i.* New York: Four Winds, 1991.

Stoddard, Hope. *Famous American Women.* New York: Crowell, 1970.

Swift, Hildegarde. *From the Eagle's Wing: A Biography of John Muir.* Illus. Lynd Ward. New York: Morrow, 1962.

Tobias, Tobi. *Marian Anderson.* New York: Crowell, 1972.

Turner, Robyn Montana. *Georgia O'Keefe.* Boston: Little, 1991.

———. *Rosa Bonheur.* Boston: Little, 1991.

Wadsworth, Ginger. *Rachel Carson: Voice for the Earth.* Minneapolis: Lerner, 1992.

Yates, Elizabeth. *Amos Fortune, Free Man.* New York: Dutton, 1950.

Yolen, Jane. *A Letter from Phoenix Farm.* Photos Jason Stemple. Katonah, NY: Richard C. Owen, 1992. (Autobiography)

Zemach, Margot. *Self-Portrait: Margot Zemach.* Reading, MA: Addison-Wesley, 1978.

CHAPTER 12

Informational Books

DEFINITION OF INFORMATIONAL BOOKS

Informational books, or nonfictional works, are not normally considered "literature," although occasionally very fine works of history, science, and biography appear. Instead, nonfictional works—at least those written for adults—are usually perceived as strictly functional and free from any aesthetic demands. We read an informational book to acquire specific knowledge, and not to be entertained. But in the field of children's literature, there has always been more than a passing interest in those books written chiefly for informational purposes—science books, history books, how-to books, and so on. One of the reasons for this interest may be that children themselves do not clearly distinguish between fiction and nonfiction. Indeed, sometimes the lines are very hazy. Holling C. Hollings's *Paddle-to-the-Sea,* for example, describes a fictional adventure of a little carved wooden canoe on its journey from Thunder Bay in the upper Great Lakes to the Atlantic Ocean. But aside from being an exciting adventure tale, this work is also a scientifically accurate book filled with a wealth of information especially about geography and natural science, and the text is accompanied by beautiful and meticulously detailed drawings.

As adults, we have unfortunately grown accustomed to expecting informational books to be merely utilitarian (and frequently dull), and we are pleasantly surprised when we find a stimulating history or geology or mathematics book. But children—who are quite tolerant when it comes to subject matter and theme—have little patience for dull books. Consequently, the writing of informational books for children requires creativity along with reasonable accuracy. We might add here that there is absolutely no reason adults should not make the same demands of their informational books as do children—but adults have come to value the *information* over the *manner* of presentation. Those adults who read some of the excellent examples of nonfiction for children may justly lament that more nonfictional works for adults do not adhere to finer literary standards.

TYPES OF INFORMATIONAL BOOKS

For the purposes of this chapter, we shall take "informational books" to mean any work that deals exclusively with factual material and is clearly intended above all to instruct young readers. In Chapter 5, we briefly discussed the first informational books children are likely to encounter—the concept books. Now we will consider the wider realm of informational books, not only for toddlers and early elementary school children but for older readers as well. Although there are informational books for young people on virtually every topic under the sun, we shall attempt to simplify our discussion by grouping these works into four broad (and occasionally overlapping) subject categories.

Lands and Peoples

Think how many of our world's problems have resulted from our failure to understand and empathize with the multiplicity of cultures that share this planet. We only dimly understand our own culture, let alone those of distant foreign peoples. By being introduced to other cultures, other civilizations, we not only learn about them, but we discover a little more about ourselves. Additionally, tolerance is a valuable byproduct of expansive knowledge, and the books describing the history, governments, customs, and religions of societies around the world can help bring young readers this knowledge. One of the purposes of books on the multiplicity of cultures is to make the young readers aware of the world and the people around them. And these books are becoming increasingly important as we realize the interdependence of humanity and the growing need for global understanding.

Through picture storybooks, such as Thomas Handforth's realistic piece, *Mei Lei,* or Gerald McDermotts's re-creation of a Navajo folk myth, *Arrow to the Sun,* young children enjoy their earliest exposure to unfamiliar cultures. These are not, of course, strictly speaking informational books, but they do help young children realize that there are other ways of life on earth. Surely one of the great advantages of folktales from around the world is that they demonstrate at once the fundamental similarities of the human race and the manifold variations that societies offer. However, in addition to the fictional works, we can find some very fine informational books written especially for the very young. Aliki (pseudonym for Aliki Brandenburg) has been among the most consistently successful in bringing stories of other lands and peoples to children in the lower grades (for example, *Mummies Made in Egypt,* in addition to accessible biographies of such people as Benjamin Franklin and George Washington Carver). The real flood of informational books comes for readers in the middle elementary years. Leonard Everett Fisher has created two outstanding series of first-rate informational books—one on colonial American crafts and one on nine-teenth-century American commerce and industry. (His *Pumpers, Boilers, Hooks and*

Ladders is suitable for a younger audience, and such works as *The Factories, The Railroads, The Schoolmasters, The Tanners, The Cabinetmakers,* and so on, are appropriate for fourth, fifth, and sixth graders.) The hallmarks of his work are a clear text and powerful illustrations, two of the most important features of any informational book for young readers.

Milton Meltzer has produced consistently high quality works on some rather complex facets of American history. His books include *In Their Own Words: A History of the American Negro; Brother Can You Spare a Dime? The Great Depression: 1929-1933;* and *Bread and Roses: The Struggle of American Labor, 1865-1915.* Meltzer's works are distinguished by their thorough scholarship. He treats his young readers with great respect, and is never condescending to them. He includes bibliographies and indexes (two features not necessarily found in informational books for young people), and he prefers to use period photographs to illustrate his works (a feature that gives them a great deal of authenticity). Meltzer's books are models of historical writing for young people.

In addition to his biographical writing mentioned in Chapter 11, Russell Freedman has written such historical works as *Cowboys of the Wild West,* presenting a fascinating history that corrects some of our misconceptions about cowboys. Through his use of photographs and an exciting writing style, Freedman suggests that the reality was even more compelling than the myth. Modern social concerns are documented in Brent Ashabranner's *Children of the Maya,* a photo-essay about Central American natives attempting to rebuild their lives in Florida after escaping from persecution in their homeland. History books for children have been sometimes notorious for their misinformation or their general inadequacy. The fact that for two centuries, history textbooks virtually ignored the contributions of African Americans and women, and hopelessly distorted the story of Native Americans is ample evidence of this careless attitude. There still remain great strides to be made toward reliable, thorough, and honest, historiography for children.

Religion is another subject we can find treated in children's books. There are some particularly useful books about Jewish traditions, such as Howard Greenfield's *Passover* and *Rosh Hashanah and Yom Kippur* or Karla Kuskin's *Jerusalem, Shining Still.* Alice Bach and J. Cheryl Exum have retold some of the stories of the Old Testament to provide a feminine point of view in *Miriam's Well: Stories about Women in the Bible.* Anton Powell's *The Rise of Islam* describes the earlier history of that important world religion. And Elizabeth Seeger's *Eastern Religions* explores the religious faith of the Orient. In an age when religion is still capable of firing passions to violence, the more knowledge we have of other faiths the more likely we are to learn tolerance for them.

Science and Nature

Millicent Selsam, herself a fine science writer for children, tells us that "a good science book is not just a collection of facts" (62). That is the shortcoming of many school textbooks—they provide voluminous, static facts, and overlook the more important total picture. (This is true of texts on all subjects, not science alone.) Or, to cite an old, but not inappropriate, cliché, these books prevent us from seeing the forest because of the trees. A good science book, Selsam contends, demonstrates the workings of the scientific method as well as conveys "something of the beauty and excitement of science" (65).

Science and nature covers as broad a spectrum as land and peoples, but the major types of books found in this category are:

1. books about the life sciences, including studies of animals and plants;
2. books about managing the environment, which combine the life sciences and the earth sciences;
3. books about the earth or physical sciences, including natural laws and outer space; and
4. books about the abstract world of mathematics.

As might be expected, informational books about animals are among the most popular of the science books—particularly with younger readers. We are told that the most frequently consulted entry in a young people's encyclopedia is "Dogs." Curiously enough, dogs are not among the most frequent subjects of informational books (dog stories tend to fall under the various categories of fiction). In recent years, a number of very good books have appeared on unusual or threatened animal species, including the puffin, the panda, the bald eagle, and some largely unheard of species, such as the hoiho in Adele Vernon's *The Hoiho: New Zealand's Yellow-Eyed Penguin,* and some surprising ones such as several breeds of American farm animals close to extinction as described in Catherine Paladino's *Our Vanishing Farm Animals.*

The plant world can be equally fascinating to younger children, as demonstrated in such books as Carol Gibbons's *From Seed to Plant* and Ruth Heller's *The Reason for a Flower.* Both books illustrated one of nature's most elemental tales, the growth of a plant from a tiny seed. Since this process can easily be witnessed in a schoolroom over a relatively short period of time, hands-on experience can follow the reading of these books. But we know that it is not only the animal world that is threatened with extinction, and we are beginning to see books alerting young children to the potential disappearance of our plant life as well. Barbara Taylor's series, which includes *Coral Life, Desert Life, Pond Life,* and *Rain Forests,* introduces the very young to the concept of the ecosystem—plants and animals working together to maintain the balance of nature and ensure the survival of the planet.

Laurence Pringle's *Living in a Risky World* encourages young readers to think about modern civilization and the implications of its lifestyle, particularly the effects of its pollutants (acid rain, carcinogens, and other environmental hazards). A book such as this demonstrates that the scientific world is not divorced from our everyday world or from the complicated ethical issues that face humanity. This work pointedly examines the ethics of science and technology in the modern world—the title suggests both the substance and the theme. As we face the ethical dilemma of humanity's responsibility to the earth, and as pollution, overpopulation, and reckless development take their toll, it becomes imperative that we begin educating our young children about the delicate ecosystem in which we live.

Books about the earth sciences include such works as Seymour Simon's *Earthquake,* which not only provides elementary scientific information on the description and cause of earthquakes but also practical information such as what to do in the event of one. They include Franklyn Branley's *Light and Darkness,* and Claire Llewellyn's *My First Book of Time,* both focusing on physics, albeit quite fundamental. Probably the most popular of these types of books are those not about the earth at all, but about the physical nature of outer space. Astronaut Sally Ride in *To Space and Back* (co-authored with Susan Okie) describes her experiences on the space shuttle flight, and this book serves a dual purpose of presenting up-to-date information of general interest and of dispelling feminine stereotyping in career choices. These works, as might be expected, date rather more rapidly than most publications, and there is the constant need for up-to-date works, as scientific discoveries reveal new facts, engender new theories, and provide for new technologies. Franklyn Branley's *Uranus: The Seventh Planet* was written in 1976 and included the most up-to-date information on our giant distant neighbor. But the visit paid to the planet in 1986 by Voyager 2 prompted Seymour Simon to write *Uranus,* since much of the earlier information on the planet had become obsolete.

David Macauley's near monumental *The Way Things Work* explores all the realms of the earth sciences—mechanics, physics (even nuclear physics), electronics, and chemistry. With amazing clarity and simplicity through hundreds of clever drawings, complex ideas and processes are revealed. This is a book with enormous appeal for adults as well as young people. Among the books on mathematical subjects are Mitsumasa Anno's imaginatively illustrated *Anno's Math Games* in two volumes and Jane Jonas Srivastava's *Statistics*, an introduction for middle elementary school children. Given the highly publicized deficiency that most American children apparently exhibit in mathematical skills, this would seem to be a ripe field for imaginative writers capable of bringing this abstract science to life.

Sometimes a science book skirts the border between science and art. Jim Arnosky's *Secrets of a Wildlife Watcher* is a firsthand account of ways to locate and observe animals in the wild. This work is also an example of how science writing can be brought to a practical level. In at least two later books, Arnosky takes his scientific knowledge and puts it to recreational use: *Fish in a Flash!: A Personal Guide to Spin-Fishing* and *Sketching Outdoors in Spring.* And so we find a segue into a new class of informational books, the fine and applied arts, never forgetting that where there is art, science is never far afield, and vice versa.

Fine and Applied Arts

The creative impulses of humanity have produced everything from architectural monuments (as illustrated by David Macauley's carefully detailed *Cathedral* and *Castle*) to oil paintings (as presented in Ernest Raboff's series, "Art for Children," on the major artists of the Western world) to such practical arts as the invention of writing (as graphically described in Leonard Everett Fisher's *Alphabet Art*). There is virtually no limit to the subject variety that can be found in these books: dance (Arnold Haskell's *The Wonderful World of Dance*), music (Langston Hughes's *The First Book of Jazz*), gardening (Marc Brown's *Your First Garden Book*), the theater (Walter Hodge's *Shakespeare's Theater*)—only begin to scratch the surface of the wealth of this field.

Picture books readily lend themselves to introductions to art and artists, for reproductions of their works can be included. Some good books to begin with are Alice Elizabeth Chase's *Looking at Art,* which describes the various ways that artists have viewed the world or Robert Hofsinde's *Indian Arts,* which reminds us that art, culture, and history are all wrapped up together. In recent years, many books for children about individual artists have appeared. It is good to see the picture-book format used to a purpose for which it is so well suited.

As there is some overlapping with books on art and books on history or culture, so there is with books on art and books on science and nature. And there is some obvious overlapping between this category and that of history. Macauley's architecture books, mentioned above, and Judith St. George's *The Brooklyn Bridge: They Said It Couldn't Be Built* both focus on remarkable human achievements, as well as give us an historical sense. In a different vein is William Jaspersohn's *Magazine: Behind the Scenes at* Sports Illustrated. This photo-essay may have an immediate appeal to sports buffs, but its focus is actually on the writing, editing, illustrating, and printing of a magazine. This is a book focusing quite clearly on an applied art—art put to a practical, everyday purpose.

In this category, we also include books on sports, which can certainly be viewed as artistic expression (indeed, a skill such as ice skating, as described in Jonah and Laura Kalb's *The Easy Ice Skating Book,* has developed into a highly refined performing art). And too, we should not forget the various craft and hobby books, such as Ferne Geller Cone's *Crazy Crocheting,* which describes a time-honored folk art form.

Human Development and Behavior

Books about human development and behavior include all those dealing with the cycle of life—especially birth, growth, sexuality, and death—and interpersonal relationships. These issues are treated frequently in picture storybooks (Martha Alexander's *Nobody Asked Me If I Wanted a Baby Sister,* and Judith Viorst's book about the death of a pet, *The Tenth Good Thing About Barney,* are two good examples). These cannot technically be considered *informational* books, the primary purpose of which is to impart fact; however, fiction is probably the most effective way of conveying complex psychological concepts to young readers. But for older readers, stories of human behavior often have a greater impact if they are factual. The success of the so-called "docu-drama," a movie based on an actual event, suggests that adults also find true stories equally as engrossing as fiction.

Eda Le Shan's *What Makes Me Feel This Way?* is written for upper elementary school children and deals with personal emotions. There are a growing number of informational books on personal responses to human predicaments. Jill Krementz specializes in writing frankly about difficult human problems. In . . . *How It Feels When Parents Divorce,* Krementz uses firsthand accounts from children of divorced parents. Appropriately, the book is illustrated with photographs, intensifying the reality of the subject.

Physical disabilities are too frequently ignored in books for children, and Ron Roy's *Move Over, Wheelchairs Coming Through!* is a welcome addition to informational books. Subtitled *Several Young People in Wheelchairs Talk About Their Lives,* this is a fascinating and moving account that provides an admirable combination of frankness and sensitivity for its topic. As was mentioned in Chapter 5, there is virtually no limit to the sort of psychological or sociological problems that children's literature might discuss. Our society's penchant for therapy has at last spilled over into the realm of children's books, but we should guard that we as adults do not allow a book to substitute for a good heart-to-heart talk with a child experiencing a personal problem.

EVALUATING INFORMATIONAL BOOKS

As with biographies, informational books must necessarily be evaluated by quite different standards from fiction, but an evaluation, nevertheless, is quite crucial. Readers, adults and children alike, have a tendency to accept unquestioningly whatever they see in print, particularly if the work purports to be "informational." The following criteria may help in evaluating these books.

Purpose

Readers expect the purpose of an informational book to be clear and manageable, and its subject treated thoroughly and objectively. Titles are important—most readers will prefer an unimaginative but accurate title to a vague showstopper that promises more than it delivers. All of us have at one time been sorely disappointed when a book's content did not live up to the hopes expressed in its title.

Naturally, the information should be appropriate to the age level of the intended audience. A good informational book ought to be challenging, but not threatening or overwhelming. Also, there should be a clear distinction made between fact and theory or supposition. Patricia Lauber, in *The Friendly Dolphins,* is quite careful to point out which details are known for sure about dolphins and which are still the best guesses of scientists. In this way, children receive valuable critical training. It is good for us all to remember that few things are certain in this world.

We expect historians to avoid stereotypes and to present a balanced view of the information (history is usually more uncertain and far less objective than science). It is also important that information be up-to-date. Informational books, as we have noted, become rather quickly dated—Lauber's book on dolphins, for example, was written in 1963 and will obviously lack important discoveries about dolphins in the intervening quarter-century. The copyright of an informational book carries far more significance than does that of a novel or poem.

Accuracy and Objectivity

A fictional writer must be a keen observer of human nature, but not necessarily an "expert" in any particular field of study. The author of an informational book, however, may need specialized training in the subject about which he or she is writing. This is less true for writers of picture concept books for preschoolers than it is for juvenile authors (one need not be a linguist to create a good alphabet book or a mathematician to create a good counting book). But it should go without saying that an informational book with glaring errors is not a good thing.

Authors of informational books for older children tend to specialize—Milton Meltzer in social history, Leonard Everett Fisher in historical crafts and trades, David Macauley in architecture, Millicent Selsam in natural history, Vicki Cobb in chemistry, to name a few. Interested readers begin to recognize familiar names and seek out books by certain writers in a field. It is also not too soon for children in the middle elementary years to become aware of the authors behind the books and to learn about their qualifications. Sometimes biographical notes in the books themselves provide this information, but additional information can be garnered from library card catalogues, books about writers (such as *Something About the Author* or the *Dictionary of Literary Biography*), and in books about children's literature. All this is not to suggest that a previously unknown writer cannot create a stunning informational book (or that a well-known writer cannot produce a bomb)—but we ought to know something about the writer if we are going to take the information he or she gives us seriously.

Objectivity in informational books is an important asset, as we have discussed in Chapter 11. We may begin to suspect undue bias if the writer portrays a subject with too great a simplicity, or with all virtues and no vices, or with all positive aspects and no negative ones. Few topics in the world are absolutely clear-cut, and nothing is perfect. There is no good reason for suggesting otherwise to young readers.

Format and Organization

The format of the informational book is extremely important. Readers prefer books that are easy to follow—and a book does not have to be simplistic to be easy to follow. Such a book is the result of clear and logical organization, moving from simple to complex ideas, or, in the case of history, developing chronologically. Organizational aids, such as headings and subheadings, supplementary aids, such as a table of contents, a glossary, an index, and a bibliography, are especially desirable in books for adolescent readers (although such supplements are surprisingly rare in older books especially).

Illustrations must be carefully placed in the text (preferably next to the material they are illustrating) and with captions if they are appropriate. We should expect illustrations both to increase our knowledge and to provide aesthetic pleasure. Photographs are frequently used to illustrate informational books, for they can provide a sense of reality and authenticity (particularly in history books, nature books, and books about people). However, we must be aware that photography is an art and that not just any photograph will do. Photographs well done can be beautiful and moving, serving more than to simply identify an object.

This is not to suggest that photographs are the only effective means of illustrating informational books. However, when graphic or painterly techniques are used to illustrate these works they ought not to trivialize the subject (can you imagine a cartoon book about divorce or the death of parent?) or to unnecessarily sentimentalize it. Leonard Everett Fisher opted for black-and-white scratchboard illustrations for his history works, for example, and they proved appropriately simple without making colonial life out to be a bed of roses—for life in the eighteenth century was very hard. Regardless of the medium and style of the illustrative material, the important thing is that the illustrations contribute to the informational value of the book. There is no substitute for clear and accurate illustrations in an informational book.

Style

As was suggested above, high school and college textbooks are notoriously dull reading—too often these books simply rattle off facts without any attention to the reader's enjoyment. The first virtue of any informational book is clarity—without this, the book is a failure. But an informational book, not only through its choice of facts, but through its choice of words (diction) and sentence structure (syntax), can be stimulating reading. A good writer will suit both diction and syntax to the intended audience's age level. (We have already noted earlier in this text that boredom results from material being either too simple or too difficult for the reader.)

Where it is appropriate, humor can add enjoyment to informational books—so long as it neither mocks nor obscures an issue. Appropriate similes and metaphors (see Chapter 7) cannot only make interesting reading, they can also clarify complicated or unfamiliar ideas. David Macauley's *The Way Things Work* treats some extremely complicated concepts, but he ties the entire work together by using cartoon figures of woolly mammoths to demonstrate the various properties and scientific principles involved. For example, the mammoths are used to represent "force" or "effort." In this way, Macauley makes use of both metaphor, to illustrate an otherwise abstract concept, and humor, to make his explanations accessible and enjoyable. Humor can enable many people to learn concepts more quickly and to remember them more easily.

INFORMATIONAL BOOKS AS LITERATURE

The entire thrust of this chapter has been to suggest that informational books for young people can be (we would like to say "ought to be") works of art. They can be books that excite young readers to further reading, and books that young readers want to return to again and again—not only for information, but for enjoyment. It is quite right to expect that a nonfictional work be well written, beautifully illustrated, imaginatively laid-out, as well as up-to-date, accurate, and thought-provoking.

When a child has a question about fish, it is simply not good enough to pick up the first book we see with a large-mouthed bass on the cover. All informational books are not equal.

We must remember that there are no dull subjects under the sun—only dull people to tell their stories. When we look for informational books, let us look for books by those writers who respect their subjects and have mastered the art of telling their stories.

SELECTED BIBLIOGRAPHY OF CRITICAL STUDIES

Bacon, Betty. "The Art of Nonfiction." *Children's Literature in Education* 14 (Spring 1981): 3–14

Carr, Jo, ed. *Beyond Fact: Nonfiction for Children and Young People.* Chicago: American Library Association, 1982.

Chamberlain, Larry. "Enchantment Isn't Everything: A New Way of Looking at Lands and Peoples." *School Library Journal* (1978): 25–26.

Fisher, Margery. *Matters of Fact: Aspects of Non-Fiction for Children.* New York: Crowell, 1972.

Kobrin, Beverly. *Eyeopeners! How to Choose and Use Children's Books About Real People, Places, and Things.* New York: Viking, 1988.

Meltzer, Milton. "Where Do All the Prizes Go? The Case for Nonfiction." *Horn Book Magazine* 52 (February 1976): 17–23.

Norris, Lynn. "Extending Curiosity: Children's Informational Books." *Idaho Librarian* (October 1975): 126–28.

Selsam, Millicent E. "Writing About Science for Children." In *Beyond Fact: Nonfiction for Children and Young People.* Ed. Jo Carr. Chicago: American Library Association, 1982, 61–65.

Sutherland, Zena. "Information Pleases—Sometimes." *Wilson Library Journal* 49 (October 1974): 17–23.

———. "Science as Literature." *Literary Trends* 22:4 (April 1974): 485–89.

SELECTED BIBLIOGRAPHY OF INFORMATIONAL BOOKS

The books in this list simply represent a cross-section of the wealth of nonfiction available for young readers. The books in this list are categorized according to the four broad classifications outlined in this chapter; however, these are only general guidelines and frequently books cross boundaries. For example, Franklyn Branley's *The Mystery of Stonehenge* may fit comfortably into both "Lands and People" as an historical work and into "Science and Nature" for its scientific explanation of that Stone Age phenomenon. This list is also in addition to those concept books listed at the end of Chapter 5.

Lands and Peoples

Aliki (pseud. for Aliki Brandenburg). *Corn Is Maise—The Gift of the Indians.* New York: Crowell, 1976.

———. *A Medieval Feast.* New York: Crowell, 1983.

———. *Mummies Made in Egypt.* New York: Crowell, 1979.

Ashabranner, Brent. *Children of the Maya.* New York: Dodd, Mead & Co., 1986.

———. *Land of Yesterday, Land of Tomorrow: Discovering Chinese Central Asia.* New York: Cobblehill, 1992.

Bach, Alice, and J. Cheryl Exum. *Miriam's Well: Stories about Women in the Bible.* New York: Delacorte, 1991.

Baylor, Byrd. *When Clay Sings.* Illus. by Tom Bakhi. New York: Scribner's, 1972.

Bealer, Alex W. *Only the Names Remain: The Cherokees and the Trail of Tears.* Boston: Little, Brown, 1972.

Berck, Judith. *No Place to Be: Voices of Homeless Children.* Boston: Houghton, 1991.

Bontemps, Arna. *Story of the Negro.* 3rd ed. New York: Knopf, 1958.

Branley, Franklyn. *The Mystery of Stonehenge.* New York: Crowell, 1969.

Caselli, Giovanni. *The First Civilizations.* New York: Bedrick, 1985.

Chaikin, Miriam, adapter. *Exodus.* Illus. Charles Mikolaycak. New York: Holiday, 1987.

———. *Sound the Shofar: The Story and Meaning of Rosh Hashanah and Yom Kippur.* Boston: Houghton-Mifflin, 1986.

Chang, Ina. *A Separate Battle: Women and the Civil War.* New York: Dutton, 1991.

Chubb, Thomas Caldecot. *The Byzantines.* Cleveland: World, 1959.

Commager, Henry Steele. *The First Book of American History.* Illus. Leonard Everett Fisher. New York: Watts, 1957.

Coolidge, Olivia. *Tales of the Crusades.* Boston: Houghton Mifflin, 1970.

Fisher, Leonard Everett. *The Factories.* New York: Holiday, 1979.

———. *The Hospitals.* New York: Watts, 1980.

———. *The Peddlers.* New York: Watts, 1968.

———. *The Railroads.* New York: Holiday, 1979.

———. *The Schoolmasters.* New York: Watts, 1967.

Foster, Genevieve. *The World of William Penn.* New York: Scribner's, 1973.

———. *The Year of the Pilgrims—1620.* New York: Scribner's, 1969.

Freedman, Russell. *Cowboys of the Wild West.* New York: Tickner & Fields, 1985.

———. *Immigrant Kids.* New York: Dutton, 1980.

———. *An Indian Winter.* New York: Holiday, 1992.

Greenfeld, Howard. *Chanukah.* New York: Holt, 1976.

———. *Passover.* New York: Holt, 1978.

———. *Rosh Hashanah and Yom Kippur.* New York: Holt, 1979.

Hughes, Langston. *The First Book of Africa.* Rev. ed. New York: Watts, 1964.

Jacobs, Francine. *The Tainos: The People Who Welcomed Columbus.* New York: Putnam, 1992.

Keegan, Marcia. *Pueblo Boy: Growing Up in Two Worlds.* New York: Dutton, 1991.

Kuskin, Karla. *Jerusalem, Shining Still.* New York: Harper, 1987.

Meltzer, Milton. *Brother Can You Spare Dime? The Great Depression: 1929–33.* New York: New American Library, 1977.

———. *The Hispanic Americans.* New York: Crowell, 1982.

Myers, Walter Dean. *Now Is Your Time!: The African-American Struggle for Freedom.* New York: HarperCollins, 1991.

Price, Christine. *Made in Ancient Egypt.* New York: Dutton, 1970.

Rylant, Cynthia. *Appalachia: The Voices of Sleeping Birds.* New York: Harcourt, 1991.

Schwartz, Alvin. *The City and Its People: The Story of One City's Government.* New York: Dutton, 1967.

Seeger, Elizabeth. *Eastern Religions.* New York: T. Crowell, 1973.

Snelling, John. *Buddhism.* New York: Watts, 1986.

Van Loon, Hendrik Willem. *The Story of Mankind.* Rev. ed. New York: Liveright, 1951.

Science and Nature

Anno, Mitsumasa. *Anno's Math Games.* New York: Philomel, 1987.

———. *Anno's Math Games II.* New York: Philomel, 1987.

Arnosky, Jim. *Secrets of a Wildlife Watcher.* New York: Lothrop, 1983.

Branley, Franklyn. *Air Is All Around You.* New York: Crowell, 1986.

———. *Light and Darkness.* New York: Crowell, 1975.

————. *Uranus: The Seventh Planet.* New York: Crowell, 1975.

Cobb, Vicki. *The Scoop of Ice Cream.* Boston: Little, Brown, 1985.

————. *Sneakers Meet Your Feet.* Boston: Little, Brown, 1985.

George, Jean Craighead. *Spring Comes to the Ocean.* New York: Crowell, 1965.

Gibbons, Gail. *From Seed to Plant.* New York: Holiday, 1991.

————. *The Puffins Are Back!* New York: HarperCollins, 1991.

————. *Recycle!: A Handbook for Kids.* Boston: Little, Brown, 1992.

Gross, Ruth Belov. *A Book about Pandas.* New York: Scholastic, 1974.

————. *Snakes.* New York: Four Winds, 1975.

Heller, Ruth. *The Reason for a Flower.* New York: Scholastic, 1983.

Brown, Laurie Krasny, and Marc Brown. *Dinosaurs to the Rescue!: A Guide to Protecting Our Planet.* Boston: Little, Brown, 1992.

Lauber, Patricia. *The Friendly Dolphins.* New York: Random, 1963.

————. *Summer of Fire: Yellowstone 1988.* New York: Watts, 1991.

————. *Tales Mummies Tell.* New York: Crowell, 1985.

Llewellyn, Claire. *My First Book of Time.* Boston: Houghton, 1992.

Macauley, David. *The Way Things Work.* Boston: Houghton Mifflin, 1988.

Machotka, Hana. *Breathtaking Noses.* New York: Morrow, 1992.

————. *What Neat Feet!* New York: Morrow, 1991.

Mendoza, George. *The Digger Wasp.* New York: Dial, 1969.

Paladino, Catherine. *Our Vanishing Farm Animals: Saving America's Rare Breeds.* Boston: Little, 1991.

Patent, Dorothy Hinshaw. *Where the Bald Eagles Gather.* Photos William Munoz. Boston: Houghton Mifflin, 1984.

Peters, Lisa Westberg. *Water's Way.* New York: Arcade, 1991.

Pringle, Laurence. *City and Suburbs: Exploring Ecosystems.* New York: Macmillan, 1975.

————. *The Hidden World: Life Under a Rock.* New York: Macmillan, 1977.

————. *Living in a Risky World.* New York: Morrow, 1989.

Ride, Sally, and Susan Okie. *To Space and Back.* New York: Lothrop, 1986.

Simon, Seymour. *Earthquakes.* New York: Morrow, 1991.

————. *Mars.* New York: Morrow, 1987.

————. *Uranus.* New York: Morrow, 1987.

Srivastava, Jane Jonas. *Statistics.* New York: Crowell, 1973.

Taylor, Barbara. *Coral Reef.* Boston: Houghton, 1992.

————. *Desert Life.* Boston: Houghton, 1992.

————. *Pond Life.* Boston: Houghton, 1992.

————. *Rain Forest.* Boston: Houghton, 1992.

Vernon, Adele. *The Hoiho: New Zealand's Yellow-Eyed Penguin.* New York: Putnam, 1991.

Fine and Applied Arts

Arnosky, Jim. *Fish in a Flash!: A Personal Guide to Spin-Fishing.* New York: Bradbury, 1991.

————. *Sketching Outdoors in Spring.* New York: Lothrop, 1987.

Batterberry, Ariane, and Michael Batterberry. *The Pantheon Story of American Art for Young People.* New York: Pantheon, 1976.

Beardsley, John. *Pablo Picasso.* New York: Abrams, 1991.

Brown, Marc. *Your First Garden Book.* Boston: Little, Brown, 1981.

Bellville, Cheryl Walsh. *Theater Magic: Behind the Scenes at a Children's Theater.* Minneapolis: Carolrhoda, 1986.

Bierhorst, John. *A Cry from the Earth: Music of the North American Indians.* New York: Four Winds, 1979.

Chase, Alice Elizabeth. *Famous Artists of the Past.* Bronx, NY: Platt & Munk, 1964.

———. *Looking at Art.* New York: T. Crowell, 1966.

Cone, Ferne Geller. *Crazy Crocheting.* Illus. Rachel Osterlof. Photos J. Morton Cone. New York: Atheneum, 1981.

Cooper, Miriam. *Snap! Photography.* New York: Messner, 1981.

Fisher, Leonard Everett. *Alphabet Art.* New York: Four Winds, 1978.

———. *Calendar Art.* New York: Four Winds, 1987.

Florian, Douglas. *A Carpenter.* New York: Greenwillow, 1991.

———. *A Potter.* New York: Greenwillow, 1991.

Greenberg, Jan, and Sandra Jordan. *The Painter's Eye: Learning to Look at Contemporary American Art.* New York: Delacorte, 1991.

Haskell, Arnold. *The Wonderful World of Dance.* New York: Doubleday, 1969.

Hodges, C. Walter. *Shakespeare's Theatre.* New York: Coward-McCann, 1964.

Hofsinde, Robert (Gray-Wolf). *Indian Arts.* New York: Morrow, 1971.

Hughes, Langston. *The First Book of Jazz.* New York: Watts, 1955.

Jaspersohn, William. *Magazine: Behind the Scenes at* Sports Illustrated. Boston: Little, Brown, 1983.

Kalb, Jonah, and Laura Kalb. *The Easy Ice Skating Book.* Illus. Sandy Kossin. Boston: Houghton Mifflin, 1981.

Kohl, Herbert. *A Book of Puzzlements: Play and Invention with Language.* New York: Schocken, 1981.

Krementz, Jill. *A Very Young Rider.* New York: Knopf, 1977.

Lasky, Kathryn. *Puppeteer.* New York: Macmillan, 1985.

Marks, Mickey K. *OP-Tricks: Creating Kinetic Art.* Philadelphia: Lippincott, 1972.

Macauley, David. *Castle.* Boston: Houghton Mifflin, 1977.

———. *Cathedral: The Story of Its Construction.* Boston: Houghton Mifflin, 1973.

———. *Pyramid.* Boston: Houghton Mifflin, 1975.

Naylor, Penelope. *Black Images: The Art of West Africa.* New York: Doubleday, 1973.

Raboff, Ernest. *Michelangelo Buonarroti.* New York: Harper, 1988.

———. *Pablo Picasso.* New York: Harper, 1987.

———. *Van Gogh.* New York: Harper, 1988.

Rodari, Florian. *A Weekend with Picasso.* New York: Rizzoli, 1991.

St. George, Judith. *The Brooklyn Bridge: They Said It Couldn't Be Built.* New York: Putnam, 1982.

———. *The Panama Canal: Gateway to the World.* New York: Putnam, 1989.

Skira-Venturi, Rosabianca. *A Weekend with Renoir.* New York: Rizzoli, 1991.

Streatfield, Noel. *A Young Person's Guide to Ballet.* London: Warne, 1985.

Tinkelman, Murray. *Rodeo: The Great American Sport.* New York: Greenwillow, 1982.

Weiss, Harvey. *How to Make Your Own Books.* New York: Crowell, 1974.

Wolf, Diane. *Chinese Writing.* New York: Holt, Rinehart & Winston, 1975.

Human Development and Behavior

Banish, Roslyn. *A Forever Family.* New York: HarperCollins, 1992.

Bernstein, Joanne, and Stephen Gullo. *When People Die.* New York: Dutton, 1977.

Cole, Joanna. *The New Baby at Your House.* New York: Morrow, 1985.

Engel, Joel. *Handwriting Analysis Self-Taught.* New York: Elsevier/Nelson, 1980.

Giblin, James Cross. *From Hand to Mouth: Or How We Invented Knives, Forks, Spoons, and Chopsticks & the Table Manners to Go with Them.* New York: Crowell, 1987.

Jennes, Aylette. *Families: A Celebration of Diversity, Commitment, and Love.* Boston: Houghton Mifflin, 1990.

Kamien, Janet. *What If You Couldn't . . . ?* New York: Scribner's, 1979.

LeShan, Eda. *What's Going to Happen to Me? When Parents Separate or Divorce.* New York: Four Winds, 1978.

——— . *When a Parent Is Very Sick.* New York: Atlantic, 1986.

Meltzer, Milton. *The Landscape of Memory.* New York: Viking, 1987.

Perl, Lila. *The Great Ancestor Hunt: The Fun of Finding Out Who You Are.* Boston: Houghton Mifflin, 1989.

Rofes, Eric E. *The Kids Book About Death and Dying.* Boston: Little, Brown, 1985.

Schwartz, Alvin. *Telling Fortunes: Love Magic, Dream Signs, and Other Ways to Learn the Future.* Philadelphia: Lippincott, 1987.

Terkel, Susan N., and Janice Rench. *Feeling Safe, Feeling Strong: How To Avoid Sexual Abuse and What to Do If It Happens to You.* Minneapolis: Lerner, 1984.

PART III

The Concerns
of Children's Literature

CHAPTER 13

Cultural and Social Diversity

Few issues are more important today than that of our adjusting to a world that is both culturally and socially diverse. It is a vast diversity that we are being asked to grapple with. Today we must be concerned about "political correctness," cross-cultural and multi-ethnic matters, gender issues, alternative family lifestyles, peoples of varying abilities, both physical and intellectual, and, a perpetual concern, censorship of children's books. Through literature, children may be brought in touch with driving issues of the day. Following is a discussion of some of the issues that concern us as students of children's literature.

CROSS-CULTURAL DIVERSITY

We live in a global world, and that means we can no longer isolate ourselves from unfamiliar cultures and peoples. If we are to live together in harmony on this planet, it is imperative that we take every opportunity to understand one another and thereby learn to accept one another. The appearance of heroes from minority cultural groups has been a belated one in children's literature—as indeed it has been in most literature. The social reality, as demographers show us, is that we are moving from a culture dominated by European Americans to one of greater ethnic diversity, and it has become imperative that our literature reflect this dramatic shift. Literature, rather than reinforcing outmoded values, can provide us with the intellectual apparatus to bring us all to greater tolerance and understanding. The critic Northrup Frye once wrote:

> So you may ask, what is the use of studying the world of imagination where anything is possible and anything can be assumed, where there are no rights

or wrongs and all arguments are equally good? One of the most obvious ones, I think, is its encouragement of tolerance. In the imagination our own beliefs are also only possibilities, but we can see the possibilities in the beliefs of others. Bigots and fanatics seldom have any use for the arts, because they're so preoccupied with their beliefs and actions that they can't see them as also possibilities. (77–78)

In the best literature, we are exposed to the world of possibilities, removed from our own narrow confines, and challenged to spread our wings. In short, literature can prepare us for the multicultural society in which we all live.

Culturally diverse literature enriches everyone. It provides the majority culture with exposure to the various minority cultures and thus helps to break down old prejudices and dispel misunderstandings. Not least, it provides the minority cultures with positive role models and bolsters cultural pride and individual dignity. There are several important features to be considered about culturally diverse literature, regardless of its subject matter. Following are some guidelines we may use in evaluating a literary work for cultural consciousness:

1. The characters are portrayed as individuals, with genuine feelings, thoughts, and beliefs, and not as types representing a specific cultural group.
2. There is no cultural stereotyping to suggest that all members of a specific cultural group share the same socio-economic status, similar occupations, and so on.
3. The culture is accurately portrayed, neither exaggerated nor romanticized.
4. The problems facing the group are dealt with seriously, faithfully, and honestly, not oversimplified.
5. All factual details are accurate, and there are no omissions or distortions that may cast an unfair light on the picture.
6. The author demonstrates a sincere understanding of and respect for the cultural group being portrayed.

We will examine some of the literature about the four principal non-European cultural groups in the United States as well as some works focusing on cultures worldwide.

African Americans

In recent years there has been an increase in children's literature about African Americans, which begins to offset the decades of sore neglect. Earlier literature tended to focus on young white, middle-class Americans of Christian backgrounds. In 1945, Jesse Jackson (not the minister/politician/activist) wrote what was considered a groundbreaking book, *Call Me Charley.* It is the story of a young African-American boy attempting to assimilate into the white middle-class neighborhood where his parents have moved. The conflict in the book is racial, and the author's intent is made clear from the very beginning when Charley responds to a boy who refers to him as "Sambo": "My name is Charles. . . . Sometimes I'm called Charley. Nobody calls me Sambo and gets away with it" (8). The story seems dated now, with its emphasis on the essentially white, middle-class values shared by Charley and his family, which we take to be the principal reason he is finally accepted as an equal in the white community. Later African Americans would decry the necessity for Charley to abandon his identity and his cultural roots in order gain entry into the white world. But Charley was only operating in accordance with the widely accepted practices of the day, when everyone believed the ideal society to be that of the melting pot in which all distinguishing cultural features were abandoned in favor of those of the dominant white culture.

It is virtually impossible to find a picture book about an African-American child published prior to the 1960s. All the widely-used elementary basal school readers of the first half of the twentieth century depicted European American families, and one reading them would never guess that the society included any people of color. Ezra Jack Keats's *The Snowy Day* and its successors, about an inner city African-American boy named Peter, are among the first to use a nonwhite as a protagonist. Lucille Clifton's touching picture books about Everett Anderson trace the joys and heartaches of a young African-American boy who experiences the separation of his parents, the remarriage of his mother, the birth of a new half-sister, and the death of his father. Such books recognize current social realities, which make them particularly appealing.

Modern writers focusing on the African-American protagonist prefer this less romanticized approach and aim at capturing what is unique about African-American culture. Among the many fine writers in this vein are Eloise Greenfield, Rosa Guy, Virginia Hamilton, Sharon Bell Mathis, Walter Dean Myers, and Mildred Taylor. At last, African-American children can choose from a generous selection of good books that speak to their life experiences, books that do not ignore the role of the African American in history or the contribution of the African American to society. And other children can at last read stories that faithfully render the African-American experience.

Rosa Guy, a distinguished writer of books for young adults (*The Friends, Ruby,* and others) and a native of the former British colony of Trinidad, remarks on her childhood education that

> everything I had learned in my young life had to do with England and nothing to do with me. We lovely children of the island remained locked into the image of our own ugliness—forever inferior, forever proud to be ruled by white rulers, striving to reach a pinnacle of success unattainable to us. (34)

This is what has been perpetrated by the the dominant European American culture: It is the stripping of personal identity, the crushing of the spirit, the deprivation of cultural pride. Alex Haley's celebrated family history, *Roots,* told African Americans that they had a history, a meaningful one, and that that history was not simply a footnote to the history of European America. It is that history that helps to define the modern African American, just as it is the history of the European immigrant that defines the modern European American. Rosa Guy speaks for all cultural groups when she says:

> I reject the young of each succeeding generation who dare to say: "I don't understand *you* people. . ." "I can't stand *those people*. . ." or, "Do you see the way *they* act. . .?" They are us! Created by us for a society which suits our ignorance.
>
> I insist that Everychild understand this. I insist that Everychild go out into the world with this knowledge: there are no good guys. There are no bad guys. We are all good guys. We are all bad guys. And we are all responsible for each other. (34)

Native Americans

The Native American (some prefer "American Indian") was, for many, the noble savage, living in harmony with the natural world and free from the corruption of society. For others, he was a brutal, uncivilized creature, prone to night raids and scalping parties. The mania for the Old West in books and movies earlier in this century only further sullied the reputation. As with the African Americans, the Native Americans' image was at the mercy of the predominant European American that had subdued them. This could hardly be expected to produce a fair billing.

Unfortunately, such early children's books as Walter Edmonds's *The Matchlock Gun,* itself a Newbery Award–winner in 1942, did much to perpetuate the prejudices, depicting Native Americans as wild and fearsome Indians. Children's picture books either ignored the Native American altogether or fell back on the stereotypes. Native Americans argue that even the modern picture books rely on the old images and fail to portray the modern American Indian realistically. Indeed, by and large, picture books on Native Americans still tend to focus on the traditional images—feathered head-dresses, teepees, tomahawks, and papooses—and ignore the fact that about two million Native Americans live today in America without these trappings. Miska Miles's *Annie and the Old One* is a rare example of a picture book about a modern Native American family, free of stereotypes.

For older children, Scott O'Dell's *Island of the Blue Dolphins* (about an Indian girl who survived alone for eighteen years on a deserted island off the California coast) and *Sing Down the Moon* (the tale of forced relocation of the Navajo nation from their Arizona homeland) are sympathetic portraits of Native Americans. Some very good novels depicting Native Americans in contemporary settings have also been written. These frequently have as their theme the cultural conflict between white America and the Native cultures. Evelyn Sibley Lampman's *The Potlatch Family* is the bittersweet story of a modern Chinook girl who must deal with the prejudices of her classmates and a difficult family situation. The Alaskan Eskimo culture has attracted considerable attention and is the subject of Scott O'Dell's *Black Star, Bright Dawn,* which focuses on a heroine, a young girl who takes her father's place in the annual dog-sled race. Jean Craighead George's *Julie of the Wolves* and Gary Paulsen's *Dogsong* both focus on modern-day Eskimos who are forced to decide between the ways of their ancestors and the encroaching white society. For older readers is Margaret Craven's *I Heard the Owl Call My Name,* which has as its protagonist a young white Anglican priest who is sent to a remote Kwiakutl village on the Pacific Coast of British Columbia where he comes to know and love the people and their ways. Jamake Highwater's *Anpao: An American Indian Odyssey* is an adaptation of native folk literature and therefore not a novel. However, it is this literature that often best captures the essence of the Native American spirit.

Partly because the numbers of Native Americans are sparser, fewer Native Americans have written books about their own culture than have African Americans written about theirs. It is important to realize that to speak of a "Native American" is about as precise as speaking of a "European." Each tribal nation enjoys its own customs, beliefs, tales, and organization, and they can be as different as the Greeks are from the Norwegians. It is time that we begin to shed the image of the mythic "Indian," the "Indian" that has become the mascot of so many athletic teams and the target in so many films and Western novels. This image of the Indian—that of the warrior Indian, whether it be the noble savage or the wild "redskin"—is one created by the enemy, and we can hardly expect it to be either fair or accurate. It is important that mainstream America begin to realize that Native Americans are still very much a part of our culture and not simply part of our historical trappings. Some of the best literature recognizes this by introducing Native Americans who are flesh-and-blood individuals living in modern America in homes (not teepees), speaking English or perhaps their native tongue (not some mock broken English that Indians never spoke to begin with), wearing modern dress, driving modern vehicles, and generally trying, like everyone else, to make a better life for themselves. A good work of literature about Native Americans will also recognize the individual tribal differences and attempt to faithfully portray the language, customs, and beliefs practiced by the various peoples. Anything less than this is dishonest and unfairly stereotypes the Native American.

Hispanic Americans

Among the largest commonly recognized minority groups in the United States is the Hispanic Americans, whose ancestry is a mingling of Spanish and Native Americans. Particularly in the southwestern states, the Hispanic American is on the way to becoming the dominant cultural group, although the literature has not yet reflected its influence. Not only are there few good books on Hispanic Americans available, studies have found that many of the books in existence present an inaccurate picture of the culture. Despite the fact that most Hispanic Americans live in cities, books more often than not depict rural people, often migrant workers, and usually living in poverty (see Wagoner). The earliest works depicting Hispanic Americans focused exclusively on the Hispanic American culture in isolation. Joseph Krumgold's . . . *and now Miguel* is the story of the coming of age of an Hispanic American boy from a family of sheepherders in northern New Mexico. Scott O'Dell's mythic tale, *The Black Pearl,* is a work transcending all age categories with its exploration of good and evil set in Baja California.

But as with the other cultural groups we have considered, a chief concern of modern-day Hispanic Americans is that of the clash of cultures and the need for both the minority and the majority group to understand each other. Scott O'Dell's *Child of Fire* is the story of an adolescent Hispanic American boy as told by a parole officer, which provides insight into the cultural disparities and the difficulties of adjustment. One of the earliest books dealing with the prejudice faced by Hispanic Americans is Hila Colman's *The Girl from Puerto Rico.* Frank Bonham's *Viva Chicano* reveals the plight of the Hispanic American in the inner city. Walter Dean Myers's *Scorpions* portrays Hispanic Americans as well as African Americans engaged in their modern-day struggle. Florence Crannell Means's *Us Maltbys* likewise focuses on both cultural groups in a story about a white family with several foster children of different backgrounds.

Given the numbers of Hispanic Americans in the United States, the dearth of literature featuring them is surprising. There are very few picture books. The writer and illustrator Leo Politi was among the first to use Hispanic Americans in picture books. His works include at least two award winners, *Pedro, The Angel of Olvera Street* (Caldecott Honor Book in 1947) and *Song of the Swallows* (Caldecott Medalist in 1950), both set in California. Marie Hall Ets's *Nine Days to Christmas,* winner of the 1960 Caldecott Medal, is another that has remained popular. Historically this negligence may be a result of widespread poverty, inadequate education, and the resulting diminished political clout of Hispanic Americans. Fortunately, we have seen important strides in all of these areas in recent years, and Hispanic Americans will unquestionably become a powerful force in the American socio-economic and political arena by the turn of the century. It is time that this presence was noted in children's literature.

Asian Americans

Asian Americans are becoming a prominent part of the American culture, and, like almost every minority in this nation's history, they too have suffered indignation at the hands of the dominant European culture. In the middle of the nineteenth century, large numbers of Chinese workers were brought to the American West where they provided cheap labor for the railroads. For the Chinese, as for the European immigrants, America promised to be a land of opportunity, but those promises did not always come to fruition. J. S. Wong's *Fifth Chinese Daughter* is among the earliest books to portray Chinese Americans with realism; it is the story of a girl growing up in San Francisco and her desire to become an artist. Laurence Yep's *Dragonwings* provides us with a view of San Francisco's Chinatown in the early 1900s through the eyes of a young Chinese immigrant, giving us valuable insight into the difficulties of assimilating two very different cultures. The same author's *The Child of the Owl* provides a modern setting with a similar theme—the clash of two cultures, out of which the protagonist learns the value of her Chinese heritage.

The Japanese too are seldom found in children's fiction, which is surprising given the economic influence of Japan in recent years. It is interesting to note that virtually no books exist on the difficulty of Japanese characters in adapting to life in America, but there are significant books on the difficulty of the Americans adapting to Japanese living in America, more specifically the cultural conflict that unjustly erupted during the Second World War. The autobiographical *Farewell to Manazar,* by Jeanne

Wakatsuki and James D. Houston, is the harrowing story of the internment of Japanese-American families during the war, a tale little-known among Americans until recent years. Yoshiko Uchida's *Journey to Topaz* is a book on the same theme, also drawn from personal experience.

World-Wide Cultures

In addition to these four, the United States can boast a myriad of cultural groups that contribute to our rich diversity. The nature of the modern world demands that we all become more aware of and sensitive to the diverse cultures found, not only in our own nation, but in the world at large. Books can be found on a wide variety of cultures from around the globe, from the Cholistan Desert tribes of Pakistan in Suzanne Fisher Staples's *Shabanu: Daughter of the Wind* to the Australian outback in Mavis Thorpe Clark's *The Min-Min* to the Welsh coal-mining district in Richard Llewellyn's *How Green Was My Valley* to modern-day Africa in Bess Clayton's *Story for a Black Night.*
Some of the most eye-opening books are those based on historical events. The moving *Anne Frank: The Diary of a Young Girl,* which recounts the horrors of Nazi occupation in The Netherlands, is among the most famous of these. Aranka Siegal's *Upon the Head of a Goat: A Childhood in Hungary, 1939-1944,* describes the Nazi atrocities against the Jews from the perspective of yet another nation. The terror of the holocaust a half-century ago was the grim culmination of centuries of persecution for the Jewish people. But anti-Semitism still thrives—most obviously, but not only, in the Middle East. Chaim Potok's *My Name Is Asher Lev,* Yuri Suhl's *The Merrymaker,* and the wonderful works of Isaac Bashevis Singer, including the autobiographical stories of *In My Father's Court,* his popular *Yentl the Yeshiva Boy,* and *The Death of Methuselah* are lovely expressions of the Jewish culture which can bring us all to a more sympathetic understanding. But persecution knows no cultural bounds as demonstrated in David Kherdian's *The Road from Home: The Story of an Armenian Girl.* This is a biographical account of the author's mother's experiences during the period of the massacre of Armenian Christians in Turkey just after World War I and brings to light one of the lesser-known, but no less horrifying, crimes against humanity. This cataloguing sounds like a grim list indeed, but perhaps keeping before us these deplorable chapters in the world's history will serve in some small way to prevent similar future atrocities.

GENDER AWARENESS

A second issue we must be aware of is that of gender roles in literature for children. For thousands of years, most of human society has been patriarchal, dominated by the male. Our patriarchal culture has effectively relegated the woman's position to one of subservience and has caused us to see feminine traits as inferior to masculine traits. Society has come to value physical strength, assertiveness, independence, power, aggression, ambition—all of which we tend to see as masculine features. Conversely, we denigrate passivity, docility, emotionalism, physical weakness, dependence, resignation—all of which we tend to see as feminine features. These values have been so ingrained in our culture that we generally accept them without question. For a woman to be taken seriously, she must perform as a man, and such behavior is just as likely to win her ridicule from both sexes. It has only been in the last half of the twentieth century that significant strides have been taken to eliminate this male bias in Western culture.

In literature, as we might expect, the bias is reflected in several ways, most notably in the prevalence of male protagonists over female, the celebration of the typically male traits of physical strength and aggression, and the perpetuation of the image of the female as weak and ineffectual. Children's books have not escaped the stereotyping, and they reflect in their own way society's subtle antifeminine bias. There are three principal ways literature conveys this negative message.

Gender-Biased Language

Language can perpetuate cultural bias, and English is particularly notable for this transgression. The use of the masculine pronoun "he" to refer to everyone, for example, effectively eliminates over at least half the human race. Compound words such as "chairman," "mailman," "policeman," and "businessman" indicate the histori-cal dominance of the male. We use "sissy" as a disparaging term, but it's seen as good for someone to stand up and take it like a "man."

Gender Roles

Society has traditionally assigned certain roles to men—generally roles of leadership and authority—and certain roles to women—generally roles of caregivers and assistants. In the past, children's books have portrayed doctors, airline pilots, school principals, and corporate executives as male, whereas nurses, stewardesses, teachers, and secretaries have been depicted as female. This is, of course, not very different from the cultural bias in which, for example, whites are depicted in leadership positions and people of color in subservient roles. Additionally, the tasks performed by women have been typically undervalued—ask those in the nursing profession or in secretarial positions, for example, two areas still largely occupied by underpaid women.

Gender Behavior

In addition to casting men and women in designated roles, society has traditionally differentiated between what it perceives to be male and female behavior or standards of conduct. Women have been cast as the fairer and weaker sex, weaker physically, emotionally, and intellectually. The male child is expected to be physically active, even mischievous. The female child who shows such traits may be labeled a "tomboy," another disparaging term. Tears are expected of a female and condemned in a male. Males are expected to be clever and inventive, but similar traits in females are often acknowledged with surprise. Studies of gender behavior in children's books will point out how often girls are depicted as passive observers, whereas the boys are actively engaged. (A boy may climb a tree, but a girl must observe from the safety of the ground, for example.)

It is important that children read books that give them positive images of women and that avoid ignorant stereotyping of roles and behavior. These might include such books as Louise Fitzhugh's *Harriet the Spy,* about a clever young girl who decides she wants to be a spy, or Jean Craighead George's *Julie of the Wolves,* about a courageous Eskimo girl with painful decisions to face, or Ouida Sebestyen's *Words by Heart,* about a young African-American girl facing prejudice in the early twentieth century. Books that provide positive adult role models are equally important, such as Peggy Mann's *Amelia Earhart, First Lady of Flight,* one of the many biographies of this pioneer pilot, or Patricia MacLachlan's *Cassie Binegar,* with its portrait of a remarkable grand-mother. Not to be neglected are books that depict males in other than stereotypical roles. John Steptoe's *My Daddy Is a Monster . . . Sometimes* depicts a nurturing father as seen through the eyes of children. And Mark Wandro and Joanie Blank's *My Daddy Is a Nurse* describes ten fathers in professions traditionally associated with women. Books in which males are depicted as sensitive, artistic, or anything other than macho sports fanatics are also helpful. Patricia MacLachlan's *Arthur, for the Very First Time* and Katherine Paterson's *Bridge to Terabithia* are two notable examples.

Two principles must be stressed here. The first is that gender bias in children's books does not create the problem, but it may reinforce it. When obvious gender bias is found in a book, we as adults should be ready to point it out to young readers and discuss it. Remember that it will inevitably be found in many of the classics that predate this era of consciousness raising. But rather than eliminate these books altogether and deprive children of some great stories, we can use the books to our advantage and show children how times have changed.

The second principle is that eliminating gender bias from our society does not help females alone. Males are just as much victims of a social bondage, weighted down with great expectations, and permitted no acceptable emotional outlet except, perhaps, for aggressive behavior on the playing fields. The liberation of women must necessarily mean the liberation of men as well, leaving all people free to choose their places in society unshackled by ignorance and bias.

Following are some guidelines we may use when evaluating a literary work for gender awareness:

1. The author uses inclusive language, avoiding the universal "he" and gender specific words like "mailman" and "chairman." (Naturally, we may not fault earlier writers for not observing this practice, for only since the 1980s has inclusive language become the norm.)
2. The author avoids blanket casting of males and females into stereotyped roles—especially roles that cast females as subservient to males (men as breadwinners, females as housewives; males as doctors, females as nurses; and so on). (Of course, this is not to suggest that all roles be reversed out of a sense of fairness, but only that we should not expect all nurses to be females, all mayors to be males, and so on.)
3. The author avoids stereotyping certain behaviors and personality traits as "feminine"—especially those suggesting weakness, docility, and passivity.
4. The author avoids stereotyping certain behaviors and personality traits as "masculine"—especially those suggesting toughness, insensitivity, and aggressiveness.

ALTERNATIVE FAMILIES AND LIFESTYLES

A third issue recognizes the fact that no longer do most children grow up in homes in the suburbs with two parents, a sibling, and a dog. No longer do most mothers don their aprons in the morning and spend their days cleaning and cooking for their families. Divorce is as common as marriage; and women virtually outnumber the men in the workforce. Modern children's books are now coming to reflect this reality. The traumas of dealing with divorce are related in Beverly Cleary's *Dear Mr. Henshaw.* Children who have stepparents, stepsiblings, and half-siblings may find comfort in books depicting other families like theirs. We must remember that many popular folktales have some very unflattering portraits of stepmothers. Rather than deprive children of the enchantment of "Cinderella," we might balance it with a book about a positive experience with stepmothers, such as Patricia MacLachlan's *Sarah, Plain and Tall.* There are also those more unconventional families, such as that depicted in Norma Klein's *Mom, the Wolfman, and Me,* which focuses on an unmarried mother and her daughter who must make adjustments to her mother's new boyfriend. Katherine Paterson's *The Great Gilly Hopkins* deals with the problems of foster care. And Cynthia Voigt's *Homecoming* and *Dicey's Song* tell the story of four children, abandoned by their mother, who seek to make a home with their formidable grandmother. Arnold Adoff's *Black Is Brown Is Tan,* a picture book for the very young, is among the few books that deal with interracial marriages. Adoff celebrates the joy of diversity in the relationship. In the future, we should expect more books for children on this subject.

Following are some guidelines we may use in evaluating books about alternative families and lifestyles:

1. The author treats the subject with sensitivity.
2. Any suggestion that the alternative family life is somehow less desirable than the so-called traditional family is avoided.
3. The author treats the subject with honesty and frankness; there is no pretense that children in these circumstances will not face problems, doubts, fears—in other words, they are treated just like all other children.

THE PHYSICALLY, EMOTIONALLY, AND INTELLECTUALLY CHALLENGED

Another change taking place in our society is the healthier and more receptive attitude toward individuals with special needs. These individuals were once virtually ignored in children's books, undoubtedly a holdover from the time when people with physical, emotional, or intellectual differences were largely hidden away from society—either institutionalized or kept secluded at home. Thankfully society is more sensitive to the needs of this group. Our laws now recognize the existence of physically challenged individuals, and our schools now are far more accommodating to the intellectually challenged. Gradually, children's books are addressing the interests of these people. We can now find books dealing with emotional needs, such as Taro Yashima's picture book, *Crow Boy,* about an inordinately shy boy, or Betsy Byars's *The Summer of the Swans,* about a boy with a mental disability and his relationship with other family members, or Virginia Hamilton's *Sweet Whispers, Brother Rush,* about a family coping with an inherited mental disorder. Physical disabilities are featured in such books as Elizabeth Fanshawe's *Rachel* and Joan Fassler's *Howie Helps Himself,* both stories about younger children in wheelchairs.

It is important that people face their fears and ignorance regarding others with special needs, and reading books is one way of overcoming prejudices and combatting stereotypes. Of course, it is important that the books we read deal fairly with disabilities and special needs. Following are some guidelines that we may use to evaluate literary works focusing on characters with special needs:

1. The characters with special needs are portrayed in a positive light without sentimentality or romanticism.
2. The characters are treated realistically and not as superhumans or as helpless children.
3. The characters are integrated naturally into the story and not depicted as anomalies or pecularities in society or comic sidekicks.
4. The author avoids using language that stereotypes or terminology such as "handicapped," "retarded," and other words that may be construed as offensive.
5. The author portrays people with special needs as capable of ordinary human feelings—love, anger, joy, hate.
6. The author avoids paralleling physical or mental disabilities with personality traits—spinal deformities as a sign of wickedness, for example.

OTHER ISSUES

Other issues to look for in children's books include old age, death and dying, war, and sexuality. Books that deal honestly with these subjects are the best. In recent years, we have seen more good books appear that portray old age in a positive light, books that present images of old people as distinctive individuals rather than cruelly stereotyped cranks, for example. Many books depict positive relationships between young people and the elderly, such as Miska Miles's *Annie and the Old One,* Tomie de Paola's *Nana Upstairs, Nana Downstairs,* and Barbara Cooney's *Miss Rumphius*—all delightful picture books. Cynthia Voigt's *Dicey's Song,* Patricia MacLachlan's *Cassie Binegar,* and Lawrence Yep's *Child of the Owl* are all excellent books that help to break down traditional stereotypes of old age.

The portrayal of death in children's literature is really nothing new. In the eighteenth century, children read books with vivid descriptions of death and dying, but usually as punishment for wickedness or godlessness or, conversely, as the gateway to the heavenly reward for a pious life. In the twentieth century, however, as life spans have lengthened and child mortality has declined, death has become far less visible—both in our lives and our literature. Earlier in this century, death was considered an unsuitable topic for children; it was simply too morbid, people seemed to feel. But we are now coming to realize what our ancestors well knew, that death is a natural part of life, and our children should not be sheltered from it. A young child's first experience with death is often with the death of an animal. Margaret Wise Brown's *The Dead Bird* is a simple story of children finding a dead bird, giving it a proper funeral, and then going about their play; death is seen as a natural part of life's cycle. Doris Buchanan Smith's *A Taste of Blackberries* is about how a boy copes with the tragic death of his best friend. It is a story both sad and beautiful.

For children approaching the middle school years—sixth, seventh, and eighth grades—even more delicate issues are broached in their reading. Judy Blume's popular *Are You There, God? It's Me, Margaret* has already been mentioned as an example of a girl exploring religious questions and anticipating the beginning of menses. Many fine books are available on the subject of war, and these are discussed in Chapter 11 with historical fiction. Children cannot long be sheltered from the highly sensitive, and today authors are even writing books for young people on the once entirely taboo subject of homosexuality (John Donovan's *I'll Get There. It Better Be Worth the Trip* and Isabelle Holland's *The Man Without a Face* are two examples.) Admittedly, these are aimed at teenagers and not technically "children's literature," but it is helpful to remind ourselves that ignoring such topics does not make them go away, and children require answers to questions that adults do not always want to hear.

Following are some general guidelines we may follow in evaluating books on such contemporary issues as death, war, old age, and sexuality:

1. The author avoids stereotyping any situation, but instead treats it as an individual experience having a specific effect on the characters involved.
2. The author avoids prejudgment, but instead allows the reader to examine the details and arrive at a conclusion.
3. The author treats the situation with sensitivity, exploring and helping the reader to understand the varied emotions as they are revealed in the characters.
4. The author treats the situation with honesty and frankness, without sentimentality, exaggeration, or romanticism.

With these and other issues that are now being confronted in books for children, our primary concern is that the subject matter is treated intelligently, sensitively, and honestly. Perhaps the most important message of this entire chapter is that children's literature can provide a positive influence on young people's lives by exposing them to the rich variety in human experience.

RECOMMENDED READINGS

Broderick, Dorothy M. *Image of the Black in Children's Fiction.* New York: Bowker, 1973.

Carlson, Ruth Kearney. *Emerging Humanity: Multi-Ethnic Literature for Children and Adolescents.* Dubuque, IA: Wm. C. Brown, 1972.

Frye, Northrup. *The Educated Imagination.* Bloomington, IN: Indiana University Press, 1964.

Gilliland, Hap. *Indian Children's Books.* Billings, MT: Montana Council for Indian Education, 1980.

Guy, Rosa. "Innocence, Betrayal, and History." *School Library Journal* (November 1985): 33–34.

Harris, Violet, ed. *Teaching Multicultured Literature in Grades K–8.* Norwood, MA: Christopher-Gordon, 1993.

Luecke, Fritz J., comp. *Children's Books: Views and Values.* Middletown, CT: Xerox Education Publications, 1973.

McCann, Donnarae, and Gloria Woodard. *The Black American in Books for Children: Readings in Racism.* Metuchen, NJ: Scarecrow, 1985.

——— . *Cultural Conformity in Books for Children.* Metuchen, NJ: Scarecrow, 1977.

McIntosh, Peggy. "White Privilege: Unpacking the Invisible Knapsack." *Peace and Freedom* (July/August 1989): 10–12.

Rudman, Masha K. *Children's Literature: An Issues Approach.* 2nd ed. New York: Longman, 1984.

Sims, Rudine. *Shadow & Substance: Afro-American Experience in Contemporary Children's Fiction.* Urbana, IL: National Council of Teachers of English, 1982.

Wagoner, Shirley A. "Mexican-Americans in Children's Literature Since 1970." *The Reading Teacher* (December 1982): 274–79.

SELECTED BIBLIOGRAPHY OF BOOKS EMPHASIZING CULTURAL AND SOCIAL DIVERSITY

The following list is only a sampling of books that address various cultural groups. See also the bibliographies following Chapters 11 and 12, which include other books about these cultural groups as well as books on women, alternative families and lifestyles, and the physically, emotionally, and intellectually challenged.

African American

Bonham, Frank. *Durango Street.* New York: Dutton, 1965.

——— . *The Nitty Gritty.* New York: Dutton, 1968.

Brooks, Bruce. *Everywhere.* New York: Harper, 1990.

Burch, Robert. *Queenie Peavy.* New York: Viking, 1966.

Cameron, Eleanor. *To the Green Mountains.* New York: Dutton, 1975.

Childress, Alice. *A Hero Ain't Nothin' But a Sandwich.* New York: Coward, 1973.

Colman, Hila. *Classmates by Request.* New York: Morrow, 1964.

Fair, R. L. *Cornbread, Earl, and Me.* New York: Bantam, 1975.

Fox, Paula. *The Slave Dancer.* New York: Bradbury, 1973.

Graham, Lorenz. *North Town.* New York: Thomas Crowell, 1965.

——— . *South Town.* New York: Thomas Crowell, 1958.

Greene, Bette. *Get on Out of Here, Philip Hall.* New York: Dial, 1981.

——— . *Philip Hall Likes Me, I Reckon Maybe.* New York: Dial, 1974.

Guy, Rosa. *The Disappearance.* New York: Delacorte, 1979.

——— . *The Friends.* New York: Holt, 1973.

——— . *Ruby.* New York: Viking, 1976.

———. *The Ups and Downs of Carl Davis.* New York: Delacorte, 1989.

Hamilton, Virginia. *The House of Dies Drear.* New York: Macmillan, 1968.

———. *M. C. Higgins, the Great.* New York: Macmillan, 1974.

———. *The Planet of Junior Brown.* New York: Macmillan, 1971.

———. *Zeely.* New York: Macmillan, 1967.

Hentoff, Nat. *Jazz Country.* New York: Harper, 1965.

Hunter, Kristin. *Guests in the Promised Land.* New York: Scribner's, 1973.

———. *The Soul Brothers and Sister Lou.* New York: Scribner's, 1968.

Jackson, Jesse. *Call Me Charley.* New York: Dell, 1945.

Jordan, June. *His Own Where.* New York: Crowell, 1971.

Lowry, Lois. *Anastasia's Chosen Career.* Boston: Houghton Mifflin, 1987.

Mathis, Sharon Bell. *Listen for the Fig Tree.* New York: Viking, 1974.

———. *Teacup Full of Roses.* New York: Viking, 1972.

Myers, Walter Dean. *Me, Mop, and the Moondance Kid.* New York: Dell, 1988.

———. *The Mouse Rap.* New York: Harper, 1990.

———. *Scorpions.* New York: Harper, 1988.

Neufeld, John. *Edgar Allan.* Chatham, NY: Phillips, 1968.

Sebastian, Ouida. *Words by Heart.* Boston: Little, 1979.

Spinelli, Jerry. *Maniac Magee.* Boston: Little, 1990.

Taylor, Mildred. *Let the Circle Be Unbroken.* New York: Dial, 1981.

———. *The Road to Memphis.* New York: Dial, 1990.

———. *Roll of Thunder, Hear My Cry.* New York: Dial, 1976.

Yates, Elizabeth. *Amos Fortune, Free Man.* New York: Dutton, 1967.

Walker, Alice. *The Color Purple.* New York: Harcourt, 1982.

Wilkinson, Brenda. *Ludell.* New York: Harper, 1975.

———. *Ludell and Willie.* New York: Harper, 1977.

Native American

Armer, Laura Adams. *Waterless Mountain.* New York: McKay, 1931.

Brown, D. *Creek Mary's Blood.* New York: Franklin Library, 1980.

Cannon, A. E. *The Shadow Brothers.* New York: Delacorte, 1990.

Clark, Ann Nolan. *Medicine Man's Daughter.* New York: Farrar, 1963.

Craven, Margaret. *I Heard the Owl Call My Name.* New York: Bantam, 1973.

Embry, Margaret. *Shadi.* New York: Holiday, 1971.

Fuller, Iola. *The Loon Feather.* New York: Harcourt, 1940.

George, Jean Craighead. *Julie of the Wolves.* New York: Harper, 1972.

———. *The Talking Earth.* New York: Harper, 1983.

———. *Water Sky.* New York: Harper, 1987.

Highwater, Jamake. *Anpao: An American Indian Odyssey.* New York: Harper, 1977.

Houston, John. *Ghost Fox.* New York: Harcourt, 1977.

Hudson, Jan. *Sweetgrass.* 1984. New York: Philomel, 1989.

LaFarge, Oliver. *Laughing Boy.* Boston: Houghton Mifflin, 1929.

Lauritzen, Jonreed. *The Ordeal of the Young Hunter.* Boston: Little, 1954.

Lampman, Evelyn Sibley. *The Potlatch Family.* New York: Crowell, 1953.

Means, Florence Crannell. *Our Cup Is Broken.* Boston: Houghton Mifflin, 1969.

O'Dell, Scott. *Black Star, Bright Dawn.* Boston: Houghton Mifflin, 1988.

———. *Island of the Blue Dolphins.* Boston: Houghton Mifflin, 1960.

———. *Sing Down the Moon.* Boston: Houghton Mifflin, 1970.

Richter, Conrad. *Light in the Forest.* New York: Knopf, 1953.
Sneve, Virginia Driving Hawk. *High Elk's Treasure.* New York: Holiday, 1972.
Speare, Elizabeth George. *The Sign of the Beaver.* Boston: Houghton Mifflin, 1983.

Hispanic American

Bonham, Frank. *Viva Chicano.* New York: Dutton, 1970.
Buss, Fran Leeper, and Daisy Cubias. *Journey of the Sparrows.* New York: Lodestar, 1991.
Colman, Hila. *Chicano Girl.* New York: Morrow, 1973.
———. *The Girl from Puerto Rico.* New York: Morrow, 1961.
Foresman, Bettie. *From Lupita's Hill.* New York: Atheneum, 1973.
Krumgold, Joseph. . . . *and now Miguel.* New York: Crowell, 1953.
Means, Florence Crannell. *Us Maltbys.* Boston: Houghton Mifflin, 1966.
Mohr, Nicholasa. *El Bronx Remembered: A Novella and Stories.* New York: Harper, 1975.
———. *Nilda.* New York: Harper, 1973.
O'Dell, Scott. *The Black Pearl.* Boston: Houghton Mifflin, 1967.

Asian American

Houston, Jeanne Wakatsuki, and James D. Houston. *Farewell to Manzanar.* New York: Bantam, 1973.
Lewis, Elizabeth Foreman. *Young Fu of the Upper Yanztze.* New York: Holt, 1932. (Chinese)
Lord, Bette Bao. *In the Year of the Boar and Jackie Robinson.* New York: Harper, 1984.
Uchida, Yoshiko. *Journey to Topaz.* New York: Scribner's, 1971.
Wong, J. S. *Fifth Chinese Daughter.* New York: Harper, 1950.
Yee, Paul. *Tales from Gold Mountain: Stories of the Chinese in the New World.* New York: Macmillan, 1990.
Yep, Laurence. *Child of the Owl.* New York: Harper, 1977.
———. *Dragonwings.* New York: Harper, 1975.

Other Cultures

Achebe, Chinua. *Things Fall Apart.* 1958. Greenwich, Connecticut: Fawcett, 1969. (Nigerian)
Beskow, Elsa. *Pelle's New Suit.* New York: Harper, 1929. (Swedish)
Boissard, J. A. *A Matter of Feeling.* Boston: Little, Brown, 1981. (French)
Case, Dianne. *Love, David.* New York: Dutton, 1991. (South African)
Clark, Ann Nolan. *Secret of the Andes.* New York: Viking, 1952. (Peruvian Indian)
Clark, M. T. *The Min-min.* New York: Macmillan, 1978. (Australian)
Cunningham, Julia. *The Silent Voice.* New York: Dutton, 1981. (French)
Degens, T. *On the Third Ward.* New York: Harper, 1990. (Chinese)
DeJong, Meindert. *The House of Sixty Fathers.* New York: Harper, 1956. (Chinese)
———. *Journey from Peppermint Street.* New York: Harper, 1968. (Dutch)
Fritz, Jean. *Homesick: My Own Story.* New York: Putnam, 1982. (Chinese)
Hall, Lynn. *Danza!* New York: Scribner's, 1981. (Puerto Rican)
Ho, Minfong. *The Clay Marble.* New York: Farrar, 1991. (Cambodian)
———. *Rice without Rain.* New York: Lothrop, 1990. (Thai)

Kherdian, David. *The Road from Home: The Story of an Armenian Girlhood.* New York: Greenwillow, 1979. (Armenian)

Lingard, Joan. *Tug of War.* New York: Lodestar, 1990. (Latvian)

Moeri, Louise. *The Forty-third War.* Boston: Houghton Mifflin, 1989. (Central American)

Naidoo, Beverley. *Chain of Fire.* New York: Lippincott, 1990. (South African)

Newth, Mette. *The Abduction.* New York: Farrar, Straus & Giroux, 1989. (Norwegian)

O'Dell, Scott. *My Name Is Not Angelica.* Boston: Houghton Mifflin, 1989. (African, Caribbean Islanders)

Orlev, Uri. *The Man from the Other Side.* Boston: Houghton Mifflin, 1991. (Jewish, Eastern European)

Potok, Chaim. *My Name Is Asher Lev.* New York: Knopf, 1972. (Jewish)

Rubinstein, Gillian. *Beyond the Labyrinth.* New York: Watts, 1990. (Australian)

Siegal, Aranka. *Upon the Head of the Goat: A Childhood in Hungary, 1939–1944.* New York: Farrar, Straus & Giroux, 1981. (Hungarian)

Singer, Isaac Bashevis. *The Death of Methuselah and Other Stories.* New York: Farrar, Straus & Giroux, 1971. (Jewish)

Sperry, Armstrong. *Call It Courage.* New York: Macmillan, 1940. (Pacific Islands)

Suhl, Yuri. *The Merrymaker.* New York: Four Winds, 1975. (Jewish)

Staples, Suzanne Fisher. *Shabanu: Daughter of the Wind.* New York: Knopf, 1989. (Pakistani)

Taylor, Sidney. *All-of-a-Kind Family.* Chicago: Follett, 1951. (Jewish)

Wojciechowska, Maia. *Shadow of a Bull.* New York: Atheneum, 1964. (Jewish)

CHAPTER 14

The Study of Literature

THE PURPOSE OF CRITICISM

An entire field of literary study wrestles with the problem of how to interpret literature, how to derive meaning from a collection of words on a page. Each generation seems compelled to devise its own theory, and we should not view this as confusion, but only as evidence that a literary text is rich and enjoys a many-faceted life. Our understanding of the various ways a piece of literature can be read and interpreted will help to make us all more perceptive readers, better judges, and wiser purveyors of literature for our children.

It was once popular to discuss the merits of a literary work in terms of how well it fit into an accepted standard—consequently, new works were compared to the "classics" (also called the "canon") to see how they measured up. In recent times, the idea of the canon has been brought to task (who decides what the classics are? what criteria are being used? what biases have crept into these criteria?). The definition of literature has been challenged (are some works "literature" and others not? whose definition is it?). But more importantly, the whole notion of how a reader approaches a piece of writing ("literature" or otherwise) has been reexamined. Whereas once a literary work was regarded "primarily as reflecting the world . . . as isolated specimens to be examined" (Purves, Rogers, and Soter 43), today it is more common to see a literary text as part of a complex structure of interrelated experiences, with the meaning varying from individual to individual and from time to time. Or, as it has been summed up: "Texts are written by authors, deal with something called 'the world,' and are read by readers" (Purves, Rogers, and Soter 43). Until we take all these factors into account, we have not fully understood the literary experience for ourselves. Of course, this theory suggests that it is not always (and perhaps it never is) possible to understand the literary experiences of others. The following discussion will review the more common approaches to studying literature and will provide just a sampling of the many ways a book or poem can be read and understood.

THE READER-RESPONSE APPROACH

Currently, the most popular approach to considering literature is the reader-response or transactional theory, which holds that each of us brings something different to our reading—different life experiences, cultural experiences, and so on; therefore, each of us has a unique interpretation of the literature we read. Further, reader-response theory recognizes that each of us will respond to the same literary work differently at different times. It is impossible then to establish a right or a wrong way to interpret a novel, a poem, a short story. This approach is one of the safest, and ultimately most rewarding, ways of using literature with children. It allows them to read, and freely explore, experiment, and discuss ideas without fear of recrimination because they do not have the "correct answer" or the "right interpretation." It can also be rewarding for the adult who is sharing the literature with children—for suddenly, a myriad of new possibilities and new ways of looking at a story are opened up for us. This approach is the basis for many of the suggestions in Chapter 15, where more will be said of reader- response theory.

THE HISTORICAL APPROACH

The historical approach to reading literature asks such questions as these:

1. Who is the author and what is his or her object in writing the work?
2. How did the political events of the time influence what the writer wrote?
3. How did the predominant social customs of the time influence the writer's outlook?
4. What is the predominant philosophy that influenced the work?
5. Were there any special circumstances under which the work was written?

In general, the historical approach looks at how the period in which a work was written has influenced the work itself. The historical approach examines the external political, social, and intellectual influences on literature. Although a grasp of this historical context is not always necessary for our enjoyment of a particular work of literature, it does give us a better understanding as to why the author wrote what he or she did. Knowing the historical context can answer some perplexing questions about a literary work.

Let's take, for example, the popular folktale of "Hansel and Gretel." How can the parents be so callous as to abandon their children? What is the significance of the gingerbread house? Why does the witch die in the oven? Because this tale in its present form is of Western European origin, some of these questions can be answered by examining the historical context out of which the tale grew.

In medieval Europe, which is the approximate setting of the tale, numerous factors contributed to widespread famine, and peasants lived on the verge of starvation. The historian Barbara Tuchman writes that during the fourteenth century "reports spread of people eating their own children, of the poor in Poland feeding on hanged bodies taken down from the gibbet" (24). In light of this ghastly information, the tale of "Hansel and Gretel" seems tame indeed. The abandonment of children might not have been so unusual a thing in a society that still did not necessarily condemn infanticide (particularly if the infant was a female). The overwhelming emphasis on food—the children drop breadcrumbs; they are enticed by a gingerbread from which they eat delicious candies; the witch is killed in her own oven where she had planned to bake Hansel—can be viewed as the product of an age when providing food indeed occupied much of the average person's daily activities.

Another example of the way society influences literature can be seen in Daniel Defoe's *Robinson Crusoe,* first published in 1719. In that story, the hero is cast upon the proverbial desert isle, and, through industry and ingenuity, he tames the wilderness and creates a virtually carefree and comfortable life. Eventually he discovers the native, Friday, who becomes his servant. To the eighteenth-century mind, nature was inexhaustible, and many people believed that the world was created entirely for the benefit of humanity, and it was the responsibility of educated people to tame the wilderness and bring salvation to the "heathen." Today, our views have changed considerably. We are much more environmentally conscious and no longer believe that nature should be bent to our wills, that wilderness needs to be tamed (and it should go without saying that we deplore the enslavement of Friday). In a twentieth-century book such as Scott O'Dell's *Island of the Blue Dolphins,* we find that the heroine, Karana, stranded on desert island, does not conquer nature, but learns to live in harmony with it. Similar messages are found in the works of Jean Craighead George (*My Side of the Mountain, Julie of the Wolves, The Talking Earth,* and others). In fact, a book published today with a hero who selfishly disregards the environment would likely be viewed as insensitive or out of touch.

These are just a few of the ways in which reading a book with the historical perspective in mind can help us to understand (and sometimes appreciate) the literary accomplishment.

THE PSYCHOANALYTICAL APPROACH

Whereas a historical reading of a work of literature examines it from the point of view of the social climate of the time in which it was written, a psychoanalytical reading examines the psychological implications of a work. The most common psychoanalytical approach is the Freudian, based on the work of Sigmund Freud, regarded as the father of modern psychoanalysis, who believed that the motivations for much of our behavior (such as our fear of heights, our compulsion to be neat, our love of a certain color) lay hidden in our unconscious minds. Freud also believed that in our dreams and our art (including literature, music, the graphic and plastic arts) these unconscious motivators appeared.

To examine a work psychoanalytically is to probe the unconscious of the characters, to determine what their actions really reveal about them. The most famous modern example in children's literature of psychoanalytical reading is Bruno Bettelheim's study of folktales, *The Uses of Enchantment* (1976). Here is a brief summary of Bettelheim's psychoanalytical interpretation of "Hansel and Gretel." He interprets the story as a symbolic representation of the child emerging from the developmental stage of oral fixation, and he points to the importance of food in the tale for his support—the children must be abandoned because of the lack of food, the children find a gingerbread house that they begin to eat, the house is inhabited by a cannibal witch. Bettelheim sees in Hansel's initial efforts to find his way back home "the debilitating consequences of trying to deal with life's problems by means of regression and denial, which reduce one's ability to solve problems" (160). The return home is seen as denial and regression—literally Hansel's denying that the parents do not want him and his desire to return to the tenuous security of home and symbolically Hansel's own resistance to move beyond the oral stage. The gingerbread house, Bettelheim contends, "stands for oral greediness and how attractive it is to give in to it" (161). He goes yet a step further in suggesting that the house is also a symbol of the body, "usually the mother's," and that the children's devouring of the house symbolically represents their nursing. The witch personifies "the destructive aspects of orality" and she also represents the threatening mother. The witch has jewels that the children inherit, but only when they have reached a higher stage of development, represented by the wisdom they use in deceiving the witch (by substituting the bone for the finger and tricking her into the oven). Bettelheim concludes:

> This suggests that as the children transcend their oral anxiety, and free themselves of relying on oral satisfaction for security, they can also free themselves of the image of the threatening mother—the witch—and rediscover the good parents, whose greater wisdom—the shared jewels—then benefit all. (162)

Bettelheim's analysis is a great deal more complex than this, but such a summary does reveal some of the basic tenets of psychoanalytical criticism.

The extent to which children would comprehend this meaning, even in an unconscious way, is questionable indeed, and Bettelheim cautions adults against attempting to interpet the way a child may feel about a given tale. But he further argues that folktales endure precisely because they do address our deepest psychological needs—"fairy tales, like all true works of art, possess a multifarious richness and depth that far transcend what even the most thorough discursive examination can extract from them" (19). In other words, as readers we may intuitively grasp some of these meanings and symbols even if we are unable to put them into words. But his comment on the witch is pertinent in a study of children's literature:

> A witch as created by the child's anxious fantasies will haunt him; but a witch he can push into her own oven and burn to death is a witch the child can believe himself rid of. As long as children continue to believe in witches

. . . they need to be told stories in which children, by being ingenious, rid themselves of these persecuting figures of their imagination. (166).

Psychoanalytical criticism causes us to examine literature from the perspective of its psychological effect on the readers and helps us to see our bond with the rest of humanity. The most evident danger is in over-reading, in seeing a symbol in every object, in seeing unconscious desires and fears lurking in every utterance.

THE FEMINIST APPROACH

Feminist criticism actually combines other critical methods while placing its focus on the questions of how gender affects a literary work, writer, or reader. The feminist approach might ask such questions as these:

1. How are women portrayed in the work? As stereotypes? As individuals?
2. How is the woman's point of view considered?
3. Is male superiority implied in the text?
4. In what way is the work different because it was written by a woman? or a man?

A major concern of feminist criticism is the masculine bias in literature. Historically most works (often even those written by women) have been written from a masculine point of view and for male audiences. Literature has traditionally celebrated the masculine traits and cast aspersion on the feminine. Among the first works to come under attack were the folktales with their stereotypically beautiful, helpless princesses who needed only a good man to set their lives aright and enable them to live happily ever after. The feminist critic looks for the presence of female stereotypes—for example, the woman as the dark-haired, sensuous, submissive, *femme fatale*, or as the fair-haired, pure plaster saint. If we look again at "Hansel and Gretel," we can see that the feminist critic might object to the portrayal of the woman as either selfish wife or cannibalistic witch. The mother/wife is, on the other hand, simply taking a desperate situation in hand, assuming authority where her ineffectual husband will not. Hansel, the boy, proves equally ineffectual, marking their path with breadcrumbs that are quickly eaten by the birds, and then finding himself imprisoned by the witch. It is Gretel who must take the decisive action and rescue them by cleverly deceiving the witch and then killing her. Gretel is, of course, an exception to the rule and refuses to fit into the traditional feminine mold. But the feminist critic looks for societal misconceptions that treat the masculine viewpoint as the norm and the feminine viewpoint as a deviation.

The issue of gender-bias as reflected in literature has been discussed in Chapter 13; our point here is to emphasize the need to challenge the way we have traditionally read literature—and that is from the point of view of a male-dominated society. The feminist critic believes that, in the words of Simone de Beauvoir, "One is not born, but rather becomes, a woman." Or, to put it another way, one critic says, "Feminists do not deny that women exhibit group characteristics. However, they do not accept the thesis that similarities in female behavior are biologically determined" (Register 13). To read a text like a woman is, according to some theorists, to read it with "the skeptical purity of an outcast from culture" (Auerbach 156). To read a text like a woman "means questioning its underlying assumptions about differences between men and women that usually posit women as inferior" (Waxman 150). Looking at a literary text from a feminist point of view can enrich a reading, making us aware of the complexity of human interaction. Feminist criticism therefore ultimately becomes cultural criticism

THE FORMALIST APPROACH

The formalist approach has long been a standard way of examining literature, and is familiar to many students for whom it was once the only way. Formalist criticism looks closely at the form of a literary work—what its parts are and how they work together to make a satisfactory whole. The true formalist critic believes that we should disregard everything except the literary elements of a work. Therefore, they believe, who the author is or the social milieu in which the author wrote are not important. A formalist approach to "Hansel and Gretel" might consider such aspects as the repeated patterns in the story, and similarity between the woodcutter's house and the witch's gingerbread cottage, and the balance between these two views of home. The formalist might examine the rising and falling action and point out the building of suspense in the children's overhearing their parents' plotting or the foreshadowing of the witch in the person of the children's mother. Or the formalist might consider the development of Gretel's character from a meek and rather helpless child into a strong and determined girl who saves both her brother and herself. The formalist might examine the sparse language and illustrate its appropriateness to the tightly constructed plot of the folktale.

THE ELEMENTS OF LITERATURE

Related, but not confined to, formalist approaches, is the consideration of the elements that make up a literary work. Partly because of the predominance of formalist criticism, the study of literature seemed at one time to be largely the study of terminology. We should recognize that classifications and terminology play only a supporting role in the study of literature and are decidedly not the end of criticism. Some of the more fundamental terminology useful in the study of literature will be discussed below. These terms can be used for fiction, drama, and poetry (although poetry also has its own specialized vocabulary that has been presented in Chapter 7).

Point of View

Every story is told from someone's point of view, and we should not assume that the narrator, the storyteller, is the author. It is important for us as readers to beaware of who is telling the story and how that narrator affects the story itself. There are essentially three types of narrators.

First-Person Narrator. If the narrator refers to him- or herself as "I" in the story, we have a *first-person narrator.* The first-person narrator is usually a character in the story and may or may not be the protagonist. Occasionally the first-person narrator is not a character in the story at all, but simply someone to whom the story has been told. Beatrix Potter *(The Tale of Peter Rabbit)* and C. S. Lewis *(The Lion, the Witch and the Wardrobe)* both use this technique, and the narrator emerges as a sort of confidante for the reader. Sometimes an author will use more than one point of view in a single work—Alice Childress's *A Hero Ain't Nothin' but a Sandwich* and Paul Zindel's *Pigman* both make use of this technique, which allows us to hear more than one side to a story.

Omniscient Narrator. An *omniscient narrator* is used when the author freely exercises godlike powers, revealing to the reader the thoughts and actions of several different characters, being able to look into the past or see into the future. The word "omniscient" means literally "all-knowing." The omniscient narrator is not a character in the story and is never referred to as "I," but instead is an outside commentator, able to delve into the hearts and minds of the characters. In E. B. White's fantasy, *Charlotte's Web,* the narrator can show us the thoughts and actions of Wilbur the pig at one time, and then, at another time, show us Mrs. Arable, a human, in a conversation with the family physician.

Limited Narrator. A *limited narrator* (also called the subjective consciousness) also tells the story from an outsider's point of view and is not a character in the tale. But unlike the omniscient narrator, the limited narrator is restricted to commenting on a single character's observations, describing only what a single character sees, knows, and feels. Laura Ingalls Wilder's popular *Little House in the Big Woods* and its sequels are told from a limited narrator's point of view. We are allowed to witness only those things that Laura experiences, although she, in fact, does not tell the story.

It is important that we realize who is telling the story and why. We should never confuse the narrator with the author, for many authors of fiction assume a *persona* (which means "mask") when they write; that is, they pretend to be someone else. Readers expect the point of view to be logical and consistent—for example, a narrator should not reveal material he or she could not have known at the time. But we must not forget that the narrator may not always be trustworthy.

Setting

The second element in the structure of a literary work is the setting, which consists of two features: place and time. Everything must happen somewhere and sometime. In some literature—novels, for instance— readers expect the setting to be believably described; in other literature it is much less important.

Place. The *place* may be either vague (a big city, a small farm) or very specific (the streets of New York, a cay in the Caribbean, even a make-believe world). Further, the place may be relatively insignificant to the story. For example, it really does not matter exactly where the comical stories of Dr. Seuss are set; they could happen virtually any place. The setting is only a *backdrop,* like scenery. On the other hand, the setting may be crucial to a story's meaning, as are Wilder's Little House books, which could only take place in the nineteenth-century American West. Fantasy fiction often requires fairly detailed descriptions of settings if the author is creating new worlds, places no one has ever seen. Ursula Le Guin's Earthsea cycle (*A Wizard of Earthsea* and others) provides a thoroughly detailed study of the geography of the mythical world of Earthsea.

Time.   The *time* described in a novel may be past, present, or even future. *Contemporary fiction* focuses on the present, which means that the author may assume that the readers have a great deal of familiarity with such things as social customs, everyday gadgetry, and so on. *Historical fiction* focuses on a specific period in history, and occasionally even includes fictional accounts of historic personages, requiring that some habits, customs, and paraphernalia peculiar to the historical period be explained as part of the narrative. *Science fiction*—much like other fantasy—usually requires detailed place descriptions, since the time is typically (but not always) set in a fantasized future, and the author must create a believable setting.

Characters

Regardless of the type of fiction, readers demand believable and memorable characters. Believable characters use convincing and natural speech patterns—or speech patterns that suit their peculiar characteristics. We expect them to speak and act according to their respective ages, social and intellectual backgrounds, and so on. The principal characters include the *protagonist,* the hero or heroine, the main character with whom we sympathize. And there is the *antagonist,* the villain, or the character who works against the protagonist. We generally want the characters to be properly *motivated,* that is, there should be believable reasons for their doing what they do, or to put it another way, the characters behave as they do because they are the kind of people they are. We usually expect the story's action to develop out of the character and not the other way around.

Static and Dynamic Characters.   All characters may be identified as either static or dynamic, and most fiction will include both types. A *static character* remains essentially the same thoughout the story and has no noticeable development. Static characters may be simple such as Mrs. Rabbit or Mr. McGregor in Potter's *The Tale of Peter Rabbit* or complex such as Charlotte the spider in *Charlotte's Web,* about whom we learn a great deal. In contrast, a *dynamic character* undergoes some significant personality adjustment during the course of the story. In children's stories, this adjustment is usually a maturing, as in Ezra Jack Keats's *Peter's Chair,* where Peter comes to accept his new baby sister as a permanent member of his family. In *Charlotte's Web,* Wilbur the pig grows from an immature, self-centered, and insecure character into a mature, caring, and confident creature.

Flat and Round Characters.   All characters may also be identified as either flat or round. A *flat character*—who is also necessarily a static character—is one who exhibits only one side of his or her personality. Usually these characters are functionaries needed to advance the plot, such as servants, police, store clerks—they might be parents (such as Fern's in *Charlotte's Web*) or siblings (such as Peter Rabbit's sisters) or teachers, gardeners, and so on. Many times a flat character will also be a *stereotype* or a *stock character,* possessing the traits considered to be typical of a group (such as disagreeable mothers-in-law, haughty English butlers, giddy school-girls, impish schoolboys, and so on). But the stereotype must be used with discretion. We might regard Templeton the rat in *Charlotte's Web* as a stereotype, behaving both selfishly and greedily as we should expect from a rat. The wise and kindly family physician is another example of a stereotype, this time a good one. Whether it be ignorance or insensitivity, no reason should excuse offensive stereotypes in modern literature.

However, we are more interested in the *round* characters, those who are fully-developed personalities—the Wilburs and Charlottes, the Huck Finns, and even the Long John Silvers (we're not only interested in the good guys). The round character experiences a range of emotions—joy, sorrow, worry, confidence, dejection, elation. It is the character we get to know best.

Foil Characters.   A *foil character* is one who possesses personality traits opposite to those of another character, often the main character. *Foil* is a jeweler's term for a gem setting, and just as the proper setting can make a diamond appear larger and more brilliant, so can certain character traits be emphasized when compared to the opposite traits in others. To use *Charlotte's Web* again, Templeton serves as a foil to Charlotte—his selfishness makes her own ultimate sacrifice that much more impressive.

Character Development and Consistency.   *Character development* is simply the means the author uses to tell us about a character. We learn about characters in a variety of ways. (1) The narrator may tell us about the characters, although this is usually the least memorable way (this is like getting our information about someone from a lecture). (2) We may hear about them through what other characters say of them, although we must be wary of possible hidden motives or prejudices and realize that what others say may not necessarily be true (this is like getting our information about someone from what their friends—and enemies—say about them). (3) We may learn about characters through what they say themselves (although we must remember that people do not always mean what they say). And, of course, (4) we may learn about characters through observing their actions. Actions, we all know, speak louder than words, and it is through actions that the most convincing evidence about character is revealed.

Character consistency means that we expect fictional characters to act in accordance with the nature of their characters as they have been revealed. Leigh Botts in Cleary's *Dear Mr. Henshaw* is seen to be a thoughtful, conscientious boy, embarrassed about the shabby home he and his mother are forced to live in, and lonely for friends his own age. He is capable of anger—as most people are—but his circumstances do not compel him to turn to crime or drugs. Such actions would be totally inconsistent with the character that Cleary has developed. Just like police investigating a crime, readers look for *motives*, the reasons behind a character's action. In *Charlotte's Web,* when Templeton the rat is persuaded to help Wilbur save Charlotte's egg sac, he does so only because he has been promised a reward. It would be totally inconsistent for the selfish Templeton to do anything otherwise. Templeton's motivation for all his actions is self-interest.

Plot and Conflict

The novelist, E. M. Forster, provides us with this definition of a plot:

> "The king died and then the queen died" is a story. "The king died, and then the queen died of grief" is a plot. (86).

The point is that a plot is more than simply a sequence of events; it is a sequence of interrelated events linked by causality. (The king's death *caused* the queen's death.) But most of us would still feel that this plot wants for something. It lacks conflict; in the most gripping plots, something must be at stake; some difficulty must be overcome; some goal must be achieved. It is to see the resolution of the conflict (which, of course, is the outcome of the plot) that most readers continue to read until the end of the story.

Types of Conflict. As the most important single feature of the plot, the conflict commonly takes one of four methods.

1. *The Individual against Another* occurs when two persons are struggling for the same goal, or perhaps one person is determined to prevent another from achieving a goal. Folktales, such as "Little Red Riding Hood," pointedly demonstrate this type of conflict, as do *The Tale of Peter Rabbit, The Wizard of Oz,* and *Treasure Island.*
2. *The Individual against Society* shows the protagonist (and sometimes the protagonist's family or close associates) pitted against the values and mores of the mainstream of society. This struggle is most evident in some of the stories of racial prejudice, such as Mildred Taylor's *Roll of Thunder, Hear My Cry* or Ouida Sebestian's *Words by Heart* and in stories dealing with such social problems as alienation, such as S. E. Hinton's story of inner-city gangs, *The Outsiders.*
3. *The Individual against Nature* is a popular conflict with older children who enjoy reading about protagonists striving to survive in a wilderness as in Elizabeth George Speare's *The Sign of the Beaver* or perhaps in the Arctic wasteland as in Jean Craighead George's *Julie of the Wolves* or on a deserted tropical island as in Theodore Taylor's *The Cay* or Scott O'Dell's *Island of the Blue Dolphins.*
4. *The Individual against Self* is the type of conflict occurring in the inner workings of the protagonist's mind. Maurice Sendak's *Where the Wild Things Are* is an interesting example of a picture-book rendition of this sort of conflict, where Max is torn by the conflicting desires to do exactly

as he pleases or to obey his mother. In Cleary's *Dear Mr. Henshaw,* Leigh Botts attempts to blame others for his problems, for his feelings of inadequacy, and for his loneliness, but he realizes eventually that these are his own problems, and ones that he alone can work out.

Another possible conflict, but one that is seldom found in children's literature, is that of the *individual against God,* stories of individuals wrestling with religious beliefs.

Plot Credibility.   Plots do not have to be realistic, but most readers insist that they be credible or believable according to the standards constructed by the author. (Naturally, for a comic work or a fantasy, those standards are different from those of a serious piece of realism.) We ask such questions as: does this action make sense in the story? Have we been sufficiently prepared for the turn of events (through foreshadowing or the dropping of hints, for example)? Is the plot unnecessarily contrived or too full of coincidences? One of the principal differences between art and life is that life is random, whereas art is often quite meticulously planned. In real life, we may receive a telephone call, during dinner or late at night, that turns out to be a wrong number, and that event may have no significance on the future course of events. However, in a novel or a play, should the telephone ring during a dinner scene, we fully expect that call to have some bearing on the action. The audience comes to expect that everything that happens has a specific purpose. Whenever a character enters a room or whenever a change in the weather is noted or whenever a cup of coffee is spilled, we may expect that that event will have some significance, whether it be to establish the atmosphere or to advance the plot or to help us evaluate a character or a situation or to reinforce the theme. In most literature, things happen for good reason.

Dramatic Plot Structure.   Plot structure may follow one of three general patterns. A *dramatic plot structure* first establishes the setting and conflict, then follows the action through to a *climax* (the peak of the action), and concludes with a *denouement* (a wrapping up of loose ends). This structure is probably the most familiar; it is the structure of most folktales, and it is adopted by most television drama. It is also the plot structure of such familiar works as *The Tale of Peter Rabbit* and *Charlotte's Web.* A dramatic plot structure is typically arranged chronologically—that is, according to time from beginning to end. For this reason, chronological plots are the easiest to understand.

Episodic Plot Structure.   An *episodic plot structure* consists of a series of loosely related incidents tied together by a common theme and a character or group of characters. Laura Ingalls Wilder's *Little House* books are organized episodically. Each chapter is capable of standing on its own much like a short story, but taken together the episodes give us a complex picture of the family relationships and other issues important to the story. Unity is provided by the predominant theme of love and family togetherness overcoming hardship. Episodic plots work best when the writer wishes to explore the personalities of the characters, the nature of their existence, and the flavor of an era. Episodic plots may be arranged chronologically—or they may be arranged using flashbacks, a technique that takes us back and forth between two or more time periods. Older readers (upper elementary school and beyond) are quite capable of handling such shifts as those found in Robert Cormier's complex *I Am the Cheese,* which freely moves back and forth in both time and place.

Parallel Plot Structure.   A parallel plot structure is typically the intertwining of two chronological dramatic plots into a single book. Often one of the plots is decidedly secondary to the main plot. Although parallel plot structure is typically found in books for older children, John Burningham's picture book, *Come Away from the Water,* Shirley, is a graphic example of parallel plot structure. It is the story of a girl going to the beach with her parents. The pictures on the left-hand side of the page show the parents relaxing in their beach chairs; the pictures on the facing page (in much more vivid color) depict the exciting imaginary games Shirley plays with herself and a dog (they find a pirate ship, fight with pirates, escape with a treasure map, and locate the treasure). The text consists only of inane remarks from Shirley's parents, parental warnings, empty promises, pointless questions. The parallel plot thus illustrated presents a dramatic contrast between reality and childhood imagination. Robert Lawson uses a parallel plot structure in his comic biography of Benjamin Franklin, *Ben and Me,* told from the point of view of Amos, a mouse (who takes most of the credit for Franklin's achievements—a good example of an unreliable first-person narrator). Paralleling the Revolutionary War activities of the humans is a similar struggle taking place among the mouse population; naturally, Amos would have us believe that the conflict among the mice is the more important of the two.

Theme

The *theme* is the principal idea behind a work of literature. In the most enduring works of literature, the theme is usually substantial, not trivial—although this does not imply that the work must be serious. Nor can we neglect the body of nonsense literature, to which we may affix Lewis Carroll's classic, *Alice's Adventures in Wonderland.* However, even in this case there are those who would argue that nonsense is a theme in itself, often a satiric intellectual or social commentary. Even though readers may prefer the theme that is good and solid over the silly and vacuous, they at the same time do *not* like to be browbeaten. Most find it much preferable to have the themes woven subtly into the fabric of the story or the poem. Literature for young readers offers many important themes (and a single book often includes several minor themes in addition to the major one). The problems of growing up and maturation are probably the most frequently found thematic issues in children's literature, including the individual's adjustment to society, the importance of love and friendship, the acceptance of a stepparent, achieving one's identity, and finding one's place in the world, among others.

Style

Style refers to the use of language, the choice of words, sentence construction, and imagery. It is not enough that a writer has a good story to tell. The story must be told well. Style consists of several elements.

Exposition.   Exposition refers to the information provided by the narrator—usually this is descriptive and background information necessary for us to understand the events. Exposition may be used to introduce a character: "Dorothy lived in the midst of the great Kansas prairies, with Uncle Henry, who was a farmer, and Aunt Em, who was the farmer's wife" (Baum, *The Wizard of Oz,* 7). Sometimes exposition is used to move the action along:

> When Laura and Mary had said their prayers and were tucked snugly under the trundle bed's covers, Pa was sitting in the firelight with the fiddle. Ma had blown out the lamp because she did not need its light. On the other side of the hearth she was swaying gently in her rocking chair and her knitting needles flashed in and out above the sock she was knitting.
>
> (Wilder, *Little House in the Big Woods*, 236)

Other times exposition is used to summarize and focus ideas presented in a scene, and to suggest future directions:

> Wilbur was merely suffering the doubts and fears that often go with finding a new friend. In good time he was to discover that he was mistaken about Charlotte. Underneath her rather bold and cruel exterior, she had a kind heart, and she was to prove loyal and true to the very end.
>
> (White, *Charlotte's Web*, 41)

Dialogue.   *Dialogue* refers to the words spoken by the characters, as opposed to exposition, the words of the narrator to the reader. Most works of fiction rely on both dialogue and exposition. Young readers, especially, enjoy dialogue as a realistic and convincing way of defining character. Dialogue allows the author to convey individual peculiarities, such as the goose's quirky speech in *Charlotte's Web* when she replies to Wibur's inquiry about the time: "Probably-obably-obably about half-past eleven . . . Why aren't you asleep, Wilbur?" (33). Charlotte's intellectual superiority over the other barnyard animals is clearly demonstrated by her greeting to Wilbur: " 'Salutations!' said [Charlotte]. Wilbur jumped to his feet. 'Salu-*what?*' he cried" (35). Dialogue makes the most sense when it is suited to the character who speaks it; otherwise it appears stilted and unnatural.

Vocabulary.   Closely aligned with both exposition and dialogue are word choice and sentence structure. In literature for children word choice is particularly important because of the child's naturally limited vocabulary. Consequently we would not expect to find sophisticated, multisyllabic and bombastic orations in a work intended for preschoolers. On the other hand, if the vocabulary of a piece of fiction never challenges the reader, boredom may set in, or worse, the reader is never given a chance to expand his or her vocabulary. Beatrix Potter is famous for not using condescending language with her young readers. In *The Tale of Peter Rabbit,* we find such words as "exert," "fortnight," and "camomile tea." Young children, just as we ourselves, discern the meanings of unfamiliar words from the context in which they appear. Of course, some abstract terms— "efficient" or "dutiful," for example—may be simply beyond the grasp of younger children, but even the very young can learn to associate such words as "iguana," "egret," or "camomile tea." We should not complain if a work requires a child to learn new words.

Denotations and Connotations.   But word choice is even more complex than that. Virtually all words we know carry more meaning than we may first suspect. Words may be used *denotatively*—that is, according to their literal definitions. When we refer to "heart" as the biological organ that pumps blood throughout the body, we are using the word denotatively. However, the words of our language are imbued with emotional overtones, and when Elizabeth Coatsworth says, "The warm of heart shall never lack a fire / However far he roam," she is using the word "heart" *connotatively,* evoking in us all the associations we generally make when we speak of the "heart." The connotations of heart are many: Sometimes the word evokes a positive quality—"She had a kind heart"—or it can indicate a weakness—"He has been blinded by his heart." It can mean generosity—"You're all heart" (but notice that *how* we say that expression may alter the meaning—with the right inflection it becomes an insult). Or, it can mean resolution—"I have the heart and stomach of a king." No word is as simple as it first appears.

Imagery.   One of the most important uses of diction in a literary work is how it is used in the imagery to create emotional response and meaning. An *image,* as explained in Chapter 7, is a verbal representation of a sensory experience. Imagery refers to a collection of images, the effect of which is to create emotional responses in the reader. Notice how L. Frank Baum uses a collection of bleak images to portray the drabness of Kansas in *The Wizard of Oz:*

> Not a tree nor a house broke the broad sweep of flat country that reached the edge of the sky in all directions. The sun had baked the plowed land into a gray mass, with little cracks running through it. Even the grass was not green, for the sun had burned the tops of the long blades until they were the same gray color to be seen everywhere. Once the house had been painted, but the sun blistered the paint and the rains washed it away, and now the house was as dull and gray as everything else. (8)

The desolation is heightened by the use of the verbs describing the sun's effects: baked, burned, blistered. Not even the sun can give joy to this scene. (For more information on imagery, see Chapter 7.)

Sentences.   Sentences, both by their length and their construction, can contribute to or inhibit our enjoyment of a work. Short sentences best convey suspense, tension, and swift action. Longer sentences work best when explanations and descriptions are needed. It is a myth that long sentences are necessarily complicated and confusing. A well-written long sentence can be just as easy to understand as a short sentence. Notice how E. B. White, in the following paragraph from *Charlotte's*

Web, effectively combines short and long sentences as he moves from describing action to thought and back to action:

> Wilbur looked everywhere. He searched his pen thoroughly. He examined the window ledge, stared up at the ceiling. But he saw nothing new. Finally he decided he would have to speak up. He hated to break the lovely stillness of dawn by using his voice, but he couldn't think of any other way to locate the mysterious new friend who was nowhere to be seen. So Wilbur cleared his throat. (34)

Prose has rhythm as well as poetry. The best writers can make a prose paragraph read as beautifully as a well-crafted poem. With the right juxtaposition of sounds, the right measure of repetition, the right variety of patterns, and the right choice of images, the author can produce a lyrical passage such as this final paragraph from Patricia MacLachlan's *Sarah, Plain and Tall:*

> Autumn will come, then winter, cold with a wind that blows like a wind off the sea in Maine. There will be nests of curls to look for, and dried flowers all winter long. When there are storms, Papa will stretch a rope from the door to the barn so we will not be lost when we feed the sheep and the cows and Jack and Old Bess. And Sarah's chickens, if they aren't living in the house. There will be Sarah's sea, blue and gray and green, hanging on the wall. And songs, old ones and new. And Seal with yellow eyes. And there will be Sarah, plain and tall. (58)

Tone

By the effective use of language and the right arrangement of literary elements, an author may convey a specific attitude toward the subject; this attitude is called the *tone.* In children's literature, a wide variety of tones are found, including humor in its numerous forms (such as the nonsense of Dr. Seuss or the comical, realistic escapades of Harriet in Fitzhugh's *Harriet the Spy*), tenderness (as in Margaret Wise Brown's favorite bedtime story, *Goodnight Moon*), didacticism (that is, instructional reading or reading with moral messages, such as Aesop's fables), and, for older readers, satire (as in Lawson's spoof, *Ben and Me*), or even cynicism (as in the novels of Robert Cormier, such as *I Am the Cheese* or *The Chocolate War*). In some books the tone may even vary from chapter to chapter, as in Childress's *A Hero Ain't Nothin' but a Sandwich.*

Critics generally frown upon some literary tones as inappropriate to children's literature (or to serious adult literature for that matter)—didacticism, sentimentalism, sensationalism, and condescension. *Didacticism* simply means that a work is intended for instructional purposes. Textbooks are didactic by design. But if a novel or a story tries too hard to teach a lesson, readers often react against it. And too often, when an author has a particular lesson in mind, some of the other literary features suffer, such as plot credibility or character development. *Sentimentalism* occurs when there is an undue amount of sentiment or emotionalism, whether tearful or joyful. In children's books, sentimentalism is seen in the "cuteness" that some authors and illustrators use to attract young readers. Sentimentalism is usually seen in opposition to logic—it is the feeling of the heart overpowering the will of the mind. However, as was noted in our discussion of feminism above, this derision of sentimentalism may be, in fact, a masculine point of view that has pervaded criticism. *Sensationalism* is akin to thrill-seeking. We call books sensational when they emphasize grisly horror or steamy passion. Little true sensationalism is found in young children's books, but in books for teenagers it has become commonplace and very popular. For some, it is an essential ingredient for a good story, for many others it is meaningless exploitation. *Condescension* is something that is found in books for the very young, and it refers to the author's talking down to the reader and treating the reader as some sort of inferior human being. Condescension can be viewed as a sort of sentimentalism (once again, the penchant toward "cuteness" in children's picture books seems to assume that young children can only handle subjects when they are sweetened and softened). Anyone who has shared some of the franker folktale versions with young children (such as Margot Zemach's *Three Little Pigs* in which the wolf devours the first two and then is himself eaten by the third) knows that children themselves love a good no-nonsense story, devoid of its sugarcoating, just as well as the rest of us.

LITERATURE AS ART

All of this may seem overwhelming at first, but the thing to remember is that literature is an art form, as are painting, sculpture, architecture, and music. The philosopher Alfred North Whitehead wrote that "Art is the imposing of a pattern on experience, and our aesthetic enjoyment in recognition of the pattern." As the painter takes lines, colors, and shapes, and imposes some order on them to create a painting, as the composer takes sounds and gives them form to create a piece of music, so the writer takes words and crafts them into a work of literature. Just as we must respond to a painting or a musical composition with both our intellect and our emotions, so must we respond to a poem, a story, or a novel with our minds and our hearts. So far as we know, human beings alone among all of creation are able to create and to enjoy art. And, if we may not all of us have the artist's creative powers, we may all be taught to love the artistic creation. This is a love we should cherish in ourselves and nurture in our children. President John Kennedy said, "When power corrupts, poetry cleanses, for art establishes the basic human truths which must serve as the touchstone of our judgment."

BIBLIOGRAPHY OF WORKS CITED

Baum, L. Frank. *The Wizard of Oz.* 1900. Ed. Michael Patrick Hearn. Illus. W. W. Denslow. New York: Schocken, 1983.

MacLachlan, Patricia. *Sarah, Plain and Tall.* New York: Harper and Row, 1985.

Purves, Alan, et al. *How Porcupines Make Love: Teaching a Response-Centered Literature Curriculum.* White Plains, NY: Longman, 1990.

Tuchman, Barbara. *A Distant Mirror: The Calamitous 14th Century.* New York: Knopf, 1978.

White, E. B. *Charlotte's Web.* Illus. Garth Williams. New York: Harper, 1952.

Wilder, Laura Ingalls. *Little House in the Big Woods.* Illus. Garth Williams. New York: Harper and Row, 1953.

RECOMMENDED READINGS

Auerbach, Nina. "Engorging the Patriarchy." In *Feminist Issues in Literary Scholarship.* Ed. Shari Benstock. Bloomington: Indiana University Press, 1987, 150–60.

Bettelheim, Bruno. *The Uses of Enchantment: The Meaning and Importance of Fairy Tales.* New York: Knopf, 1976.

Carlson, Ruth Kearney. *Emerging Humanity: Multi-Ethnic Literature for Children and Adolescents.* Dubuque, IA: Wm. C. Brown, 1972.

Cullinan, Bernice, and Carolyn Carmichael, eds. *Literature and Young Children.* Urbana, IL: National Council of Teachers of English, 1977.

Forster, E. M. *Aspects of the Novel.* New York: Harcourt, Brace, 1954.

Hilkick, Wallace. *Children and Fiction.* Cleveland: World, 1971.

Lukens, Rebecca J. *A Critical Handbook of Children's Literature.* 4th ed. Glenview, IL: Scott, Foresman, 1990.

Nodelman, Perry. *The Pleasures of Children's Literature.* New York: Longman, 1992.

Otten, Charlotte F., and Gary D. Schmidt, eds. *The Voice of the Narrator in Children's Literature: Insights from Writers and Critics.* New York: Greenwood, 1989.

Purves, Alan C., and Dianne L. Monson. *Experiencing Children's Literature.* Glenview, IL: Scott, Foresman, 1984.

Register, Cheri. "American Feminist Literary Criticism: A Bibliographic Introduction." In *Feminist Literary Criticism: Explorations in Theory.* Ed. Josephine Donovan. Lexington: University Press of Kentucky, 1975, 1–28.

Rosenblatt, Louise. *The Reader, the Text, and the Poem.* Carbondale, IL: Southern Illinois Press, 1978.

Shapiro, Jon, ed. *Using Literature & Poetry Affectively.* Chicago: International Reading Association, 1979.

Smith, James Steel. *A Critical Approach to Children's Literature.* New York: McGraw-Hill, 1967.

Smith, Lillian. *The Unreluctant Years.* 1953. New York: Viking, 1967.

Stewig, John Warren, and Sam L. Sebesta, eds. *Using Literature in the Elementary Classroom.* Urbana, IL: National Council of Teachers of English, 1978.

Waxman, Barbara Frey. "Feminist Theory, Literary Canons, and the Construction of Textual Meanings." In *Practicing Theory in Introductory College Literature Courses.* Eds. James M. Cahalan and David B. Downing. Urbana, IL: National Council of Teachers of English, 1991, 149–60.

CHAPTER 15

Literature in the Classroom

SHARING LITERATURE WITH CHILDREN

Perhaps the principal responsibility of adults when it comes to children and books is simply to make sure that children and books come together often, and to see that, when they do, the experience is a happy one and a stimulating one. So it is crucial that we do everything we can to make our children readers, lovers of books, and seekers of knowledge. To ensure this, we must see to it that the experiences young readers have with books are as pleasurable as possible.

Happily, the trend in most schools today is moving away from using textbooks to teach reading and toward using much of the fine literature—fiction, poetry, and nonfiction—that is currently available for young people. Books are an integral part of every excellent preschool and elementary school classroom. There are books on shelves, teachers provide book clubs through which children can purchase their own books, and reading both silently and aloud is part of the daily exercise. Our goal should be that every classroom have plenty of books on hand, both fiction and nonfiction; that ample time for sharing books, reading aloud, and silent reading is scheduled; and that children look forward to the time when they can read. Simply put, books should be seen as an inseparable part of education, an invaluable part of life.

Elementary children are also ripe for learning library skills (how to find favorite books, how to locate information). Here is where students learn that a library is both for enjoyment and for discovering information. The library should represent not a silent, awesome sepulcher for books, but a busy, exciting marketplace of ideas and entertainment, a place where students can browse for luxuries or shop for necessities for the mind and spirit.

But schools alone cannot be expected to create a generation of readers. To nurture in children a healthy attitude toward reading requires above all good adult role models. If they never see their parents reading, children can hardly be expected to pick up the habit—and it is a habit. A family reading time can be an effective way of instilling that habit. Reading engenders more reading, as ideas and pleasures in one book encourage us to seek others. It is important for adults to establish the habit of reading in children, to provide an atmosphere free from the persistent interference of television cartoons, sitcom reruns, and other mindless distractions. It is not a bad idea for every home to begin its own modest library. Inexpensive books can still be found on the sale tables in bookstores, and many schools sponsor book swaps and participate in paperback book clubs. Parents should not rely on the teachers alone to acquaint their children with books. Frequent family visits to the public library on a regular schedule are excellent supplements to reading experiences at home and in school. In short, the task of creating a literate society rests with all of us—and it may be the most important educational task we undertake.

THE READER-CENTERED APPROACH TO LITERATURE

As revealed in Chapter 14, a reader-centered approach to talking and writing about literature has as its emphasis the individual as reader-responder. Because of what we may call its reader-friendly attitude, this approach is ideal for use in the elementary classroom. Purves, Rogers, and Soter have identified four "Objectives" of the reader-centered approach: (1) to encourage individual readers to feel comfortable with their own responses to a literary work; (2) to encourage the readers to seek out the reasons for their responses and thereby come to understand themselves better; (3) to encourage the readers to recognize, in the responses of others, the differences among people and to respect those differences; and (4) to encourage readers to recognize, in the responses of others, the similarities among people (47). Such an approach does not attempt to "teach" literature; rather, its primary goal is to bring children and literature together.

In a response-centered approach, as adults interested in the interaction of children with books, we do a variety of things: (1) we bring children and books together; (2) we give them as many different types of literature as possible; (3) we encourage honest and open responses; (4) we challenge them to explore those responses and learn something about themselves; (5) we provide them with the critical language so that they might clearly express their responses; (6) we encourage tolerance; and (7) we encourage mutual understanding (Purves et al. 56).

The following activities are possible ways for bringing about a connection between children and the books they read. This is in no way an exhaustive list, but rather a suggestive one. We are limited only by our own imaginations.

Reading Aloud

From the parent's gentle singing of a lullaby while rocking an infant to sleep, to the reading of such childhood classics as *Alice in Wonderland* or *Pinocchio,* sharing literature orally with children can be one of the most fulfilling human experiences.

The relaxing moments of story time with two-, three-, and four-year-olds are among the most cherished memories of parenthood. But the times are equally magical when young children themselves want to read the stories to us. Jim Trelease's *Read-Aloud Handbook* is a excellent resource for adults who wish to cultivate the skill of effective reading aloud. And, as Trelease points out, reading aloud to children need not stop when children acquire the ability to read for themselves. Many of us can remember those pleasurable times when a beloved teacher read to us in elementary school. It is unfortunate that more reading aloud is not done in the upper grades—no one is too old to relish a good story read well.

If the book is a picture book, then we have to take care that the illustrations can be easily seen by everyone in the audience. This is easy enough with one or two children, but somewhat more difficult when sharing a picture storybook with a classroom of thirty. Books in small formats, such as Beatrix Potter's, are clearly intended for an intimate story time and not especially suited for large groups. It is possible to buy "giant" books now, books in very large format for kindergarten and first grade classes; however, the selection is limited, and we should not feel that standard-sized books are inadequate for group situations. Of course, an alternative is to break larger classes into small groups for story sharing.

Selecting books for children in the upper elementary grades requires just as much care. But there is surely no shortage of good books available (as attested to by the bibliographies in this volume). The story ought to be one that the reader enjoys as well as the listener. It is not all that easy to pretend to like a book, and the reader risks passing on his or her distaste by reading a work that is less than a favorite. It pays to select the book thoughtfully, considering the emotional level of the children and their primary social and psychological concerns; even the time of year may have an impact on the selection. This is also a great opportunity to introduce subjects and themes that children may not ordinarily seek, but would find rewarding.

Of course, reading aloud entails something more than simply pronouncing the words on the page. The proper inflections, the correct tone, the meaningful pause—all these help to make the experience more rewarding for reader and listener alike. Reading aloud is not, however, acting, and exaggerated threatrics may actually detract from the story itself and defeat the entire purpose. Generally, the best reading is slow and deliberate—listening audiences miss a great deal of what is said to them anyway, and reading too rapidly only increases the chances of their becoming lost or confused. The effective reading is also carefully enunciated, with a natural voice that provides inflection, cadence, and pace to the story. A lower-pitched voice is usually more pleasant to listen to than a higher-pitched one, and, although we cannot always control pitch, it is possible to modify this feature to some extent.

And finally, nothing beats rehearsing the story ahead of time, practicing the pronunciation and making certain there are no words to stumble over. The reward—a grateful and delighted audience—is well worth the effort.

Storytelling

Storytelling, the art of narrating a tale from memory rather than reading it, is one of the oldest of all art forms—undoubtedly reaching back to prehistoric times. Through storytellers, virtually all the traditional folktales were preserved for centuries, having only been committed to paper in the past two or three centuries. To be an effective storyteller, one must be something of a performer, for the delivery is crucial and requires considerable preparation and rehearsal. But the reward— the wide eyes and broad smiles of delight—is generally worth the effort.

Folktales are natural sources for storytellers. They include easily memorized patterns, ample dialogue to enliven the story; and they are brief enough to be relayed in a single sitting. Also, they lend themselves well to adaptation so the storyteller can adjust the tale to the audience. Of course, a rich, mellifluous voice is an asset to any would-be storyteller, but few of us are so blessed. However, this means only that we need to develop some other assets—effective body movement, eye contact, clear enunciation, meaningful inflection, and appropriate pauses. And, with practice (particularly with deep breathing from the diaphragm), it is possible to develop a greater vocal range and a voice that will project. Much of the storyteller's skill derives from knowing how to pace the telling, when to slow down, when to speed up, when to talk in near whispers, when to shout, and so on.

For the storyteller, movement on a staging area is important. Natural body gestures (and at times even exaggerated ones, depending on the nature of the story) and direct eye contact help to totally engage the audience.

At least part of the success of storytelling lies in the choice of an effective story. Action and dialogue are usually preferable to lengthy description or exposition; consequently, the fast pace of the folktales make them particularly suitable. The inclusion of regional speech patterns or dialect can be very effective, but this places a further burden on the storyteller to pronounce the words convincingly. A good storytelling narrative builds up to a climax and then ends quickly while the audience's interest is still at a peak. It is important that the storyteller tells stories that he or she finds thoroughly enjoyable—for delight is contagious.

It is not important that all young people become storytellers themselves; that is not the point. What is important is that they have known the joy of hearing a good story told well, and that may encourage them to seek out other goods stories to read on their own.

Book Discussions

One of the most common classroom approaches to literature is the book discussion, which, if successful, will go beyond a simple series of questions from the teacher and the expected "correct" answers from the students. A good book discussion evolves and metamorphoses as it proceeds. It should be stimulating and provocative, and to ensure that it is, the leader of the discussion needs to be prepared.

A thought-provoking discussion of a book depends upon the types of questions that are asked. If the questions require only that the respondent regurgitate facts from the story, little discussion (and less thinking) will arise. But the proper questions asked in the proper order may result in a lively exchange of ideas. Educators have identified many different levels of questions, but for most practical purposes four levels will suffice.

(1) *Memory or factual questions* ask the audience to recall facts from the story or poem: plot incidents, character identifications, details of the setting, and so on. It is

good to begin a discussion with memory questions for they can help determine if the readers understand the basic elements of the work.

An example of a good memory question might be, "In Beatrix Potter's *The Tale of Peter Rabbit,* what happened to Peter's father?" The answer to this question has a direct bearing on the theme of the story, since it shows that Peter was aware of the dangers of entering Mr. McGregor's garden. In a discussion of E. B. White's classic book, *Charlotte's Web,* for example, we may begin with memory questions such as these: Why was Wilbur's life in danger? How did Fern save Wilbur? How did Charlotte save Wilbur? How did Wilbur repay Charlotte? All these questions can be answered factually from a reading of the book, and all have some thematic significance focusing on the relationships between the various characters. It would be unproductive to ask such questions as: What color was Wilbur? or What was Charlotte's oldest child's name? These details have little bearing on the story, and there is no reason to expect a reader to recall every bit of minutiae. There is no virtue in memory questions that seem designed to trick even the most careful reader; if we can think of no good reason for asking a question, it probably should not be asked.

Memory questions tend to be the easiest type of questions, and they can help to loosen up the audience by giving early positive reinforcement. Memory questions tend to focus on matters of plot and setting. Good memory questions direct our attention to significant points rather than minor details, and they require something beyond "yes" or "no" responses. Unfortunately, some discussion leaders seldom get beyond these types of questions.

(2) The second level of questioning consists of *interpretation questions:* questions requiring the readers to make inferences and draw conclusions from the facts of the story or poem. These questions may require *analysis* (lifting individual facts from the story and examining them carefully) or *synthesis* (putting together disparate facts in a new way). "Why does Peter's mother not punish him for his disobedience?" might be a good interpretative question, for it will lead into a discussion of one of the major ideas of the story. For *Charlotte's Web,* we might ask such questions as these: How does the relationship between Fern and Wilbur change over the course of the book? How does Wilbur's character change from the beginning to the end of the book? In any case, it is important that readers understand that any conclusions they draw be based soundly on the evidence found in the work itself. Simple personal opinions are not adequate if they cannot be supported by hard facts. Interpretation questions focus on matters of character motivation and theme.

(3) The third level of questioning is that of *application:* questions that ask the readers to consider the work in a larger context. They tend to focus on further extensions of the theme as well as on matters of style, imagery, symbolism, and so on. Application refers to the transfer of information acquired from the literary work to another experience (one's own life, for example, or another literary work). Children might be asked to compare *The Tale of Peter Rabbit* with Potter's *The Tale of Benjamin Bunny,* or they might be asked to discuss a time when they were in a situation similar to Peter's. While discussing *Charlotte's Web,* students might be asked in what ways Templeton, Charlotte, and Wilbur remind them of people they know. Application questions should ultimately help us to see the relationships between literature and life, and should, when possible, ask us to draw on our own experiences.

Here are where the personal responses to literature come into play. These questions can result in some of the more meaningful and exciting discussions.

(4) Ultimately, we may bring young readers to the *critical evaluation questions.* As children read more and more and become sophisticated in their literary knowledge, we can ask them to make critical judgments about the works they read. It is not realistic to expect the very young to read at this level, but with older children we might ask them to compare *Charlotte's Web* with Kenneth Grahame's *Wind in the Willows* or with Robert Lawson's *Rabbit Hill.* How are they alike? How are they different? Which is most believable and why? Compare *Charlotte's Web* with another of E. B. White's fantasies—*Stuart Little* or *Trumpet of the Swan.* What similarities do you see? What differences? If you prefer one over another, why? Asking young readers which of two books they prefer is only useful if we can get them to articulate their reasons and thereby help them to understand their own tastes a little better. This is also the beginning of the acquisition of critical taste and judgment. It is good to remember that with most interpretation and evaluation questions, there are no clear right or wrong answers, only answers that are more convincingly supported than others.

Writing Experiences

As early as second grade, most children are capable of responding to literature through writing, and, certainly by the time they reach the middle elementary grades, children should be writing as a regular part of their total curriculum. Several possibilities are available at all grade levels.

Journals. Keeping journals in which they are free to record their feelings without fear of a recriminating grade can be a very effective way for children to become more thoughtful readers. When we have to commit our ideas to writing we are compelled to think them through more thoroughly and to impose more order on them than when these ideas are freely (and perhaps aimlessly) floating about in our heads. Writing, in other words, can help us to analyze and evaluate our thoughts.

Journal sharing can be a rewarding variation on this exercise. Students can share journal entries with others, who can then write back to them their own feelings. This can be effectively done by drawing a line down the middle of the page with the original writer using the left-hand side and the respondent using the right-hand side. It can also be done by using facing pages in a spiral notebook. Teachers can also be respondents. It is important that children fully understand the nature of the journal assignment before they write—an entry in a private journal will be much different from an entry intended for another reader.

Journal writing is only effective, however, if it becomes habitual and if the individual entries eventually attain a reasonable length.

Reader-Response Essays. Other writing exercises might include reader-response essays, in which young readers are asked to record various responses to their reading. These responses may be emotional, responding to particular characters or situations, especially as they relate to their own lives and experiences. They may be interpretative, as when a reader makes an inference about what he or she reads, or draws some conclusion based on the evidence in a story. Or responses may be critical, as when a reader makes some judgment about the literary quality of a written work—such as the language, the story content, or the plot construction. When a child states that a story is boring, we are hearing an immature critical response, but when the child can explain why he or she thinks the story is boring (such as, not enough action, too repetitious, too predictable), we are getting closer to a true critical response. Also, a response may be evaluative, when a reader attempts to demonstrate the literary quality of a work, its emotional appeal, or its moral or ethical significance. These kinds of responses are (like the evaluative questions) the most sophisticated. They often explain why a work is good or not, whether the theme or central idea or philosophy of the work is valid or useful, or if the writer is successful in accomplishing a purpose.

The reader-response essay, if used as an informal writing assignment, can provide readers with the opportunity to thoughtfully consider their reading. As with the journal, if we have to write our thoughts down, we are required to do more serious thinking than if we are simply asked to answer one or two questions in class. The best reader-response essays are those in which children draw on concrete examples from the reading to support their ideas. Not incidentally, the reader-response essays can be good exercises in preparing children for more formal critical analyses in later years.

Another interesting writing experiment is to have young readers write a preliminary essay in preparation for a reading assignment. For example, prior to reading Natalie Babbitt's *Tuck Everlasting,* middle school students might be asked to write on the following topic: "If you discovered the fountain of immortality, would you drink from it? Why or why not?" Then, once the students have read the book, in which such a question is actually posed to the protagonist, they might be asked to write a follow-up essay reconsidering the same issue but with the new light shed by the novel. A comparison of the two responses—before and after—can be quite interesting.

Book Reports: Variations on an Old Theme.

There are countless imaginative exercises available to replace the old "book report." Children may enjoy making up their own endings to stories, for example, or writing new episodes with their favorite characters (Peggy Parrish's *Amelia Bedelia* series or Beverly Cleary's *Ramona* books provide wonderful starting points for younger readers). Children might be asked to review a book, much like the movie critics review movies on television. Newspaper stories based on events in books can also be fun to write (Roald Dahl's *James and the Giant Peach* or *Charlie and the Chocolate Factory* offer some delightful opportunities here). Some children may enjoy reading and writing about the life of a favorite author. It should be pointed out that whereas most writers enjoy receiving fan mail, bundles of form letters written by entire school classes as part of a writing assignment tend to lack sincerity and hold little meaning for the writer. There is nothing wrong, however, with having students write open letters to authors—living or dead—in which the students discuss their own attitudes and opinions toward a book. They do not need to be mailed. (Read Beverly Cleary's *Dear Mr. Henshaw* for an example of the value of letter writing, even if those letters are not mailed.) Writing the imaginary diary of a fictional character, such as Laura from Laura Ingalls Wilder's *Little House* series, can help children understand the concept of point of view. Having children create a story from their own life experiences can help them gain firsthand knowledge of plot. Scriptwriting, in which children must devise dialogue for characters, can enrich their understanding of language differences, characterization, and setting.

Whatever the project may be, it is useful and good to integrate writing into the reading program—for writing and reading naturally complement one another. A good writer must necessarily be a good reader. And a good reader can help to produce a good writer. Both will result in a good thinker.

Creating Books. A particularly enjoyable activity for children of all ages is that of making their own books. Very young children can create alphabet, counting, or concept books, or do takeoffs on favorite nursery rhymes or poems. Older children may want to experiment with ghost stories, adventure stories, family stories, or poetry. Of course, much of the fun lies in illustrating the books, and a variety of media can be used—crayon, watercolor, collage, montage, pencil, and so on.

Binding the books can be as simple as fastening them in a loose-leaf folder or as elaborate as sewing the leaves and making cloth-covered cardboard covers. Not only does this project give children firsthand experience in designing books and laying out pages, it can also result in an attractive finished product that is fit for a gift or a keepsake. Such a project is a rewarding way of bringing a writing exercise to a climax, and the children see themselves as young authors.

Dramatic Responses to Literature

Dramatic responses to literature include a wide range of activities, from oral interpretation (a one-person performance of a piece of literature) to creative dramatics and role-playing (which are really impromptu inventions of the actors). We will briefly consider a few of these approaches.

Oral Interpretation. Oral interpretation typically involves a one-person performance of a poem or brief prose passage, usually, but not necessarily, memorized. The effectiveness of oral interpretation lies in the performer's vocal talents and meaningful gestures. It is very much like storytelling, except that oral interpretation does not allow for variants in its material. That is, the speaker is expected to recite the words with faithful accuracy. Oral interpretation is generally not suitable for use with young children, but by the fourth or fifth grades most children should be ready to orally recite a passage. Many wonderful, humorous poems are available that might make this experience a pleasurable one for both performer and audience. Whenever possible, children should be allowed to select their own material for oral interpretation. The principal emphasis should be on careful pronunciation and enunciation of the words, projection, and, to the extent possible, appropriate feeling. Shyness is inevitable with many students, but it can be overcome only with continued practice and experience. Since this is a rather sophisticated approach to literature, it is perhaps best used sparingly in the elementary years—but there is no need to completely avoid it.

Story Theater.   Story theater is a pantomime accompanied by a narrator who reads or tells the story while others act out the plot. Since even inanimate objects (such as a tree) might be portrayed by an actor, story theater allows for a very flexible number of performers (some children may enjoy the idea of portraying the moon, for example). The performance can be as simple or elaborate as the means dictate. Pantomime does not require line memorizing, making it one of the least threatening dramatic forms for children. It does require one good reader, however, and some uninhibited actors. Since the youngest children tend to be the least inhibited, story theater is a good exercise to begin in the early elementary years. The best tales for a story theater presentation are those with plenty of action, otherwise the pantomimers would be little more than furniture. Many folktales provide wonderful opportunities for story theater, particularly the farcical tales, such as "Clever Gretel," where action rather than dialogue dominates. Story theater can be enhanced by costumes, scenery, and props, and can thus serve as an introduction to play production.

Reader's Theater.   Reader's theater, as the name implies, involves the reading of a script as opposed to acting it out. The participants assume various speaking roles in a story—usually one reader for each speaking character and one narrator to read the exposition. True reader's theater is traditionally performed without any action whatever, with the readers sitting on chairs and using only their voices to convey meaning. The old-time radio dramas were, in essence, reader's theater, and that is very much the effect good reader's theater has. All the audience's attention is directed to the language, so the readers must be expressive and must read with clarity and precision.

To avoid distraction from the reading, performers in true reader's theater wear nondescript, but uniform clothing—usually in black or black and white. Since no memorization, physical movement, scenery, or properties are involved, reader's theater provides a ready outlet for self-expression. But this does not mean that it is simple. Without the advantage of action—as with story theater—greater responsibility is placed on the readers to discover the voice of their respective characters. For this reason, practice in oral interpretation is good preparation for reader's theater. Although reader's theater is designed for the reading of plays, suitable plays for elementary children are often hard to locate. But many stories can be adapted to reader's theater, including (once again) many folktales. It is important that each reader have a substantial part—and there is no reason a single person cannot read more than one part. But stories of few speaking parts may leave most of the reading for the narrator, with little for the other readers to do—"The Three Bears" is an example of a story that is primarily narration; there is really very little for the characters to say. The best reader's theater stories are those with several speaking parts, ample dialogue, a fairly easy vocabulary but with expressive language, and, finally, a good conflict. "Hansel and Gretel" might adapt easily, since several parts are rather substantial. It is always possible to edit the tales as well, abbreviating the narration or even replacing narration with dialogue.

Creative Dramatics.   Creative dramatics is the dramatization of a story with improvised dialogue. This allows children to perform their own versions of stories without strict adherence to script (although in creative dramatics, the actors are expected to remain faithful to the storyline). This activity requires considerable preparation and may be as elaborate in setting, props, and theatrical accouterments as the director desires. Creative dramatics can be less threatening than a more traditional play since there is no need for memorization. It also allows for more individual expression than either story or reader's theater, providing children with the opportunity to update old stories and give them their own peculiar twists. At the same time, since the actors must have a firm grasp of plot and character, this exercise can result in a more meaningful consideration of character, plot, and theme. One of the great advantages of creative dramatics is that many folktales and other short stories or even chapters from favorite books (*Winnie-the-Pooh* or *The Wind in the Willows* come to mind) can be readily adapted to the form.

Role-Playing. Role-playing is similar to creative dramatics, but it removes us one step further from the literary source, for the actors assume specific character roles and are expected to invent not only the dialogue but the action as they proceed. Typically, a problem is posed, and through the role-playing exercise the children arrive at a solution. Consequently, in the experience they are allowed to examine the issues through the eyes of others. Role-playing is only marginally connected with literature, but is a widely-used and effective method of exploring personal and social values. And, of course, since these values are usually a part of literature, role-playing can be adapted as a response to literature. Children, for example, could be assigned the roles of various characters (such as those from Cleary's *Ramona* books), and they could then be presented with a dilemma to solve. The important element in a successful role-playing exercise is to be sure that each assigned role is a distinct personality type who will respond appropriately as the personality suggests. This exercise, as with many of the dramatic responses, works best with children in the middle or upper elementary grades, since younger children have not yet grasped the fundamental concepts of drama.

Puppet Theater. Puppet theater is a favorite medium of children and combines both dramatic and artistic responses to literature. An elaborate and time-honored art form, puppetry can be very simple (with puppets made from a sock or decorated paper bag stuck on a hand) or very complex (with string-operated marionettes with movable hands, feet, eyes, and mouth). Puppet-making is an art in itself, but one in which children can readily participate. In addition to socks and paper bags, puppets can be made from construction paper and sticks, vegetables (they make wonderful puppets, but don't wait too long to do the show), cardboard boxes, rubber balls and cloth, cardboard cylinders (such as paper towel tubes), and shadow puppets (created by using overhead projectors, with great possibilities available through the use of colored acetate sheets for background).

Once the puppet is made, the dramatic part of the experience begins. Stories with ample dialogue and action work best. Since lines need not be memorized and since the puppeteers are hidden from the audience's view, puppet theater can be an ideal form for beginning thespians. It is also ideal for shy children, for behind the mask of the puppet, many have found an exhilarating outlet for their deepest feelings.

Art and Literature

Another popular means of extending literature is through art. As soon as they can handle a crayon or pencil, even the youngest children can be asked to draw pictures in response to a story. The means by which art can enrich the literary experience are limited only by the imaginations of those involved. A few of the more widely used methods will be discussed here.

The Graphic Arts.   Children love working with paints, watercolors, crayons, and pencil. These are usually the simplest art projects, requiring rather basic tools and minimal instruction to get started. And they allow for a great deal of originality. Even having young children draw pictures suggested by picture storybooks can be a means of getting them to explore different artistic styles as they try to copy Sendak's impressionistic style in Zolotow's *Mr. Rabbit and the Lovely Present,* or Potter's delicate representational style in *The Tale of Peter Rabbit,* or the expressionistic style of Ludwig Bemelmans in *Madeline.* Allowing children to draw pictures after hearing stories read to them can result in some of the most highly individualistic creations, however, for they do not have another artist's work to imitate.

Collage, not technically a "graphic" method except that it can make use of pens, pencils, and other drawing instruments, is a picture created from nonpainterly materials (cloth, wood, cotton, leaves, rocks, and so on). These materials are typically fixed to a posterboard to make a unified work. This was the favorite method of Ezra Jack Keats (*The Snowy Day, Peter's Chair* and many other fine picture books) and Leo Lionni (*Frederick* and *Inch by Inch,* among others). Creating a collage about a favorite story is especially appealing for young children since it does not require highly developed drawing skills. The materials used and their arrangement may be suggested by the story itself.

Similar to the collage is the *montage:* a collection of pictures arranged into a single composite. Both the collage and the montage can be used as responses to literature if children are asked to create, for example, a poster that reflects their feelings about a particular work. Doing this, young readers are being asked to focus on a specific aspect of the literature—usually either a character or theme. This is the great advantage of incorporating artwork into the literature program, for the readers are encouraged to distill all their thoughts on a story into a single visual image. The result may be that they understand the work's plot or theme or characterization a little bit better than when they began.

The Plastic Arts.   The plastic arts include the three-dimensional, nonpainterly artforms, such as sculpture. The *diorama* is a three-dimensional scene easily created from a shoebox or other carton and decorated with cardboard cutouts, plastic figures, or any other suitable objects. It is really a sort of primitive doll house and can be seen as an extension of the montage and collage in that it requires the maker to focus on a single thematic idea. By a further extension of the diorama, children can create miniature stages and puppet figures with which to reenact a story, thus combining an artistic and a dramatic response to literature. A natural development of the miniature stage is for the children to create stories of their own to dramatize. The diorama requires attention to detail, which is why this form is used so frequently for social studies projects (creating a diorama of the Ice Age or of Colonial America). Children may have to read more closely and pay attention to every detail in order to create an effective three-dimensional scene.

Mobiles are free forms, usually cut from paper or cardboard, interconnected and suspended by string or wire so that when hung they turn freely in the breeze. These are popular with children from infancy, and many babies enjoy some form of mobile hung over their cribs. *Stabiles* are similar to mobiles in that they are abstract sculptural forms, but stationary. Modeling with clay or working with other craft materials, such as popsicle sticks, can provide further imaginative outlets as responses to stories or poems. These projects, like the montages and collages, can help children see relationships in a story, and they can help them to consider such things as character, plot, and theme more seriously. As with any art project associated with literature, such projects are extensions of the literary study, not just meaningless time-fillers.

Cooking.   A recently popularized extension to literature is cooking, which can be considered an art form in itself, one in which the artistic creation is eaten. Some children's books even include recipes suitable for children, and there are, in fact, some very fine cookbooks written for children (Virginia Ellison's *Pooh's Cookbook* is for the very young). Jean Fritz's *George Washington's Breakfast* readily lends itself to a cooking experience as a capstone to the reading.

Regardless of the art project, it is important to remember that if the art is seen as a true extension of the literature it should not be regarded as the end itself. In other words, we are not reading *Pinocchio* for the purpose of making our own puppet when we are finished. And, if the art is to be a true extension of the literature, it should not be simply gratuitous—"Now that we have read *Pinocchio,* let's all draw a picture of his nose." If the art project cannot become a meaningful part of the study of the literature, helping children to better focus on the ideas and the structure of the work itself, it is perhaps best not to fabricate a relationship between the art and the literature. Both, after all, are valuable in their own right, and neither should be regarded as a handmaiden to the other.

CHILDREN'S BOOKS AND THE CENSOR

A regrettable fact that many educators ultimately have to face is the self-proclaimed censor wielding a swift and wrathful sword against the "dangerous" ideas presented in books. Literature, as we have noted, is not for the bigot, for literature encourages tolerance as it presents to us endless possibilities. The bigot and the despot both fear literature because it helps to keep people's minds open and receptive to new ideas. It is no coincidence that the bigots and despots are also the bookburners and censors.

There is no justification for censorship of any literature, and that includes children's literature. Many well-meaning people have sought to protect children from the unsavory in literature, but of course the problem is that not everyone agrees with what ought to be forbidden. We have seen the folktales tidied up and rid of much of their gore, and that may be to accommodate delicate modern tastes (usually of adults). But we have also seen the banning of such books as E. B. White's *Charlotte's Web* (some groups have found the whole concept of talking animals unnatural), William Steig's *Sylvester and the Magic Pebble* (the author made the mistake of portraying the police in this animal fantasy as pigs), Robert Cormier's *I Am the Cheese* (too negative a view of society), J. D. Salinger's *The Catcher in the Rye* (all those four-letter words)—the list is exhaustive. Censorship is alive and well in the United States. We should view this with alarm, for it threatens our intellectual freedom, our personal freedom, and undermines one of the most fundamental tenets of our Constitution. It can, at its worst, threaten democracy.

Our problem as purveyors of children's literature is to be prepared to defend our choices if parents or the community objects to any literature we might wish to use. It is wise for teachers to have a written justification prepared for each book in the curriculum. We should try to anticipate possible objections and be ready to address them if it becomes necessary. Perhaps the last word on censorship should be the reminder that censoring a book typically fails and often has the effect of making the forbidden book immediately popular. The fact of the matter seems to be that there is absolutely no evidence that essentially good children are turned into bad by reading the wrong kinds of books—just as there is no evidence that reading the "right" books will correct a willful child's behavior.

THE INFLUENCE OF LITERATURE

Literature does influence us. It influences us in the very best way because it compels us to think, to examine our lives, to regard those around us, to imagine better (and sometimes worse) worlds. It broadens our experiences far beyond what any of us could hope to accomplish in a lifetime; it takes us to places we will never go and to places that do not even exist outside the imagination.

Our success in introducing children to books can only be measured when the children are grown and on their own. Have we provided them with the necessary tools so that they are able to read with competence? Have we nurtured in them the necessary intellectual curiosity so that they will want to keep on reading and learning? Have we allowed them the necessary opportunity to discover the joy of reading? Whether we are parents, teachers, or interested adults, we have these challenges before us. The seventeenth-century English thinker Sir Francis Bacon wrote, "Some books are to be tasted, others to be swallowed, and some few to be chewed and digested." The various responses to literature we have discussed are meant to suggest ways in which we can help children taste, swallow, and, in some cases, chew and digest the books they read. If we have done our jobs well, the young people in our care will look forward to a feast of rich and pleasurable reading, lasting throughout their entire lives.

RECOMMENDED READINGS

Aquino, John. *Fantasy in Literature.* Washington, DC: National Education Association, 1977.
Bauer, Caroline Feller. *This Way to Books.* Bronx, NY: Wilson, 1982.
Barton, Bob, and David Booth. *Stories in the Classroom.* Portsmouth, NH: Heinemann, 1990.

Blatt, Gloria T., ed. *Once Upon a Folktale: Capturing the Folklore Process with Children.* New York: Teachers College Press, 1993.

Bosma, Betty. *Fairy Tales, Fables, Legends, and Myths: Using Folk Literature in Your Classroom.* 2nd ed. New York: Teachers College Press, 1992.

Bromley, Karen D'Angelo. *Webbing with Literature: Creating Story Maps with Children's Books.* Boston: Allyn and Bacon, 1991.

Bruno, Janet, and Peggy Dakan. *Cooking in the Classroom.* Belmont, CA: Fearon Pitman, 1974.

Chambers, Aidan. *Introducing Books to Children.* 2nd ed. Boston: The Horn Book, 1983.

———. *The Reluctant Reader.* Elmsford, NY: Pergamon, 1969.

Cioni, Alfred J., ed. *Motivating Reluctant Readers.* Newark, DE: International Reading Association, 1981.

Coody, Betty. *Using Literature with Young Children.* 4th ed. Dubuque, IA: Wm. C. Brown, 1992.

Cook, Elizabeth. *The Ordinary and the Fabulous: An Introduction to Myths, Legends and Fairy Tales.* 2nd ed. New York: Cambridge, 1969.

Cullinan, Bernice. *Literature and the Child.* 2nd ed. San Diego, CA: Harcourt, 1989.

Currell, David. *The Complete Book of Puppetry.* Boston: Plays, 1975.

Donelson, Kenneth L., and Alleen Pace Nilsen. *Literature for Today's Young Adults.* 2nd ed. Glenview, IL: Scott, Foresman, 1985.

Gillies, Emily. *Creative Dramatics for All Children.* Wheaton, MD: Association for Childhood Education International, 1973.

Hanford, Robert Ten Eyck. *Puppets and Puppeteering.* New York: Sterling, 1981.

Huck, Charlotte S., Susan Hepler, and Janet Hickman. *Children's Literature in the Elementary School.* 5th ed. New York: Holt, Rinehart & Winston, 1993.

Hurst, Carol. "What to Do with a Poem." *Early Years* (February 1980): 28–29, 68.

Leonard, Charlotte. *Tied Together: Topics and Thoughts for Introducing Children's Books.* Metuchen, NJ: Scarecrow, 1980.

MacDonald, M. R. *The Storyteller's Sourcebook: A Subject, Title and Motif Index to Folklore Collections for Children.* Detroit, MI: Heal-Schuman, 1982.

Pellowski, Ann. *World of Storytelling.* Ann Arbor: R. R. Bowker, 1977.

Purves, Alan, et al. *How Porcupines Make Love: Teaching a Response-Centered Literature Curriculum.* White Plains, NY: Longman, 1990.

Routman, Regie. *Transitions: From Literature to Literacy.* Portsmouth, NH: Heinemann, 1988.

Rudman, Masha, ed. *Children's Literature: Resource for the Classroom.* 2nd ed. Norwood, MA: Christopher-Gordon, 1993.

Sadler, Glenn Edward, ed. *Teaching Children's Literature: Issues, Pedagogy, Resources.* New York: Modern Language Association of America, 1992.

Sawyer, Ruth. *The Way of the Storyteller.* New York: Penguin, 1942.

Shapiro, Jon E., ed. *Using Literature & Poetry Affectively.* Newark, DE: International Reading Association, 1971.

Shedlock, Marie. *The Art of the Storyteller.* 1915. New York: Dover, 1951.

Sloan, Glenna Davis. *The Child as Critic: Teaching Literature in Elementary and Middle Schools.* 3rd ed. New York: Teachers College Press, 1991.

Trelease, Jim. *The New Read-Aloud Handbook.* New York: Penguin, 1989.

Troeger, Virginia Bergen. "Student Storytelling." *Teaching K–8* (March 1990): 41–43.

Watson, Dorothy J., ed. *Ideas and Insights: Language Arts in the Elementary School.* Urbana, IL: National Council of Teachers of English, 1987.

Yopp, Ruth Helen, and Hallie Kay Yopp. *Literature-Based Reading Activities.* Boston: Allyn and Bacon, 1992.

Children's Book Awards

Every year numerous book awards are presented to works of children's literature, both for writing and for illustration. These awards are sponsored by various organizations, each with its own set of criteria. In addition, several awards are presented to individuals recognizing lifetime achievement in children's literature. Included below are some of the more prestigious awards. Unless otherwise indicated, the author is also the illustrator for these books. The award-selection process is not infallible, and often some excellent works have been overlooked whereas some award-winning works have not stood the test of time. In general, these lists can suggest—in addition to specific titles—authors and illustrators who produce works of high quality. But we should not be slaves to book award lists.

Included in the following lists are not only awards presented to writers in English, but some international awards. It is good that we make a concerted effort to acquaint ourselves not only with American and English children's authors, but with writers the world over. Perhaps in time, more of these foreign language books for children will be available in translation as we realize how important intercultural communication is to global understanding.

AMERICAN BOOK AWARDS

The Newbery Medal

The Newbery Medal was named for John Newbery, the British entrepreneur who pioneered children's book publishing in the eighteenth century. The award is, however, an American award, presented annually by the American Library Association to the most distinguished contribution to children's literature published in the United

States. Runners-up are termed Honor Books. As with any such award, there has not always been general agreement with the decisions. However, the list does include some of the finest writing for young people over the last seventy years.

1922 *The Story of Mankind* by Hendrik Willem van Loon, Liveright
 Honor Books: *The Great Quest* by Charles Hawes, Little, Brown; *Cedric the Forester* by Bernard Marshall, Appleton; *The Old Tobacco Shop: A True Account of What Befell a Little Boy in Search of Adventure* by William Bowen, Macmillan; *The Golden Fleece and the Heroes Who Lived before Achilles* by Padraic Colum, Macmillan; *Windy Hill* by Cornelia Meigs, Macmillan

1923 *The Voyages of Doctor Dolittle* by Hugh Lofting, Lippincott
 Honor Books: No record

1924 *The Dark Frigate* by Charles Hawes, Little, Brown
 Honor Books: No record

1925 *Tales from Silver Lands* by Charles Finger, Doubleday
 Honor Books: *Nicholas: A Manhattan Christmas Story* by Anne Carroll Moore, Putnam; *Dream Coach* by Anne Parrish, Macmillan

1926 *Shen of the Sea* by Arthur Bowie Chrisman, Dutton
 Honor Book: *Voyagers: Being Legends and Romances of Atlantic Discovery* by Padraic Colum, Macmillan

1927 *Smoky, the Cowhorse* by Will James, Scribner
 Honor Books: No record

1928 *Gayneck, The Story of a Pigeon* by Dhan Gopal Mukerji, Dutton
 Honor Books: *The Wonder Smith and His Son: A Tale from the Golden Childhood of the World* by Ella Young, Longmans; *Downright Dencey* by Caroline Snedeker, Doubleday

1929 *The Trumpeter of Krakow* by Eric P. Kelly, Macmillan
 Honor Books: *Pigtail of Ah Lee Ben Loo* by John Bennett, Longmans, Green (McKay); *Millions of Cats* by Wanda Gag, Coward, McCann & Geoghegan; *The Boy Who Was* by Grace Hallock, Dutton; *Clearing Weather* by Cornelia Meigs, Little, Brown; *Runaway Papoose* by Grace Moon, Doubleday; *Tod of the Fens* by Elinor Whitney, Macmillan

1930 *Hitty, Her First Hundred Years* by Rachel Field, Macmillan
 Honor Books: *Daughter of the Seine: The Life of Madame Roland* by Jeanette Eaton, Harper; *Pran of Albania* by Elizabeth Miller, Doubleday; *Jumping-off Place* by Marian Hurd McNeely, Longmans, Green (McKay); *Tangle-coated Horse and Other Tales: Episodes from the Fionn Saga* by Ella Young, Longmans, Green (McKay); *Vaino: A Boy of New England* by Julia Davis Adams, Dutton; *Little Blacknose* by Hildegarde Swift, Harcourt Brace Jovanovich

1931 *The Cat Who Went to Heaven* by Elizabeth Coatsworth, Macmillan

Honor Books: *Floating Island* by Anne Parrish, Harper; *The Dark Star of Itza: The Story of a Pagan Princess* by Alida Malkus, Harcourt Brace Jovanovich; *Queer Person* by Ralph Hubbard, Doubleday; *Mountains Are Free* by Julia Davis Adams, Dutton; *Spice and the Devil's Cave* by Agnes Hewes, Knopf; *Meggy Macintosh* by Elizabeth Janet Gray, Doubleday; *Garram the Hunter: A Boy of the Hill Tribes* by Herbert Best, Doubleday; *Ood-Le-Uk the Wanderer* by Alice Lide and Margaret Johansen, Little, Brown

1932   *Waterless Mountain* by Laura Adams Armer, Longmans, Green (McKay)
Honor Books: *The Fairy Circus* by Dorothy P. Lathrop, Macmillan; *Calico Bush* by Rachel Field, Macmillan; *Boy of the South Seas* by Eunice Tietjens, Coward, McCann & Geoghegan; *Out of the Flame* by Eloise Lownsbery, Longmans, Green (McKay); *Jane's Island* by Marjorie Allee, Houghton Mifflin; *Truce of the Wolf and Other Tales of Old Italy* by Mary Gould Davis, Harcourt Brace Jovanovich

1933   *Young Fu of the Upper Yangtze* by Elizabeth Foreman Lewis, Winston
Honor Books: *Swift Rivers* by Cornelia Meigs, Little, Brown; *The Railroad to Freedom: A Story of the Civil War* by Hildegarde Swift, Harcourt Brace Jovanovich; *Children of the Soil: A Story of Scandinavia* by Nora Burglon, Doubleday

1934   *Invincible Louisa: The Story of the Author of "Little Women"* by Cornelia Meigs, Little, Brown
Honor Books: *The Forgotten Daughter* by Caroline Snedeker, Doubleday; *Swords of Steel* by Elsie Singmaster, Houghton Mifflin; *ABC Bunny* by Wanda Gag, Coward, McCann & Geoghegan; *Winged Girl of Knossos* by Erik Berry, Appleton; *New Land* by Sarah Schmidt, McBride; *Big Tree of Bunlahy: Stories of My Own Countryside* by Padraic Colum, Macmillan; *Glory of the Seas* by Agnes Hewes, Knopf; *Apprentice of Florence* by Ann Kyle, Houghton Mifflin

1935   *Dobry* by Monica Shannon, Viking
Honor Books: *Pageant of Chinese History* by Elizabeth Seeger, Longmans, Green (McKay); *Davy Crockett* by Constance Rourke, Harcourt Brace Jovanovich; *Day on Skates: The Story of a Dutch Picnic* by Hilda Van Stockum; Harper

1936   *Caddie Woodlawn* by Carol Ryrie Brink, Macmillan
Honor Books: *Honk, the Moose* by Phil Strong, Dodd, Mead; *The Good Master* by Kate Seredy, Viking; *Young Walter Scott* by Elizabeth Janet Gray, Viking; *All Sail Set: A Romance of the Flying Cloud* by Armstrong Sperry, Winston

1937   *Roller Skates* by Ruth Sawyer, Viking
Honor Books: *Phoebe Fairchild: Her Book* by Lois Lenski, Stokes; *Whistler's Van* by Idwal Jones, Viking; *Golden Basket* by Ludwig Bemelmans, Viking; *Winterbound* by Margery Bianco, Viking; *Audubon* by Constance Rourke, Harcourt Brace Jovanovich; *The Codfish Musket* by Agnes Hewes, Doubleday

1938   *The White Stag* by Kate Seredy, Viking
        Honor Books: *Pecos Bill* by James Cloyd Bowman, Little, Brown; *Bright Island* by Mabel Robinson, Random House; *On the Banks of Plum Creek* by Laura Ingalls Wilder, Harper

1939   *Thimble Summer* by Elizabeth Enright, Holt, Rinehart and Winston
        Honor Books: *Nino* by Valenti Angelo, Viking; *Mr. Popper's Penguins* by Richard and Florence Atwater, Little, Brown; *"Hello the Boat!"* by Phillis Crawford, Holt, Rinehart and Winston; *Leader by Destiny: George Washington, Man and Patriot* by Jeanette Eaton, Harcourt Brace Jovanovich; *Penn* by Elizabeth Janet Gray, Viking

1940   *Daniel Boone* by James Daugherty, Viking
        Honor Books: *The Singing Tree* by Kate Seredy, Viking; *Runner of the Mountain Tops: The Life of Louis Agassiz* by Mabel Robinson, Random House; *By the Shores of Silver Lake* by Laura Ingalls Wilder, Harper; *Boy with a Pack* by Stephen W. Meader, Harcourt Brace Jovanovich

1941   *Call It Courage* by Armstrong Sperry, Macmillan
        Honor Books: *Blue Willow* by Doris Gates, Viking; *Young Mac of Fort Vancouver* by Mary Jane Carr, Crowell; *The Long Winter* by Laura Ingalls Wilder, Harper; *Nansen* by Anna Gertrude Hall, Viking

1942   *The Matchlock Gun* by Walter D. Edmonds, Dodd, Mead
        Honor Books: *Little Town on the Prairie* by Laura Ingalls Wilder, Harper; *George Washington's World* by Genevieve Foster, Scribner; *Indian Captive: The Story of Mary Jemison* by Lois Lenski, Lippincott; *Down Ryton Water* by Eva Roe Gaggin, Viking

1943   *Adam of the Road* by Elizabeth Janet Gray, Viking
        Honor Books: *The Middle Moffat* by Eleanor Estes, Harcourt Brace Jovanovich; *Have You Seen Tom Thumb?* by Mabel Leigh Hunt, Lippincott

1944   *Johnny Tremain* by Esther Forbes, Houghton Mifflin
        Honor Books: *The Happy Golden Years* by Laura Ingalls Wilder, Harper; *Fog Magic* by Julia Sauer, Viking; *Rufus M.* by Eleanor Estes, Harcourt Brace Jovanovich; *Mountain Born* by Elizabeth Yates, Coward, McCann & Geoghegan

1945   *Rabbit Hill* by Robert Lawson, Viking
        Honor Books: *The Hundred Dresses* by Eleanor Estes, Harcourt Brace Jovanovich; *The Silver Pencil* by Alice Dalgliesh, Scribner; *Abraham Lincoln's World* by Genevieve Foster, Scribner; *Lone Journey: The Life of Roger Williams* by Jeanette Eaton, Harcourt Brace Jovanovich

1946   *Strawberry Girl* by Lois Lenski, Lippincott
        Honor Books: *Justin Morgan Had a Horse* by Marguerite Henry, Rand McNally; *The Moved-Outers* by Florence Crannell Means, Houghton Mifflin; *Bhimsa, the Dancing Bear* by Christine Weston, Scribner; *New Found World* by Katherine Shippen, Viking

1947   *Miss Hickory* by Carolyn Sherwin Bailey, Viking

Honor Books: *Wonderful Year* by Nancy Barnes, Messner; *Big Tree* by Mary and Conrad Buff, Viking; *The Heavenly Tenants* by William Maxwell, Harper; *The Avion My Uncle Flew* by Cyrus Fisher, Appleton; *The Hidden Treasure of Glaston* by Eleanore Jewett, Viking

1948   *The Twenty-One Balloons* by William Pene du Bois, Viking
Honor Books: *Pancakes-Paris* by Claire Huchet Bishop, Viking; *Le Lun, Lad of Courage* by Carolyn Treffinger, Abingdon; *The Quaint and Curious Quest of Johnny Longfoot, The Shoe-Kings Son* by Catherine Besterman, Bobbs-Merrill; *The Cow-tail Switch, and Other West African Stories* by Harold Courlander, Holt, Rinehart and Winston; *Misty of Chincoteague* by Marguerite Henry, Rand McNally

1949   *King of the Wind* by Marguerite Henry, Rand McNally
Honor Books: *Seabird* by Holling C. Holling, Houghton Mifflin; *Daughter of the Mountains* by Louise Rankin, Viking; *My Father's Dragon* by Ruth S. Gannett, Random; *Story of the Negro* by Arna Bontemps, Knopf

1950   *The Door in the Wall* by Marguerite de Angeli, Doubleday
Honor Books: *Tree of Freedom* by Rebecca Caudill, Viking; *The Blue Cat of Castle Town* by Catherine Coblentz, Longmans, Green (McKay); *Kildee House* by Rutherford Montgomery, Doubleday; *George Washington* by Genevieve Foster, Scribner; *Song of the Pines: A Story of Norwegian Lumbering in Wisconsin* by Walter and Marion Havighurst, Winston

1951   *Amos Fortune, Free Man* by Elizabeth Yates, Aladdin
Honor Books: *Better Known as Johnny Appleseed* by Mabel Leigh Hunt, Lippincott; *Gandhi, Fighter without a Sword* by Jeanette Eaton, Morrow; *Abraham Lincoln, Friend of the People* by Clara Ingram Judson, Follett; *The Story of Appleby Capple* by Anne Parrish, Harper

1952   *Ginger Pye* by Eleanor Estes, Harcourt Brace Jovanovich
Honor Books: *Americans before Columbus* by Elizabeth Baity, Viking; *Minn of the Mississippi* by Holling C. Holling, Houghton Mifflin; *The Defender* by Nicholas Kalashnikoff, Scribner; *The Light at Tern Rock* by Julia Sauer, Viking; *The Apple and the Arrow* by Mary and Conrad Buff, Houghton Mifflin

1953   *Secret of the Andes* by Ann Nolan Clark, Viking
Honor Books: *Charlotte's Web* by E. B. White, Harper; *Moccasin Trail* by Eloise McGraw, Coward, McCann & Geoghegan; *Red Sails to Capri* by Ann Weil, Viking; *The Bears on Hemlock Mountain* by Alice Dalgliesh, Scribner; *Birthdays of Freedom,* Vol. 1, by Genevieve Foster, Scribner

1954   *. . . and Now Miguel* by Joseph Krumgold, Crowell
Honor Books: *All Alone* by Claire Huchet Bishop, Viking; *Shadrach* by Meindert DeJong, Harper; *Hurry Home Candy* by Meindert DeJong, Harper; *Theodore Roosevelt, Fighting Patriot* by Clara Ingram Judson, Follett; *Magic Maize* by Mary and Conrad Buff, Houghton Mifflin

1955   *The Wheel on the School* by Meindert DeJong, Harper

Honor Books: *The Courage of Sarah Noble* by Alice Dalgliesh, Scribner; *Banner in the Sky* by James Ullman, Lippincott

1956   *Carry On, Mr. Bowditch* by Jean Lee Latham, Houghton Mifflin
Honor Books: *The Secret River* by Marjorie Kinnan Rawlings, Scribner; *The Golden Name Day* by Jennie Linquist, Harper; *Men, Microscopes, and Living Things* by Katherine Shippen, Viking

1957   *Miracles on Maple Hill* by Virginia Sorensen, Harcourt Brace Jovanovich
Honor Books: *Old Yeller* by Fred Gipson, Harper; *The House of Sixty Fathers* by Meindert DeJong, Harper; *Mr. Justice Holmes* by Clara Ingram Judson, Follett; *The Corn Grows Ripe* by Dorothy Rhoads, Viking; *Black Fox of Lorne* by Marguerite de Angeli, Doubleday

1958   *Rifles for Watie* by Harold Keith, Crowell
Honor Books: *The Horsecatcher* by Mari Sandoz, Westminster; *Gone-away Lake* by Elizabeth Enright, Harcourt Brace Jovanovich; *The Great Wheel* by Robert Lawson, Viking; *Tom Paine, Freedom's Apostle* by Leo Gurko, Crowell

1959   *The Witch of Blackbird Pond* by Elizabeth George Speare, Houghton Mifflin
Honor Books: *The Family under the Bridge* by Natalie Savage Carlson, Harper; *Along Came a Dog* by Meindert DeJong, Harper; *Chucaro: Wild Pony of the Pampas* by Francis Kalnay, Harcourt Brace Jovanovich; *The Perilous Road* by William O. Steele, Harcourt Brace Jovanovich

1960   *Onion John* by Joseph Krumgold, Crowell
Honor Books: *My Side of the Mountain* by Jean George, Dutton; *America Is Born* by Gerald W. Johnson, Morrow; *The Gammage Cup* by Carol Kendall, Harcourt Brace Jovanovich

1961   *Island of the Blue Dolphins* by Scott O'Dell, Houghton Mifflin
Honor Books: *America Moves Forward* by Gerald W. Johnson, Morrow; *Old Ramon* by Jack Schaefer, Houghton Mifflin; *The Cricket in Times Square* by George Selden, Farrar, Straus & Giroux

1962   *The Bronze Bow* by Elizabeth George Speare, Houghton Mifflin
Honor Books: *Frontier Living* by Edwin Tunis, World; *The Golden Goblet* by Eloise McCraw, Coward, McCann & Geoghegan; *Belling the Tiger* by Mary Stolz, Harper

1963   *A Wrinkle in Time* by Madeleine L'Engle, Farrar, Straus & Giroux
Honor Books: *Thistle and Thyme: Tales and Legends from Scotland* by Sorche Nic Leodhas, Holt, Rinehart and Winston; *Men of Athens* by Olivia Coolidge, Houghton Mifflin

1964   *It's Like This, Cat* by Emily Cheney Neville, Harper
Honor Books: *Rascal* by Sterling North, Dutton; *The Loner* by Ester Wier, McKay

1965   *Shadow of a Bull* by Maia Wojciechowska, Atheneum
Honor Book: *Across Five Aprils* by Irene Hunt, Follett

1966   *I, Juan de Pareja* by Elizabeth Borten de Trevino, Farrar, Straus & Giroux

Honor Books: *The Black Cauldron* by Lloyd Alexander, Holt, Rinehart and Winston; *The Animal Family* by Randall Jarrell, Pantheon; *The Noonday Friends* by Mary Stolz, Harper

1967   *Up a Road Slowly* by Irene Hunt, Follett
Honor Books: *The King's Fifth* by Scott O'Dell, Houghton Mifflin; *Zlateh the Goat and Other Stories* by Isaac Bashevis Singer, Harper; *The Jazz Man* by Mark H. Weik, Atheneum

1968   *From the Mixed-Up Files of Mrs. Basil E. Frankweiler* by E. L. Konigsburg, Atheneum
Honor Books: *Jennifer, Hecate, Macbeth, William McKinley, and Me, Elizabeth* by E. L. Konigsburg, Atheneum; *The Black Pearl* by Scott O'Dell, Houghton Mifflin; *The Fearsome Inn* by Isaac Bashevis Singer, Scribner; *The Egypt Game* by Zilpha Keatley Snyder, Atheneum

1969   *The High King* by Lloyd Alexander, Holt, Rinehart and Winston
Honor Books: *To Be a Slave* by Julius Lester, Dial Press; *When Shlemiel Went to Warsaw and Other Stories* by Isaac Bashevis Singer, Farrar, Straus & Giroux

1970   *Sounder* by William H. Armstrong, Harper
Honor Books: *Our Eddie* by Sulamith IshKishor, Pantheon Books; *The Many Ways of Seeing: An Introduction to the Pleasures of Art* by Janet Gaylord Moore, World; *Journey Outside* by Mary Q. Steele, Viking

1971   *Summer of the Swans* by Betsy Byars, Viking
Honor Books: *Kneeknock Rise* by Natalie Babbitt, Farrar, Straus & Giroux; *Enchantress from the Stars* by Sylvia Louise Engdahl, Atheneum; *Sing Down the Moon* by Scott O'Dell, Houghton Mifflin

1972   *Mrs. Frisby and the Rats of NIMH* by Robert C. O'Brien, Atheneum
Honor Books: *Incident at Hawk's Hill* by Allan W. Eckert, Little, Brown; *The Planet of Junior Brown* by Virginia Hamilton, Macmillan; *The Tombs of Atuan* by Ursula K. Le Guin, Atheneum; *Annie and the Old One* by Miska Miles, Little, Brown; *The Headless Cupid* by Zilpha Keatley Snyder, Atheneum

1973   *Julie of the Wolves* by Jean Craighead George, Harper
Honor Books: *Frog and Toad Together* by Arnold Lobel, Harper; *The Upstairs Room* by Johanna Reiss, Crowell; *The Witches of Worm* by Zilpha Keatley Snyder, Atheneum

1974   *The Slave Dancer* by Paula Fox, Bradbury
Honor Book: *The Dark is Rising* by Susan Cooper, Atheneum

1975   *M. C. Higgins, the Great* by Virginia Hamilton, Macmillan
Honor Books: *Figgs & Phantoms* by Ellen Raskin, Dutton; *My Brother Sam Is Dead* by James Lincoln Collier and Christopher Collier, Four Winds; *The Perilous Gard* by Elizabeth Marie Pope, Houghton Mifflin; *Philip Hall Likes Me. I Reckon Maybe* by Bette Greene, Dial Press

1976   *The Grey King* by Susan Cooper, Atheneum

Honor Books: *The Hundred Penny Box* by Sharon Bell Mathis, Viking; *Dragonwings* by Lawrence Yep, Harper

1977   *Roll of Thunder, Hear My Cry* by Mildred D. Taylor, Dial Press
Honor Books: *Abel's Island* by William Steig, Farrar, Straus & Giroux; *A String in the Harp* by Nancy Bond, Atheneum

1978   *Bridge to Terabithia* by Katherine Paterson, Crowell
Honor Books: *Ramona and Her Father* by Beverly Cleary, Morrow; *Anpao: An American Indian Odyssey* by Jamake Highwater, Lippincott

1979   *The Westing Game* by Ellen Raskin, Dutton
Honor Book: *The Great Gilly Hopkins* by Katherine Paterson, Crowell

1980   *A Gathering of Days: A New England Girl's Journal 1830–32* by Joan Blos, Scribner
Honor Book: *The Road from Home: The Story of an American Girl* by David Kherdian, Greenwillow (Morrow)

1981   *Jacob Have I Loved* by Katherine Paterson, Crowell
Honor Books: *The Fledgling* by Jane Langton, Harper; *A Ring of Endless Light* by Madeleine L'Engle, Farrar, Straus & Giroux

1982   *A Visit to William Blake's Inn: Poems for Innocent and Experienced Travelers* by Nancy Willard, Harcourt Brace Jovanovich
Honor Books: *Ramona Quimby, Age 8* by Beverly Cleary, Morrow; *Upon the Head of the Goat: A Childhood in Hungary, 1939–1944* by Aranka Siegal, Farrar, Straus & Giroux

1983   *Dicey's Song* by Cynthia Voigt, Atheneum
Honor Books: *Blue Sword* by Robin McKinley, Morrow; *Dr. DeSoto* by William Steig, Farrar, Straus & Giroux; *Graven Images* by Paul Fleischman, Harper; *Homesick: My Own Story* by Jean Fritz, Putnam; *Sweet Whisper, Brother Rush* by Virginia Hamilton, Philomel (Putnam)

1984   *Dear Mr. Henshaw* by Beverly Cleary, Morrow
Honor Books: *The Wish Giver* by Bill Brittain, Harper; *Sugaring Time* by Kathryn Lasky, Macmillan; *The Sign of the Beaver* by Elizabeth George Speare, Hougton Mifflin; *A Solitary Blue* by Cynthia Voigt, Atheneum

1985   *The Hero and the Crown* by Robin McKinley, Greenwillow (Morrow)
Honor Books: *The Moves Make the Man* by Bruce Brooks, Harper; *One-Eyed Cat* by Paula Fox, Bradbury; *Like Jake and Me* by Mavis Jukes, Knopf

1986   *Sarah, Plain and Tall* by Patricia MacLachlan, Harper
Honor Books: *Commodore Perry in the Land of the Shogun* by Rhoda Blumberg, Lothrop; *Dogsong* by Gary Paulsen, Bradbury

1987   *The Whipping Boy* by Sid Fleischman, Greenwillow (Morrow)
Honor Books: *On My Honor* by D. Bauer, Clarion; *Volcano: The Eruption and Healing of Mount St. Helens* by Patricia Lauber, Bradbury; *A Fine White Dust* by Cynthia Rylant, Bradbury

1988   *Lincoln: A Photobiography* by Russell Freedman, Clarion/Houghton Mifflin

Honor Books: *After the Rain* by Norma Fox Mazer, Morrow; *Hatchet* by Gary Paulsen, Bradbury

1989   *Joyful Noise: Poems for Two Voices* by Paul Fleischman, Harper
Honor Books: *In the Beginning* by Virginia Hamilton, Harcourt Brace Jovanovich; *Scorpions* by Walter Dean Myers, Harper

1990   *Number the Stars* by Lois Lowry, Houghton Mifflin
Honor Books: *Afternoon of the Elves* by Janet Taylor Lisle, Orchard Books/Watts; *The Winter Room* by Gary Paulsen, Orchard Books/Watts; *Shabanu: Daughter of the Wind* by Suzanne Fisher Staples, Knopf

1991   *Maniac Magee* by Jerry Spinelli, Little, Brown
Honor Book: *The True Confessions of Charlotte Doyle* by Avi, Orchard

1992   *Shiloh* by Phillis Reynolds Naylor, Atheneum
Honor Books: *Nothing But the Truth* by Avi, Orchard; *The Wright Brothers: How They Invented the Airplane* by Russell Freedman, Holiday

1993   *Missing May* by Cynthia Ryland, Orchard
Honor Books: *The Dark-Thirty: Southern Tales of the Supernatural* by Patricia McKissack, Knopf; *Somewhere in the Darkness* by Walter Dean Myers, Scholastic; *What Hearts* by Bruce Brooks, HarperCollins

The Caldecott Medal

Named for the British illustrator Randolph Caldecott, the Caldecott Medal has been awarded annually since 1938 by the American Library Association to the most distinguished picture-book published in America. Runners up are given Honor Awards. Although the passage of time has not always validated the awards and many fine books have been overlooked, the awards list does provide a roll call of some of the best in children's books. The Caldecott Award is given to the illustrator and honors the pictorial art rather than the text.

1938   *Animals of the Bible* by Helen Dean Fish, illustrated by Dorothy P. Lathrop, Stokes
Honor Books: *Seven Simeon: A Russian Tale* by Boris Artzybasheff, Viking; *Four and Twenty Blackbirds: Nursery Rhymes of Yesterday Recalled for Children of To-Day* by Helen Dean Fish, illustrated by Robert Lawson, Stokes

1939   *Mei Li* by Thomas Handforth, Doubleday
Honor Books: *The Forest Pool* by Laura Adams Armer, Longmans, Green (McKay); *Wee Gillis* by Munro Leaf, illustrated by Robert Lawson, Viking; *Snow White and the Seven Dwarfs* by Wanda Gag, Coward, McCann & Geoghegan; *Barkis* by Clare Newberry, Harper; *Andy and the Lion: A Tale of Kindness Remembered or the Power of Gratitude* by James Daugherty, Viking

1940   *Abraham Lincoln* by Ingri and Edgar Parin d'Aulaire, Doubleday

Honor Books: *Cock-a-Doodle Doo: The Story of a Little Red Rooster* by Berta and Elmer Hader, Macmillan; *Madeline* by Ludwig Bemelmans, Simon & Schuster; *The Ageless Story* by Lauren Ford, Dodd, Mead

1941   *They Were Strong and Good* by Robert Lawson, Viking
Honor Book: *April's Kittens* by Clare Newberry, Harper

1942   *Make Way for Ducklings* by Robert McCloskey, Viking
Honor Books: *An American ABC* by Maud and Miska Petersham, Macmillan; *In My Mother's House* by Ann Nolan Clark, illustrated by Velino Herrera, Viking; *Paddle-to-the-Sea* by Holling C. Holling, Houghton Mifflin; *Nothing at All* by Wanda Gag, Coward, McCann & Geoghegan

1943   *The Little House* by Virginia Lee Burton, Houghton Mifflin
Honor Books: *Dash and Dart* by Mary and Conrad Buff, Viking; *Marshmallow* by Clare Newberry, Harper

1944   *Many Moons* by James Thurber, illustrated by Louis Slobodkin, Harcourt Brace Jovanovich
Honor Books: *Small Rain: Verses from the Bible* selected by Jessie Orton Jones, illustrated by Elizabeth Orton Jones, Viking; *Pierre Pigeon* by Lee Kingman, illustrated by Arnold E. Bare, Houghton Mifflin; *The Mighty Hunter* by Berta and Elmer Hader, Macmillan; *A Child's Good Night Book* by Margaret Wise Brown, illustrated by Jean Charlot, W. R. Scott; *Good Luck Horse* by Chih-Yi Chan, illustrated by Plato Chan, Whittlesey

1945   *Prayer for a Child* by Rachel Field, illustrated by Elizabeth Orton Jones, Macmillan
Honor Books: *Mother Goose: Seventy-Seven Verses with Pictures,* illustrated by Tasha Tudor, Walck; *In the Forest* by Marie Hall Ets, Viking; *Yonie Wondernose* by Marguerite de Angeli, Doubleday; *The Christmas Anna Angel* by Ruth Sawyer, illustrated by Kate Seredy, Viking

1946   *The Rooster Crows . . . ,* illustrated by Maud and Miska Petersham, Macmillan
Honor Books: *Little Lost Lamb* by Golden MacDonald, illustrated by Leonard Weisgard, Doubleday; *Sing Mother Goose* by Opal Wheeler, illustrated by Marjorie Torrey, Dutton; *My Mother Is the Most Beautiful Woman in the World* by Becky Reyher, illustrated by Ruth Gannett, Lothrop; *You Can Write Chinese* by Kurt Wiese, Viking

1947   *The Little Island* by Golden MacDonald, illustrated by Leonard Weisgard, Doubleday.
Honor Books: *Rain Drop Splash* by Alvin Tresselt, illustrated by Leonard Weisgard, Lothrop; *Boats on the River* by Marjorie Flack, illustrated by Jay Hyde Barnum, Viking; *Timothy Turtle* by Al Graham, illustrated by Tony Palazzo, Viking; *Pedro, The Angel of Olvera Street* by Leo Politi, Scribner; *Sing in Praise: A Collection of the Best Loved Hymns* by Opal Wheeler, illustrated by Marjorie Torrey, Dutton

1948   *White Snow, Bright Snow* by Alvin Tresselt, illustrated by Roger Duvoisin, Lothrop

Honor Books: *Stone Soup: An Old Tale* by Marcia Brown, Scribner; *McElligot's Pool* by Dr. Seuss, Random House: *Bambino the Clown* by George Schreiber, Viking; *Roger and the Fox* by Lavinia Davis, illustrated by Hildegard Woodward, Doubleday; *Song of Robin Hood* edited by Anne Malcolmson, illustrated by Virginia Lee Burton, Houghton Mifflin

1949　*The Big Snow* by Berta and Elmer Hader, Macmillan
Honor Books: *Blueberries for Sal* by Robert McCloskey, Viking; *All Around the Town* by Phyllis McGinley, illustrated by Helen Stone, Lippincott; *Juanita* by Leo Politi, Scribner; *Fish in the Air* by Kurt Wiese, Viking

1950　*Song of the Swallows* by Leo Politi, Scribner
Honor Books: *America's Ethan Allen* by Stewart Holbrook, illustrated by Lynd Ward, Houghton Mifflin; *The Wild Birthday Cake* by Lavinia Davis, illustrated by Hildegard Woodward, Doubleday; *The Happy Day* by Ruth Krauss, illustrated by Marc Simont, Harper; *Bartholomew and the Oobleck* by Dr. Seuss, Random House; *Henry Fisherman* by Marcia Brown, Scribner

1951　*The Egg Tree* by Katherine Milhous, Scribner
Honor Books: *Dick Whittington and His Cat* by Marcia Brown, Scribner; *The Two Reds* by William Lipkind, illustrated by Nicholas Mordvinoff, Harcourt Brace Jovanovich; *If I Ran the Zoo* by Dr. Seuss, Random House; *The Most Wonderful Doll in the World* by Phyllis McGinley, illustrated by Helen Stone, Lippincott; *T-Bone, the Baby Sitter* by Clare Newberry, Harper

1952　*Finders Keepers* by William Lipkind, illustrated by Nicholas Mordvinoff, Harcourt Brace Jovanovich
Honor Books: *Mr. T. W. Anthony Woo: The Story of a Cat and a Dog and a Mouse* by Marie Hall Ets, Viking; *Skipper John's Cook* by Marcia Brown, Scribner; *All Falling Down* by Gene Zion, illustrated by Margaret Bloy Graham, Harper; *Bear Party* by William Pene du Bois, Viking; *Feather Mountain* by Elizabeth Olds, Houghton Mifflin

1953　*The Biggest Bear* by Lynd Ward, Houghton Mifflin
Honor Books: *Puss in Boots* by Charles Perrault, illustrated and translated by Marcia Brown, Scribner; *One Morning in Maine* by Robert McCloskey, Viking; *Ape in a Cape: An Alphabet of Odd Animals* by Fritz Eichenberg, Harcourt Brace Jovanovich; *The Storm Book* by Charlotte Zolotow, illustrated by Margaret Bloy Graham, Harper; *Five Little Monkeys* by Juliet Kepes, Houghton Mifflin

1954　*Madeline's Rescue* by Ludwig Bemelmans, Viking
Honor Books: *Journey Cake, Ho!* by Ruth Sawyer, illustrated by Robert McCloskey, Viking; *When Will the World Be Mine?* by Miriam Schlein, illustrated by Jean Charlot, W. R. Scott; *The Steadfast Tin Soldier* by Hans Christian Andersen, illustrated by Marcia Brown, Scribner; *A Very Special House* by Ruth Krauss, illustrated by Maurice Sendak, Harper; *Green Eyes* by A. Birnbaum, Capitol

1955   *Cinderella, or the Little Glass Slipper* by Charles Perrault, translated and illustrated by Marcia Brown, Scribner

Honor Books: *Book of Nursery and Mother Goose Rhymes,* illustrated by Marguerite de Angeli, Doubleday; *Wheel on the Chimney* by Margaret Wise Brown, illustrated by Tibor Gergely, Lippincott; *The Thanksgiving Story* by Alice Dalgliesh, illustrated by Helen Sewell, Scribner

1956   *Frog Went A-Courtin* edited by John Langstaff, illustrated by Feodor Rojankovsky, Harcourt Brace Jovanovich

Honor Books: *Play with Me* by Marie Hall Ets, Viking; *Crow Boy* by Taro Yashima, Viking

1957   *A Tree Is Nice* by Janice May Udry, illustrated by Marc Simont, Harper

Honor Books: *Mr. Penny's Race Horse* by Marie Hall Ets, Viking; *1 Is One* by Tasha Tudor, Walck; *Anatole* by Eve Titus, illustrated by Paul Galdone, McGraw-Hill; *Gillespie and the Guards* by Benjamin Elkin, illustrated by James Daugherty, Viking; *Lion* by William Pene du Bois, Viking

1958   *Time of Wonder* by Robert McCloskey, Viking

Honor Books: *Fly High, Fly Low* by Don Freeman, Viking; *Anatole and the Cat* by Eve Titus, illustrated by Paul Galdone, McGraw-Hill

1959   *Chanticleer and the Fox* adapted from Chaucer and illustrated by Barbara Cooney, Crowell

Honor Books: *The House That Jack Built: A Picture Book in Two Languages* by Antonio Frasconi, Harcourt Brace Jovanovich; *What Do You Say, Dear?* by Sesyle Joslin, illustrated by Maurice Sendak, Scott; *Umbrella* by Taro Yashima, Viking

1960   *Nine Days to Christmas* by Marie Hall Ets and Aurora Labastida, illustrated by Marie Hall Ets, Viking

Honor Books: *Houses from the Sea* by Alice E. Goudey, illustrated by Adrienne Adams, Scribner; *The Moon Jumpers* by Janice May Udry, illustrated by Maurice Sendak, Harper

1961   *Baboushka and the Three Kings* by Ruth Robbins, illustrated by Nicolas Sidjakov, Parnassus

Honor Book: *Inch by Inch* by Leo Lionni, Obolensky

1962   *Once a Mouse . . .* by Marcia Brown, Scribner

Honor Books: *The Fox Went Out on a Chilly Night: An Old Song* by Peter Spier, Doubleday; *Little Bear's Visit* by Else Holmelund Minarik, illustrated by Maurice Sendak, Harper; *The Day We Saw the Sun Come Up* by Alice E. Goudey, illustrated by Adrienne Adams, Scribner

1963   *The Snowy Day* by Ezra Jack Keats, Viking

Honor Books: *The Sun Is a Golden Earring* by Natalia M. Belting, illustrated by Bernarda Bryson, Holt, Rinehart and Winston; *Mr. Rabbit and the Lovely Present* by Charlotte Zolotow, illustrated by Maurice Sendak, Harper

1964   *Where the Wild Things Are* by Maurice Sendak, Harper

Honor Books: *Swimmy* by Leo Lionni, Pantheon Books; *All in the Morning Early* by Sorche Nic Leodhas, illustrated by Evaline Ness, Holt, Rinehart and Winston; *Mother Goose and Nursery Rhymes* illustrated by Philip Reed, Atheneum

1965   *May I Bring a Friend?* by Beatrice Schenk de Regniers, illustrated by Beni Montresor, Atheneum

Honor Books: *Rain Makes Applesauce* by Julian Scheer, illustrated by Marvin Bileck, Holiday; *The Wave* by Margaret Hodges, illustrated by Blair Lent, Houghton Mifflin; *A Pocketful of Cricket* by Rebecca Caudill, illustrated by Evaline Ness, Holt, Rinehart and Winston

1966   *Always Room for One More* by Sorche Nic Leodhas, illustrated by Nonny Hogrogian, Holt, Rinehart and Winston

Honor Books: *Hide and Seek Fog* by Alvin Tresselt, illustrated by Roger Duvoisin, Lothrop; *Just Me* by Marie Hall Ets, Viking; *Tom Tit Tot* by Evaline Ness, Scribner

1967   *Sam, Bangs & Moonshine* by Evaline Ness, Holt, Rinehart and Winston

Honor Book: *One Wide River to Cross* by Barbara Emberley, illustrated by Ed Emberley, Prentice-Hall

1968   *Drummer Hoff* by Barbara Emberley, illustrated by Ed Emberley, Prentice-Hall

Honor Books: *Frederick* by Leo Lionni, Pantheon Books; *Seashore Story* by Taro Yashima, Viking; *The Emperor and the Kite* by Jane Yolen, illustrated by Ed Young, World

1969   *The Fool of the World and the Flying Ship* by Arthur Ransome, illustrated by Uri Shulevitz, Farrar, Straus & Giroux

Honor Book: *Why the Sun and the Moon Live in the Sky: An African Folktale* by Elphinstone Dayrell, illustrated by Blair Lent, Houghton Mifflin

1970   *Sylvester and the Magic Pebble* by William Stieg, Windmill (Simon & Schuster)

Honor Books: *Goggles!* by Ezra Jack Keats, Macmillan; *Alexander and the Wind-Up Mouse* by Leo Lionni, Panthen Books; *Pop Corn and Ma Goodness* by Edna Mitchell Preston, illustrated by Robert Andrew Parker, Viking; *Thy Friend, Obadiah* by Brinton Turkle, Viking; *The Judge: An Untrue Tale* by Harve Zemach, illustrated by Margot Zemach, Farrar, Straus & Giroux

1971   *A Story—A Story: An African Tale* by Gail E. Haley, Atheneum

Honor Books: *The Angry Moon* by William Sleator, illustrated by Blair Lent, Little, Brown; *Frog and Toad Are Friends* by Arnold Lobel, Harper; *In the Night Kitchen* by Maurice Sendak, Harper

1972   *One Fine Day* by Nonny Hogrogian, Macmillan

Honor Books: *If All the Seas Were One Sea* by Janina Domanska, Macmillan; *Moja Means One: Swahili Counting Book* by Muriel Feelings, illustrated by Tom Feelings, Dial Press; *Hildilid's Night* by Cheli Duran Ryan, illustrated by Arnold Lobel, Macmillan

1973   *The Funny Little Woman* retold by Arlene Mosel, illustrated by Blair Lent, Dutton

           Honor Books: *Anansi the Spider: A Tale from the Ashanti* adapted and illustrated by Gerald McDermott, Holt, Rinehart and Winston; *Hosie's Alphabet* by Hosea Tobias and Lisa Baskin, illustrated by Leonard Baskin, Viking; *Snow White and the Seven Dwarfs* translated by Randall Jarrell, illustrated by Nancy Ekholm Burkert, Farrar, Straus & Giroux; *When Clay Sings* by Byrd Baylor, illustrated by Tom Bahti, Scribner

1974   *Duffy and the Devil* by Harve Zemach, illustrated by Margot Zemach, Farrar, Straus & Giroux

           Honor Books: *Three Jovial Huntsmen* by Susan Jeffers, Bradbury; *Cathedral: The Story of Its Construction* by David Macauley, Houghton Mifflin

1975   *Arrow to the Sun* adapted and illustrated by Gerald McDermott, Viking

           Honor Book: *Jambo Means Hello: A Swahili Alphabet Book* by Muriel Feelings, illustrated by Tom Feelings, Dial Press

1976   *Why Mosquitoes Buzz in People's Ears* retold by Verna Aardema, illustrated by Leo and Diane Dillon, Dial Press

           Honor Books: *The Desert Is Theirs* by Byrd Baylor, illustrated by Peter Parnall, Scribner; *Strega Nona* retold and illustrated by Tomie de Paola, Prentice-Hall

1977   *Ashanti to Zulu: African Traditions* by Margaret Musgrove, illustrated by Leo and Diane Dillon, Dial Press

           Honor Books: *The Amazing Bone* by William Steig, Farrar, Straus & Giroux; *The Contest* retold and illustrated by Nonny Hogrogian, Greenwillow (Morrow); *Fish for Supper* by M. B. Goffstein, Dial Press; *The Golem: A Jewish Legend* by Beverly Brodsky McDermott, Lippincott; *Hawk, I'm Your Brother* by Byrd Baylor, illustrated by Peter Parnall, Scribner

1978   *Noah's Ark* by Peter Spier, Doubleday

           Honor Books: *Castle* by David Macaulay, Houghton Mifflin; *It Could Always Be Worse* retold and illustrated by Margot Zemach, Farrar, Straus & Giroux

1979   *The Girl Who Loved Wild Horses* by Paul Goble, Bradbury

           Honor Books: *Freight Train* by Donald Crews, Greenwillow (Morrow); *The Way to Start a Day* by Byrd Baylor, illustrated by Peter Parnall, Scribner

1980   *Ox-Cart Man* by Donald Hall, illustrated by Barbara Cooney, Viking

           Honor Books: *Ben's Trumpet* by Rachel Isadora, Greenwillow (Morrow); *The Treasure* by Uri Shulevitz, Farrar, Straus & Giroux; *The Garden of Abdul Gasazi* by Chris Van Allsburg, Houghton Mifflin

1981   *Fables* by Arnold Lobel, Harper

           Honor Books: *The Bremen-Town Musicians* by Ilse Plume, Doubleday; *The Grey Lady and the Strawberry Snatcher* by Molly Bang, Four Winds; *Mice Twice* by Joseph Low, Atheneum; *Truck* by Donald Crews, Greenwillow (Morrow)

1982   *Jumanji* by Chris Van Allsburg, Houghton Mifflin

Honor Books: *A Visit to William Blake's Inn: Poems for Innocent and Experienced Travelers* by Nancy Willard, illustrated by Alice and Martin Provensen, Harcourt Brace Jovanovich; *Where the Buffaloes Begin* by Olaf Baker, illustrated by Stephen Gammell, Warne; *On Market Street* by Arnold Lobel, illustrated by Anita Lobel, Greenwillow (Morrow); *Outside Over There* by Maurice Sendak, Harper

1983   *Shadow* by Blaise Cendrars, illustrated by Marcia Brown, Scribner

Honor Books: *When I Was Young in the Mountains* by Cynthia Rylant, illustrated by Diane Goode, Dutton; *Chair for My Mother* by Vera B. Williams, Morrow

1984   *The Glorious Flight: Across the Channel with Louis Blériot July 25, 1909* by Alice and Martin Provenson, Viking

Honor Books: *Ten, Nine, Eight* by Molly Bang, Greenwillow (Morrow); *Little Red Riding Hood* by Trina Schart Hyman, Holiday House

1985   *Saint George and the Dragon* by Margaret Hodges, illustrated by Trina Schart Hyman, Little, Brown

Honor Books: *Hansel and Gretel* by Rika Lesser, illustrated by Paul O. Zelinsky, Dodd, Mead; *The Story of the Jumping Mouse* by John Steptoe, Lothrop; *Have You Seen My Duckling?* by Nancy Tafuri, Greenwillow (Morrow)

1986   *The Polar Express* by Chris Van Allsburg, Houghton Mifflin

Honor Books: *The Relatives Came* by Cynthia Rylant, illustrated by Stephen Gammell, Bradbury; *King Bidgood's in the Bathtub* by Audrey Wook, illustrated by Don Wood, Harcourt Brace Jovanovich

1987   *Hey, Al* by Arthur Yorinks, illustrated by Richard Egielski, Farrar, Straus & Giroux

Honor Books: *The Village of Round and Square Houses* by Ann Grifalconi, Little, Brown; *Alphabatics* by Suse MacDonald, Bradbury; *Rumpelstiltskin* by Paul O. Zelinsky, Dutton

1988   *Owl Moon* by Jane Yolen, illustrated by John Schoenherr, Philomel (Putnam)

Honor Books: *Mufaro's Beautiful Daughter* by John Steptoe, Lothrop

1989   *Song and Dance Man* by Karen Ackerman, illustrated by Stephen Gammell, Knopf

Honor Books: *Goldilocks* by James Marshall, Dial Press; *The Boy of the Three-Year Nap* by Dianne Snyder, illustrated by Allen Say; *Mirandy and Brother Wind* by Patricia McKissack, illustrated by Jerry Pinkney, Knopf; *Free Fall* by David Wiesner, Lothrop

1990   *Lon Po Po: A Red-Riding Hood Story from China* by Ed Young, Philomel (Putnam)

Honor Books: *Hershel and the Hanukkah Goblins* by Eric Kimmel, illustrated by Trina Schart Hyman, Holiday; *Color Zoo* by Lois Ehlert, Lippincott; *Bill Peet: An Autobiography* by Bill Peet, Houghton Mifflin; *The Talking Eggs* retold by Robert D. San Souci, illustrated by Jerry Pinkney, Dial

1991   *Black and White* by David Macaulay, Houghton
              Honor Books: *Puss 'n Boots* by Charles Perrault, illustrated by Fred Marcellino, Farrar; *"More, More, More," Said the Baby: 3 Love Stories* by Vera Williams, Greenwillow

1992   *Tuesday* by David Wiesner, Clarion
              Honor Book: *Tar Beach* by Faith Ringgold, Crown

1993   *Mirette on the High Wire* by Emily Arnold McCully, Putnam
              Honor Books: *Seven Blind Mice* by Ed Young, Philomel; *The Stinky Cheese Man and Other Fairly Stupid Tales* by Jon Scieszka, illustrated by Lane Smith, Viking; *Working Cotton* by Sherley Anne Williams, illustrated by Carole Byard, Harcourt

Boston Globe–Horn Book Awards

Awarded annually since 1967 and sponsored jointly by the *Boston Globe* and *Horn Book Magazine,* two prizes originally were given—one to recognize the outstanding text and one the outstanding illustration. Beginning in 1976, the categories were redefined: Outstanding Fiction or Poetry, Outstanding Nonfiction, and Outstanding Illustration.

1967   Text: *The Little Fishes* by Erik Haugaard, Houghton Mifflin
              Illustration: *London Bridge Is Falling Down* by Peter Spier, Doubleday

1968   Text: *The Spring Rider* by John Lawson, Crowell
              Illustration: *Tikki Tikki Tembo* by Arlene Mosel, illustrated by Blair Lent, Holt, Rinehart and Winston

1969   Text: *A Wizard of Earthsea* by Ursula K. Le Guin, Houghton Mifflin
              Illustration: *The Adventures of Paddy Pork* by John S. Goodall, Harcourt Brace Jovanovich

1970   Text: *The Intruder* by John Rowe Townsend, Lippincott
              Illustration: *Hi, Cat!* by Ezra Jack Keats, Macmillan

1971   Text: *A Room Made of Windows* by Eleanor Cameron, Little, Brown
              Illustration: *If I Built a Village* by Kazue Mizumura, Crowell

1972   Text: *Tristan and Iseult* by Rosemary Sutcliff, Dutton
              Illustration: *Mr. Gumpy's Outing* by John Burningham, Holt, Rinehart and Winston

1973   Text: *The Dark Is Rising* by Susan Cooper, McElderry/Atheneum
              Illustration: *King Stork* by Trina Schart Hyman, Little, Brown

1974   Text: *M. C. Higgins, the Great* by Virginia Hamilton, Macmillan
              Illustration: *Jambo Means Hello* by Muriel Feelings, illustrated by Tom Feelings, Dial Press

1975   Text: *Transport 7-41-R* by T. Degens, Viking
              Illustration: *Anno's Alphabet* by Mitsumasa Anno, Crowell

1976   Fiction: *Unleaving* by Jill Paton Walsh, Farrar, Straus & Giroux

Nonfiction: *Voyaging to Cathay: Americans in the China Trade* by Alfred Tamarin and Shirley Glubok, Viking

Illustration: *Thirteen* by Remy Charlip and Jerry Joyner, Parents

1977   Fiction: *Child of the Owl* by Laurence Yep, Harper

Nonfiction: *Chance, Luck and Destiny* by Peter Dickinson, Little, Brown

Illustration: *Granfa' Grig Had a Pig and Other Rhymes* by Wallace Tripp, Little, Brown

1978   Fiction: *The Westing Game* by Ellen Raskin, Dutton

Nonfiction: *Mischling, Second Degree: My Childhood in Nazi Germany* by Ilse Koehn, Greenwillow (Morrow)

Illustration: *Anno's Journey* by Mitsumasa Anno, Philomel (Putnam)

1979   Fiction: *Humbug Mountain* by Sid Fleischman, Little, Brown

Nonfiction: *The Road From Home: The Story of an Armenian Girl* by David Kherdian, Greenwillow (Morrow)

Illustration: *The Snowman* by Raymond Briggs, Random House

1980   Fiction: *Conrad's War* by Andrew Davies, Crown

Nonfiction: *Building: The Fight Against Gravity* by Mario Salvadori, McElderry/Atheneum

Illustration: *The Garden of Abdul Gasazi* by Chris Van Allsburg, Houghton Mifflin

1981   Fiction: *The Leaving* by Lynn Hall, Scribner

Nonfiction: *The Weaver's Gift* by Kathryn Lasky, Warne

Illustration: *Outside Over There* by Maurice Sendak, Harper

1982   Fiction: *Playing Beatie Bow* by Ruth Park, Atheneum

Nonfiction: *Upon the Head of the Goat: A Childhood in Hungary, 1939–1944* by Aranka Siegal, Farrar, Straus & Giroux

Illustration: *A Visit to William Blake's Inn: Poems for Innocent and Experienced Travelers* by Nancy Willard, illustrated by Alice and Martin Provensen

1983   Fiction: *Sweet Whispers, Brother Rush* by Virginia Hamilton, Philomel (Putnam)

Nonfiction: *Behind Barbed Wire: The Imprisonment of Japanese-Americans During World War II* by Daniel S. David, Dutton

Illustration: *A Chair for My Mother* by Vera B. Williams, Greenwillow (Morrow)

1984   Fiction: *A Little Fear* by Patricia Wrightson, McElderry/Atheneum

Nonfiction: *The Double Life of Pocahontas* by Jean Fritz, Putnam

Illustration: *Jonah and the Great Fish* retold and illustrated by Warwick Hutton, McElderry/Atheneum

1985   Fiction: *The Moves Make the Man* by Bruce Brooks, Harper

Nonfiction: *Commodore Perry in the Land of the Shogun* by Rhoda Blumberg, Lothrop

Illustration: *Mama Don't Allow* by Thatcher Hurd, Harper

1986   Fiction: *In Summer Light* by Zibby Oneal, Viking/Kestrel

Nonfiction: *Auks, Rocks and the Odd Dinosaur* by Peggy Thompson, Crowell

Illustration: *The Paper Crane* by Molly Bang, Greenwillow (Morrow)

1987   Fiction: *Rabble Starkey* by Lois Lowry, Houghton Mifflin
Nonfiction: *Pilgrims of Plimouth* by Marcia Sewall, Atheneum
Illustration: *Mufaro's Beautiful Daughters* by John Steptoe, Lothrop

1988   Fiction: *The Friendship* by Mildred Taylor, Dial Press
Nonfiction: *Anthony Burns: The Defeat and Triumph of a Fugitive Slave* by Virginia Hamilton, Knopf
Illustration: *The Boy of the Three-Year Nap* by Diane Snyder, Houghton Mifflin

1989   Fiction: *The Village by the Sea* by Paula Fox, Franklin Watts
Nonfiction: *The Way Things Work* by David Macaulay, Houghton Mifflin
Illustration: *Shy Charles* by Rosemary Wells, Dial

1990   Fiction: *Maniac Magee* by Jerry Spinelli, Little, Brown
Nonfiction: *The Great Little Madison* by Jean Fritz, Putnam
Illustration: *Lon Po Po: A Red-Riding Hood Story* retold and illustrated by Ed Young, Philomel

1991   Fiction: *The True Confessions of Charlotte Doyle* by Avi, Orchard
Nonfiction: *Appalachia: The Voices of Sleeping Birds* by Cynthia Rylant, illustrated by Barry Moser, Harcourt
Illustration: *The Tale of the Mandarin Ducks* retold by Katherine Paterson, illustrated by Leo and Diane Dillon, Lodestar

1992   Fiction: *Missing May* by Cynthia Rylant, Orchard
Nonfiction: *Talking with Artists* by Pat Cummings, Bradbury
Illustration: *Seven Blind Mice* by Ed Young, Philomel

The Mildred L. Batchelder Award

Presented annually by the American Library Association, this award recognizes the most outstanding children's book originally translated from a language other than English. (Unless otherwise indicated, the author is also the translator.)

1968   *The Little Man* by Erich Kastner, translated by James Kirkup, illustrated by Rich Schreiter, Knopf, 1966

1969   *Don't Take Teddy* by Babbis Friis-Baastad, translated by Lise Somme McKinnon, Scribner, 1967

1970   *Wildcat under Glass* by Alki Zei, translated by Edward Fenton, Holt, Rinehart and Winston, 1968

1971   *In the Land of Ur: The Discovery of Ancient Mesopotamia* by Hans Baumann, Stella Humphries, illustrated by Hans Peter Renner, Pantheon Books, 1969

1972   *Friedrich* by Hans Peter Richter, translated by Edite Kroll, Holt, Rinehart and Winston, 1970

1973   *Pulga* by Siny Rose Van Iterson, translated by Alexander and Alison Gode, Morrow, 1971

1974   *Petros' War* by Alki Zei, translated by Edward Fenton, Dutton, 1972

1975   *An Old Tale Carved Out of Stone* by Aleksandr M. Linevski, translated by Maria Polushkin, Crown, 1973

1976   *The Cat and Mouse Who Shared a House* by Ruth Hurlimann, translated by Anthea Bell, Walck, 1974

1977   *The Leopard* by Cecil Bodker, illustrated by Gunnar Poulsen, Atheneum, 1975

1978   No award

1979   *Konrad* by Christine Nostlinger, translated by Anthea Bell, illustrated by Carol Nicklaus, Watts, 1977

       Rabbit Island by Jorg Steiner, translated by Ann Conrad Lammers, illustrated by Jorg Muller, Harcourt Brace Jovanovich, 1978

1980   *The Sound of Dragon's Feet* by Alki Zei, translated by Edward Fenton, Dutton, 1979

1981   *The Winter When Time Was Frozen* by Els Pelgrom, translated by Raphael and Maryka Rudnik, Morrow, 1980

1982   *The Battle Horse* by Harry Kullman, translated by George Blecher and Lone Thygesen-Blecher, Bradbury, 1981

1983   *Hiroshima no Pika* by Toshi Maruki, Lothrop, 1982

1984   *Ronia, the Robber's Daughter* by Astrid Lindgren, translated by Patricia Crampton, Viking, 1983

1985   *The Island on Bird Street* by Uri Orlev, translated by Hillel Halkin, Houghton Mifflin, 1984

1986   *Rose Blanche* by Christophe Gallaz and Roberto Innocenti, translated by Martha Coventry and Richard Graglia, illustrated by Roberto Innocenti, Creative Education, 1985

1987   *No Hero for the Kaiser* by Rudof Frank, translated by Patricia Crampton, illustrated by Klaus Steffans, Lothrop, 1986

1988   *If You Didn't Have Me* by Ulf Nilsson, illustrated by Eva Ericksson, translated by Lone Thygesen-Blecher and George Blecher, McElderry

1989   *Crutches* by Peter Hartling, Lothrop

1990   *Buster's World* by Branner og Korch, Dutton

1991   *A Handful of Stars* by Rafik Schami, translated by Rika Lesser, Dutton

       Honor Book: *Two Short and One Long* by Nina Ring Aamundsen, Houghton

1992   *The Man from the Other Side* by Uri Orlev, translated by Hillel Halkin, Houghton

The Laura Ingalls Wilder Award

Named in honor of the beloved author of the *Little House* books (who was also its first recipient), this award is presented by the Association of Library Service to Children of the American Library Association to the individual, either author or illustrator, whose work has over the years proved to be a significant contribution to children's literature. Originally awarded every five years, it has since 1980 been given every three years.

1954	Laura Ingalls Wilder
1960	Clara Ingram Judson
1965	Ruth Sawyer
1970	E. B. White
1975	Beverly Cleary
1980	Theodore Geisel (Dr. Seuss)
1983	Maurice Sendak
1986	Jean Fritz
1989	Elizabeth George Speare
1992	Marcia Brown

National Council of Teachers of English Award for Excellence in Poetry for Children

This award is presented every three years (from 1977 through 1982 it was awarded annually) by the National Council of Teachers of English and was established to recognize a living poet's lifetime contribution to poetry for children.

1977	David McCord
1978	Aileen Fisher
1979	Karla Kuskin
1980	Myra Cohn Livingston
1981	Eve Merriam
1982	John Ciardi
1985	Lilian Moore
1988	Arnold Adoff
1992	Valerie Worth

The Phoenix Award

Since 1985, the Children's Literature Association has annually presented this award to a book, published twenty years before, that did not receive any major award, but has proved, through the test of time, to be a work of enduring excellence.

1985	*Mark of the Horse Lord* by Rosemary Sutcliff, Walck
1986	*Queenie Peavy* by Robert Burch, Viking

1987   *Smith* by Leon Garfield, Constable
1988   *The Rider and His Horse* by Eric Christian Haugaard, Houghton Mifflin
1989   *The Night Watchman* by Helen Cresswell, Macmillan
1990   *Enchantress from the Stars* by Sylvia Engdahl, Macmillan
1991   *A Long Way from Verona* by Jane Gardam, Macmillan
1992   *A Sound of Chariots* by Mollie Hunter, Harper
1993   *Carrie's War* by Nina Bawden, Lippincott

The Coretta Scott King Award

Presented annually by the Social Responsibilities Round Table of the American Library Association, this award recognizes an African-American text and illustration (since 1974) that has made an outstanding contribution to literature for children in the preceding year. The award is named for the widow of civil rights leader and Nobel Peace Prize winner, Dr. Martin Luther King, Jr., and it acknowledges the humanitarian work of both Dr. and Mrs. King.

1970   *Martin Luther King, Jr., Man of Peace* by Lillie Patterson, Garrard
1971   *Black Troubadour: Langston Hughes* by Charlemae Rollins, Rand
1972   *17 Black Artists* by Elton C. Fax, Dodd
1973   *I Never Had It Made* by Jackie Robinson (as told to Alfred Duckett), Putnam
1974   Text: *Ray Charles* by Sharon Bell Mathis, Crowell
        Illustration: *Ray Charles* by Sharon Bell Mathis, illustrated by George Ford, Crowell
1975   Text: *The Legend of Africana* by Dorothy Robinson, Johnson
        Illustration: *The Legend of Africana* by Dorothy Robinson, illustrated by Herbert Temple, Johnson
1976   Text: *Duey's Tale* by Pearl Bailey, Harcourt
        Illustration: No award
1977   Text: *The Story of Stevie Wonder* by James Haskins, Lothrop
        Illustration: No award
1978   Text: *Africa Dream* by Eloise Greenfield, Day/Crowell
        Illustration: *Africa Dream* by Eloise Greenfield, illustrated by Carole Bayard, Day/Crowell
1979   Text: *Escape to Freedom* by Ossie Davis, Viking
        Illustration: *Something on My Mind* by Nikki Grimes, illustrated by Tom Feelings, Dial
1980   Text: *The Young Landlords* by Walter Dean Myers, Viking
        Illustration: *Cornrows* by Camille Yarbrough, illustrated by Carole Bayard, Coward
1981   Text: *This Life* by Sidney Poitier, Knopf
        Illustration: *Beat the Story-Drum, Pum-Pum* by Ashley Bryan, Atheneum

1982   Text: *Let the Circle Be Unbroken* by Mildred D. Taylor, Dial
        Illustration: *Mother Crocodile: An Uncle Amadou Tale from Senegal* adapted by Rosa Guy, illustrated by John Steptoe, Delacorte

1983   Text: *Sweet Whispers, Brother Rush* by Virginia Hamilton, Philomel
        Illustration: *Black Child* by Peter Mugabane, Knopf

1984   Text: *Everett Anderson's Good-Bye* by Lucile Clifton, Holt
        Illustration: *My Mama Needs Me* by Mildred Pitts Walter, illustrated by Pat Cummings, Lothrop

1985   Text: *Motown and Didi* by Walter Dean Myers, Viking
        Illustration: No award

1986   Text: *The People Could Fly: American Black Folktales* by Virginia Hamilton, Knopf
        Illustration: *Patchwork Quilt* by Valerie Flournoy, illustrated by Jerry Pinckney, Dial

1987   Text: *Justin and the Best Biscuits in the World* by Mildred Pitts Walter, Lothrop
        Illustration: *Half Moon and One Whole Star* by Crescent Dragonwagon, illustrated by Jerry Pinkney, Macmillan

1988   Text: *The Friendship* by Mildred D. Taylor, Dial
        Illustration: *Mufaro's Beautiful Daughters: An African Tale* retold and illustrated by John Steptoe, Lothrop

1989   Text: *Fallen Angels* by Walter Dean Myers, Scholastic
        Illustration: *Mirandy and Brother Wind* by Patricia McKissack, illustrated by Jerry Pinkney, Knopf

1990   Text: *A Long Hard Journey* by Patricia and Frederick McKissack, Walker
        Illustration: *Nathaniel Talking* by Eloise Greenfield, illustrated by Jan Spivey Gilchrist, Black Butterfly Press

1991   Text: *Road to Memphis* by Mildred D. Taylor, Dial
        Illustration: *Aida* retold by Leontyne Price, illustrated by Leo and Diane Dillon, Harcourt

1992   Text: *Now Is Your Time! The African-American Struggle for Freedom* by Walter Dean Myers, HarperCollins
        Illustration: *Tar Beach* by Faith Ringgold, Crown

1993   Text: *The Dark-Thirty: Southern Tales of the Supernatural* by Patricia McKissack, Knopf
        Illustration: *The Origin of Life on Earth: An African Creation Myth* by David A. Anderson, illustrated by Kathleen Atkins Wilson, Sight Productions

The Scott O'Dell Award for Historical Fiction

Established by the noted children's novelist, Scott O'Dell, and administered by the Advisory Committee of the Bulletin of the Center for Children's Books, this award is presented to the most distinguished work of historical fiction set in the New World and written by a citizen of the United States.

| 1984 | *The Sign of the Beaver* by Elizabeth George Speare, Houghton |

1984   *The Sign of the Beaver* by Elizabeth George Speare, Houghton

1985   *The Fighting Ground* by Avi, Harper

1986   *Sarah, Plain and Tall* by Patricia MacLachlan, Harper

1987   *Streams to the River, River to the Sea: A Novel of Sacagawea* by Scott O'Dell, Houghton

1988   *Charlie Skedaddle* by Patricia Beatty, Morrow

1989   *The Honorable Prison* by Lyll Becerra de Jenkins, Lodestar

1990   *Shades of Gray* by Carolyn Reeder, Macmillan

1991   *A Time of Troubles* by Pieter van Raven, Scribner's

1992   *Stepping on the Cracks* by Mary Downing Hahn, Clarion

1993   *Morning Girl* by Michael Dorris, Hyperion

INTERNATIONAL AWARDS

The Hans Christian Andersen Award

This medal, named for the great Danish storyteller, is presented every two years by the International Board on Books for Young People to a living author and (since 1966) living illustrator whose works have made a significant, international contribution to children's literature.

1956   Eleanor Farjeon (Great Britain)

1958   Astrid Lindgren (Sweden)

1960   Erich Kastner (Germany)

1962   Meindert DeJong (United States)

1964   Rene Guillot (France)

1966   Author: Tove Jansson (Finland)
          Illustrator: Alois Carigiet (Switzerland)

1968   Authors: James Kruss (Germany) and Jose Maria Sanches-Silva (Spain)
          Illustrator: Jiri Trnka (Czechoslovakia)

1970   Author: Gianni Rodari (Italy)
          Illustrator: Maurice Sendak (United States)

1972   Author: Scott O'Dell (United States)
          Illustrator: Ib Spang Olsen (Denmark)

1974   Author: Maria Gripe (Sweden)
          Illustrator: Farsid Mesghali (Iran)

1976   Author: Cecil Bodker (Denmark)
          Illustrator: Tatjana Mawrine (USSR)

1978   Author: Paula Fox (United States)
          Illustrator: Otto S. Svend (Denmark)

1980   Author: Bohumil Riha (Czechoslovakia)
          Illustrator: Suekichi Akaba (Japan)

1982   Author: Lygia Gojunga Nunes (Brazil)
           Illustrator: Zbigniew Rychlicki (Poland)

1984   Author: Christine Nostlinger (Austria)
           Illustrator: Mitsumasa Anno (Japan)

1986   Author: Patricia Wrightson (Australia)
           Illustrator: Robert Ingpen (Australia)

1988   Author: Annie M. G. Schmidt (Netherlands)
           Illustrator: Dusan Kallay (Yugoslavia)

1990   Author: Tormod Haugen (Norway)
           Illustrator: Lisbeth Zwerger (Austria)

1992   Author: Virginia Hamilton (United States)
           Illustrator: Kveta Pacovská (Czechoslovakia)

The Carnegie Medal

Awarded by the British Library Association to an outstanding book first published in the United Kingdom, this medal has been awarded annually since it was established in 1937 (the first award being presented to a book published in the preceding year).

1936   *Pigeon Post* by Arthur Ransome, Jonathan Cape

1937   *The Family from One End Street* by Eve Garnett, Muller

1938   *The Circus Is Coming* by Noel Streatfeild, Dent

1939   *Radium Woman* by Eleanor Doorly, Heinemann

1940   *Visitors from London* by Kitty Barne, Dent

1941   *We Couldn't Leave Dinah* by Mary Treadgold, Penguin Books

1942   *The Little Grey Men* by B. B., Eyre & Spottiswoode

1943   No award

1944   *The Wind on the Moon* by Eric Linklater, Macmillan

1945   No award

1946   *The Little White Horse* by Elizabeth Goudge, Brockhampton Press

1947   *Collected Stories for Children* by Walter de la Mare, Faber

1948   *Sea Change* by Richard Armstrong, Dent

1949   *The Story of Your Home* by Agnes Allen, Transatlantic

1950   *The Lark on the Wind* by Elfrida Vipont Foulds, Oxford University Press

1951   *The Wool-Pack* by Cynthia Harnett, Methuen

1952   *The Borrowers* by Mary Norton, Dent

1953   *A Valley Grows Up* by Edward Osmond, Oxford University Press

1954   *Knight Crusader* by Ronald Welch, Oxford University Press

1955   *The Little Bookroom* by Eleanor Farjeon, Oxford University Press

1956   *The Last Battle* by C. S. Lewis, Bodley Head

1957   *A Grass Rope* by William Mayne, Oxford University Press

1958	*Tom's Midnight Garden* by Philippa Pearce, Oxford University Press
1959	*The Lantern Bearers* by Rosemary Sutcliff, Oxford University Press
1960	*The Making of Man* by I. W. Cornwall, Phoenix
1961	*A Stranger at Green Knowe* by Lucy Boston, Faber
1962	*The Twelve and the Genii* by Pauline Clarke, Faber
1963	*Time of Trial* by Hester Burton, Oxford University Press
1964	*Nordy Banks* by Sheena Porter, Oxford University Press
1965	*The Grange at High Force* by Philip Turner, Oxford University Press
1966	No award
1967	*The Owl Service* by Alan Garner, Collins
1968	*The Moon in the Cloud* by Rosemary Harris, Faber
1969	*The Edge of the Cloud* by K. M. Peyton, Oxford University Press
1970	*The God Beneath the Sea* by Leon Garfield and Edward Blishen, Kestrel
1971	*Josh* by Ivan Southall, Angus & Robertson
1972	*Watership Down* by Richard Adams, Rex Collings
1973	*The Ghost of Thomas Kempe* by Penelope Lively, Heinemann
1974	*The Stronghold* by Mollie Hunter, Hamilton
1975	*The Machine-Gunners* by Robert Westall, Macmillan
1976	*Thunder and Lightnings* by Jan Mark, Kestrel
1977	*The Turbulent Term of Tyke Tiler* by Gene Kemp, Faber
1978	*The Exeter Blitz* by David Rees, Hamish Hamilton
1979	*Tulku* by Peter Dickinson, Dutton
1980	*City of Gold* by Peter Dickinson, Gollancz
1981	*The Scarecrows* by Robert Westall, Chatto & Windus
1982	*The Haunting* by Margaret Mahy, Dent
1983	*Handles* by Jan Mark, Kestrel
1984	*The Changeover* by Margaret Mahy, Dent
1985	*Storm* by Kevin Crossley-Holland, Heinemann
1986	*Granny Was a Buffer Girl* by Berlie Doherty, Methuen
1987	*The Ghost Drum* by Susan Price, Faber
1988	*A Pack of Lies* by Geraldine McCaughrean, Oxford University Press
1989	*My War with Goggle-Eyes* by Ane Fine, Joy Street
1990	*Wolf* by Gillian Cross, Oxford University Press

The Kate Greenaway Medal

Named for the celebrated nineteenth-century children's illustrator, this medal is awarded annually by the British Library Association to the most distinguished illustrated work for children first published in the United Kingdom during the preceding year.

1956   *Tim All Alone* by Edward Ardizzone, Oxford University Press

1957   *Mrs. Easter and the Storks* by V. H. Drummond, Faber

1958   No award

1959   *Kastanka and a Bundle of Ballads* by William Stobbs, Oxford University Press

1960   *Old Winkle and the Seagulls* by Elizabeth Rose, illustrated by Gerald Rose, Faber

1961   *Mrs. Cockle's Cat* by Philippa Pearce, illustrated by Anthony Maitland, Kestrel

1962   *Brian Wildsmith's ABC* by Brian Wildsmith, Oxford University Press

1963   *Borka* by John Burningham, Jonathan Cape

1964   *Shakespeare's Theatre* by C. W. Hodges, Oxford University Press

1965   *Three Poor Tailors* by Victor Ambrus, Hamilton

1966   *Mother Goose Treasury* by Raymond Briggs, Hamilton

1967   *Charlie, Charlotte & the Golden Canary* by Charles Keeping, Oxford University Press

1968   *Dictionary of Chivalry* by Grant Uden, illustrated by Pauline Baynes, Kestrel

1969   *The Quangle-Wangle's Hat* by Edward Lear, illustrated by Helen Oxenbury, Heinemann
        Dragon of an Ordinary Family by Margaret May, illustrated by Helen Oxenbury, Heinemann

1970   *Mr. Gumpy's Outing* by John Burningham, Jonathan Cape

1971   *The Kingdom under the Sea* by Jan Pienkowski, Jonathan Cape

1972   *The Woodcutter's Duck* by Krystyna Turska, Hamilton

1973   *Father Christmas* by Raymond Briggs, Hamilton

1974   *The Wind Blew* by Pat Hutchins, Bodley Head

1975   *Horses in Battle* by Victor Ambrus, Oxford University Press
        Mishka by Victor Ambrus, Oxford University Press

1976   *The Post Office Cat* by Gail E. Haley, Bodley Head

1977   *Dogger* by Shirley Hughes, Bodley Head

1978   *Each Peach Pear Plum* by Janet and Allan Ahlberg, Kestrel

1979   *Haunted House* by Jan Pienkowski, Dutton

1980   *Mr. Magnolia* by Quentin Blake, Jonathan Cape

1981   *The Highwayman* by Alfred Noyes, illustrated by Charles Keeping, Oxford University Press

1982   *Long Neck and Thunder Foot* by Michael Foreman, Kestrel
        Sleeping Beauty and Other Favorite Fairy Tales by Michael Foreman, Gollancz

1983   *Gorilla* by Anthony Browne, Julia McRae Books

1984   *Hiawatha's Childhood* by Errol LeCain, Faber

1985	*Sir Gawain and the Loathly Lady* by Selina Hastings, illustrated by Juan Wijngaard, Walker
1986	*Snow White in New York* by Fiona French, Oxford University Press
1987	*Crafty Chameleon* by Adrienne Kennaway, Hodder & Stoughton
1988	*Can't You Sleep, Little Bear?* by Martha Waddell, illustrated by Barbara Firth, Walker
1989	*War Boy: A Country Childhood* by Michael Foreman, Arcade
1990	*The Whale's Song* by Dyan Sheldon, illustrated by Gary Blythe, Dial

Australian Children's Book of the Year Award

This has been awarded annually since 1946 to the most distinguished children's book by an Australian citizen. Occasionally, more than one book in a given year will be so honored, and occasionally no award is presented.

1946	*Karrawingi, the Emu* by Leslie Rees, Sands
1947	No award
1948	*Shackleton's Argonauts* by Frank Hurley, Angus & Robertson
1949	*Whalers of the Midnight Sun* by Alan Villiers, Angus & Robertson
1950	No award
1951	*Verity of Sydney Town* by Ruth Williams, Angus & Robertson
1952	*The Australia Book* by Eve Pownall, Sands
1953	*Aircraft of Today & Tomorrow* by J. H. and W. D. Martin, Angus & Robertson
	Good Luck to the Rider by Joan Phipson, Angus & Robertson
1954	*Australian Legendary Tales* by K. L. Parker, Angus & Robertson
1955	*The First Walkabout* by H. A. Lindsay and N. B. Tindale, Kestrel
1956	*The Crooked Snake* by Patricia Wrightson, Angus & Robertson
1957	*The Boomerang Book of Legendary Tales* by Enid Moodie-Heddle, Kestrel
1958	*Tiger in the Bush* by Nan Chauncy, Oxford University Press
1959	*Devil's Hill* by Nan Chauncy, Oxford University Press
	Sea Menace by John Gunn, Constable
1960	*All the Proud Tribesmen* by Kylie Tennant, Macmillan
1961	*Tangara* by Nan Chauncy, Oxford University Press
1962	*The Racketty Street Gang* by H. L. Evers, Hodder & Stoughton
	Rafferty Rides a Winner by Joan Woodbery, Parrish
1963	*The Family Conspiracy* by Joan Phipson, Angus & Robertson
1964	*The Green Laurel* by Eleanor Spence, Oxford University Press
1965	*Pastures of the Blue Crane* by Hesba F. Brinsmead, Oxford University Press
1966	*Ash Road* by Ivan Southall, Angus & Robertson

1967   *The Min Min* by Mavis Thorpe Clark, Landsdowne

1968   *To the Wild Sky* by Ivan Southall, Angus & Robertson

1969   *When Jays Fly to Barbmo* by Margaret Balderson, Oxford University Press

1970   *Uhu* by Annette Macarther-Onslow, Ure Smith

1971   *Bread and Honey* by Ivan Southall, Angus & Robertson

1972   *Longtime Passing* by Hesba F. Brinsmead, Angus & Robertson

1973   *Family at the Lookout* by Noreen Shelly, Oxford University Press

1974   *The Nargun and the Stars* by Patricia Wrightson, Hutchinson

1975   No award

1976   *Fly West* by Ivan Southall, Angus & Robertson

1977   *The October Child* by Eleanor Spence, Oxford University Press

1978   *The Ice Is Coming* by Patricia Wrightson, Hutchinson

1979   *The Plum-Rain Scroll* by Ruth Manley, Hodder & Stoughton

1980   *Displaced Person* by Lee Harding, Hyland House

1981   *Playing Beatie Bow* by Ruth Park, Nelson

1982   *The Valley Between* by Colin Thiele, Rigby

1983   *Master of the Grove* by Victor Kelleher, Penguin Books

1984   *A Little Fear* by Patricia Wrighton, Hutchinson

1985   *The True Story of Lillie Stubeck* by James Aldridge, Hyland House

1986   *The Green Wind* by Thurley Fowler, Rigby

1987   *Pigs Might Fly* by Emily Rodda, illustrated by Noela Young, Angus & Robertson

1988   *My Place* by Nadia Wheatley and Donna Rawlins, Collins Dove

1989   *The Best-Kept Secret* by Emily Rodda, Angus & Robertson

1990   *Pigs and Honey* by Jeanie Adams, Omnibus

1991   *Finders Keepers* by Emily Rodda, Omnibus

1992   *The Magnificent Nose and Other Marvels* by Anna Fienberg and Kim Gamble, Allen and Unwin

Australian Picture Book of the Year

Beginning in 1956, an additional award was established for the most distinguished Australian picture book of the year.

1956   *Wish the Magic Nut* by Peggy Barnard, illustrated by Shelia Hawkins, Sands

1957   No award

1958   *Piccaninny Walkabout* by Axel Poignant, Angus & Robertson

1959–1964   No awards

1965   *Hugo's Zoo* by Elisabeth MacIntyre, Angus & Robertson

1966–1968   No awards

1969   *Sly Old Wardrobe* by Ivan Southall, illustrated by Ted Greenwood, Cheshire

1970   No award

1971   *Waltzing Matilda* by A. B. Paterson, illustrated by Desmond Digby, Collins

1972–1973   No awards

1974   *The Bunyip of Berkeley's Creek* by Jenny Wagner, illustrated by Ron Brooks, Kestrel

1975   *The Man from Ironbark* by A. B. Paterson, illustrated by Quentin Hole, Collins

1976   *The Rainbow Serpent* by Dick Roughsey, Collins

1977   *ABC of Monsters* by Deborah Niland, Hodder & Stoughton

1978   *John Brown, Rose and the Midnight Cat* by Jenny Wagner, illustrated by Ron Brooks, Kestrel

1979   *The Quinkins* by Percy Trezise and Dick Roughsey, Collins

1980   *One Dragon's Dream* by Peter Pavey, Nelson

1981   No award

1982   *Sunshine* by Jan Ormerod, Kestrel

1983   *Who Sank the Boat?* by Pamela Allen, Nelson

1984   *Bertie and the Bear* by Pamela Allen, Nelson

1985   (Commended) *Home in the Sky* by Jeannie Baker and Junko Morimoto (retelling by Helen Smith), Collins

1986   *Felix and Alexander* by Terry Denton, Oxford University Press

1987   *Kojuro and the Bears* adapted by Helen Smith, illustrated by Junko Morimoto, Collins

1988   *Crusher Is Coming!* by Bob Graham, Lothian

1989   *Drac and the Gremlins* by Allan Baillie, illustrated by Jane Tanner, Viking/Kestrel
        The Eleventh Hour by Graeme Base, Viking/Kestrel

1990   *The Very Best of Friends* by Margaret Wild, illustrated by Julie Vivas, Margaret Hamilton

1991   *Greetings from Sandy Beach* by Bob Graham, Lothian

1992   *Window* by Jeannie Baker, Julia MacRae

The Canadian Library Award

Presented by the Canadian Library Association since 1947, this award recognizes the most distinguished children's book by a Canadian citizen. Beginning in 1956, an additional award has been presented to a distinguished work published in French. The association also has presented, since 1971, the Amelia Frances Howard-Gibbon Medal for outstanding illustration by a Canadian illustrator in a children's book published in Canada. In some years no award may be given.

1947	*Starbuck Valley Winter* by Roderick Haig-Brown, Collins
1948	*Kristi's Trees* by Mabel Dunham, Hale
1949	No award
1950	*Franklin of the Arctic* by Richard S. Lambert, McClelland & Stewart
1951	No award
1952	*The Sun Horse* by Catherine Anthony Clarke, Macmillan of Canada
1953	No award
1954	*Mgr. de Laval* by Emile S. J. Gervais, Comité des Fondateurs de l'Église Canadienne
1955	No award
1956	*Train for Tiger Lily* by Louise Riley, Macmillan of Canada
1957	*Glooskap's Country* by Cyrus Macmillan, Oxford University Press
1958	*Lost in the Barrens* by Farley Mowat, Little, Brown
	The Chevalier du Roi by Beatrice Clement, Les Éditions de l'Atelier
1959	*The Dangerous Cove* by John F. Hayes, Copp Clark
	Un Drôle de Petit Cheval by Helen Flamme, Editions Lemeac
1960	*The Golden Phoenix* by Marius Barbeau and Michael Hornyansky, Walck
	L'Été Enchanté by Paule Daveluy, Les Éditions de l'Atelier
1961	*The St. Lawrence* by William Toye, Oxford University Press
	Plantes Vagabondes by Marcelle Gauvreau, Centre de Psychologie et de Pedagogie
1962	*Les Îles du Roi Maha Maha II* by Claude Aubry, Les Éditions du Pelican
1963	*The Incredible Journey* by Sheila Burnford, Little, Brown
	Drôle d' Automne by Paule Daveluy, Les Éditions du Pelican
1964	*The Whale People* by Roderick Haig-Brown, William Collins of Canada
	Feerie by Cecile Chabot, Librairie Beauchemin Ltée
1965	*Tales of Nanabozho* by Dorothy Reid, Oxford University Press
	Le Loup de Noel by Claude Aubry, Centre de Psychologie de Montreal
1966	*Tikta'Liktak* by James Houston, Kestrel
	Le Chêne des Tempêtes by Andre Mallet-Hobden, Fides
	The Double Knights by James McNeal, Walck
	Le Wapiti by Monique Corriveau, Jeunesse
1967	*Raven's Cry* by Christie Harris, McClelland & Stewart
1968	*The White Archer* by James Houston, Kestrel
	Legendes Indiennes du Canada by Claude Melancon, Éditions du Jour
1969	*And Tomorrow the Stars* by Kay Hill, Dodd, Mead
1970	*Sally Go Round the Sun* by Edith Fowke, McClelland & Stewart
	Le Merveilleuse Histoire de la Naissance by Lionel Gendron, Les Éditions de l'Homme

1971   *Cartier Discovers the St. Lawrence* by William Toye, Oxford University Press

         La Surprise de Dame Chenille by Henriette Major, Centre de Psychologie de Montreal

1972   *Mary of Mile 18* by Ann Blades, Tundra

1973   *The Marrow of the World* by Ruth Nicholas, Macmillan of Canada

         Le Petit Sapin Qui A Pousse sur une Étoile by Simone Bussieres, Presses Laurentiennes

1974   *The Miraculous Hind* by Elizabeth Cleaver, Holt, Rinehart and Winston of Canada

1975   *Alligator Pie* by Dennis Lee, Macmillan of Canada

1976   *Jacob Two-Two Meets the Hooded Fang* by Mordecai Richler, Knopf

1977   *Mouse Woman and the Vanished Princess* by Christie Harris, McClelland & Stewart

1978   *Garbage Delight* by Dennis Lee, Macmillan

1979   *Hold Fast* by Kevin Major, Clarke, Irwin

1980   *River Runners: A Tale of Hardship and Bravery* by James Houston, McClelland & Stewart

1981   *The Violin Maker's Gift* by Donn Kushner, Macmillan of Canada

1982   *The Root Cellar* by Janet Lunn, Lester & Orpen Dennys

1983   *Up to Low* by Brian Doyle, Groundwood

1984   *Sweetgrass* by Jan Hudson, Tree Frog Press

1985   *Mama's Going to Buy a Mockingbird* by Jean Little, Penguin Books

1986   *Julie* by Cora Taylor, Western

1987   *Shadow in Hawthorn Bay* by Janet Lunn, Scribner

1988   *A Handful of Time* by Kit Pearson, Viking

1989   *Easy Avenue* by Brian Doyle, Groundwood

1990   *The Sky Is Falling* by Kit Pearson, Penguin

1991   *Redwork* by Michael Bedard, Dennys

Amelia Frances Howard-Gibbon Medal

Awarded since 1971 by the Canadian Library Association, this medal honors excellence in children's illustration in a book published in Canada. The award must go to a citizen or resident of Canada.

1971   *The Wind Has Wings,* edited by Mary Alice Downie and Barbara Robertson, illustrated by Elizabeth Cleaver, Oxford University Press

1972   *A Child in Prison Camp* by Shizuye Takashima, Tundra

1973   *Au Delà du Soleil/Beyond the Sun* by Jacques de Roussan, Tundra

1974   *A Prairie Boy's Winter* by William Kurelek, Tundra

1975   *The Sleighs of My Childhood/Les Traineaux de Mon Enfance* by Carlos Italiano, Tundra

1976   *A Prairie Boy's Summer* by William Kurelek, Tundra

1977   *Down by Jim Long's Stage: Rhymes for Children and Young Fish* by Al Pittman, illustrated by Pam Hall, Breakwater

1978   *The Loon's Necklace* by William Toye, illustrated in Elizabeth Cleaver, Oxford University Press

1979   *A Salmon for Simon* by Betty Waterton, illustrated by Ann Blades, Douglas & McIntyre

1980   *The Twelve Dancing Princesses* by Laszlo Gal, Methuen

1981   *The Trouble with Princesses* by Douglas Tait, McClelland & Stewart

1982   *Ytek and the Arctic Orchid: An Innuit Legend* by Heather Woodall, Douglas & McIntyre

1983   *Chester's Barn* by Lindee Climo, Tundra

1984   *Zoom at Sea* by Tim Wynne-Jones, illustrated by Ken Nutt, Douglas & McIntyre

1985   *Chin Chiang and the Dragon's Dance* by Ian Wallace, Groundwood

1986   *Zoom Away* by Tim Wynne-Jones, illustrated by Ken Nutt, Douglas & McIntyre

1987   *Moonbeam on a Cat's Ear* by Marie-Louise Gay, Stoddard

1988   *Rainy Day Magic* by Marie-Louise Gay, Hodder & Stoughton

1989   *Amos's Sweater* by Janet Lunn, illustrated by Kim LaFaye, Douglas & McIntyre

1990   *Til All the Stars Have Fallen: Canadian Poems for Children* selected by David Booth, illustrated by Kady MacDonald Denton, Kids Can Press

1991   *The Orphan Boy* by Tololwa M. Mollel, illustrated by Paul Morin, Oxford

INDEX

A Is for Always (Anglund), 64
A to Z Picture Book (Fujikawa), 64
ABC (Dr. Seuss), 62, 64
ABC Bunny (Gag), 62
Abraham Lincoln (Daugherty), 150
Abstractionism, 39–40
Accommodation, Piaget's concept of, 21
Accuracy
  in biography, 153–154
  in informational books, 171
Across Five Aprils (Hunt), 146, 148
Acrylics, 45
Adams, Henry, 156
Adams, William Taylor, 14
Adaptation, concept of, 21
Adoff, Arnold, 67, 190
Adventures of Huckleberry Finn, The (Twain),
  13, 134
Adventures of Tom Sawyer, The (Twain), 13, 34
Adventure stories, 13–14, 134–135, 146
Aeneid (Virgil), 4
Aesthetic development, 75–76
African Americans, 182–184, 189
  depiction in picture books, 54–55
  family stories of, 135–136, 137
  in historical fiction, 149
  mystery story, 135
Aiken, Joan, 123, 128, 145
Alcott, Louisa May, 14, 135
Alex, the Kid with AIDS (Girard), 68
Alexander, Lloyd, 124
Alexander, Martha, 170

Alexander and the Wind-up Mouse (Lionni),
  121
Alger, Horatio, Jr., 14, 137
Alice's Adventures in Wonderland (Carroll), 12,
  119, 122–123, 208
Aliki, 166
All About You (Anholts), 67
Allard, Harry, 42
Allen, Jeffrey, 54
Alliteration, 95
All Kinds of Families, 67
All Shapes and Sizes (Hughes), 67
All Year Long (Tafuri), 67
Alphabet (Anno), 62, 66
Alphabet Art (Fisher), 169
Alphabet books, 61–65
Alphabet rhymes, 74
Alphabet Tale, The (Garten), 62
"Altar, The" (Herbert), 91
Amelia Bedelia series (Parrish), 221
Amelia Earhart, First Lady of Flight (Mann), 189
Analysis, questions to encourage, 219
Anansi the Spider (McDermott), 35, 37, 42
Ancient literature
  Greek , 3, 105
    animal fantasies, 139
    myths, 107–108
    tragedy, 111–112
  narrative poems, 89
  Roman, 3
    myths, 107–108
Andersen, Hans Christian, 12, 119, 120

And now Miguel (Krumgold), 185
Angeli, Marguerite de, 81
Anglund, Jane Walsh, 64
Anholt, Catherine, 67
Anholt, Laurence, 67
Animal tales, 5
    fantasies, 120–121
    in folk literature, 104–105
    informational books, 168
    realistic, 139–140
Anne of Green Gables (Montgomery), 14, 136
Annie and the Old One (Miles), 184, 191
Anno, Mitsumasa, 31, 32, 62, 66, 169
Another, the individual in conflict with, 206
Anpao: An American Indian Odyssey
    (Highwater), 185
Antagonist, 204
Anthologies of poetry, 97
Anthropomorphism in myths of gods and
    goddesses, 108
Application questions, 219–220
Apricot ABC (Miles), 62
Ardizzone, Edward, 22
Are You There, God? It's Me, Margaret (Blume),
    138, 192
Arnosky, Jim, 169
Arrow to the Sun (McDermott), 35, 166
Art Deco, 43
Arthur, for the Very First Time (MacLachlan),
    189
Arthurian legends, 5
Artistic elements of folk literature, 109–112
Arts
    fine and applied, 225–226
        books about, 169
    literary, 212
    plastic, 225–226
    storytelling, 217–218
Ascham, Roger, 7
Ashabranner, Brent, 167
Ashanti to Zulu: African Traditions (Musgrove),
    42, 62, 63
Asian Americans, 186–187
Assimilation, Piaget's concept of, 21
Assonance, 95
"At Sea" (Cunningham), 93
Auditory images, 92–93
Authenticity
    of biography, 150–151, 153–154
    of historical fiction, 147–148
    of informational books, 167
Autobiography, 150, 152
    fictionalized, 149
    special characteristics of, 156
Autonomy versus doubt, stage of, 23–24
Averitt, Eleanor, 94
Awards for children's literature. *See also*
        Caldecott Medal; Newbery Medal
    Amelia Frances Howard-Gibbon Medal, 259–260
    Australian Children's Book of the Year,
        255–256

    Australian Picture Book of the Year, 256–257
    Boston-Globe-Horn Book, 244–246
    Canadian Library, 257–259
    Carnegie Medal, 252–253
    Coretta Scott King, 249–250
    Hans Christian Andersen, 251–252
    Kate Greenaway Medal, 253–255
    Laura Ingalls Wilder, 248
    Mildred L. Batchelder, 246–248
    National Council of Teachers of English Award
        for Excellence in Poetry for Children, 248
    Phoenix, 248–249
    Scott O'Dell, 250–251

Babbitt, Natalie, 128, 221
Baby's Opera, The (Crane), 15
Bach, Alice, 167
Backdrop, setting as, 204
Bacon, Sir Francis, 227
Balance, in biography, 154–155
Ballads, 89–92
"Bam, Bam, Bam" (Merriam), 92–93
Bang, Molly, 66
Banks, Lynn Reid, 125
"Barbara Allen's Cruelty", 89
Barbauld, Anna Laetitia, 11
Barrie, James, 123
Baum, L. Frank, 13, 120, 123, 209, 210
Believability
    of fantasy, 127–128
    of historical fiction, 147
    of a plot, 207
Bemelmans, Ludwig, 39, 40, 51, 54, 225
Ben and Me (Lawson), 151, 208, 211
Benjamin Bunny (Potter), 50
Benjamin Franklin (Meltzer), 155
Ben's Trumpet (Isadora), 43
Beowulf, 5, 109
Bettelheim, Bruno, 114, 200
Beyond the Chocolate War (Cormier), 137
Bible
    the Gospels, 150
    Puritan, 7
Biographical fiction, 151
Biography, 150–157
    complete and partial, 152
    of women, 189
Black Hearts of Battersea (Aiken), 123, 145
Black Is Brown Is Tan (Adoff), 67, 190
Black Pearl, The (O'Dell), 185
Black Star, Bright Dawn (O'Dell), 184
Blank, Joanie, 189
Blos, Joan, 147
Blubber (Blume), 22
Blueberries for Sal (McCloskey), 34, 51
Blue Fairy Book, The (Lang), 12
Blume, Judy, 22, 23, 138, 192
Boccaccio, 5, 113
Boke Named the Governor (Elyot), 7
Bolliger, Max, 152
Bonham, Frank, 186

Book discussion, 218–220
Book of Martyrs (Foxe), 7, 109
Book reports, 221–222
Books, creating in the classroom, 222
Books of Courtesy, 7
Boredom, reasons for, 53
Borrowers, The (Norton), 9, 123
Boston, Lucy, 125
Boy: Tales of Childhood (Dahl), 157
Brandenburg, Aliki. *See* Aliki
Branley, Franklyn, 169
*Bread and Roses: The Struggle of American
    Labor* (Meltzer), 167
Bridge to Terabithia, A (Paterson), 138, 189
Briggs, Raymond, 81
Bright, Robert, 125
Brooke, L. Leslie, 78
Brooklyn Bridge, The (St. George), 170
Brother Can You Spare a Dime? (Meltzer), 167
Brothers of the Heart (Blos), 147
Brown, Marc, 169
Brown, Marcia, 32
Brown, Margaret Wise, 23, 52, 54, 67, 192, 211
Browning, Robert, 15, 89
Buckmaster, Henrietta, 153
Bumblebees Fly Anyway (Cormier), 23, 137
Bunyan, John, 9
Burnett, Frances Hodgson, 135
Burnford, Sheila, 139
Burningham, John, 41, 45, 67, 208
Burns, Robert, 93
Burton, Virginia, 21, 50
Byars, Betsy, 138, 157, 191
By the Great Horn Spoon (Fleischman), 122, 145

Cabinetmakers, The (Fisher), 167
Caldecott, Randolph, 13, 15
Caldecott Medal, 13, 15, 41, 186, 237–244
Call Me Charley (Jackson), 182
Call of the Wild (London), 139
Canterbury Tales, The (Chaucer), 113
Carrick, Carol, 41
Carrick, Donald, 41
Carroll, Lewis (Charles Dodgson), 12, 22, 119,
    208
Carry On, Mr. Bowditch (Latham), 151
Cartoon art, 41–42, 81
    Dr. Seuss's ABC, 62
Cassie Binegar (MacLachlan), 22, 189, 191
Castle (Macauley), 169
Catcher in the Rye, The (Salinger), 227
Cathedral (Macauley), 169–170
Cay, The (T. Taylor), 134, 206
Censorship, 55, 226–227
Chalk drawings, 45
Chanticleer and the Fox (Cooney), 5
Character
    development of, in role-playing, 224
    eccentric, in fantasy, 122, 123
    exploring in episodic plots, 207–208
    in folktales, 110, 204–206

    in narrative poems, 89
    in picture books, 52
Charlie and the Chocolate Factory (Dahl), 123,
    221
Charlotte's Web (White), 121, 203, 204, 209,
    210–211, 219, 227
Chase, Alice Elizabeth, 170
Chase, Richard, 107
Chaucer, Geoffrey, 5
Child development, 19–26
Child of Fire (O'Dell), 186
Child of the Owl, The (Yep), 186, 191
Children of the Maya (Ashabranner), 167
Children of Odin, The (Colum), 108
Children's Homer, The (Colum), 109
Childress, Alice, 203, 211
Chocolate War, The (Cormier), 14, 137, 211
Chronology, and age of the reader, 51
"Cinderella", 105
Cinderella (Brown), 32
Cinquain, 90
"City" (Hughes), 93–94
Clarity, in informational books, 173
Clark, Mavis Thorpe, 187
Classics, 197–198
    Greek, 3
Classroom, literature in, 215–227
Clayton, Bess, 187
Cleary, Beverly, 22, 24, 136, 140, 190, 205–206,
    207, 221
Cleaver, Bill, 136
Cleaver, Vera, 136
Clemens, Samuel. *See* Twain, Mark
"Clever Gretel", 223
Clifton, Lucille, 51, 54–55
Coatsworth, Elizabeth, 146, 210
Cobb, Vicki, 172
Cognitive development
    and concept books, 67
    and content of alphabet books, 64
    and Mother Goose rhymes, 74–75
    theory of (Piaget), 20–23
Collage, 46, 225
Collective biographies, 152–153
Collier, Christopher, 146, 147
Collier, James Lincoln, 146, 147
Collodi, Carlo, 120, 121
Colman, Hila, 186
Color, in illustrations, 34–35
Colum, Padraic, 108, 109
Come Away from the Water Shirley
    (Burningham), 45, 208
Comenius, John, 7
Coming of age in realistic fiction, 140
Composition. *See also* Styles
    of illustrations, 37–38
Conan Doyle, Arthur, 134
Concept books, 61, 67–68
Concrete operations, period of (Piaget), 22
    parallel with conventional level, 25
Concrete poetry, 91

Condescension, 212
Cone, Ferne Geller, 170
Conflict
  cultural, 184, 185–186
  protagonist and antagonist in literature, 204, 206
  racial, 182–183
  reader's theater use of, 223
  resolution of
    in folktales, 111–112
    in narrative, 51, 206–207
Connotation, 210
Conservation of quantity (Piaget), 21
Consistency
  in character development, 205–206
  in fantasy, 127
Consonance, 95
Content
  of alphabet books, 62, 64
  of counting books, 66
Context
  historical, of literature, 198–199
  questions for examining, 219–220
Contractual/legalistic orientation, 25–26
Conventional level of development, 25
Cooking, as an extension of literature, 226
Cooney, Barbara, 5, 45, 51, 191
Cooper, Susan, 124
Coral Life (Taylor), 168
Cormier, Robert, 14, 23, 137, 211, 227
Counting books, 61, 65–66
Counting House (Anno), 66
Count and See (Hoban), 42
Country Noisy Book, The (Brown), 67
Cowboys of the Wild West (Freedman), 167
Crane, Walter, 15
Crapsey, Adelaide, 90
Craven, Margaret, 185
Crayon, 45
Crazy Crocheting (Cone), 170
Creation stories, 106, 107
Creative dramatics, 223–224
Credibility, 207. *See also* Believability
Crews, Donald, 67
Criticism, 197–198
  written, 221
Crow Boy, The (Yashima), 55, 191
Cruikshank, George, 15
Cubism, 41, 43
Cultural diversity, 181–187
Culture. *See also* Folktales; Religion
  African, *Ashanti to Zulu: African Traditions*, 62
  Alaskan Eskimo, 184
  American, tall tales in, 107
  Armenian, 187
  Australian, 187
  Chinese, 35
    Mei Lei, 51
    Story About Ping, 51
  family stories, 135–136

French, *Madeline*, 51
  informational books about, 165–167
  Japanese, 186–187
  Jewish, 187
  and mythology, 109
  Pakistani, 187
  preliterate, folk literature in, 103
  sources of folk art, 42
  stereotyping in picture books, 54–55
  Swahili counting book (*Moja Means One*), 66
  Welsh, 124, 187
Cumulative tales, 106
Cunningham, Alan, 93

Daddy Is a Monster . . . Sometimes (Steptoe), 37, 43, 44, 189
Dahl, Roald, 123, 157, 221
Daisy Chain, The (Yonge), 135
Daniel Boone (Daugherty), 150
Dante, Gabriel Rosetti, 93
da Paola, Tomi, 55, 191
Dark Is Rising, The (Cooper), 124
Daugherty, James, 150
David (Bolliger), 152
Day Jimmy's Boa Ate the Wash, The (Noble), 42
Day No Pigs Would Die, A (Peck), 136
Dead Bird, The (M. W. Brown), 192
de Angeli, Marguerite, 80, 148
Dear Mr. Henshaw (Cleary), 22, 136, 140, 190, 205–206, 207, 221
Death, portrayal in literature, 191–192
Death of Arthur, The (Malory), 109
Death of Methuselah, The (Singer), 187
de Beauvoir, Simone, 201
Decameron, The (Boccaccio), 113
Defoe, Daniel, 9, 134, 199
de la Mare, Walter, 92
Del Rey, Lester, 126
Denotation, 210
Desert Life (Taylor), 168
Design
  of alphabet books, 64–65
  of concept books, 68
  of counting books, 66
Detail in fantasies, 127
Developmental psychology, uses of, 26
Dewey, John, 24
Dialogue, 209
  for reader's theater, 223
Diary of a Young Girl, The (Frank), 152, 187
Dicey's Song (Voight), 190
Dickens, Charles, 15, 137
Dick Whittington and His Cat (Cooney), 45
Diction of informational books, 173
Didactic books
  fables, 53, 105
  Puritan, 7, 9
  Rousseau's, 11
  science fiction, 126
  tone of, 211
Dillon, Diane, 42, 62, 63

Dillon, Leo, 42, 62, 63
Diorama, 225–226
Direct images, 92–93
Diversity, 181–192
Dodgson, Charles. *See* Carroll, Lewis
Dogsong (Paulsen), 184–185
Domestic stories, 14
  historical, 145
Donovan, John, 23, 192
Don Quixote (Cervantes), 134
Door in the Wall, The (de Angeli), 148
Double Life of Pocahontas, The (Fritz), 155
Dove in the Eagle's Nest, The (Yonge), 146
Dragon Slayer, The (Sutcliff), 5, 109
Dragonwings (Yep), 186
Dramatic responses to literature, 222–226
Dr. Doolittle (Loftis), 122
Dr. Seuss books, 42, 64
Drummer Boy, The (Garfield), 146
Drummer Hoff (Emberley), 45
du Bois, William Pene, 123
Duffy and the Devil (Zemach), 32, 33, 34, 42, 44
"Dying Cowboy, The", 89
Dynamic characters, 204–205

Earthquake (Simon), 168–169
Earthsea cycle (Le Guin), 24, 124, 204
Eastern Religions (Seeger), 167
"Easter Wings" (Herbert), 91
Easy Ice Skating Book, The (Kalb), 170
Edgeworth, Maria, 11
Edmonds, Walter, 184
Education
  in the European Middle Ages, 4
  in the European Renaissance, 6
  Locke's theory of *tabula rasa*, 9
  Rousseau's moral philosophy, 11
Education of Henry Adams, The, 156
Eggleston, Edward, 14
El Cid, 5
Ellison, Virginia, 226
Elsie Dinsmore (Finlay), 14
Elyot, Sir Thomas, 7
Emberley, Barbara, 45
Emberley, Ed, 45
Emile (Rousseau), 11
Emotional development, 191
  and nursery rhymes, 76
Emotions, poetry's appeal to, 95–96
Enchantress from the Stars (Engdahl), 126
Encyclopedia Brown (Sobol), 22, 134
Endless Steppe: Growing Up in Siberia, The
  (Hautzig), 152
Engdahl, Sylvia, 126
English Fairy Tales (Jacobs), 12
Enright, Elizabeth, 136
Epics, 109
  medieval, 4–5
Episodic plot structure, 207–208
Erikson, Erik, 19, 23–24
Expressionistic art, 225

Estes, Eleanor, 25, 136
Ets, Marie Hall, 186
European Americans, 149
Evaluation
  of books about alternative families and
    lifestyles, 190
  of books about contemporary issues, 192
  of books about special needs, 191
  critical, questions for, 220
  of informational books, 171
Exposition, 209
Expressionism, 39–41, 80
External forms of poetry, 88–92
Exum, J. Cheryl, 167

Fables, 53, 105
Fables (Aesop), 4, 5–6, 7, 53, 105
Fact, distinguishing from fiction, 51, 75–76
Factories, The (Fisher), 167
Fairy tales, 103, 105
  literary, 120
  psychoanalytic interpretation of, 200
Fairy Tales (Andersen), 12
Families
  diversity in organization of, 190
  stories about, 135–136
Fanshawe, Elizabeth, 191
Fantasy, 49, 50, 119–128
Farewell to Manazar (Wakatsuki), 186–187
Far Side of Evil, The (Engdahl), 126
Fauves, Les, 43, 44
Feelings, Muriel, 66
Feelings, Tom, 66
Feminist approach to literary criticism, 201–202
Ferdinand the Bull (Leaf and Lawson), 34
Fessler, Joan, 191
Fiction, distinguishing fact from, 51, 75–76
Fictionalized biography, 151
Field, Rachel, 122
Fifth Chinese Daughter (Wong), 186
Finlay, Martha, 14
First Book of Jazz, The (Hughes), 169
First-person narrator, 203
Fisher, Leonard Everett, 45, 169, 172–173
"Fisherman and His Wife, The", 104
Fish in a Flash!: A Personal Guide to
  Spin-Fishing (Arnosky), 169
Fish Is Fish (Lionni), 46
Fitzhugh, Louise, 189, 211
Five Little Peppers and How They Grew, The
  (Sidney), 135
Flat characters, 204–205
Fleischman, Sid, 122, 145
"Fog" (Sandburg), 92
Foil characters, 205
Folk art, 42
Folk literature, 103–115
  Mother Goose rhymes, 73
Folktales, 12, 49, 218, 226–227. *See also* Culture
  African
    Anansi the Spider, 35, 37, 42

Folktales (*continued*)
   Ashanti to Zulu: African Traditions, 42
   dramatic plot structure in, 207
   individual against Another, 206
   origins of, 104
   using for reader's theater, 223
   using for story theater, 223
Foot (rhythmical pattern), 94
Footsteps (Garfield), 145
Forbes, Esther, 146
Formalism in literary criticism, 202
Formal operations, period of (Piaget), 22–23
Format, of informational books, 172
Forster, E. M., 206
Foster care, 190
Fox, Paula, 146, 149
Foxe, John, 7, 109
Frank, Anne, 152
Frankenstein (Shelley), 125
Franklin Delano Roosevelt (Freedman), 154
Frederick (Lionni), 46, 225
Freedman, Russell, 150–151, 152, 154, 155, 167
Free verse, 92
Freight Trains (Crews), 67
Freud, Sigmund, 199
Friendly Dolphins, The (Lauber), 171
Friends, The (Guy), 183
Fritz, Jean, 150, 154, 155, 226
Frog He Would A-Wooing Go, The, 13
Frog and Toad Are Friends (Lobel), 50
Froman, Robert, 91
From Earth to the Moon Direct (Verne), 125
From Seed to Plant (Gibbons), 168
From the Mixed-Up Files of Mrs. Basil E. Frankweiler (Konigsburg), 134
Frye, Northrup, 181–182
Fujikawa, Gyo, 64

Gag, Wanda, 34, 54, 62
Gammage Cup, The (Kendall), 9, 123
Garfield, Leon, 145, 146
Garne, S. T., 66
Garner, Alan, 125
Garten, Jan, 62
Gathering of Days, A (Blos), 147
Gayneck, the Story of a Pigeon (Mukerji), 139
Geisert, Arthur, 66
Gender
   and child development, 19–20
   and criticism of tone, 212
   emphasis in literature for children, 187–189
   stereotyping in folk tales, 113
   stereotyping in picture books, 54
   in traditional literature, 201–202
Gender behavior, 188–189
George, Jean Craighead, 134, 184, 189, 199, 206
George Washington's Breakfast (Fritz), 226
Georgie and the Robbers (Bright), 125
Gesta Romanorum, 5
Ghost in the Noonday Sun, The (Fleischman), 122

Ghost of Thomas Kempe, The (Lively), 125
Ghost stories, 107, 125
Gibbons, Carol, 168
Gilgamesh, 89
"Gingerbread Boy, The", 106
Girard, Linda Walvoord, 67–68
Girl from Puerto Rico, The (Colman), 186
Golden Fleece, The (Colum), 109
Goodnight Moon (M. W. Brown), 23, 52, 54, 211
Goodsell, Jane, 153
Gouache, 44
Grahame, Kenneth, 13, 119, 120, 121, 220
Gramatky, Hardy, 21, 50
Graphics, 45–46, 225
Great Gilly Hopkins, The (Paterson), 24, 138, 190
Greenaway, Kate, 15, 82
Greenfield, Howard, 167
Green Knowe (Boston), 125
Grimm, Jacob, 12
Grimm, Wilhelm, 12
Gulliver's Travels (Swift), 9, 123, 134
Gustatory images, 93
   cooking as an extension of literature, 226
Guy, Rosa, 183, 184

Haiku, 90
Hale, Lucretia, 122
Haley, Alex, 183
Hall, Donald, 45, 51, 149
Hamilton, Virginia, 24, 107, 135, 136, 191
Handforth, Thomas, 51, 166
Handley-Taylor, Geoffrey, 74
"Hansel and Gretel", 198–199, 200
"Hans in Luck", 106
Harold and the Purple Crayon (Johnson), 50
Harriet and the Promised Land (Lawrence), 45
Harriet and the Runaway Book (J. Johnston), 152
Harriet the Spy (Fitzhugh), 189, 211
Harvard College, founding of, 7
Haskell, Arnold, 169
Hautzig, Esther, 152
Heidi (Spyri), 135
Heller, Ruth, 168
Henry, Marguerite, 139
Henty, G. A., 14, 146
Herbert, George, 91
Hero, 204
Hero Ain't Nothin' but a Sandwich, A (Childress), 203, 211
Heroic fantasy, 124–125
Highwater, Jamake, 185
"Highwayman, The" (Noyes), 89
Hinton, S. E., 23, 26, 137, 206
Hispanic Americans, 185–186
Historical approach to literature, 198–199
Historical fiction, 22, 50–51, 145–149, 204
History of the Fairchild Family (Sherwood), 11
History of the Robins (Trimmer), 11

Hitty, Her First Hundred Years (Field), 122
Hoban, Russell, 50, 66
Hoban, Tana, 42, 68
Hodge, Walter, 169
Hofsinde, Robert, 170
Hoibo: New Zealand's Yellow-Eyed Penguin, The
    (Vernon), 168
Holland, Isabelle, 192
Hollings, Holling C., 165
Homecoming (Voigt), 190
Homer, 3
Hoosier School Boy, The (Eggleston), 14
Hoosier Schoolmaster, The (Eggleston), 14
Horn books, 7, 9
House of Dies Drear, The (Hamilton), 135
Housman, A. E., 95
How Green Was My Valley (R. Llewellyn), 187
How High Is Up? (Kon), 67
How I Came to Be a Writer (Naylor), 157
Howie Helps Himself (Fassler), 191
How It Feels When Parents Divorce (Krementz),
    170
Huckleberry Finn. See Adventures of
    Huckleberry Finn, The (Twain)
Hughes, Langston, 93–94, 169
Hughes, Shirley, 67
Hughes, Thomas, 14
Human development, 170–171
Humor, 211
    development of, 75
    in poetry, limericks, 91
Hunt, Irene, 138, 146, 148
Hymns in Prose for Children (Barbauld), 11

I Am the Cheese (Cormier), 23, 137, 211, 227
Identity versus role confusion, stage of, 24
I Heard the Owl Call My Name (Craven), 185
Iliad (Homer), 3, 89, 109
I'll Get There, It Better Be Worth the Trip
    (Donovan), 23, 192
Illusion in narrative art, 32
Illustrated books
    concept books, 68
    informational, 172
    matching illustrations to text for authenticity,
        154
    nineteenth century, 15
    Orbis Sensualium Pictus, 7
    versus picture books, 31
Imagery, 88, 210
    in poetry, 92–94
Impressionism, 41, 225
Inch by Inch (Lionni), 225
Incredible Journey, The (Burnford), 139
Indian Arts (Hofsinde), 170
Indian in the Cupboard, The (Banks), 125
Indirect images, 93–94
Individual, conflicts of, 206–207
Indoor Noisy Book, The (Brown), 67
Industry versus inferiority, stage of, 24
    parallel with the conventional level, 25

Influence of literature, 227
Informational books, 45, 165–173
    concept books as, 68
    photographs in, 42
Initiative versus guilt, stage of, 24
Ink drawings, 45
Instructional books in the European Renaissance,
    6–7
Instrumental/relativist orientation, 25
In Summer's Light (Oneal), 138
Intellectual development, Piaget's theory of,
    20–23
Intellectually challenged, 190–191
Interpretation questions, 219
    writing about, 221
In the Beginning: Creation Stories from Around
    the World (Hamilton), 107
In the Moonlight, Waiting (C. Carrick), 41
In Their Own Words:A History of the American
    Negro (Meltzer), 167
Intuitive stage of development, 22
Ionesco, Eugene, 41
Ira Sleeps Over (Waber), 52
Isadora, Rachel, 43
Islam, 167
Island of the Blue Dolphins (O'Dell), 134, 184,
    199, 206
Island Keeper, The (Mazer), 134
Island of the Skog, The (Kellogg), 42
Iwamatsu, Jun. *See* Yashima, Taro

Jackson, Jesse, 182
"Jack Sprat", 77, 78, 79, 80, 81
Jacob Have I Loved (Paterson), 136
Jacobs, Joseph, 12, 114
James and the Giant Peach (Dahl), 123, 221
Janssen, Tove, 123
Jaspersohn, William, 170
Jeremy's First Haircut (Girard), 67–68
Jerusalem, Shining Still (Kuskin), 167
John Gilpin's Ride, 15
Johnny Tremain (Forbes), 146
Johnson, Crocket, 50
Johnston, Johanna, 152
Journals, 220
Journey (Anno), 31
Journey to Topaz (Uchida), 146, 187
Judaism, 167
Julie of the Wolves (George), 134, 184, 189,
    199, 206
Jumanji (Van Allsburg), 34, 35, 37, 41, 45
Jump tales, 107

Kalb, Jonah, 170
Kalb, Laura, 170
Keats, Ezra Jack, 24, 46, 54, 62, 66, 183, 204,
    225
Kellogg, Steven, 42
Kendall, Carol, 9, 123
Kendall, Paul Murray, 150
Kennedy, John F., 153

Kherdian, David, 187
Kidnapped (Stevenson), 146
Kinesthetic images, 93
King's Fifth, The (O'Dell), 146
Kingsley, Charles, 13, 123
King of the Wind (Henry), 139
Kipling, Rudyard, 146
Klein, Norma, 138, 190
Knight, Eric, 139
Knowles, John, 14
Kohlberg, Lawrence, 19
  theory of moral judgment, 24–26
Kon, Bernice, 67
Konigsburg, E. L., 67, 134
Krementz, Jill, 170
Krumgold, Joseph, 185
Kunhardt, Dorothy, 21
Kuskin, Karla, 167

Lampman, Evelyn Sibley, 184
Lang, Andrew, 12, 114
Language
  gender-biased, 188
  in historical fiction, 148
  of poetry, 92–95
  sound of, 54, 75–76, 94–95
  in poetry, 88
Language of Goldfish, The (Oneal), 138
Lantern Bearers, The (Sutcliff), 146
Lassie Come Home (Knight), 139
Latham, Jean Lee, 151
Lauber, Patricia, 171
"Law and order" orientation", 25
Lawrence, Jacob, 45
Lawson, Robert, 151, 208, 211, 220
Layout, picture book, 46
Learning, from reading, and from experience, 53
Legends, 49, 109
Le Guin, Ursula, 24, 124, 127, 204
L'Engle, Madeleine, 126, 136
Le Shan, Eda, 170
Lessons for Children (Barbauld), 11
Lewis, C. S., 16, 124, 203
Libraries
  learning to use, 215
  in the Middle Ages, 4
  public, family visits to, 216
Lifestyles, diversity in, 190
Light Beyond the Forest, The (Sutcliff), 109
Light and Darkness (Branley), 169
Lightfoot, Edmund, 89
Light Princess, The (MacDonald), 120
Limericks, 91
Limited narrator, 203
Lincoln: A Photobiography (Freedman), 151,
  152, 154
Lindgren, Astrid, 122
Line, in illustrations, 32
Linocuts, 45
Lion, the Witch and the Wardrobe, The (Lewis),
  124, 127, 203

Lionni, Leo, 46, 121, 225
Lipsyte, Robert, 138
Literature
  informational books as, 173
  study of, 197–212
Little Goody Two Shoes, 11
Little House, The (Burton), 50
Little House in the Big Woods, The (Wilder),
  203, 209
Little House series (Wilder), 22
"Little Miss Muffet", 77, 81, 82, 83, 84
Little Pretty Pocket Book, 11
"Little Red Riding Hood", 104
Little Tim and the Brave Sea Captain
  (Ardizzone), 22
Little Toot (Gramatky), 21, 50
Little Women (Alcott), 14, 135
Lively, Penelope, 125
Living in a Risky World (Pringle), 168
Livingston, Myra Cohn, 90
Llewellyn, Claire, 169
Llewellyn, Richard, 187
Lobel, Arnold, 50
Local legends, 109
Locke, John, 9
Loftis, Hugh, 122
London, Jack, 139
Longfellow, Henry Wadsworth, 89
Look Again (Hoban), 42
Looking at Art (Chase), 170
Lord of the Rings (Tolkien), 124
Lowry, Lois, 22, 147, 149
Lullabies, 73
Lyric poetry, 89, 90–92
Lytle, Ruby, 90

Macauley, David, 169, 172, 173
MacCann, Donnarae, 34
McCloskey, Robert, 22, 34, 36, 37, 38, 46, 51
McDermott, Gerald, 35, 37, 42, 166
MacDonald, George, 13, 120
MacLachlan, Patricia, 22, 55, 146, 189, 190, 191,
  211
Madeline (Bemelmans), 39, 40, 51, 54, 225
*Magazine: Behind the Scenes at Sports
  Illustrated* (Jaspersohn), 170
Magic in folktales, 110, 112
Malory, Thomas, 5
Mama One, Mama Two (MacLachlan), 55
Mann, Peggy, 189
Man Without a Face, The (Holland), 192
Many Moons (Thurber), 49, 120
Märchen, 105
Mark of the Horse Lord (Sutcliff), 146
Marshall, James, 42, 54
Mary Alice, Operator Number Nine (Allen and
  Marshall), 54
Mary Poppins (Travers), 122
Matchlock Gun, The (Edmonds), 184
Math Games (Anno), 169
Mayo Brothers, The (Goodsell), 153

Mazer, Harry, 134
M. C. Higgins, the Great (Hamilton), 24, 136
Meaning in poetry, 95–96
Means, Florence Crannell, 186
Media, artistic, 43–46
Medieval literature, 4–6
Meet the Austins (L'Engle), 136
Mei Lei (Handforth), 51, 166
Meltzer, Milton, 154, 155, 167, 172
Memory questions for classroom discussion,
    218–219
Merriam, Eve, 92–93
Merry Adventures of Robin Hood, The (Pyle), 5,
    146
Merrymaker, The (Suhl), 187
Merry tales, 106
Metamorphoses (Ovid), 4
Metaphor, 93–94
    for describing poetry, 87
    in informational books, 173
Meter, 94
Mike Mulligan's Steamshovel (Burton), 21, 50
Miles, Miska, 62, 184, 191
Millions of Cats (Gag), 34, 54
Milne, A. A., 119, 120, 122
Min-Min, The (Clark), 187
*Miriam's Well: Stories about Women in the
    Bible* (Bach and Exum), 167
Miss Nelson Is Missing (Allard), 42
Miss Rumphius (Cooney), 191
Misty of Chincoteague (Henry), 139
Mobiles, 226
Moffats, The (Estes), 25
Moja Means One (Feelings), 66
Mom, the Wolf Man and Me (Klein), 138, 190
Monjo, F. N., 152
Monochrome illustrations, 34
Monogenesis, 104
Montage, 46, 225
Montgomery, Lucy Maude, 14, 136
Moon and I, The (Byars), 157
Moral development, theory of, 24–26
Morality in children's literature, 11
More, Hannah, 11
Morte d'Artur (Malory), 5
Mother Goose rhymes, 73–84
    imagery in, 88
Motifs
    of folktales, 112
    journey, 122–123
Move Over, Wheelchairs Coming Through!
    (Roy), 170
Mowat, Farley, 139
Mr. Gumpy's Outing (Burningham), 41
Mr. Rabbit and the Lovely Present (Zolotow),
    41, 225
Mukerji, Dhan Gopal, 139
Mummies Made in Egypt (Aliki), 166
Musgrove, Margaret, 42, 62, 63
Music in poetry, 88
My Brother Sam Is Dead (Colliers), 146, 147

My Daddy Is a Nurse (Wandro and Blank), 189
Myers, Walter Dean, 186
My Father's Court (Singer), 187
My First Book of Time (Llewellyn), 168
My Friend Flicka (O'Hara), 139
My Name Is Asher Lev (Potok), 187
My Side of the Mountain (George), 199
Mystery stories, 134–135
Myths, 49, 107–109

Nana Upstairs, Nana Downstairs (da Paola), 55,
    191
Narrative
    in picture books, 51
    in poetry, 89–92
Narrative art, 32
Narrator
    exposition by, 209
    point of view in literature, 202–203
Native Americans, 184–185
    Navajo story, *Arrow to the Sun*, 35, 149, 166
    pourquoi tales, 106
    stereotyping of, in picture books, 55
Nature
    books about, 167–169
    the individual in conflict with, 206
Naylor, Phyllis Reynolds, 157
Need for others in realistic fiction, 140
Newbery, John, 11
Newbery Medal, 15, 135, 136, 149, 151, 184,
    229–237
New England Primer, The, 9, 10
New realism, 137
Nicholson, Margery, 121–122
Nicols, Jeannette, 95
Nine Days to Christmas (Ets), 186
Noble, Trinka, 42
Nobody Asked Me If I Wanted a Baby Sister
    (Alexander), 170
Nonfiction. *See* Autobiography; Biography;
    Informational books
Nonsense
    in cumulative tales, 106
    literature using, 208
    versus reality
        learning in Mother Goose rhymes, 75
        in verse, 87
Noodlehead tales, 106
Norse mythology, 108
Norton, Mary, 9, 123
"November Night" (Crapsey), 90
Noyes, Alfred, 89
Number the Stars (Lowry), 22, 147, 149
Nursery rhymes, 73
    rhythms in, 94–95

Obesity, *One Fat Summer*, 138
Objectivity in informational books, 171
Object permanence, 20–21
O'Dell, Scott, 134, 146, 149, 184, 185, 186, 199,
    206

Odyssey (Homer), 3, 9, 89, 109, 122
O'Hara, Mary, 139
Oil paint, 45
Olfactory images, 93
Oliver Twist (Dickens), 15
Omniscient narrator, 203
Oneal, Zibby, 138
One Fat Summer (Lipsyte), 138
O'Neill, Mary, 93
One Morning in Maine (McCloskey), 22, 34, 36, 37, 38–39, 46
One White Sail (Garne), 66
Opposites, concept of, 67
Opposites (Burningham), 67
Optic, Oliver, pseudonym for William Taylor Adams, 14
Oral interpretation, dramatic, 222
Oral literature, ancient, 3
Orbis Sensualium Pictus (Comenius), 7, 8
Originality in fantasy, 127
Otto of the Silver Hand (Pyle), 146
Our Vanishing Farm Animals (Paladino), 168
Outdoor Noisy Book, The (Brown), 67
Outsiders, The (Hinton), 23, 26, 137, 206
Over in the Meadow (Keats), 62
Ovid, 4
Owl Moon (Yolen), 41
Owl Service (Garner), 125
Owls in the Family (Mowat), 139
Ox-Cart Man, The (Hall and Cooney), 45, 51, 54, 149

Pacing in picture books, 54
Paddle-to-the-Sea (Hollings), culture, 165
Paladino, Catherine, 168
Pantomime, 223
Parallel plot structure, 208
Parrish, Peggy, 221
Passover (Greenfield), 167
Pastels, 45
Paterson, Katherine, 24, 136, 138, 189, 190
Pat the Bunny (Kunhardt), 21
Paulsen, Gary, 184
Peaceable Kingdom: The Shaker Abecedarius (Provensens), 42, 65
Pearce, Philippa, 125
Peck, Robert Newton, 136
Pedro, the Angel of Olvera Street (Politi), 186
Pencil drawings, 45
Perrault, Charles, 12, 73–85, 114
Personification, 94
Perspective in illustrations, 37–38
Peterkin Papers, The (Hale), 122
Peter Pan (Barrie), 123, 127
Peter's Chair (Keats), 24, 204, 225
Phonetic sounds versus spelling, 64
Photography
    as an art, 42
    for illustrating informational books, 172–173
Physical development in cooperative play based on nursery rhymes, 76–77

Physical disability, 170–171, 190–191
Physically challenged, 190–191
Piaget, Jean, 19, 20–23, 24
Picture book, 8
    about art and artists, 170
    biography in, 152
    depiction of Hispanic Americans, 186
    depiction of Native Americans, 184
    the illustrations, 31–46
    Mother Goose, selecting, 77
    reading aloud from, 217
    the story, 49–55
Pied Piper of Hamelin, The (Browning), 15, 89
Pigman (Zindel), 203
Pigs from 1 to 10 (Geisert), 66
Pilgrim's Progress, A (Bunyan), 9
Pinocchio (Collodi), 120, 121
Pippi Longstocking (Lindgren), 122
Place, 203–204
Plants, informational books, 168
Plastic arts, 225–226
Plot, 51, 206–208
    credibility of, 207
    in folktales, 111
    in "Little Miss Muffet", 75–76
    in mysteries, 134
    in narrative poetry, 89
Poe, Edgar Allan, 134
Poetry, 87–98. *See also* Rhymes; Rhythm
Pointillism, 43
Polar Express, The (Van Allsburg), 50
Politi, Leo, 186
Pollyanna (Porter), 135
Polygenesis, 104
Pond Life (Taylor), 168
Pooh's Cookbook (Ellison), 226
Poor Richard (Daugherty), 150
Poor Richard in France (Monjo), 152
Pop-up books, 32
Porter, Eleanor, 135
Postconventional level of development, 25–26
Poster color, 45
Potlatch Family, The (Lampman), 184
Potok, Chaim, 187
Potpourri book, 62
Potter, Beatrix, 23–24, 38, 39, 43, 50, 203, 204, 209, 219, 225
Pourquoi tales, 106
Powell, Anton, 167
Preconceptual period of development, 21
Preconventional period of development, 25
Preferences of children in poetry, 96
Preoperational period of development, 21–22, 25
Princess and the Curdie, The (MacDonald), 13, 120
Princess and the Goblin, The (MacDonald), 13, 120
Princess and the Lion, The (Coatsworth), 146
Pringle, Laurence, 168
Printing press, 6
Profiles in Courage (Kennedy), 153

Protagonist, 204
Provensen, Alice, 42, 65, 84
Provensen, Martin, 42, 65, 84
Prydain cycle, 124
Psychoanalytical approach to literature, 199–201
Psychological novels, 137–139
   historical, 146
Psychosocial development
   and concept books, 67–68
   Erikson's theory of, 23–24
Puck of Pook's Hill (Kipling), 146
Pumpers, Boilers, Hooks and Ladders (Fisher), 166–167
Punishment/obedience orientation, 25
Puppet theater, 224
Puritanism, educational philosophy, 7, 9
"Purple Jar, The" (Edgeworth), 11
Pyle, Howard, 5, 146

Quest fantasy, 124–125

Rabbit Hill (Lawson), 220
Raboff, Ernest, 169
Rachel (Fanshawe), 191
Rack, Marjorie, 51
Rackham, Arthur, 83
Raftery, Gerald, 95
Ragged Dick (Alger), 14
Railroads, The (Fisher), 167
Rain Forests (Taylor), 168
Ramona books (Cleary), 24, 136, 221
Raskin, Ellen, 135
Rawlings, Marjorie Kinnan, 139
Rawls, Wilson, 139
Read-Aloud Handbook (Trelease), 217
Reader-centered approach, 216–226
Reader-response approach, 198
   reader's theater, 223
   writing essays, 220–221
Reading
   encouraging with Mother Goose rhymes, 75
   as a habit, 216
   impact of early cognitive development on, 21
   reinforcement of beliefs with, 55
Reading aloud, 216–217
   from picture books, 54
   of poetry, 96–97
Realism
   in adventure and survival stories, 134–135
   domestic, 135–136
Realistic fiction, 50–51, 133–141
Reality
   developing a sense of, from fiction, 75–76
   root of fantasy in, 127
Reason for a Flower, The (Heller), 168
Rebecca of Sunnybrook Farm (Wiggin), 135
Recording of folktales, 113–114
Red Fairy Book, The (Lang), 12
Red Fox (Roberts), 139
Religion, 167. *See also* Culture

books discussing, 192
conflict of the individual against God, 207
the Gospels as biography, 150
life of King David, 152
myths of, 107–108
Shakers, in America, 65, 136
and violence, 7
Representational art, 36, 38–39, 80, 225
Response-centered approach, 216
Restraint in fantasy, 127
Retardation, 190–191
   The Summer of the Swans, 138
Reversibility of operations (Piaget), 21
Reynard the Fox, 5, 7
Rhymes
   counting, 66
   Mother Goose, 73–84
   in poetry, 95
Rhythm
   development of a sense of, 75
   of haiku, 90
   in limericks, 91
   in poetry, 88, 94–95
   in prose, 211
Richard, Olga, 34
Ride, Sally, 169
Rise of Islam, The (Powell), 167
Ritual, and folktales, 111
Road from Home: The Story of an Armenian Girl, The (Kherdian), 187
Roberts, Charles G. D., 139
Robinson Crusoe (Defoe), 9, 134, 199
Roche, Paul, 87
Rojankovsky, Feodor, 66
Role-playing, 224
Roles, gender, 188
Roll of Thunder, Hear My Cry (Taylor), 23, 137, 147, 206
Romances, medieval, 5
Romantic Movement, nineteenth century, 12–15, 146
Roots (Haley), 183
Rosh Hashanah and Yom Kippur (Greenfield), 167
Round characters, 205
Rousseau, Jean Jacques, 11
Roy, Ron, 170–171
Ruby (Guy), 183
Rumpelstiltskin (Zelinsky), 45
Runaway Robot, The (Del Ray), 126
Rylant, Cynthia, 149

St. George, Judith, 170
Saints' legends, 109
Salinger, J. D., 227
Samuel Todd's Book of Great Colors (Konigsburg), 67
Sandburg, Carl, 92, 95
Sarah, Plain and Tall (MacLachlan), 22, 146, 190, 211
Sasek, Miroslav, 43

Satire, 211
  on the fairy tale, 120
Scarry, Richard, 38
Schoenherr, John, 41
Scholemaster, The (Ascham), 7
Schoolmasters, The (Fisher), 167
School stories, 14
Science books, 167–169
Science fiction, 125–126, 204
Scoppettone, Sandra, 23
Scorpions (Myers), 186
Scratchboard technique, 45
Sebastian, Ouida, 189, 206
Secret Garden, The (Burnett), 135–136
Secrets of a Wildlife Watcher (Arnosky), 169
Seeger, Elizabeth, 167
"Seeing Poem, A" (Froman), 91
Self in conflict, 206
Self-Portrait: Erik Blegvad, 157
Self-Portrait: Margot Zemach, 157
Selsam, Millicent, 167–168, 172
Sendak, Maurice, 41, 44, 46, 50, 53, 206–207,
  225
Sensimotor period, 20–21
Sensitivity in historical fiction, 148
Sentences, construction of, 210
Sentimentalism, tone of, 211–212
Separate Peace, A (Knowles), 14
Sequential-story book, alphabet books, 62
Seton, Ernest Thompson, 139
Setting
  in folktales, 110
  in literary works, 203–204
  in picture books, 52
Seurat, Georges, 43
Sexuality, books discussing, 192
Shabanu: Daughter of the Wind (Staples), 187
Shakespeare, William, 93
Shakespeare's Theater (Hodge), 169
Shape, in illustrations, 34
Shapes and Things (Hoban), 68
Shelley, Mary, 125
Sherwood, Mrs., 11
Sidney, Margaret, 135
Siegal, Aranka, 147, 187
Sign of the Beaver, The (Speare), 206
Silver Pony, The (Lynd), 31, 44
Simile, 93
  in informational books, 173
Simon, Seymour, 168, 169
Simple Susan (Edgeworth), 11
Simpleton tales, 106
Sing Down the Moon (O'Dell), 149, 184
Singer, Isaac Bashevis, 187
Sketching Outdoors in Spring (Arnosky), 169
Slave Dancer, The (Fox), 146, 149
"Sleeping Beauty", 105
Smith, Doris Buchanan, 192
Smith, William Jay, 95
Smith (Garfield), 146
Snowbound (Mazer), 134

"Snow White and the Seven Dwarfs", 105
Snowy Day, The (Keats), 46, 54, 183, 225
Snyder, Zilpha, 126
Sobol, Donald, 134
Social concerns, depicted in picture books,
  54–55
Social development, 76–77
Social realism, 137
Society. *See also* Culture
  changes in the European Renaissance, 6
  the individual in conflict with, 206
Some of the Days of Everett Anderson (Clifton),
  51
"Song of Hiawatha, The" (Longfellow), 89
Song of Roland, The, 5, 109
"Song of Sherwood, A" (Noyes), 89
Space Cat (Todd), 126
Space fantasy, 125–126
Space, in illustrations, 32, 34
Speare, Elizabeth George, 146, 206
Spyri, Johanna, 135
Srivastava, Jane Jonas, 169
Stabiles, 226
Staples, Suzanne Fisher, 187
Static characters, 204–205
Statistics (Srivastava), 169
Steig, William, 227
Stephens, James, 94
Steptoe, John, 43, 44, 189
Stereotyping. *See also* Culture; Gender
  in folktales, 110, 113
  in picture books, 54–55, 184, 204–205
Stevenson, Robert Louis, 13, 146
Stone lithography, 46
Stories in picture books, 49–55
Stories of King Arthur and His Knights, 5
Story About Ping (Rack), 51
Story for a Black Night (Clayton), 187
Story Number 1 (Ionesco), 41
Story Number 2 (Ionesco), 41
Storytelling, 217–218
Story theater, 223
Street Life in New York (Alger), 14
"Streets of Laredo, The", 89
Structure, dramatic, of a plot, 207
Stuart Little (White), 220
Stupids Die, The (Allard), 42
Styles. *See also* Composition
  artistic, 38–43
  in folktales, 112
  in informational books, 173
  literary, 208–211
    in biographies, 155
    in picture books, 53–54
Subject
  in biography, 153
  in picture books, 52
Subjective consciousness, 203
Suhl, Yuri, 187
Summer of the Swans, The (Byars), 138, 191
Sundial (Anno), 32

Supernatural
   in fantasy, 125
   in märchen, 105
Surrealism, 41
Survival stories, 134–135
Sutcliff, Rosemary, 5, 109, 146
Sweet Whispers, Brother Rush (Hamilton), 191
Swift, Jonathan, 9, 123
Sylvester and the Magic Pebble (Steig), 227
Symbolism in animal fantasies, 121
Syntax of informational books, 173
Synthesis, questions to encourage, 219

Tactile images, 92
Tafuri, Nancy, 67
Tale of Peter Rabbit, The (Potter), 23–24, 34,
   38, 39, 43, 50, 53, 203, 204, 209, 219,
   225
Tales of a Fourth Grade Nothing (Blume), 22
Tales from Moominvalley (Janssen), 123
Tales from Mother Goose (Perrault), 12, 73–84,
   114
Talking Earth, The (George), 199
Tall tales, 107
Tanners, The (Fisher), 167
Taste of Blackberries, A (Smith), 192
Taylor, Barbara, 168
Taylor, Mildred, 23, 137, 147, 206
Taylor, Theodore, 134, 206
Telling time, concept books, 67
Tempera, 43–44
Ten, Nine, Eight (Bang), 66
Tenth Good Thing About Barney, The (Viorst),
   170
Ten What? A Mystery Counting Book (Hoban),
   66
Texture, in illustrations, 37
Theme, 208
   in alphabet books, 62
   in biography, 155–156
   in folktales, 111–112
   in picture books, 53
   in realistic fiction, 140
Then Again, Maybe I Won't (Blume), 23
"This Is the House that Jack Built", 106
This Is New York (Sasek), 43
Thompson, Stith, 112
Thoughts Concerning Education (Locke), 9
Three Little Pigs (Zemach), 212
"Three Wishes, The", 106
Thurber, James, 49, 120
Thy Friend, Obadiah (Turkle), 51, 149
Time
   fantasies of, 125, 146
   in historical fiction, 145
   setting for dramatic plots, 207
   setting for literature, 204
Todd, Ruthven, 126
Tom Brown's School Days (Hughes), 14
Tom Sawyer. See Adventures of Tom Sawyer, The
   (Twain)

Tom's Midnight Garden (Pearce), 125
Tone, 211–212
To Space and Back (Ride with Okie), 169
Toy fantasy, 121–122
Traditional literature. *See* Folk literature
Transactional theory, 198
Travers, P. L., 122
Treasure Island (Stevenson), 13, 134, 145
Trelease, Jim, 217
Trimmer, Sarah, 11
Trompe d'oeil artwork, 62
Trucks (Crews), 67
Trumpet of the Swan (White), 220
Trust versus mistrust, stage of, 23
Trying Hard to Hear You (Scoppettone), 23
Tuchman, Barbara, 199
Tuck Everlasting (Babbitt), 128, 221
Turkle, Brinton, 50–51, 149
"Turnip, The", 106
Twain, Mark, 13
Twenty-One Balloons (du Bois), 123
Twenty Thousand Leagues under the Sea
   (Verne), 120, 125

Uchida, Yoshiko, 146, 187
Unclaimed Treasures (MacLachaln), 22
Uncle Tom's Cabin (Stowe), 152
Universal/ethical/principle orientation, 26
Up a Road Slowly (Hunt), 138
*Upon the Head of the Goat: A Childhood in
   Hungary* (Siegal), 147, 187
Uranus (Simon), 169
Uranus: The Seventh Planet (Branley), 169
Uses of Enchantment, The (Bettelheim), 76, 200
Us Maltbys (Means), 186

Values
   ethics of science and technology, 168
   in folktales, 111
   reinforcement in myths, 107
Van Allsburg, Chris, 34, 35, 37, 41, 45, 50
Velveteen Rabbit, The (Nicholson), 121–122
Verne, Jules, 120, 125
Vernon, Adele, 168
Villain, 204
Violence, 7
   ethnic, 187
   in fantasies, 125
   in folk literature, 113
   historical context, 199
   in nursery rhymes, 74, 76
Viorst, Judith, 170
Virgil, 4
Visual images, 92
Viva Chicano (Bonham), 186
Vocabulary
   choice of, 209–210
   in nursery rhymes, 74–75
   in picture books, 53–54
Voigt, Cynthia, 190, 191

2
, 186–187
89
, 44
The (Kingsley), 13, 123
43
Work, The (Macauley), 169, 173
Leonard, 67
ame, The (Raskin), 135
kes Me Feel This Way? (Le Shan), 170
he Big Idea, Ben Franklin? (Fritz), 154
Was Young in the Mountains (Rylant), 149
e the Lilies Bloom (Cleavers), 136, 137
re the Red Fern Grows (Rawls), 139
ere Was Patrick Henry on the 29th of May? (Fritz), 155
There the Wild Things Are (Sendak), 44, 46, 50, 53, 206–207
White, E. B., 121, 203, 209, 210–211, 219, 220, 227
White Fang (London), 139
Whitehead, Alfred North, 212
Wiggin, Kate Douglas, 135
Wild Animals I Have Known (Seton), 139
Wilder, Laura Ingalls, 22, 149, 203, 207–208, 209, 221–222
Wildsmith, Brian, 41, 43
William's Doll (Zolotow), 138
Wind in the Willows, The (Grahame), 13, 119, 120, 121, 220
Winnie-the-Pooh (Milne), 119, 120, 122, 127
Witch of Blackbird Pond, The (Speare), 146
With Clive in India (Henty), 14

Wizard of Oz, The (Baum), 13, 120, 123, 127, 209, 210
Wolves of Willoughby Chase, The (Aiken), 123
Women Who Shaped History (Buckmaster), 153
Wonderful World of Dance, The (Haskell), 169
Wonder tales, 105
Wong, J. S., 186
Woodblocks, 8, 45–46
Wordless picture books, 31
Words by Heart (Sebestian), 189, 206
"World According to Mother Goose, The" (Bremner), 76
"Wreck of the Edmund Fitzgerald" (Lightfoot), 89
Wreck of the Zephyr, The (Van Allsburg), 45
Wright, Blanche Fisher, 78
Wrinkle in Time, A (L'Engle), 126
Writing
poetry, 96–97
about literature, 220–222

Yashima, Taro, 55, 191
Yearling, The (Rawlings), 139
Yentl the Yeshiva Boy (Singer), 187
Yep, Laurence, 186, 191
Yolen, Jane, 41
Yonge, Charlotte, 135, 146
Your First Garden (Marc Brown), 169

Zelinsky, Paul O., 45
Zemach, Margot, 32, 33, 42, 44, 212
Zindel, Paul, 203
Zolotow, Charlotte, 41, 138, 225
Z Was Zapped (Van Allsburg), 64–65